CW01024223

COLONEL WILLIAM PRESCOTT

PRESCOTT

Heroic Commander of the Battle of Bunker Hill

DONALD R. RYAN

CASEMATE

Pennsylvania & Yorkshire

Published in the United States of America and Great Britain in 2025 by
CASEMATE PUBLISHERS
1950 Lawrence Road, Havertown, PA 19083, USA
and
47 Church Street, Barnsley, S70 2AS, UK

Hardcover Edition: ISBN 978-1-63624-568-3
Digital Edition: ISBN 978-1-63624-569-0

A CIP record for this book is available from the British Library

Printed and bound in the United Kingdom by CPI Group (UK) Ltd, Croydon, CR0 4YY
Typeset in India by DiTech Publishing Services

For a complete list of Casemate titles, please contact:

CASEMATE PUBLISHERS (US)
Telephone (610) 853-9131
Fax (610) 853-9146
Email: casemate@casematepublishers.com
www.casematepublishers.com

CASEMATE PUBLISHERS (UK)
Telephone (0)1226 734350
Email: casemate@casemateuk.com
www.casemateuk.com

Cover image: Statue of William Prescott in Bunker Hill National Historical Park, Charlestown, MA,
dedicated June 17, 1881. (Wikimedia Commons)

The Publisher's authorised representative in the EU for product safety is Authorised Rep Compliance Ltd.,
Ground Floor, 71 Lower Baggot Street, Dublin D02 P593, Ireland.
www.arccompliance.com

Contents

To my wife, Mary Ann Kavanaugh, with my enduring love. I'm ever grateful for her support and patience through this highly consuming effort.

And to my three wonderful daughters—Katherine, Eileen, and Allie—who have been a source of constant joy in my life and who have inspired and encouraged me to pursue my passions.

Acknowledgments

As I expected, writing a book, and particularly a nonfiction book, requires a lot of help from a lot of people. I've been fortunate to have a terrific group of supporters. That support started with my family, to whom I've dedicated this book. So, first and foremost, I want to extend my heartfelt thanks to my wife, Mary, and daughters, Katherine, Eileen, and Allie. Their constant enthusiasm fueled my efforts.

I also must acknowledge a number of historians and authors who responded to my outreach to them, encouraged my work, and passed along very valuable advice. Prolific revolutionary era expert John Ferling was generous with his time and offered useful recommendations that propelled my research into areas I hadn't initially considered. Paul Lockhart was another early supporter, noting the gap in the historical record with respect to Colonel William Prescott. I would be remiss if I did not give a shout out to Nat Philbrick, Bob Allison, Gordon Wood, and Christian DiSpigna, who also quickly replied to my inquiries. Their supportive words meant a great deal to this first-time author.

Jonathan Nourse of Westborough, Massachusetts, was a fount of knowledge regarding colonial farming, which opened my eyes to the extreme rigors of that life. His input enabled me to envision the difficulties and challenges William Prescott encountered in managing a large farm in an often inhospitable environment. Similarly, Brian Donahue of Brandeis University also contributed keen insights about town development and land use in early New England.

I owe a debt of gratitude to my high school classmate and West Point grad, Mike Johnson. Now retired, Mike introduced me to James Scudieri, former colonel and now senior researcher for the U.S. Army War College, who directed me to candid assessments of American military history. Understanding how the Army has viewed the battle of Bunker Hill was a great addition to the story. Interestingly, in the course of this investigation, I discovered that Mike is a descendant of Major John Buttrick, the militia commander who ordered the volunteers at the Concord Bridge in April 1775 to return fire on the British troops. It marked the first time militia troops had been given such an order, and helped to ignite the War of Independence.

Tony Mayo, a former colleague, and Nancy Koehn, both of Harvard University, aided me in fleshing out my thoughts on leadership. In similar fashion, Cynthia Pury of Clemson University was instrumental in my examination of the psychology of courage, while Daniela Schiller of the Mount Sinia School of Medicine in New York instructed me on the neuroscience behind it.

I received wonderful support from a number of U.S. National Park Service rangers, including Dan Gagnon, Bill Parrow, and Patrick Boyce, who provided useful details regarding musket firing, the battle of Bunker Hill, and Bunker Hill National Historical Park. Likewise, Eric Schnitzer of Saratoga National Park was a vital resource on the tide-turning battle there and the role of militias such as William Prescott's unit.

Julie Hall and Arthur Hurley of the Charlestown Historical Society enthusiastically endorsed this project. Having their backing was very gratifying and, with the 250th anniversary of the battle of Bunker Hill nearing, pushed me to tell Prescott's story.

I enjoyed tremendous assistance from a number of people from the town of Pepperell, Massachusetts, where William Prescott lived in his adult life. Ron Karr, Wendy Cummings, Franek Kulik, and Tony Saboliauskas provided important details about Prescott that I hadn't found otherwise.

Debra Spratt, Tina McCoy, and Mary Cook of the Lawrence Library in Pepperell facilitated my review of original town records from the revolutionary period, which proved enormously valuable in learning about William Prescott's activities before, during, and after the Revolutionary War. They were always available when I needed them and couldn't have been more pleasant to work with. Joan Ladik of the Pepperell Town Hall also enabled me to access long-undisturbed historical files about Prescott's role in the community.

Librarians at the Massachusetts Historical Society, the Boston Public Library, and the American Antiquarian Society also supplied much-needed aid in locating and retrieving relevant historical documents, newspapers, letters, and books. Librarians are, indeed, the unsung heroes of our learned society.

Caitlin Ramos and Conor Snow of the Massachusetts Archives were willing partners in my detective work, instantly responding to my many requests. Mike Ducrow at the South Middlesex County Registry of Deeds good-naturedly walked me through the complex system of its digital records to find revealing transactions of the Prescott family.

Jonathan Feltner, a descendant of the first Prescotts in America, came to my rescue when important details were missing from Prescott's life story. Linda Geiger, a certified genealogist and another descendant in the Prescott line, unearthed critical information about the Prescott ancestry and Colonel Prescott's military service.

Kara Fossey of the Groton Historical Society assisted me in digging into William Prescott's early life in Groton. Tom Callahan, also of Groton, was another cheerful supporter of my work and educated me about the opposing stances of the neighboring Shattuck and Prescott families during Shays's Rebellion.

I worked with two editors during initial drafts of the book. Melanie Viets, a nonfiction editor in Vermont, carefully reviewed my first manuscript, prompting a new approach to how I told the story. Rachel Carter of Onion River Press also did a wonderful job editing a later draft of the book, pointing out, with fine-toothed comb exactness, where the narrative could be improved and streamlined.

Finally, I need to thank my agent, Roger Williams, for his steady guidance and patience throughout this yearslong project, and for finding a distinguished publisher for this book. Indeed, I worked with a wonderful team at Casemate Publishers, including Ruth Sheppard, Isobel Fulton, Lizzy Hammond, and Declan Ingram, along with consultant Julie Frederick. I am enormously indebted to them for bringing this work to fruition.

Without the collaboration of all these individuals, and the interest of other family and friends, this book would never have been possible. For that, I am eternally grateful. They made the final product immeasurably better with myriad suggestions and corrections. All remaining inaccuracies and errors are mine.

Introduction

In 2018, as my professional career was winding down, I began a volunteer job with the U.S. National Park Service in Boston. This was shortly after my wife, Mary, and I had left our longtime home in the suburbs of central Massachusetts and moved into a condominium in Charlestown, on the northern side of the Charles River, where we lived until April 2024. Our apartment was across the street from Bunker Hill Monument National Park, the site of the majestic, 180-year-old granite memorial. Every day, we looked at the 221-foot obelisk through our living room windows and, if we walked through the park, also saw the distinctive statue of Colonel William Prescott, the leading American field commander on that fateful Saturday, June 17, 1775, when the battle of Bunker Hill was fought.

The Prescott statue is the only one on the Breed's Hill battlefield (yes, the battle of Bunker Hill was fought on Breed's Hill, not Bunker's Hill), and it is an arresting sight. Prescott, perched on a six-foot-high plinth, towers over the main walkway leading up to the monument and is depicted striking a rather stern, martial pose. I have a small, black-and-white photograph from 1938 of my father standing in front of the Prescott statue, which was taken while he was in his mid-20s and on a road trip with some pals from his native Bronx, New York. I was startled to find that old photo when cleaning out some boxes during our move, and it was somewhat ironic, or perhaps prophetic, that I ended up living no more than about a hundred yards from where he had stood so long ago.

As a docent and guide at Monument Park, I greet visitors, answer questions (sometimes just about the nearest bathroom), and retell the story of the battle of Bunker Hill. It can be a busy job, especially when tour buses or school groups descend on the site. The National Park Service reports that, in a typical year, over 300,000 visitors come to the park.[1] These visitors, spanning all ages and backgrounds, are not only from every corner of the United States including Alaska and Hawaii—but from all reaches of the world. In the height of the summer, it isn't uncommon to find tourists from Western and Eastern Europe, the Middle East, Russia, Asia, Africa, and South America listening to ranger talks and snapping pictures in front of the Bunker Hill Monument and the Prescott statue. The more motivated visitors will also climb the 294 steps of the monument to enjoy the panoramic view from the top.

To no surprise, a large number of visitors are from England and France, respectively an enemy and an ally in the war. In particular, many of the Brits want to discuss, often with a touch of remorse, what happened back in the latter part of the 18th century that led to the separation of the colonies from the king's realm. These are fun conversations, without any detection of hard feelings. But the more intriguing interactions are with citizens from other parts of the world who have not enjoyed the democratic experience in their own countries or have only experienced it fleetingly. When I ask them why they have come, these visitors routinely point to the site's importance in America's early history and the revolution. They want to hear about the origin of the United States, a country they clearly admire. They want to know the secret of the nation's success in securing liberty and self-determination.

One place visitors tend to congregate is at the statue of Colonel Prescott, and that is where I have had many rich discussions with them. The questions I have been asked about Prescott—and those I have asked myself—compelled me to look further into his life in the context of the broader struggle for American independence. To my delight, I found an enormously interesting character and an inspiring story.

William Prescott was a witness to, and vital participant in, a number of critical moments during America's unlikely journey to independence. Through this turbulent era and beyond, Prescott was also a prominent civic leader, giving his all to ensure that, first and foremost, his town (Pepperell) and his state (Massachusetts) would endure and thrive after the separation from England. As I came to understand, few Americans could claim to have Prescott's breadth of experiences during a formidable time in the country's history.

Despite the approbation he garnered from his actions, particularly at Bunker Hill, Prescott's fame, like that of so many champions of distant wars, has dimmed nearly to extinction. As each successive generation has passed on, the personal connections to that momentous event in Charlestown have loosened and frayed. More than two centuries have now passed since that gory, chaotic clash, and there is generally little remembrance of the importance of Bunker Hill and Colonel Prescott's role in it. Moreover, even less is known about how Prescott contributed to the revolutionary effort both before and after that fateful event.

If Bunker Hill did not happen—or worse, if it was an American catastrophe, as the British expected it would be—William Prescott likely would have remained in obscurity, and the colonists' drive for liberty may have been permanently derailed right then and there. The battle was enormously consequential. However, this book is not solely the retelling of a famous battle. It is a view into the life of an extraordinary American who, through his repeated, undaunted courage, played an emblematic role in the birth of a nation.

I have long been enamored with individuals who have shown exceptional courage. Courage is a noble, animating trait (some think the most virtuous trait), and anyone, from the highest-perceived leader to the most ordinary individual, can possess it. Courage is overcoming one's fear to achieve a greater good, and it can manifest itself in various ways. Philosophers and psychologists talk about moral, physical, civil, social, emotional, and spiritual courage. We can all think of examples of these types of courage and be inspired by them. It was, in fact, William Prescott's courage that drew me to him. In multiple ways in multiple situations, he overcame his fear, thought about more than himself, and took principled action. Such behavior is hard to ignore.

After my talks in Bunker Hill National Historical Park, visitors often approach me to say they are glad to know more about the battle, and about Prescott. William Prescott led an outsized life, but he was a humble man of generous spirit. He was not a self-promoter. Yet, while Prescott would be the last person to ask for more public praise and acclaim, he undoubtedly deserves it.

My objective here is to make Prescott's incredible, and very American, story available to a broad audience. With various commemorative anniversaries from the revolutionary era already being observed, people's interest in the birth of the United States has been heightened. I'd like William Prescott to be one of the individuals from that time whom we remember and honor. Therefore, in accordance with these milestones, this book retells key aspects of William Prescott's life, principally over its last 25 years when he took up the cause of liberty, fought in the Revolutionary War, and then returned home to pursue civic duties aimed to ensure future tranquility.

Through Prescott's example, I hope the book also reminds Americans of the astonishing efforts and sacrifices made by many Americans to obtain the country's freedom. William Prescott was a significant actor in this struggle, but he certainly was not the only one. Everyday Americans, from all walks of life, whose names have long been forgotten, came together in common cause, suffered enormous hardships, and all too many paid the highest price for their beliefs. They deserve our sincere and everlasting appreciation.

Because this book covers a period over two hundred years ago when records were not assiduously maintained, it is part history/part detective story. It moves back and forth in time, describing the events and the environment that shaped

Prescott's life, as well as my efforts to resurrect his past. I dug into original, primary source documents (some probably for the first time), went to the locations of Prescott's most memorable activities, and leveraged the knowledge of scholars who have studied the dynamic times when Prescott made his mark. Out of this, I have tried to create a portrait of a true American hero.

In the end, when all is said and done, I can say that Prescott's life was big and multifaceted, exciting and inspirational. It was also undoubtedly consequential and therefore worthy of examination. Prescott's legacy and fame have been largely washed away by time. I hope this book will revive both.

Chronology

February 20, 1726: William Prescott is born in Groton, Massachusetts, the fourth of seven children of Benjamin and Abigail Prescott.

1744–48: William Prescott joins a military unit from Massachusetts during King George's War.

January 1756–63: The French and Indian War is fought. William Prescott fights as part of a Massachusetts regiment.

April 5, 1764: Great Britain's Parliament passes the Sugar Act, the first tax to raise revenue from the colonists.

March 22, 1765: The Stamp Act is enacted by Parliament, also to raise revenue from the colonies.

June 15–July 2, 1767: The Townshend Acts are implemented to pay for British soldiers in the colonies and to exert authority over the citizens.

March 5, 1770: The Boston Massacre occurs; five Americans are shot and killed by British troops in Boston during a confrontation.

May 10, 1773: The Tea Act is passed in Parliament, requiring the colonists to purchase English tea during a glut on the world market.

December 16, 1773: The Boston Tea Party occurs, in which angry citizens dump English tea in the city's harbor.

Spring 1774: Parliament passes the Coercive (Intolerable) Acts. General Thomas Gage becomes Military Governor of Massachusetts.

April 19, 1775: Paul Revere's midnight ride. Bloody fighting erupts between British troops and colonial militias at Lexington and Concord.

June 17, 1775: William Prescott leads provincial soldiers at the battle of Bunker Hill.

July 2, 1775: George Washington arrives in Cambridge, Massachusetts, as Commander in Chief of the Continental Army.

March 5, 1776: American troops and cannonry on Dorchester Heights force the British to evacuate Boston on March 17.

April 4, 1776: George Washington heads to New York to defend the city. William Prescott leads the 7th Continental Regiment.

July 1776: General William Howe and Admiral Richard Howe arrive in New York harbor with plans to capture the city.

August 29, 1776: General Washington evacuates his army from Brooklyn Heights to avoid capture and eventually flees New York.

January 1777: William Prescott retires from the army and returns to his farm in Pepperell, Massachusetts.

October 1777: William Prescott rejoins the army as a volunteer and participates in the siege of Burgoyne's army at Saratoga.

Winter 1777/78: A bedraggled Continental Army camps at Valley Forge.

March 1, 1781: The Articles of Confederation, the nation's first frame of government, goes into effect.

October 19, 1781: British General Cornwallis surrenders to General Washington at Yorktown.

September 3, 1783: The Treaty of Paris is signed, ending the Revolutionary War.

August 1786: Shays's Rebellion, an anti-tax insurrection, erupts in Massachusetts, threatening to overthrow the government.

May–September 1787: The Constitutional Convention convenes in Philadelphia and creates a new United States government.

June 21, 1788: The U.S. Constitution is adopted when New Hampshire becomes the ninth state to ratify the Constitution.

April 30, 1789: George Washington is sworn in as the first President of the United States of America.

October 13, 1795: William Prescott dies in Pepperell, Massachusetts.

"When future generations shall inquire where are the men who gained the highest prize of glory in the arduous contest which ushered in our nation's birth, upon Prescott and his companions in arms will the eye of history beam."
(Light Horse Harry Lee, Revolutionary War general, referring to William Prescott's actions at the battle of Bunker Hill)

"Prescott lived to the last loved and honored in his own town not merely for what he had done, but for what he was, a man who could not help charming all who knew him."
(U.S. Congressman William Everett, in an 1895 oration celebrating the centennial of William Prescott's death)

Prologue

The concussive boom of cannons broke the early morning silence, causing the American troops atop Breed's Hill in Charlestown, Massachusetts, to cringe reflexively and halt working on the dirt fort they were building. Their aim on this chilly morning was to construct a defensive barrier against an anticipated British attack. The enemy cannon shots were an unmistakable and foreboding message to the Americans that their efforts would not be allowed to stand. It was a little after 4:30 a.m. on Saturday, June 17, 1775.

When the provincial soldiers cast their eyes southeastward toward the source of the sound in the Charles River, they saw clouds of white smoke billowing from the HMS *Lively*, one of His Majesty's warships that sat between Charlestown and Boston proper. At the same time, the solid iron projectiles from the ship's cannons—likely 24-pounders or more—arced toward the American fort, screaming louder and louder as they descended from the pinnacles of their trajectories. The balls landed with distinctive thuds on the hillside beneath the fort, which, even though they did not hit their target, provided little comfort for the Americans.

More blasts followed and more cannonballs filled the sky. The firing came principally from three men-of-war, a number of floating batteries, and an artillery placement on Copp's Hill in Boston.[1] Panic and dread spread through the Americans. With each blast, the troops instinctively ducked for cover behind the walls of the redoubt, which they had started working on only a few hours before. Fortunately, these additional cannonballs were also falling harmlessly on the hillside. The troops, most of them unaccustomed to battle, couldn't help but look toward the source of the blast each time the ground shook with the impact.

Colonel William Prescott, their commander, tried to assure his men that they were going to be alright. But he was probably just as alarmed as they were. Then, as suddenly as it had started, the cannonade stopped. Admiral Samuel Graves, in command of British naval forces in the region, had ordered the ships to cease firing. Now, with the quiet, all that remained was the dissipating remnants of the white smoke from the ships' guns hanging over the water. No one was quite sure what was going to happen next.

As reddish streaks of sunlight started to illuminate the area, the 49-year-old Prescott could now quite plainly see the precariousness of his troops' position on Breed's Hill. The British could also see more clearly what the Americans were up to. The night before, Prescott and his men had been given written orders by Major General Artemas Ward, leader of the New England military forces, to take possession of and fortify Bunker's Hill, which is why he and his men, numbering about 1,100, were in Charlestown at this time.[2]

Recognizing that, if attacked by the British Army, the redoubt could be easily flanked on both sides, Prescott made adjustments. He placed snipers in the evacuated buildings of Charlestown village along the Charles River on the redoubt's south side and ordered a breastwork to be built on the north side, running down the hill toward the Mystic River on the opposite side of the peninsula. At the sight of these added defensive maneuvers on Breed's Hill, Graves resumed the cannon barrage.

Despite this disturbing development, Prescott remained outwardly calm, encouraging his men to keep working as whistling cannonballs, affectionately called tea kettles, traced purposeful parabolas toward the fort. Luckily, the British could not elevate their cannon high enough to reach the redoubt, and the cannonballs consistently fell without the desired effect, embedding themselves in the field below the fort's walls.[3]

Prescott, who had fought with the British in both King George's War in the 1740s and the French and Indian War (referred to as the Seven Years' War in Europe) in the mid-1750s, kept his men low behind the ramparts when the firing was going on. But he had them recommence their digging whenever there was a break in the cannonade.[4] This seemed to settle the men. Unfortunately, one of the streaking cannonballs, coming in on a more acute angle, did not implant itself in the field as the others had. Instead, it skipped along the ground like a stone on a lake before popping up and killing a 35-year-old soldier, Asa Pollard of Billerica, taking off his head.[5] Prescott later recounted the gruesome scene when Pollard was hit, saying, "He was so near to me that my clothes were besmeared with his blood and brains, which I wiped off, to some degree, with a handful of fresh earth. The sight was so shocking to many of the men that they left their posts and ran to view him. I ordered them back, but in vain."[6]

Pollard's terrifying death sent a shock through the provincial soldiers, most of whom had never been involved in a battle before. Incomprehensibly, given the events that were unfolding, they implored Prescott to allow them to hold a full religious service for Pollard before laying his body in a hastily dug grave. But Prescott knew there was no time for this and limited the service so his men could resume working. "Bury him," directed the tall and athletically built Prescott sharply, and he strode off, turning his attention back to the redoubt.[7]

However, seeing that his troops were quite shaken, Prescott then did a remarkable thing. He mounted the redoubt and strolled across the top, again urging the men to keep working, telling them they were safe, and demonstrating, by exposing his own body to the firing, that there was nothing to worry about.[8] The imposing, six-foot-two Prescott had by then taken off the heavy overcoat he'd worn in the night in favor of a long, lightweight banyan one. He also carried a straight, triangular-bladed, American-made short sword that symbolized his superior rank. The sword was good for thrusting and was called the "thirsty sword" because of the devastating, bloody wound it inflicted.[9] Atop the six-foot-high redoubt wall, Prescott was an inviting target for the British cannon. Who willingly exposes himself to such danger? What did his men think? Were they reassured and inspired, or did they think their commander was a bit crazy? Did Prescott value the cause greater than his own life?

Prescott exhorted the men to work quickly, knowing full well that if the British soldiers—who were just a mile away across the Charles River—decided to take action against them, they would have a real fight on their hands. No doubt, Prescott's forceful presence and bravery made an impression on the men. As did his moxie. At one point during his stroll on top of the redoubt, Prescott reputedly turned toward the British in Boston and, in a defiant gesture, waved his hat toward them.[10]

A good one hundred yards to Prescott's left, Captain Thomas Knowlton of the Connecticut militia, also sensing vulnerability, took it upon himself to expand the defenses on the grassy slope leading down toward the Mystic River. Knowlton, 33 years old, was born into a military family in West Bedford, Massachusetts. His family moved permanently from the Bay Colony when he was eight and settled in Ashford, Connecticut. Like Prescott and some others on Breed's Hill, Knowlton had served in the French and Indian War on the side of the British.

Almost immediately after that protracted war, a rift with Britain had opened up in the colonies that, year after year, gradually built to an ineluctable boil. Massachusetts might have been a hotbed of that animosity, but other colonies were also implicated in the growing conflict. In Connecticut, when revolutionary war clouds gathered in the mid-1770s and there was a call for provincial troops to be assembled, Thomas Knowlton not only volunteered but was unanimously chosen to be captain of a local militia unit—which is how he ended up in Charlestown facing this terrifying British naval bombardment.

Knowlton surveyed the hillside and saw an existing livestock fence made of rails that was assembled with a method known as stake-and-rider and ran on the slope in a zigzag pattern. He quickly realized it offered another useful barrier to possible British advances.[11] Knowlton's men expanded and reinforced the southwestern length of the fence with additional rails and posts taken from nearby fields and stuffed the gaps between the rails with haycocks and bundles of cut grass. They also added several freestanding fleches—small, triangular-shaped works—which would allow Knowlton's men to fire on an attacking British force from several directions. These defenses might not have been as formidable and protective as the fort atop Breed's Hill, but it gave the Connecticut troops a decent barricade to crouch behind and from which to fire upon the British. At the time of the battle, a gap of about 200 feet remained in the provincials' defensive line between the rail fence and the redoubt's breastwork. The Americans had done what they could, and they hoped that it would be enough.

Prescott's primary aim was to get the fort built before the British could launch a ground attack later in the morning. According to author Richard Frothingham, after the battle, Prescott was frequently heard remarking that "his great anxiety was to have a screen raised, however slight, as he knew it would be difficult, if not impossible, to make raw troops, however full of patriotism, to stand, in an open field, against artillery and well-armed and well-disciplined soldiers."[12] This was why Prescott urged on the work so forcefully, pressing his men to strain at the task even to the point of exhaustion. After such an effort, it was fair to say that the Americans were not then in the best shape to fight a strenuous battle, which they would find themselves doing in a matter of hours.

Still early in the day, General Thomas Gage, the British Military Governor who had been installed in Massachusetts by King George III in May 1774, came to Copp's Hill in Boston's North End, directly across the river from Charlestown, to see firsthand what the Americans were doing.[13] With him was Colonel Abijah Willard, a Massachusetts loyalist who was a high-ranking aide. Gage handed Willard his spyglass and asked him to view what was going on in Charlestown, saying, "Who is this person who appears to command?"[14] Remarkably, given the distance, Willard told Gage, "It's Prescott."[15] Willard knew it was Prescott because he was his brother-in-law, having married Prescott's older sister, Elizabeth. In a conversation at Prescott's house a number of weeks earlier, Willard had tried to reason with him, noting that if he took up arms against the British his life and estate would be forfeited for treason.

Prescott had replied, "I have made up my mind on that subject. I think it probable I may be found in arms, but I will never be taken alive. The Tories shall never have the satisfaction of seeing me hang."[16]

Gage asked Willard, "Will he fight?" Willard confirmed Prescott would, saying, "Yes, sir. He is an old soldier and he will fight as long as there is a drop of blood in his veins."[17] In another version of the exchange, cited by historian Richard Ketchum, Willard was reported to have said, "I cannot answer for his men, but Prescott will fight you to the gates of hell."[18] And, in the Prescott genealogical history compiled many years after the war, Willard's alleged response to Gage was even more prophetic: "It is my brother-in-law, Prescott. Yes, that man will fight, and if his men are like him, you will have bloody work today."[19] Whichever account is correct (maybe all bear some truth) is of little consequence, as the intent was clear: Prescott and the Americans would stand their ground. Gage's response was short and to the point: "The works must be carried."

Escalation

Recognizing the seriousness of the situation in Charlestown, Gage then assembled his leading generals—William Howe, Henry Clinton, and John Burgoyne—who had arrived a month earlier in Boston on the aptly named warship, HMS *Cerberus*, to form a plan of attack.[20] As author Rick Atkinson notes, once in Boston, the three prestigious officers had wasted little time in undercutting Gage's authority, with Burgoyne haughtily pointing out that "it was no reflection to say he [Gage] is unequal to his present station, for few characters in the world would be fit for it. It requires a genius of the very first class."[21] Burgoyne referred to the three generals as "the triumvirate of reputation," and their presence seemed to have forced Gage to act more decisively.[22]

Huddled together with Gage, General Clinton proposed a combined naval and land assault in which the British would sail past the Breed's Hill redoubt and deploy their troops near the narrow Charlestown Neck connecting the peninsula to Cambridge on the west.[23] Clinton's idea was to cut off the provincials' escape route and trap them where they stood. General Howe had a different plan, however. He pushed for a frontal assault on the redoubt after landing his troops on the Charlestown waterfront. Gage, fearing that if his troops disembarked near the Neck they might be attacked from both sides, agreed with Howe, and that became the strategy. Later, Clinton, piqued at Gage's decision, would say that Gage was inclined to ignore anyone, like him, who lacked fighting experience in America.[24] In reality, Howe's reputation as a field commander was nonpareil, which added weight to his recommendation, and which likely sealed the decision in Gage's mind.

Gage and Howe felt very strongly that the volunteer provincial soldiers could not repulse their trained troops and a brazen frontal assault would therefore demonstrate to the Americans that their opposition was foolish.[25] As writer Samuel Adams Drake noted in his 1875 summary of the battle, "If the Americans really meant to offer battle with the hope of deciding the fate of Boston, it was an exhibition of singular hardihood, as they had no officers capable of leading large bodies of troops."[26] This was exactly why the British were convinced that the Americans would be easily overmatched. Although William Prescott had distinguished himself years earlier while fighting with the British, there is no indication that Gage, Howe, Clinton, or Burgoyne knew anything about him at the time of the battle or that they were worried about how he and his troops would perform.

In making his decision to attack Charlestown, Gage might have also been reacting to some prevailing views back in England that he was too soft on the provincials and hadn't been decisive enough when hostilities had broken out. Gage had married a wealthy American woman from New Jersey—Margaret Kemble—which could have affected his view of the colonists and caused him to be more measured. Feeling pressure to act, Gage might have wanted to impress his three recently arrived, decorated generals. Thus, punishing the provincials in a direct assault would do two things—eliminate the American threat in a dramatic way and simultaneously repair his image.[27]

Gage assigned the 45-year-old Howe to command the troops that would assault Charlestown.[28] Like Prescott, Howe was relatively tall, standing about six feet. And much like the Americans' soon-to-be-famous general, George Washington, Howe had gained his primary military leadership experience during the French and Indian War. As with Washington, too, Howe had miraculously survived several bloody battlefield actions without being killed or wounded while his fellow soldiers were cut down or maimed all around him. For instance, as a young officer, Howe had led the attack on the Plains of Abraham at Quebec, which ended up being the decisive engagement in the final battle of the French and Indian War.[29] Later, Howe had developed a reputation as a master of light infantry tactics, which rely on speed and maneuverability. When this brilliance and agility had been displayed at the battle of Havana in 1762, Howe was regarded as the most dazzling commander of the British Army.[30]

That Howe was even in America was a surprise, however. Howe possessed a conciliatory posture toward the Americans, even telling the constituents in his district in England that he did not believe the British Army could defeat them.[31] For this and other reasons, Howe had also said he would decline a command in the colonies. Nonetheless, eventually King George, looking for a strong military leader in America, had pressed the issue and persuaded Howe to take the assignment.

Before the attack on June 17, Howe had written to his brother, Richard, the respected admiral, and relayed General Gage's plan. The action was slated for Sunday, June 18—first to occupy and fortify Dorchester Heights and then, if possible, to advance across Roxbury to secure Boston from that side. Afterwards, from Roxbury, the British were to march to Charlestown and "attack the Rebels at Cambridge from the [Charlestown] Heights."[32] Now, circumstances would force a change in those plans and make Charlestown the first objective.

When Howe was given the responsibility of removing the Americans from Charlestown, he assembled about 1,550 men in his initial landing force. This was a sizable number—about a quarter of all the British troops in Boston—and was deemed sufficient to dispatch the Americans from their fortifications. On the other hand, while field cannons were also meant to play a significant role in the attack, the artillery units that accompanied the troops to Charlestown were initially supplied with the wrong-sized cannonballs and, though this was corrected eventually, the cannon did not factor into the early fighting.

Despite the British advantage in firepower, with dozens of heavy guns blasting away from anchored warships and field cannons at Howe's disposal, the Bunker Hill fight turned out to be a classic infantry battle, the prevailing, and more prosaic, military tactic of the period.[33] The key concept was to bring as many guns together as were available and to fire upon the enemy simultaneously. The attackers would form three lines, and they would load and fire their muskets in succession to maintain a steady barrage. Quick reloading would make it nearly impossible for the other side to withstand the intensity of the fire. Eventually, the stronger side would prevail and the losers would abandon the field. Usually, the winners would not pursue the retreating troops, as the pursuit would more often than not collapse into disarray. Once the field was theirs, that was good enough.

Another element of normal tactics at the time was something called "the melee." It consisted of the use of bayonets both to incite fear at the start of the fighting and to rout the enemy with consistent, overwhelming pressure when the fighting became hand-to-hand. This was the plan Howe would employ against the Americans, and he had absolutely no doubt that he would crush the inexperienced provincial troops in Charlestown. While the British troops were trained with the bayonet, Prescott's troops by and large were not, and few even had the weapon.

Committed to acting honorably despite his understandable anger with the Americans and his determination to strike a punishing blow, Gage ended his conference with his three generals with a pointed order that "Any man who shall quit his ranks on any pretense, or shall dare to blunder or pillage, will be executed without mercy."[34] Gage may or may not have known just how fully his reputation was on the line that day, but he was not going to sacrifice all of his principles in seeking victory. He wanted his troops to behave nobly, and anyone who didn't abide by that would suffer the most severe consequences.

After working hard all night on the fort, the provincials were hungry, thirsty, and dog-tired. Some also began to leave. One of the soldiers, Peter Brown, described the situation when writing to his mother in Rhode Island: "We began to feel almost beat out, being tired by our labor and having no sleep the night before."[35] Brown added, "The danger we were in made us think there was treachery, and that we were brought here to be all slain."[36]

The men who had toiled through the night to construct the redoubt were beginning to get discouraged and even to feel abandoned—as they had been told that fresh troops would relieve them in the morning and, so far, none had arrived. Prescott's officers repeatedly begged him to send for reinforcements. Initially, Prescott held off, declaring, "The men who raised these works are the best able to defend them."[37] He would eventually change this stubborn stance, but his original bravado and resolve, as shortsighted as it was, may have had a confidence-building effect on his men and impressed upon them that they would indeed be able to fight the British.

At nine o'clock, after consulting with his officers, Prescott finally relented and sent Major John Brooks of Medford, the ranking officer in Ebenezer Bridge's command, back to Cambridge for reinforcements and supplies.[38] Brooks did not have a horse and could not secure one, so he was forced to make the three-and-a-half-mile trek on foot. This would mean additional troops would probably not arrive for at least another couple of hours at best. Around this time, Colonel Richard Gridley of Massachusetts, a 65-year-old veteran of the French and Indian War, and who had designed the redoubt, left the battlefield to see if he could get some cannon. But Gridley never returned (later reports indicated he had been injured), prompting an angry Prescott to say, "The engineer forsook me."[39]

Meanwhile, another provincial commander in Charlestown, the legendary General Israel Putnam of Connecticut, was also scarce to be found. Without

Gridley or Putnam with him, Prescott was likely feeling very isolated standing in the redoubt, knowing full well the British would come, and come in force. He must have also been more than a bit anxious, since he was a battle-tested veteran and knew the British capabilities from his experience fighting with them earlier in his life.

Throughout the morning and into the afternoon, Prescott and the other soldiers on Breed's Hill could see the British in Boston preparing to come to Charlestown and confront the Americans. Every hour that the British delayed their assault gave Prescott more time to prepare. Prescott finally got some cannon in the afternoon, which initially gave him a measure of hope against the British firepower.[40] But, in the haste to build the redoubt, they had forgotten to create embrasures for the cannon (small openings in a fort's walls) and they didn't bring any wood to create gun platforms. Eventually, during the early part of the fighting, the artillery crew fired a few pitiful rounds to no effect, and the cannon were ultimately abandoned on the field.

Putnam, who spent much of the day riding between Bunker's Hill and Breed's Hill—which were about a half mile apart—came to the redoubt during the morning cannonade. Suspecting British troops would soon be arrayed against them, Putnam urged Prescott to send the entrenching tools to the rear to avoid them being taken by the British.[41] Prescott did not want to do this, fearing that the men engaged in this task would not come back. Prescott ultimately allowed Putnam to take the equipment, but, as he suspected, the men who left never returned. (Most of the entrenching tools fell into the hands of the British anyway.)[42]

Prescott did indicate to Putnam, however, that he desperately needed reinforcements, as his men were fatigued and needed nourishment. Putnam promptly set off by horse for Cambridge, overtaking the previously dispatched Major Brooks and arriving at headquarters a little after nine o'clock in the morning. In no uncertain terms, Putnam informed General Ward that Prescott was in danger and needed more troops.[43] Ward was upset when he learned that the fort had been built on Breed's Hill, not Bunker's Hill, and that Prescott wanted more men, as well as food and water.[44] Not long after Putnam headed back to Charlestown, Major Brooks finally reached Ward at the Hastings House headquarters, where he reiterated Prescott's dire circumstance.

While there, Brooks discovered that Dr. Joseph Warren, head of the Massachusetts provincial government and one of the leading figures against British rule in the colony, was also at Hastings House, stretched out on an upstairs bed with a splitting headache.[45] Upon hearing about the anticipated battle, the 34-year-old Dr. Warren immediately mixed himself an elixir to suppress his headache and prepared to make his way to Charlestown. Several friends and associates tried to dissuade him from joining the coming battle, but he rejected those pleas and rushed toward the impending fight.[46]

Warren did not have formal military training, but he had done some drills while a student at Harvard and had long seen himself serving the colony in a high-level military capacity.[47] In fact, three days earlier, he had been voted major general of the New England forces. One advantage that Warren did bring to the battle was that he knew the terrain in Charlestown very well—certainly better than the other commanders there, having lived in Boston his entire life and provided medical services to the broad population.

As for Ward, his problem was that he wasn't sure if the British were also going to attack Dorchester Heights, as earlier intelligence indicated, or maybe somewhere between the two elevations where they could isolate the provincials into two sections and finish off each in turn.[48] Ward also hadn't intended to engage the British in a major fight at this time, and so he hesitated to supply the requested reinforcements. Ward was worried that he only had 27 half-barrels of powder in his arsenal, which was about enough for 40,000 cartridges, or only about 20 shots per soldier.[49]

As the hours passed before the battle, Prescott periodically checked to see if any reinforcements were coming. So far, none were. As the sun got higher and the day warmer, the troops in Charlestown were worn out and getting more and more worried. It was hard to argue against the supposition that they had been abandoned and left to fight the British on their own.

While the provincials were preparing their defenses, Howe was still getting his troops in order in Boston and moving them toward the harbor. Howe's General Orders that morning eliminated any doubt about the seriousness of the action when he repeated Gage's forceful admonition about deserting or pillaging.[50] Finally, at one o'clock, roughly eight and a half hours after the Americans were initially spotted on Breed's Hill, General Howe had gotten his troops organized and loaded on 28 barges arrayed in two columns that would ferry the men to Charlestown in successive round trips.[51]

As the barges made their way across the Charles River, David Avery, a Connecticut chaplain on top of Breed's Hill, watched in amazement and then raised both arms to heaven, asking God's mercy on a "scene most awful and tremendous."[52] Amos Farnsworth, the celebrated diarist from Groton, was a little more matter of fact about the scene when he wrote in his diary:

> The Enemy appeared to be much Alarmed on Saturday Morning when they discovered Our operations and immediately began a heavy Cannonading from a battery on Corps [sic] Hill Boston and from the Ships in ye Harbor…we with little loss Continued to Carry on our

works till 1 o'clock when we discovered a large Body of the Enemy Crossing Charles-River from Boston…they landed on a Point of land about a Mile Eastward of our Intrenchment And immediately disposed their army for an attack previous to which they Set fire to the town of Charlestown.[53]

Initially, Howe's troops landed at Morton's Point (also referred to as Moulton's Hill), which was another small elevation along the edge of the Charlestown waterfront, roughly three-quarters of a mile from Breed's Hill. No one contested the landing and, after a rest, Howe eventually formed his troops there in the customary three battle lines: the grenadiers and light infantry constituted the first line, the 38th and 5th Regiments the second line, and the 52nd and 43rd the third line.[54]

Reinforcements, Finally

Around two o'clock, having received the consent of the Committee of Safety, General Ward agreed to send to Charlestown additional troops from the New Hampshire militia, which was encamped in Medford about four miles north along the Mystic River. There was little time to spare. Ward gave reinforcement orders to Colonels John Stark and James Reed, who quickly sent an advance detachment of two hundred New Hampshire militia—about one-third of Stark's regiment—to support Prescott.[55] Stark also had the rest of his troops, most of whom he had recruited since arriving in Medford, draw ammunition from a local house that had been converted into an armory. Each soldier was to get 15 musket balls, a flint, and about five ounces of gunpowder. These men were also sent forward, along with all of Colonel Reed's regiment, at about 11 o'clock.[56]

Colonel John Stark, the New Hampshire commander, was a five-foot-ten, square-jawed, 47-year-old of Scottish ancestry.[57] He had deep-set, light-blue eyes and was so serious some wondered if he had any sense of humor. An accomplished farmer and tradesman with a successful timber business, Stark was physically fit and fiercely independent. Although he was not talkative, he was very comfortable speaking his mind to anyone. A tough, fearless fighter, he was characterized as "the sort who caused others to sense that they were in the presence of a dangerous individual."[58] An immensely popular commander, Stark had been elected colonel by a unanimous show of hands in a local New Hampshire tavern, and so many men decided to enlist under his command that 13 companies were formed in his regiment.[59] As a result, Stark led one of the largest regiments yet to be assembled in the young patriot army.

Like Prescott, Stark had impressed the British during the French and Indian War as a second lieutenant in the famed regiment of Major Robert Rogers, called Rogers' Rangers.[60] While part of this well-regarded group, Stark had gained invaluable experience and detailed knowledge of the northern frontier. Earlier in his life, he had demonstrated his fierce nature when he was captured by Abenaki Indians and brought to Canada.[61] Forced to run the gauntlet where one would ordinarily be beaten by clubs and sticks, Stark had grabbed the weapon out of the hands of the first Indian in the line and began beating him with it. The tribe's chief was so impressed he'd stopped the affair and adopted Stark into the tribe. Later, when Rogers' Rangers went on a raiding mission to the village of Saint Francis in Quebec where the Abenaki resided, Stark had maintained his allegiance to the tribe and refused orders to attack them.

Now in Massachusetts, Stark was surprised when his son, Caleb, not yet 17 years old, joined him in Medford, looking to fight alongside his father.[62] Annoyed at first, Stark let his son stay and directed one of his officers to give him something to do. Caleb's instinct for action was not unlike his father's. John had been energized by the news of Lexington and Concord in April and wanted to get involved, just as his son did now. Indeed, as it was recorded, after the earlier fighting, John abruptly left his family and home, "hastening forward from his sawmill in his shirt sleeves...to ride on horseback nearly seventy miles to Cambridge to join the patriot army there."[63]

Once Stark got his instructions from Ward on the afternoon of June 17, he hurried his men to the Charlestown battlefield. At the Charlestown Neck, the narrow isthmus connecting Cambridge to Charlestown, he came upon provincial troops who were afraid to cross because artillery fire from British warships threatened their passage. This thin land formation was perhaps the weakest part of the provincials' position in Charlestown since the Americans crossing to and from the peninsula could be mercilessly attacked there from one or more warships in the river.[64] However, Stark didn't procrastinate and ordered these idle men to stand aside. Yet when his captain, Henry Dearborn, tried to hustle the New Hampshire men across the Neck and out of danger, Stark told him to slow down, saying, "One fresh man in action is worth ten fatigued men."[65] Stark then marched his troops calmly up the steep rise of Bunker's Hill singing "Yankee Doodle."[66]

Stark did not know whether he would arrive in time to make a difference. But the British attack was running behind schedule due to low tide around Charlestown, which postponed their debarkation from Boston.[67] Stark's troops arrived at Prescott's position on Breed's Hill without suffering a single casualty, increasing the strength of the American force eventually, when more New Hampshire troops came, perhaps to at least 1,600 men.[68] However, Artemas Ward's hesitancy, his lack of decisiveness to rush more men into the fray, meant his supporting action, in hindsight, wasn't as robust as it should have been.[69]

When Stark reached Breed's Hill, less than an hour before the commencement of fighting, he could see that, despite the addition of the breastwork and the rail fence barrier, the Americans were still vulnerable to a flank attack on the northern side of the redoubt and particularly along the Mystic River. Stark had read General Howe's mind exactly, as the British commander's plan was to send a contingent of his troops under Brigadier Robert Pigot up from the waterfront on a direct assault on the eastern side of the redoubt, while Howe himself would lead a large body of soldiers along the Mystic River in a classic flanking move.[70] Pigot's action on the open field would merely be a feint, meant to detract attention from Howe's men on the far right. Prescott agreed with Stark and told him to take whatever actions he felt fit.

Immediately, Stark ordered his men to fill in the space to the left of Knowlton's Connecticut troops all the way to the Mystic River beach. On Stark's orders, Captain John Moore led his company down an eight-foot riverbank and hastily started stacking fieldstones to construct a thick stone wall for his marksmen to shelter behind.[71] At the other end of their line, they also added to Knowlton's formation a contiguous rail fence made from timbers taken from the nearby fields, and stuffed this barrier with hay and grass as Knowlton's men had done. This gave the New Hampshire men at least some cover. It was really the only thing they could do in the brief time they had, and, as it turned out, it was amazingly effective.

One of Stark's key officers was Major Andrew McClary, born in Ulster, Ireland, and now a tavern owner in Londonderry, New Hampshire, who led a company of 80 men.[72] McClary had acquired his military experience years earlier, directing expeditions against hostile Indians in the New Hampshire frontier, and he was also part of Rogers' Rangers during the French and Indian War. An ardent patriot, he distinguished himself in leading an attack against British troops in Portsmouth, New Hampshire, in December 1774, overpowering the British contingent at Fort William and Mary, hauling down the British colors, and making off with roughly one hundred kegs of gunpowder.[73] With a strong, stentorian voice, the six-foot-six McClary was said to be a natural leader who inspired great morale among the New Hampshire militia. McClary now took his place behind the fortifications and awaited the British attack.

Had Howe known Prescott was about to receive the New Hampshire reinforcements that would shore up his left flank, he might have decided to strike the redoubt right then and there.[74] Instead, more time passed as the British soldiers ate, rested, and waited for instructions. Howe reconnoitered the area to obtain a better idea of the strength of the American position and, sensing a larger opposition, sent a request to Boston for more troops.[75] Howe's request was immediately answered, and he was given the 47th Regiment, 1st Marine Battalion, and some additional light infantry and grenadiers.[76] Even more troops would come later when it was clear the resistance was far stronger than expected, making the British total for the day at least 2,300 men.

Amos Farnsworth, who had scouted the Charlestown waterfront with Prescott and Putnam on Friday night and who had taken part in other prior actions, penned an entry about Saturday, June 17 in his diary. He described the situation from his vantage point in the redoubt:

> They [the British] landed on a point of land about a mile east-ward of our entrenchment and immediately disposed their army for an attack, previous to which they set fire to Charlestown. It is supposed the enemy intended to attack us under the cover of the smoke from the burning houses: the wind favoring them in such a design; while on the other side their army was extending northward towards Mystic River with an apparent design of surrounding our men in the works and cutting off any assistance intended for our relief.[77]

Then, just before Howe's troops moved out toward the redoubt, a second British cannonball fired from offshore killed an American soldier. This time it was Lieutenant Joseph Spaulding from Massachusetts, who was by Prescott's side.[78] The shot sheared off Spaulding's head, splattering his brains on Prescott. Prescott, ever composed, brushed away the blood and matter as he had done before and cleaned his hands with some loose dirt. His focus remained unbroken.

CHAPTER I

Searching for a Forgotten American Hero

Who was William Prescott? Where was he from? Did he survive the Charlestown battle? What else did he do in the Revolutionary War? How long did he live? Why is his statue the only one on Breed's Hill? Is he known for having done anything else?

As a volunteer with the National Park Service at Bunker Hill Monument National Park in Charlestown, Massachusetts, I routinely get asked these questions—which is not surprising since I had the same questions when I first began to prepare for my docent duties. What I quickly found out was that while a lot has been written about other primary American figures who participated in the battle of Bunker Hill and the revolutionary era more generally—especially Artemas Ward, Israel Putnam, John Stark, and Dr. Joseph Warren—there is very little available about William Prescott, and certainly no work that has consolidated what is known about his life in one comprehensive volume. This struck me as rather odd, since Prescott was the principal commander in one of the most consequential military actions in American history.

There is no doubt that few Americans would be able to identify who Colonel William Prescott was, what his role at Bunker Hill had been, or what he did beyond that famous confrontation. Prescott is not unique in this regard. Other American military commanders and once-celebrated soldiers throughout America's wars, who exhibited extreme bravery and achieved great renown, have similarly faded from the national memory. Joshua Lawrence Chamberlain of the Civil War, Sergeant Alvin York of World War I, and Audie Murphy of World War II come to mind. There are no doubt scores of others. But Prescott's current anonymity, especially during today's revival of early American history, is particularly egregious. Bunker Hill was a pivotal battle as the country was beginning to contemplate independence. Independence would not be won with this battle, but there was a real possibility that it could be derailed, perhaps permanently. Rarely does one person make a major difference in the course of history, but Prescott's actions at Bunker Hill formed an inflection point in American history that few others could claim.

One partial answer to the lack of scholarly attention paid to Prescott is that he was not a man of letters. Prescott did not leave a diary, a memoir, or a raft of correspondence that explained his views, actions, or his memorable life. Potential biographers have comparatively little with which to work. This is not surprising, as relatively few people in Prescott's era had the time or took the time to record their thoughts for posterity. For most, it was hard enough to get by all the travails of living in that age, when days were physically demanding and there were few hours to spare for leisure or writing history.

Thus, to learn about Prescott in the absence of a rich collection of revelatory writings, I had to do a bit of detective work. Actually, more than a bit as it turned out; a lot would be the correct description. To say something new about Prescott, I knew I had to locate as many primary sources as I could that had not been tapped by others before me. I had to engage with historians and other individuals who knew something about Prescott or the era in which he lived. I had to assemble leads that could answer the questions I had, as well as the additional questions that would surface from my efforts. Then, ultimately, I had to sift through the findings and form a portrait of Prescott that would bring him to life and satisfy my proposition that he was an important figure who should be remembered and honored.

However, because William Prescott's voice does not reverberate from the written page, to understand him more fully I had to look for clues in his behavior and the key decisions he made. This would help me determine why he did what he did. As contemporary behavioral scientists have discovered, the choices individuals make—their actual deeds—generally best explain their personal philosophies, everyday preferences, attitudes toward risk, and other elements of their personalities.[1] While it is useful to know what a particular individual has said or written about to understand his nature, it is often better to examine what that individual actually did in the course of his life. Unfortunately, even here the details of Prescott's actions are somewhat limited and are not spread evenly over his life. Rather, he comes in and out of focus. This was not ideal, but my attitude was that it was worth the effort to try to develop a meaningful portrait of this once-acclaimed, now largely forgotten, American. Prescott was a significant actor in one of the most consequential military engagements in the history of the United States. As the visitors to Bunker Hill National Historical Park ask: Shouldn't we know more?

One woman with a couple of youngsters in tow thanked me for my talk, then with firmness in her voice and pointing her finger at me for emphasis, added, "Our children in grade school should know more about this battle and its commander. It would make them appreciate American history more and the importance of our freedom."

So, in the spring of 2020, as the world was shutting down due to the rise of the Covid-19 virus, I set out on a "search" to find William Prescott, the hero of Bunker Hill. My first objective was to learn about his ancestry, as well as about the time in which he lived, the circumstances that he had to confront, and the hardships he had to endure. My plan then was to trace his actions across the revolutionary era and also dig into his life after the war. I wanted to know if Bunker Hill was Prescott's one, shining moment—to use a popular current phrase—or if there were other noteworthy moments to remember and acknowledge.

As my quest to learn about William Prescott transformed from a casual curiosity into a full-fledged book project, I knew it would be as much a detective story as straightforward history. I also knew I'd have to accept that some facets of Prescott's persona, his attitudes, and his activities might remain fuzzy or downright obscure unless and until new details were discovered. It would be a challenge, but I felt it was an important one.

My Search Begins

The first step in my investigation was to check the catalogs of the venerable Boston Public Library and its Charlestown branch where I thought there might be a collection of Bunker Hill books, files, and other primary source materials involving Prescott.[2] I also did Google searches and accessed online booksellers to see what I could find. Turned out, not much—aside from a few popular books about the battle of Bunker Hill, as well as commemorative speeches and other monographs celebrating Prescott. Even the Bunker Hill Museum across the street from the battlefield had only a few books on the battle, such as well-known works by Paul Lockhart and Nathaniel Philbrick, which I had already read.

After coming up essentially empty-handed in my initial outreach, I made the first of a number of forays to the Massachusetts Historical Society (MHS) in downtown Boston. As its website says, the Society is "the oldest organization in the United States devoted to the collection of materials for the study of American history." The MHS opened its doors in 1791, when it was called simply The Historical Society, a straightforward name that seemed to indicate its founders didn't expect another historical society to be established.

The MHS is located in a stylish building at the top of Boylston Street, a major artery heading west out of Boston's downtown. Several long vertical banners hang above the few steps leading up to the entrance doors, which are bordered with Doric columns, underscoring the MHS's serious nature. As required due to Covid precautions, I had made an appointment to work in the research library and had already browsed ABIGAIL—the MHS's rich online catalog named after Abigail Adams—in order to request material about William Prescott.

Inside, I was directed at the check-in desk to place my belongings, including my shoulder bag, notebooks, pens, and jacket, in a keyed locker in a small room off the lobby. Paper and pencils would be available to me inside. I was allowed to bring in my phone and could take pictures of the materials I would be studying, but everything else had to remain in the locker. I headed up the carpeted ramp to the research library, pushed through the glass doors, and found a vacant table where I could receive the material I had requested online days earlier.

There were three others in the research room, spaced out and hunched over assorted files and other materials. I would soon assume their posture, focused on centuries-old documents and buried deep in thought. I was provided soft, angled book props on which to rest my fragile materials, as well as string weights to keep the opened pages in place. The room was quiet, and bright sunlight streamed in through the tall windows on the long wall to the right of my table.

Settled in, I was hoping I might come upon a treasure trove of Prescott material that would quickly satisfy my accumulating curiosities. I did find a treasure trove, but it was associated with another William Prescott—William Hickling Prescott, the Colonel's grandson and a renowned historian, who had left a large volume of his papers to the MHS.[3] In those papers, I located only a handful of documents dealing with the Colonel. Fortunately, I did find Prescott's wartime orderly book and his personal paybook of wartime and non-wartime financial transactions. This was very useful information, but, as interesting as it was, it didn't tell me anything close to what I was looking for.

Based on recommendations from various writers, historians, and researchers, I then visited the massive home of the Massachusetts Archives at Columbia Point in the Dorchester section of Boston. The 100,000-square-foot building, designed to look like a colonial-era fort, had opened in 1985, replacing the basement of the State House as the core repository of Massachusetts' historical records. The sturdy, granite-blocked Archives is nestled between the campus of the University of Massachusetts/Boston, the John F. Kennedy Presidential Library, and the Edward M. Kennedy Institute. As its Wikipedia page explains, the Archives "works to ensure the preservation and accessibility of government records, and helps protect the Commonwealth's historic heritage for its citizens, students, and scholars."

Among other historic documents, the facility contains copies of the 1629 English Charter of the Bay Colony, the Declaration of Independence, the Bill of Rights, 1780 Massachusetts Constitution, and a host of Revolutionary and Civil War documents. It has numerous documents signed by luminaries including John Adams, John Hancock, Thomas Jefferson, and George Washington, as well as treaties made with Native American tribes and a compilation of slave records. Researchers, officials, and everyday citizens also have access to 11.8 billion vital records of births, marriages, and deaths in the state. There are also treasury records, census schedules, tax lists, judicial actions, and legislative orders covering the history of the state. It is, without exaggeration, the mother lode of Massachusetts history.

When I presented myself at the long, oak check-in desk, a laminated badge was made for me and I was directed, just like at the MHS, to put my belongings in a locker just off the main lobby. I sharpened a few of the pencils that were provided and was ready to go. There was only one other person in the bright and inviting research room, so I easily found a quiet place to sit among the half-dozen or so wide tables and made a list of the topics I wanted to pursue. Behind me was a wall of five-foot-tall, wooden card catalogs with slide-out trays, like the ones you see in old public libraries. These trays are the keys to the repository's collection.

Only a few other researchers filtered in, so I had virtually the full attention of several of the Archives' staff. Caitlyn Ramos, Head of Reference, Conor Snow, Reference Archivist, and Amber Hayward, a Northeastern University Co-op student, helped me navigate the online databases and answered questions I had about the files. These three showed an earnestness and focus that belied the stereotype of the languid government worker. Much to my delight, the youthful trio got instantly engaged in my detective work and hopped from card catalog to computer screen and back again to try to track down my inquiries into Massachusetts' colonial past. With their help, I combed through the FamilySearch database, period letters, muster rolls, government reports, and more.

By all rights, this expansive repository should have offered a deep vein of materials related to someone like William Prescott who, due to his command at Bunker Hill alone, should have been considered one of the most important figures in the early history of the state. Distressingly, the online files were tough to work with, as many of the scanned pages were imperfect images of hard-to-read and deteriorated documents. I scrolled back and forth through the material, but on this first visit only found a few useful items.

Furthermore, as anyone who has worked with primary source documents from the colonial period knows, even when you locate a relevant document, it is frequently a challenge to decipher what had been written on those disintegrating sheets. The task is made harder by illegible handwriting, fanciful lettering, gross misspellings, and faded ink. The imprecise nature of colonial recordkeeping also contributes to the problem.

Despite these hurdles, however, I was determined to plow on. The detective search was unfolding slowly, but I wanted to get to the bottom of Prescott's story. What were the factors that influenced his behavior and formed his character? How did he feel about the growing tensions with the British troops in Boston and the Parliament in London? Was he for or against separation from England? In other words, was he a patriot? How did he feel about the war effort? Ultimately, was he happy with the outcome of the struggle for liberty? Did he favor a national government or a federal republic, or did he simply prefer that Massachusetts remain an independent state?

After several painstaking hours, I left the Archives, wondering if its files did not have what I was looking for or if I simply could not find what was there. I drove out of the parking lot very discouraged. Two historical repositories down, two disappointing experiences. Faced with a paucity of material on William Prescott, I began to feel like a paleontologist at an archeological dig sifting through a collection of calcified bones in an attempt to construct a prehistoric skeleton. And like the more unfortunate ones who only find a few remains—an arm bone here, a femur there, and maybe a jawbone somewhere nearby—I knew right away that this was going to be a harder task than I had hoped.

Then, only days later, a breakthrough occurred. This came about after I explained my dilemma to the National Park Service's Lead Ranger in Charlestown—Dan Gagnon—who supervised my volunteer activities at Bunker Hill National Historical Park. Dan, now retired, sent me a link that he had found to a genealogical history of the Prescott family published in 1870 by descendant William Prescott, M.D. (one of a long line of William Prescotts). As best I can determine, much of what is known about the Prescotts' arrival in America and their early years in the Commonwealth comes from this document.

While the Prescott family history may be presumed to be accurate, you never know when exaggeration or myth may creep into the lore. Ultimately, however, this compilation is the best available information on the Prescott lineage and, although I have no reason to question its accuracy, it should be taken for what it is. What I really needed, too, was to locate, if I could, living descendants on the Prescott family tree to verify the facts (to the extent they would be able) and to supply other information that might not be in the 1870 history. And this is where some serendipity came in.

While working on other aspects of my research and still running down a host of leads, Julie Hall, the energetic president of the Charlestown Historical Society, texted me excitedly, saying that at a local Society event she had met "a gentleman who said he is a descendant of Prescott!" Julie sent me his contact information, and I quickly got in touch with Jonathan (Jon) Prescott Feltner, a Massachusetts native, who informed me of his heritage and expressed interest in my work. While Jon is not in the direct line descending from Colonel William Prescott, he is a 10th-generation Prescott following a parallel line from namesake Captain Jonathan Prescott (1643–1721). In other words, he is a cousin. Perhaps the most notable ancestor in Jon's lineage is Dr. Samuel Prescott, who, as we will hear later, rode with Paul Revere and William Dawes from Lexington on April 19, 1775 to alert the citizens of Concord that British troops were heading their way.

Jon very enthusiastically offered me his help and became a timely and useful resource in my efforts. I discovered only weeks afterward that Jon is, like other ancestral Prescotts, a distinguished military veteran, with two Purple Hearts and a Bronze Star for his actions in the Vietnam War, as well as a Navy Commendation Medal for later activity. A true Prescott, Jon, who had a successful legal career, has also dedicated much of his life to community service.

"I heard about your project and thought I'd reach out to see if I could help," Jon said in our first telephone meeting. "Tell me to go away, if you can't use me," he added. "I don't want to impose on you."

"I need all the help I can get," I told Jon and quickly reviewed some of the topics I was exploring. "Right now, I'm trying to learn about William Prescott's ancestors, to see if they provide any clues to his behavior and attitudes."

"That's a good assignment for me," Jon responded, "as I've already done some research into the Prescott line in America; they are an interesting bunch."

Jon quickly provided information about William Prescott's relatives in Middlesex County, located some detailed material on the Provincial Army, and offered some anecdotes about various Prescotts. He also introduced me to Linda Geiger of Connecticut, who is another Prescott descendant in the same original line as Jon. Lucky for me, Linda is a certified genealogist and was able to confirm various details of the Prescott descendancy. Linda shared with me her files of William Prescott's military service records, probate records, and other original documents. Between Jon and Linda, I had stumbled upon a couple of dedicated Prescott sleuths who expanded my research team. I got right to work piecing together Prescott's heritage.

CHAPTER 2

Frontier Family

William Prescott was a fourth-generation American. He was born on February 20, 1726, in the eastern district of Groton, Massachusetts, roughly 40 miles northwest of Boston. In those days Groton was still considered the frontier; the land was virgin and Native Americans were prevalent. Prescott's ancestors arrived in America about 86 years earlier, making it one of the earliest European families in the colonies. Over this time, the Prescotts were able to build a decent life through hard work and a willingness to take on more and more responsibilities. They had not succumbed to the typical trials and tribulations associated with life in what was, in reality, a young and fragile territory; they rose to the top of their communities, eventually living in relative comfort and security.

The Prescott lineage can be traced back in England to at least the time of Queen Elizabeth, known as the Virgin Queen, who was the last of the five monarchs of the House of Tudor and who reigned from 1558 to 1603. The name Prescott, derived from the concatenation of two Saxon words—priest and cottage—has long been known in England. In fact, Prescot (with one "t") is the name of a market town in northern England about eight miles east of Liverpool that is renowned for the manufacture of watches and watch tools.[1]

The genealogical history of the Prescotts begins in the mid-16th century with James Prescott, William Prescott's great-great-grandfather, who was "one of the gentlemen who were required by an Order of Queen Elizabeth, signed in August 1564, to keep in readiness horsemen and armor to defend the Crown."[2] In order words, James had to provide military support if the queen were in need of it. This presumably meant that he was deemed to be a capable fighter, one who could lead men in battle. This recognition would have been considered a high honor, and James would have been admired and respected by his neighbors and associates because of it.

It was James's son, John, a Puritan born around 1604, who left England for America. Like most of the early Puritan emigrants to New England, this was probably to escape religious persecution. John, William Prescott's great-grandfather, had been born in Lancaster County, England, about two hundred miles from London. In 1638, while in his mid-30s, John set out from Yorkshire and headed southwestward across the ocean, visiting several British colonies, including Barbados, where he first settled.[3]

Barbados had been a popular destination for English refugees since 1625, most of whom were indentured. These were joined later by English Civil War veterans of the 1640s.[4] Interestingly, two such veterans were Lewis and Richard Morris, who fought on Oliver Cromwell's side in the war against King Charles I. The two Morrises migrated to New York from Barbados and in time became quite wealthy. They were also ancestors of Bronx-born Gouverneur Morris, a founding father and author of the U.S. Constitution.[5] Emigrants to Barbados received free land as an inducement, which may have attracted John Prescott, as it had attracted others. So John's circuitous route to a new future in America was not so unique.

The promise of opportunity in the new, northern colonies made John Prescott's stay in Barbados relatively short. He and his young family sailed to Boston in 1640, when that city was only 10 years old and when the American colonies in general were still very young. But because the port of Boston was on its way to establishing itself as a significant trading center in New England, it was a popular site for migrating Europeans.

John first settled in Watertown, one of Boston's emerging communities about four miles inland from the coast, where he pursued his trade as a blacksmith. There, John accumulated an estate of 126 acres and seemed poised to settle down for the long-term. However, John soon decided to venture further westward in the colony when a promising business arrangement presented a chance to expand his fortunes.

About eight years before the English arrived at Plymouth, Massachusetts in 1620, many Native American tribes had been decimated by a terrible pestilence, reducing their populations dramatically.[6] The Nashaway tribe of Algonquins in Central Massachusetts was particularly affected by this plague. The Nashaways were also involved in various conflicts with the Mohawks, an Iroquoian-speaking tribe that had communities in southeastern Canada and northern New York State. The Mohawks became the scourge of other New England tribes. This unbearable situation persuaded Sholan, the peaceful sachem of the Nashaways, to seek friendship with the English settlers in the region, whom they hoped would protect them.

Sholan occasionally visited Watertown on the western edge of Boston in order to trade with a Mr. Thomas King, an immigrant from England, who lived there. Sholan recommended to King that an area called Nashawogg, near the central Massachusetts town of Sterling, was a suitable place for a plantation. Upon inspecting the land, the impressed King formed an association with several investors to purchase a tract almost 80 miles square. This group included Harmon Garrett of Charlestown, Thomas Skidmore and Stephen Day of Cambridge, and John Prescott, King's neighbor in Watertown.

The transfer of Sholan's property to the Americans was approved by the Massachusetts General Court (more formally known then as the Great and General Court).[7] However, various obstacles slowed the growth of the plantation. As a result, all of the members of the association, except John Prescott, ended up not fulfilling their contracts to develop the area. As was reported, "Only one of the associates, John Prescott the stalwart blacksmith, was faithful among the faithless. He turned not back, but vigorously pursued the interests of the plantation till his exertions were crowned with success."[8]

John Prescott, young and ambitious, then chose the Nashawogg area for his future home, selling all his property holdings in Watertown. John purchased a remote trading post at a crossing of the Nashua River, roughly 25 miles from the nearest English settlement.[9] He opted for this area not only for the perceived economic opportunity it offered, but, with his Baptist leanings and advocacy of religious tolerance, he felt he was not welcome in Watertown.

To have the Nashawogg territory declared a town, John had to appeal to the General Court, which, in addition to promulgating laws, also sat as the judicial court of appeals. According to the Prescott genealogical history, the court, for unknown reasons, treated the settlement at Nashawogg with "indifference and culpable neglect."[10] Being so far from Boston, perhaps it was a case of out of sight, out of mind. The court also objected to the proposal to name the area Prescott, saying, "It smacked too much of man worship or man-service." Eventually, however, the transaction was completed, and on May 18, 1653, the territory was incorporated as the new township of Lancaster, named in honor of John Prescott's birthplace in England.

Seduced by the Indians' recommendation that the area was a fine location for a plantation, another part of John's business interest in the region was related to iron ore deposits that were found there. Because of those ores, many of the early settlers in the territory ended up becoming gunsmiths and blacksmiths like John Prescott was.

Although the area held great promise, there was no denying that in the 17th and 18th centuries colonists throughout Massachusetts faced harsh winters, crop failures, and other hardships that made life extremely difficult. On the frontier, inhabitants had to work together to ensure that new settlements would take root. Religion also played an outsized role in the survival of those settlements, and conformity was a vital ingredient of success. Town elders kept an attentive eye on mavericks, dissenters, and other troublemakers who could fracture the critical foundation of the community. A good example of this was the case of Anne Hutchinson of Boston, who was banished from Massachusetts in 1637 for religious views that were deemed heretical and contrary to those held by the town elders.[11]

New England towns secured needed capital improvements and commercial development by awarding monopolies to leading town founders, like John Prescott, who would then invest their own financial resources and expertise.[12] This stimulated growth. For instance, at the time Lancaster was incorporated, there were just nine families in the town. By the spring of the following year, 1654, 20 families inhabited the area.

Lancaster granted John 70 acres of land, a five-pound loan for the purchase of iron for a mill, and a seven-year abatement of taxes.[13] From the start, John was considered a man of high character, and an influential member of the original Puritan stock of the region. Like many contemporaries, John devoted most of his time to building mills and farming the rich soil into productive fruit fields and meadows. His hard work, integrity, perseverance, and high morals were prominent traits that many of his descendants would exhibit generation after generation.[14]

In 1652, John swore an oath of fidelity to the town and later was admitted a freeman. This meant he was no longer a "common" and could now join a church and become a member of the local governing body to enact and enforce laws, as well as to judge various civil and criminal matters. The following year, John was awarded a land grant by the citizens of Lancaster on the condition that he build a corn mill for the town.[15] Soon after that, John also constructed a sawmill.

Unfortunately, Lancaster, like other frontier towns, occasionally suffered at the hands of Native American tribes, particularly when there was war between England, the Americans' mother country, and France, England's frequent opponent. In 1675, only about 20 years after the town was incorporated, eight inhabitants of Lancaster were killed in a raid.[16] A year later, roughly 1,500 Native Americans attacked again, this time more intent on decimating the town. Lancaster had about 50 families then, and more than four dozen people were killed or captured during this raid, in which the town was destroyed.

Despite these tragic events, John Prescott was not intimidated and did not abandon the region. On the contrary, he went on to have several memorable, if not hair-raising, interactions with local tribesmen in defense of his land and property. To start with, John had brought with him from England a coat of mail, armor, and medieval habiliments (clothing) that were worn by ancient warriors.[17] From this, it was inferred that some of John's English ancestors, perhaps including his father, James, had been knighted warriors. It was also believed by the family that John himself had served under Oliver Cromwell. Connection to Cromwell would have embellished John's reputation even more and that of the Prescotts in general.

Whenever John had difficulty with Native Americans, he would don his coat of mail, helmet, cuirass (breastplate and backplate), and gorget (steel collar to protect the throat), which not only offered protection but made him look fierce and intimidating.[18] On one occasion, John, in all his armor and looking like some kind of alien, chased after the men who had stolen his horse. Another time, the tribesmen set fire to his barn and he again put on his armor and drove them off his property. But a third incident, perhaps embellished by family lore and sounding like the unlikely script from a B movie, was his most remarkable encounter. This time, the tribesmen attacked him while he was inside his house, and he tricked them into thinking that they were fighting not just him but a group of men. As the attackers advanced on his home, John moved about the house shouting orders as if he had additional men with him. John had several muskets, which his wife, the former Mary Gawkroger Platts, kept loaded throughout the engagement. John fired at the approaching men through various openings in the house, hitting more than a few of them. John and Mary kept up the deception for half an hour. Fooled, the attackers decided to withdraw, carrying off their dead and wounded with them.

Notwithstanding the troubles with the local natives, John fortunately lived to see the town rebuilt and returned to prosperity.[19] John and his wife had nine children—four sons and five daughters.[20] Large families were the norm then, as disease, accidents, and other causes of death often reduced the size of families, sometimes by as much as 50 percent. John finally passed away in 1683, nearly 45 years after arriving in the new world, having made his mark and setting the tone for succeeding generations of Prescotts. He was 75 years old.

By the time of John's death, the growing clan of Prescotts were solidly rooted in the region. In addition to founding Lancaster, Prescotts were among the first settlers of the Massachusetts towns of Sudbury, Concord, and Groton.[21] It was John's youngest son, Jonas, born in June 1648, who ended up settling in Groton, which the General Court made a township on

May 25, 1655, just two years after Lancaster was founded.[22] The tract was named after the town of Groton in Suffolk, England, and sat roughly 14 miles northeast from Lancaster. When the grant was made, and in keeping with the prevailing practice, it was specifically stipulated that "Mr. Jonathan Danforth of Cambridge [an early inhabitant], with others as he desired, should with all convenient speed secure the services of a minister, whom the selectmen of the town should pay with a fair salary." Hiring a minister was a sure indication that a town's citizens were committed to its development.

At the time of its incorporation, Groton was the northwestern-most town in the Bay Colony and it is where Jonas, William Prescott's grandfather, decided to establish his own farm.[23] The area was blessed with rugged and unspoiled beauty, marked by rivers, meadows, and forested thickets. Roads were cut to farms, pastures, and woodlots, and a church was erected in the town center. Still, those living there knew well the dangers that the local Native Americans represented. As a result, settlers gathered in garrison-style homes—large, well-built structures that could house many families. Militia troops patrolled the area and guards stood watch. Staying safe was a group effort.

As his father had done, Jonas took advantage of the natural resources in the region and built the first ironworks in nearby Forge Valley, beginning that area's long history of industrial activity. And, again like his father, Jonas became a blacksmith. He was also Groton's first miller.[24]

Groton was known for its excellent fishing and farming. The region started with the trading post of a settler named John Tinker, whose activities brought him in close contact with various indigenous tribes—and, unfortunately, the area did not remain peaceful. During King Philip's War, from 1675 to 1678, Native Americans raided and burned all the buildings in the town except for four structures.[25] Naturally, the killings and destruction of the village put everyone on edge and sowed doubt into the long-term viability of the community. After the destruction of Lancaster and Groton, the towns were abandoned for two years. But, eventually resigned to the danger, many in the region felt "this venture into the wilderness was their destiny and that they had been called on a mission to establish a kingdom of Puritan righteousness."[26] Consequently, they rebuilt the towns, accepted hard work and physical risk as part of God's way of testing their faith, and attributed anything that happened to them as God's will.[27]

Jonas's personal life was no less complicated. He courted a young woman named Mary Loker, the daughter of John Loker, who was the head of a wealthy family in Sudbury, situated to the southeast of Groton.[28] Mary's parents did not want her to wed a blacksmith, a mere tradesman. Instead, they preferred her spouse be a lawyer, and therefore forbade Jonas from entering their house, hoping to break up the romance. The Lokers also barred Mary's windows to try to prevent Jonas from even speaking with Mary. Still, Jonas persisted, and the Lokers, in desperation, felt compelled to move Mary to Chocksett, a pleasant locale near the town of Sterling, a fair distance away. Jonas kept up his pursuit and located Mary, who had vowed to marry only him. The couple finally married on December 14, 1672, with the Loker family so distressed they did not provide a customary dowry. This financial snub was only a minor setback for Jonas, who poured himself into his work. Jonas and Mary were blessed with four sons and eight daughters.

Jonas mined bog-ore in Groton to be smelted into iron at a mill site on Stony Brook.[29] The iron was used for making candlesticks, farm tools, and household items. Then, at a Groton town meeting in the 1670s, it was agreed that Jonas would grind the town's corn, designating it would be done on the second and sixth day of each week. Following this decree, in 1681, Groton also granted Jonas permission to set up his own corn mill at Stony Brook. Later, he was also asked to operate a sawmill. This was almost an exact replica of his father's life.

Also reminiscent of his father, Jonas was prominent in the military and the civic affairs in Groton.[30] In 1689, Jonas was appointed lieutenant of the militia by the colonial government and was also a selectman, town clerk, surveyor of highways, and a commissioner devoted to trying small, legal cases. As evidence of his substantial reputation, Jonas represented Groton in the Massachusetts General Assembly later in life. He was also captain of the Military Company of Groton in King William's War, which ran from 1688 to 1697.[31] In all, Jonas lived a remarkably productive life thanks to his indefatigable hard work and tenacity, prominent traits that seemed to mark all Prescotts both before and after him. Jonas died on December 31, 1723 at the age of 75, three years before his grandson, William, would be born.[32]

It was Jonas's youngest son, Benjamin—William's father—who became the second proprietor of the Prescott farm in Groton. Benjamin was born on January 4, 1696, and, similarly to his father and grandfather before him, was an accomplished and active man. Benjamin, a member of the third generation of Prescotts in America, was considered by his neighbors and other townsfolk to be a man of "superior mental endowments and of commanding appearance." He had an enviable reputation and was noted for his "sagacity, sound judgment and decision of character." In 1723, the year his father died, Benjamin was elected to represent Groton in the General Court for the first time. He was only 27 years old. He stayed on the court for eight years, winning a series of reelections. He was also commissioned a justice of the peace.

Then, in 1732, as his tenure on the General Court was ending, Benjamin was made lieutenant colonel in the local militia. Thus, he maintained the military tradition of his forbears. Three years after that, Benjamin was appointed a justice of the Superior Court. He was also asked to represent the province at the Court of Great Britain, but he declined the post, saying that he had never had smallpox and was fearful of contracting it during his travels. Perhaps his reluctance was a bit of clairvoyance, as his replacement, the Honorable Edmund Quincy, died of smallpox on his mission.

Benjamin married Abigail Oliver of Cambridge on June 11, 1718, when he was 23 years old. The Olivers were large landowners and among the wealthiest families in the region. This marriage inducted the Prescotts into an elite class in the colony. Benjamin and Abigail had seven children: three sons and four daughters. Their first child was a daughter, Abigail, born on April 23, 1719, who tragically died when she was a youthful 20-year-old. As was often the case with women of that era, little was documented about her life. Their second child, James, was born almost two years after Abigail. James went on to marry his cousin, Susanna Lawrence—not an unusual event in those times—on June 18, 1752, when he was 31 years old. James was highly accomplished and heavily engaged in public affairs, maintaining that longstanding pattern for Prescott men. James sat on the General Court for 14 years and was also a member of the Senate and the Massachusetts Supreme Executive Council. In addition, James served as sheriff of Middlesex County and was a member of the militia, rising through the ranks to colonel.

At the beginning of the Revolutionary War, James was a member of the Provincial Congress and the Board of War. After the war, he was named a judge on the Court of Common Pleas. For the last 50 years of his life, he was Groton's clerk of the proprietor and was employed by the town to lay out and divide the common lands. This gave him the opportunity to select the best lots to enhance his personal landholdings and thus his wealth. James died on February 15, 1800, at the advanced age of 79. Unfortunately, due to unfavorable economic conditions during and after the Revolutionary War, as well as excessive spending, James was insolvent at the time of his death. His wife, Susanna, survived him by six years.

Benjamin Prescott's third child was another daughter, Elizabeth, who was born on October 1, 1723. In an event that would have implications over 50 years later, she married Abijah Willard of Lancaster in December 1747. In the French and Indian War, Mr. Willard had led a company of soldiers mainly from the towns of Lancaster, Harvard, and Lunenburg against a French fortress on the Bay of Fundy. Willard reluctantly carried out orders he'd received to remove the Acadian inhabitants from their villages, marched off the men, and burned down all their buildings, leaving the women and children to fend for themselves.[33] During the Revolutionary War, Mr. Willard would make an unusual cameo on the side of the British. Elizabeth died in December 1751, at the age of 28, and so was not alive to witness that upsetting turn of events.

Three years after Elizabeth was born, Benjamin and Mary had their fourth child, William, the future colonel. Three more children would also follow William, which made him the middle child in the lineup. The first of these final three was William's younger sister, Lucy, who was born on February 25, 1729, when William was three years old. Again, like the other women of the family, little is known about Lucy other than that she lived for 36 years before dying in August 1765 of a "malignant throat distemper," or what we'd refer to today as strep throat.

Lucy was followed a little over two years later by Oliver, who was born on April 27, 1731. Oliver graduated from Harvard, a member of the Class of 1750, and became a respected medical doctor. Approximately six feet tall and somewhat corpulent, Oliver was initially appointed a major in the militia by King George, then advanced to lieutenant colonel, and eventually colonel. Like his older brothers, James and William, he took an early role in the American Revolution when he was appointed a brigadier general for Middlesex County and was chosen as a member of the Board of War.

In 1777, two years after the battle of Bunker Hill, Oliver was elected a member of the Supreme Executive Council and shortly thereafter was named a third major general of the militia throughout the Commonwealth. After the Revolutionary War, Oliver was heavily involved in trying to squelch a violent tax revolt called Shays's Rebellion that threatened the state. (Much more on that later.)

Oliver was a member of various scientific societies and was named a Fellow of the Academy of Arts and Sciences in 1786. Oliver was also one of the trustees of the Groton Academy and its first board president. Brothers James and William were supporters of the academy as well, and William was also an early board member. In addition, Oliver held the position of Groton Town Clerk for 13 years from 1765 to 1777. In 1779, he was appointed a probate judge for Middlesex County, a post Oliver retained until his own death of a heart attack on November 17, 1804. Oliver was three months shy of 74 at the time of his death. It was said that Oliver was "devoted to the cause of Christianity and the social virtues that he and his wife, Lydia Baldwin, walked together and adorned their profession by a well-ordered life and godly conversation." Moreover, in language that would echo that attributed to William, Oliver was described as a man who "possessed and ever practiced a peculiar suavity and politeness of manners, and a gentlemanly deportment, which strongly endeared him to the people, always commanding esteem and respect." It was also said he "possessed uncommon powers and versatility of mind, showing himself in all manner of difficulty, at once competent to its development and elucidation, by which he was enabled to dispatch business with surprising rapidity."

Mary was the last of William's siblings, the seventh child of Benjamin and Abigail. She was born on August 7, 1735 and died on October 25, 1751, just past her 16th birthday. Her death was again a reminder of the fragility of life in the colonial era. Early deaths were a hazard of the times; it seemed like no family was immune from them and their accompanying grief and sorrow.

William Prescott's Youth

Just three years after Mary, his last child, was born, Benjamin, the head of the household, became sick after working vigorously in the field during a rainstorm. He died seven days later on August 3, 1738. Benjamin was only 42 years old; his sudden and untimely death struck a significant blow to the family. This was not lost on William, who was only 12 years old, nor on his remaining siblings, who now had to shoulder a bigger load in caring for the family and making ends meet. There were eight mouths to feed in the household and no time to sulk or whine about their misfortune. Everyone had to pull their own weight.

William did his part and matured quickly, taking on more chores and keeping his head about him. Fortuitously, in November 1735, a grant of 3,000 acres of land was made by the General Court to Benjamin's three sons—James, William, and Oliver—out of a larger grant of 10,800 acres in that region.[34] This land, which was compensation for land lost in a dispute over the border with New Hampshire, would get the Prescott boys on their feet financially and help secure their futures.

William never knew his paternal grandfather and had lost his father before becoming a teenager. However, he did have the benefit of living close to his cousins, who could have helped mentor him as he grew into adulthood. A probate record also indicates that William Lawrence and Benjamin Bancroft of Groton were granted guardianship on September 29, 1742, of Elizabeth Prescott, age 19, and William Prescott, age 17. There was no mention of any of William's other siblings. This record suggests that William had supplemental adult supervision as he approached his 20s.

William's mother, Abigail, was still relatively young at 42 when Benjamin died, but she never remarried. She lived another 27 years before passing away on September 13, 1765, at the age of 69, succumbing to strep throat, which was a deadly epidemic at that time. Abigail saw all four of her daughters die relatively young, but her three sons survived her by at least 30 years. She also did not witness the tumult in America that would turn into a revolution against England; nor would she be alive for the famous battle in Charlestown in 1775 that would, in many ways, define her son William's legacy.

After his father died, William grew to be a strapping young man, standing a lanky six feet, two inches, which meant he was about a half-foot taller than most men of that time. William was also lean and athletic, with sinewy arms and a sturdy torso, and when he moved, it was with grace and self-assurance. He had brown hair and blue eyes, with strong, if ordinary, facial features.[35] As an adult, William was slightly bald and wore a tie-wig. Like many citizens, he had a rather limited formal education, but he was said to be "a man of vigorous mind, not much indebted to the advantages of education in early life, though he preserved to the last a taste for reading."[36]

According to people who knew him, William was an open, warm, garrulous, and popular figure. One such admirer was William's great-niece, Sarah (Chaplin) Rockwood, who described William this way:

> [H]e was a tall and well-proportioned man...he usually wore a skull cap and he parted his hair in the middle, wearing it long behind, braided loosely and tied in a "club" with a black ribbon, as was common in those days...he had a pleasant countenance, and was remarkably social, and full of fun and anecdote...he was dignified in his manner and had the bearing of a soldier.[37]

In keeping with this description, Prescott was known to have a lively sense of humor and his personal integrity was unassailable. One trait that certainly aided him during his military service was that he never seemed to be in a hurry or was unduly excited. He was cool, calm, and self-possessed during times of commotion and danger.

In many respects, William had a fairly typical childhood in a frontier town. Life was hard, especially in the northern New England colonies, and he knew the difficulties of living in a small community distant from the center of commerce and development. The winters were cold and inhospitable. There were almost constant dangers caused by the harsh weather, the potential for crop failures, the threat of rampant disease, and the periodic conflicts with Native American tribes. Homes were smoky from wood burning and often drafty. Roofs leaked, and the lack of indoor plumbing made supplying the home with water arduous. Outhouses were used to collect human waste. Like most families, Prescott's family relied on him to provide much-needed labor to sustain itself. So, as a young man, William worked the Prescott farm in Groton with his brothers and other hired men.

Following the examples of his ancestors, throughout much of his life, William was both a farmer and a soldier, and he alternated between those two occupations as circumstances dictated. His first military experience was as a 19-year-old when he was part of the British forces in 1745 that took the French fortress at Louisbourg in Nova Scotia during King George's War (1744–48)—the main event of that conflict.[38] Massachusetts Governor William Shirley planned the attack to capture the French citadel, which guarded the Gulf of St. Lawrence near Cape Breton Island. The Massachusetts Assembly allocated money for a military expedition, and other New England colonies were offered the opportunity to join the force, marking the first time the colonies began to cooperate for a common purpose.[39]

William Pepperrell (spelled with a double "r") was chosen commander in chief of the Massachusetts force, holding the rank of major general. Pepperrell was not a professional military man but rather a leading merchant who had excellent organizational skills and was very popular. William Prescott enlisted in the company of Captain William Lawrence and left Boston on March 24, 1745, heading north. The attack on Louisbourg occurred two months later, on May 26. Prescott acquitted himself well during the attack. In fact, his bravery during his enrollment did not go without notice, as years later, following his service in the French and Indian War, the British afterward offered him a commission in its army.[40] Prescott declined that offer, however, opting to return to Groton and his life of farming and civic duty. Still, Prescott gained valuable military experience from his service, learning firsthand how to handle the rigors of war, as well as battlefield tactics, discipline, and the importance of military cohesion.

Then, in 1746, back from the war, and when he was barely out of his teens, William moved from his childhood home and relocated a few miles up the road to establish his own homestead in Groton's West Parish.[41] Prescott's property was in an area known as the Groton Gove, part of a region that would later become its own district in 1753 and eventually the separate town of Pepperell in 1775, named after the beloved American general from King George's War.[42] This land was situated at the confluence of the Nissitissit and Nashua Rivers northwest of Boston, on a long dormant volcano that helped shape much of New England's geography. The region was noted for its good soil and orchards, which, in addition to the local mining and milling possibilities, attracted settlers there.

On His Own

Now, as a 20-year-old, William felt ready to strike out on his own. He built a large, garrison-style house on 120 acres of land he inherited from his father, which he eventually expanded to a substantial, sprawling farm of 250 acres.[43] The property was about two miles from the center of the West Parish, situated in a very quiet and bucolic site surrounded by woods. Prescott's farm sat on a rise that descended gently to the Nissitissit River, an attractive waterway that wound through the region.

William's brothers, James and Oliver, ages 23 and 15 respectively when William left, stayed in the main part of Groton, which was not very far away. For many men in that period, however, life was very orderly and predictable, and moving away from family was a significant development. As historian Robert Gross describes it, in colonial times, it was not unusual for a man to live on his native land, farm as his father had farmed, marry his cousin, and raise a large family.[44] The contours of one's life were essentially preordained.

A farmer's children were a precious labor resource, and they were usually kept close. Throughout the year, except when a farmer's son was in school, he worked alongside his father tilling crops, alleviating his chores, and helping to generate income for the family.[45] Thus, his world was typically very localized and rather circumscribed. Moving away gave a young man a chance to get out from under the thumb of his parents (especially his father), expand his horizons, and explore other possibilities. William did not seem to be motivated in this way, albeit his life certainly would turn out differently than this stereotypical depiction. Frankly, because of the proximity of the West Parish, his move was not likely a big deal to the family.

Where William Prescott came to live was closer to the settlements of sometimes aggressive Native Americans. When men in the area went into the field to plow, they took with them their rifles, which they stood against nearby trees or posts so they could be easily retrieved. This practice made them very familiar with the handling and use of guns. One report based on this hazardous situation said of Prescott that, "Living among the savages, an unmarried man, it seems early to have given him soldier-like habits and tastes."[46]

At its core, the colonial New England town was a tight-knit community and a prime example of democratic practice. The town claimed authority over anything that happened within its borders.[47] In Groton and Pepperell, most of the residents were the children and grandchildren of Puritans who had emigrated from England. As an observer had put it, the settlers saw themselves as "modern Israelites, agents in a noble cause at a pivotal moment in history—working to establish the true faith in the new world."[48]

One of the first and most important acts of a new town was to recruit a minister to preach to its citizens fundamental virtues of a moral life. While religion was less formal on the frontier, it was still a critical component responsible for the development of a new town.[49] Securing and keeping a minister was one of the first tasks in a new settlement. In 1690, Groton's minister left the community, and it took several years to find a replacement. The rugged frontier was not the easiest sell to a young man of the cloth, and towns closer to the larger cities were definitely more enticing. Because of this, each year a top item on the town meeting agenda was the amount of money to be appropriated for the town minister.

In keeping with this practice, one of the first things Prescott's new district prioritized was finding a minister for the West Parish. This was accomplished on February 25, 1747, when 23-year-old Reverend Joseph Emerson of Malden, near Boston, was ordained and "settled in the gospel ministry over the church and parish."[50] As part of his contract, Reverend Emerson received a grant of 40 acres of land close to the area's newly built meetinghouse and a sum of 120 English pounds. He also got 35 cords of firewood annually, to be cut and delivered to his door, plus a salary of 62 pounds, 10 shillings. This monetary compensation was to be increased by 12 pounds and 10 shillings, or roughly 20 percent, when the parish contained 100 ratable families, up from the existing 72. Emerson's salary was also adjusted by the rate of inflation from year to year.

Reverend Emerson's employment in the West Parish and later in Pepperell helped ensure that the area's population would continue to grow, and it helped stabilize the community for William Prescott, his neighbors, and their descendants. Emerson would remain on the job for 28 years. It was entirely fitting and unsurprising that William was a member of the town's Congregational Church, and he attended services regularly.[51]

After relative calm for nearly a decade, William's farming activities and involvement in town matters were abruptly interrupted when, in the mid-1750s, he signed up to fight with the British during the rapidly developing French and Indian War. It was the patriotic thing to do, and he did not hesitate. The partisan sentiment in the region was exemplified by a speech Reverend Emerson gave in 1758 to a company of Pepperell soldiers as they prepared to march off to war.[52] "Boldly, then, advance into the heart of your enemies country," said Emerson. "Fear them not; let it never be said of a New England soldier,—let it never be said of a Pepperell soldier,—that he was afraid to face his enemies, or that he turned his back on them, and cowardly deserted the cause of his country."

William may have also had another motive for enlisting. There is no doubt that he was a patriot, but it was also true that, as part of the landed gentry, he would naturally want to protect his own financial interests. He had a lot at stake. He had significant landholdings, and the prevailing systems of government favored such landholders. But whereas some affluent men avoided fighting by spending money to raise troops to send off to war in their stead—a practice that existed all the way through at least the American Civil War—William was willing to enter the fight himself.

William served as a lieutenant in the Provincial Army under the command of General John Winslow, who was himself a member of one of the most prominent families in New England.[53] Military commanders for many years were often given military commissions because they were wealthy and leading men in their communities. Prior wartime experience was certainly a nice-to-have but not required. Winslow had been appointed by William Shirley, who was then serving as Massachusetts's governor for the second time. Winslow was one of those rarities who was a popular leader and an experienced officer. Given these credentials, Winslow was given the rank of major general of the combined provincial forces from Massachusetts and Connecticut.[54] The Massachusetts legislature had agreed to raise 3,000 of the required total of 7,500 men from the northern colonies. William Prescott, perhaps because of his charisma and heroic stature, turned out to be a very active recruiter of soldiers for this force, drafting 25 men.[55]

In 1754, the French seized several forts along the Ohio River. After a severe military triumph against a force consisting substantially of American-born troops, they sent a young and relatively inexperienced British military officer named George Washington trudging back to his home in Virginia. Setbacks like that prompted British General James Wolfe to label his North American troops "the worst soldiers in the universe."[56]

William Prescott fared better. He was part of the expedition that removed the French from Nova Scotia in the spring of 1755. The local Acadians were unsuspicious of anything untoward by the victorious British. They assembled in churches in accordance with military directives and, without being able to return to their homes, were marched onto ships at bayonet-point and scattered throughout the American colonies. With no regard to the inhumanity of these actions, many families were separated—wives from husbands, children from parents—never to see each other again.[57] After his fighting was done, Prescott put down his musket and returned to his farm. While on his return from that expedition, Prescott was also promoted to captain. This transition from farmer to soldier to farmer was a pattern that Prescott would repeat even during the Revolutionary War.

In 1758, Prescott was back attending the West Parish's district town meetings, where he again was named a selectman. In that same year, nearly 20 years after his father's death and more than a decade after moving to West Parish, Prescott finally established his own family when he married 25-year-old Abigail Hale of the central Massachusetts town of Sutton, on April 13, 1758. He was 32 at the time. The couple lived on William's sprawling farm, which he called "The Highlands," about 45 miles northwest of Boston and proximate to the southern border of New Hampshire. Most of the farms at the time were not lucrative commercial properties but merely provided sustenance for the landowner's family. Occasionally, during especially good harvests, some extra crops were sold or used to barter for other local goods or services, which seems to be the case with respect to Prescott's farm.

According to late-18th-century author, politician, and commentator William Everett, Prescott's wife was deeply religious and "one of those remarkable New England matrons who loved to exercise their minds over the most tremendous problems of the relation between God and man."[58] Abigail was a friend and correspondent of Jonathan Edwards, the Yale-educated revivalist minister, philosopher, and Congregationalist Protestant theologian, who focused his work on concepts of harmony, beauty, and ethical fitness. Edwards, the grandfather of Aaron Burr, had a critical role in a social-religious movement called the First Great Awakening, which gave rise to a distinct school of theology known as New England Theology. The Great Awakening extended over a number of periods of religious revival that made religion intensely personal for the average person. It fostered a deep sense of spiritual conviction of personal sin and the need for redemption while encouraging introspection and a commitment to a new standard of personal morality.

Abigail's approach to life and her strong religious views, built upon her experience and the tenets of the Great Awakening, were likely in concert with William's views, and therefore how he conducted himself and interacted with his peers. While not much is definitively known about Colonel Prescott's religious opinions, it appears that he also possessed strong moral principles. Some of that comes through in the limited writings he left behind and in various comments made about him during his life.

For whatever reason, and contrary to the practice of most families in those days who had large families, William and Abigail had only one child. William Jr. was born on August 19, 1762. Single-child families were indeed rare in the colonial era and may have indicated that William and Abigail had trouble conceiving or carrying another child to birth.

Although Abigail lived a full life, she apparently suffered from chronic feeble health, which, according to Everett, was "the fate of generations of New England wives and mothers, before they understood that it is better to live for one's dear fathers, brothers, and sons than to die for them by inches, freezing and starving one's self to keep them fed and clothed."[59] William's ancestors had large families, so he may have been inclined to have one as well. Perhaps Abigail's delicate health ineluctably ruled this out.

By available accounts, despite her poor health, Abigail ruled her household firmly, and with love and care. She was also very concerned about the welfare of the young men in her community and invited them into her kitchen for additional educational help and instruction.[60] In one anecdote, she would tell friends how she had been called out of the room in the middle of a spelling lesson one day, and when she returned, she found her six-year-old son had taken her place in front of a class of young men in their late teens.[61] Abigail is described as being an exceedingly amiable, prudent, and estimable woman, a well-suited match for her husband, having the "rare combination of virtues of thrift without selfishness, and frugality without parsimony."[62]

As for William Jr., being an only child, he received enormous attention from his parents and, as recorded in the family genealogical history, was "guided in a way to ensure a long and prosperous life."[63] At the age of 14, he was placed under the instruction of Master Moody, a celebrated teacher at Drummer Academy in Newbury, Massachusetts, on the north shore. He studied there for three years before entering Harvard College, from which he graduated in 1783 with high honors. To help pay for his education, William Jr. took charge of an academy in Beverly, another town on Massachusetts's northern coastline. He was admitted to the bar in 1787 and began his legal practice there.

William Jr. remained in Beverly for only two years because the area did not provide a broad enough legal field for his purposes and aspirations.[64] So, in 1789, William Jr. moved to the adjacent town of Salem, where his prospects seemed greater. This put him about 50 miles from his childhood farm in Pepperell and no doubt reduced the amount of time he spent with his parents. It was in Salem where William Jr. set down his roots and where he remained for 19 years. It was also where he gained considerable renown as a legal scholar. As a sign of his educational and professional achievement, at some time along the way George Washington (possibly during his presidency) offered William Jr. the position of confidential secretary. He declined the role but instead recommended his friend and Harvard classmate, Colonel Tobias Lear.[65]

After four years in the bustling, notorious town of the Witch Trials of the early 1690s, William Jr. married Catherine Green Hickling of Boston.[66] They were together for 51 years and had seven children between 1795 and 1806, although four of the children died within one year of birth.

Starting in 1798, William Jr. represented Salem in the General Court, and in 1805 he was voted senator of Essex County. Despite serving successfully, he declined reelection and three years later the family moved to Boston. William Jr. then represented Boston in the General Court for a number of years. He was twice nominated for a seat on the Massachusetts Supreme Court, once when he lived in Salem in 1806 and a second time in Boston in 1813, but he turned down the position each time. However, he was also elected and twice served in the Massachusetts State Senate.

William Jr. was nearly entangled in an explosive political controversy while at the height of his fame. In December 1814, near the end of the War of 1812, the Federal Party, which had opposed the war and held other political grievances, organized a three-week convention of delegates from the New England states in Hartford, Connecticut.[67] The convention discussed a number of controversial issues, including abolishing the three-fifths compromise in the U.S. Constitution and removing the two-thirds supermajority in Congress to admit new states, make declarations of war, and pass new laws restricting trade. It aired grievances against the Louisiana Purchase and the Embargo of 1807. But, in its most controversial move, it shockingly discussed whether the New England states should secede from the Union and start their own country.[68] The Prescott genealogical history mentions that William Jr. was a delegate to the convention, but claimed that he accepted the appointment mostly because he feared that rash measures might be taken at the convention that could adversely affect the Union. The Hartford Convention did irreparable damage to the Federal Party—the party of George Washington, John Adams, and Alexander Hamilton—however, no one ever doubted the patriotism of William Jr., and his reputation weathered the storm.

In 1818, William Jr. was appointed a judge on the Court of Common Pleas for Boston, but he resigned from that post within a year. He was also elected to be one of the delegates from Boston at a convention in 1820 for revising and amending the Constitution of Massachusetts. And the honors kept coming. In 1824, Harvard College conferred on him the degree of Doctor of Laws. Four years later, he retired from the bar after 40 years of service. He died on December 8, 1844; he was 82 years old. When Daniel Webster announced Prescott's death to the State Supreme Court, he said that "at the moment of retirement from the bar of Massachusetts [William Jr.] stood as head for legal learning and attainments."[69]

One other family member of William Prescott is worth mentioning—his grandson, William Hickling Prescott. W. H. also had a brilliant career, although the Colonel was not alive to witness it. William Hickling Prescott, one of William Jr. and Catherine's three surviving children, was born on May 4, 1796, about six months after Colonel Prescott's death.

Like his father, W. H. attended Harvard College, graduating in 1814. While there, he had a devastating injury that caused him to lose sight in one eye and impaired the other. But as the family genealogical history declares, due to "his heroic courage and undaunted resolution, combined with an ardent aspiring mind, an abundant native energy, strong natural genius and indefatigable perseverance, he was able to overcome his difficulties and establish for himself a brilliant reputation as an internationally regarded literary figure and historian.[70] He authored many successful works on European and South American history, which were translated into French, German, Spanish, Italian, and Dutch.

On May 4, 1820, W. H. married Susan Amory, the daughter of Hannah Linsee and Thomas Amory, a successful Boston merchant. In an ironic turn of events, the couple's grandfathers, Colonel Prescott and Captain John Linsee, were on opposite sides in the American Revolution and even fought against one another during the battle of Bunker Hill. John Linsee skippered the HMS *Falcon*, one of the warships that bombarded Charlestown on June 17, 1775. The swords of the erstwhile combatants were passed down through their families until they came together in W. H.'s marriage to Susan. They were mounted on a walnut plaque, crossed together, and hung over the books in W. H.'s library in the old homestead where he ended up residing. After his death, the swords were transferred to the Massachusetts Historical Society in Boston where they still hang today.

W. H. Prescott received many honors and was elected to a number of professional organizations, including the Massachusetts Historical Society, the American Antiquarian Society, and the American Academy of Arts and Sciences. Prescott was also an honorary member of historical societies in Rhode Island, New Hampshire, New York, and a host of European societies. He died on January 28, 1859, at the age of 62.

Neither William Jr. nor W. H. Prescott carried on the military tradition of the family. Both were highly accomplished citizens, but due to the timing of their births, they were not of prime age when either the Revolutionary War or the War of 1812 were being waged. Similarly, W. H. Prescott was only about

16 at the start of the War of 1812, but, in any event, his very poor eyesight would have disqualified him from military service.

It was easy to see a pattern in the lives of the Prescotts. The values of hard work, integrity, service-oriented were common attributes of one ancestor after another. They were farmers, blacksmiths, and millers. Military involvement and leadership were also repeated traits. While William Prescott is best remembered for his military exploits, he had another, more common occupation that engaged much of his time, and it was to this pursuit that I next turned in my research.

CHAPTER 3

Colonial Farmer

Like roughly 90 percent of New England citizens in the 1700s, William Prescott was a farmer.[1] Moreover, after expanding his initial, inherited property to 250 acres, he had one of the largest landholdings in the north central region of Massachusetts.[2] Being an inveterate urbanite, I know very little about agriculture, next to nothing about taking care of large animals like cows, sheep, and oxen, and even less about the rigors of a farming life, especially one during colonial America. So, to learn what Prescott's farm life was probably like, I resorted to Jonathan Nourse, a friend, former neighbor, and lifelong farmer in Westborough, Massachusetts. My wife and I got to know Jonathan when we settled in Westborough to raise our family and ended up staying for nearly three decades.

Westborough, situated about 30 miles due west of Boston, was founded in 1675 and began as an early agricultural community in America with a notable history, including being the birthplace of Eli Whitney. Jonathan's ancestors settled there in 1722, a couple of generations into its development. William and Ebenezer Nurse (no "o") founded the Nourse Farm (spelled today with an "o") after the Nurse family fled from Salem Village following the infamous Witch Trials. That's when, in 1692, 71-year-old Rebecca Nurse was among a group of citizens accused of witchcraft and subsequently, and unjustly, put to death. Most were hanged, like Rebecca Nurse, but some were crushed with heavy stones or simply died in jail. Rebecca Nurse was made famous by Arthur Miller's highly acclaimed 1953 play *The Crucible*, although this is not something that Jonathan is quick to mention when you first meet him.

Jonathan currently manages his 140-acre family farm, which he is proud to point out is the 13th oldest continuously operating family business in America. Jonathan is an affable, industrious man of 75, who has lived and worked on the farm for his entire life (save for when he was a student at the University of Massachusetts), sharing the land the last 50 years with his wife, Marsha, an educator. While Jonathan is known as an able farmer, Marsha has a reputation as a top-notch baker—a nice combination. It is worth a trip to the farm to pick up some of their fruit pies and jams, along with their usual assortment of organically grown berries and vegetables. Jonathan and Marsha have two grown children, Rachel and Samantha, who, in true colonial fashion, also worked on the farm while they were growing up. It is no exaggeration to say they have farming in their veins. If anyone was going to help me understand colonial farming and Prescott's agricultural situation, it was Jonathan.

Jonathan and I met on his farm on a windswept March day in 2023 and, after catching up on our respective family doings, we got down to business. Jonathan started by noting Prescott's small family, reiterating that most farmers in colonial America had large families, as children were a key source of labor. Jonathan pointed out that a farmer's children would be put to work as soon as they were able, although they generally did not handle the most difficult tasks until they were in their teens. Boys were usually given physical labor, while girls would most frequently support the matriarch of the family with stereotypically female tasks. There was never a shortage of things to do, even in the non-planting and non-harvesting seasons.

Jonathan acknowledged that Prescott must have sought supplemental laborers to make the farm viable. For instance, in colonial times, some farmers used indentured servants as workers and, in some cases, slaves—even in Puritan New England.[3] Because of the need to ensure enough food was being produced in the area, another way in which a community could harvest vital crops was through impressed labor. In these cases, able-bodied men, including shop owners and artisans, were rounded up by constables, forced to put down their own work, and escorted to large farms to assist the owner. Often, however, farmers just hired the laborers they needed. This seems to be the case for William Prescott. There is no evidence that Prescott had indentured servants and, as far as it is known, he did not own slaves. Thus, he probably hired farmhands, most likely out of a pool of local, available men. Abigail, Prescott's wife, would also have needed consistent, dependable help to assist her with her duties, especially while her husband was away fighting in various wars.

Jonathan suggested that, given the size and nature of his farm, Prescott would have needed to hire workers year-round, not just in the growing and harvesting seasons from April to November. At a minimum, Prescott would have probably employed at least three workers to help with the farming duties and perhaps another two as blacksmiths, toiling in the two ironworks he owned. If Prescott was lucky, the workers he hired would have come back to the farm year after year, until they got too old and were unable to do the labor anymore. A good, reliable, long-term worker was worth a great deal to a landowner like Prescott.

Hired laborers generally were not well-off and typically did not own land, which was a main source of colonial income. Working as farm laborers was one of the principal ways they could make a living. Farming was an extremely hard life in the mid-18th century, even after several generations had worked the land and made it productive. The daily routine of an average farmer would follow this generalized schedule:

04:45–05:00 a.m.	Rise and tend to the livestock
05:00–06:30 a.m.	Work in the fields
06:30–07:00 a.m.	Eat breakfast
07:00–11:00 a.m.	Work in the fields
11:00–11:30 a.m.	Take a cider break
11:30–02:00 p.m.	Work in the fields
02:00–03:00 p.m.	Eat dinner
03:00–06:00 p.m.	Work in the fields, tend livestock, repair tools
06:00–07:00 p.m.	Eat supper
08:30 p.m.	Go to bed[4]

Day after day, the farmer and his laborers would get up in the early morning and, for maybe weeks on end, repeatedly do the same tasks, depending on what season it was. Sunday, a traditional day of rest, might provide their only relief. This schedule was not for the faint of heart. The hours were long, and the work was often backbreaking. Even with hired labor, William Prescott would have likely contributed some of his time to tasks around the farm, while also juggling other important civic activities in Pepperell as one of its prominent leaders.

As I learned from Jonathan, before Prescott's farm was fully developed, a lot of effort would have been expended cutting down trees and removing tree stumps, either by digging or burning them out. The land had to be prepared for whatever Prescott planned to grow. On a positive note, wood was exceedingly important as a building material, as the primary component of wagons and tools, and as a key fuel source until the introduction of coal burning. Fortunately, land in the colonies in the 1700s was relatively virgin and so trees were plentiful, not like in Europe where the land had supported populations for centuries and forests had been thinned out. The dense woods of New England offered an ample resource, but it required concerted physical labor to harvest. Since green wood does not burn, felled trees would have to age for two years before they were ready for use. Prescott had to manage the wood on his land, just like other natural resources such as fresh water and fertile soil. Rocks, which were plentiful in the New England soil, also needed to be removed. As you can imagine, this was not easy without the benefit of the heavy equipment that would be employed in later years.

Warming to his subject, Jonathan noted that Prescott had lots of other issues to worry about as well. Every day his cows needed milking. Since this was an age before refrigeration, milk had to be used before it spoiled. In the winter, ice would have been cut out of ponds or lakes and the frozen blocks put in ice houses to help preserve assorted perishable foods. This was a strenuous chore, and moving large chunks of ice was no mean feat. Plus, without proper gear, such as rubber boots and waterproof gloves, the ice cutters typically got very wet while working with the ice. It was taxing labor that required a high tolerance for discomfort. Without ice, storing milk was impossible and drinks had to be consumed warm—a prospect that I, a cold drink obsessive, cannot imagine.

Prescott was fortunate to have a steady supply of fresh water on his property from the Nissitissit River and a number of ponds and other brooks. Land that contained fresh lakes or ponds, or that had clear streams running through it, was especially valuable. Those that did not have fresh water available would have had to dig wells or collect rainwater in barrels, maybe even both. However it was obtained, this collected water was used solely for family and animal needs; it was not used to nourish trees, plants, or crops, which simply had to rely on naturally occurring precipitation or the capacity of deep roots to bring water where it was needed.

After painting a colorful, if stark, picture of colonial farming life, Jonathan then helped me probe deeper into the specifics regarding Prescott's property and its outputs. I shared with him information from the Massachusetts Tax Valuation List of 1771. This report came out of a law passed by the General Court in July of that year called "An Act for Enquiring into the Rateables Estate of this Province."[5] In accordance with this regulation, each town elected assessors who then compiled a list of all taxpayers and taxable property in their town. The residents worked with the assessors, providing them with an inventory of their property as of September 1 of that year. This information was then to be updated every seven years for reapportioning tax requirements for each town. (The Revolutionary War would interrupt this periodic accounting.)

The valuation was circumscribed by certain qualifying factors. For example, only "improved land" was counted, meaning native forest was not reported.

Small gardens, where landowners grew potatoes, squash, pumpkins, peas, beans, turnips, and possibly other items, were also not reported. There were also some other qualifiers. For instance, only adult animals were included, which thus vastly undercounted the number of animals on each farm. The unqualified were oxen under four years of age, cows and horses under three, and goats, sheep, and pigs under one. In addition, in the report, grain meant wheat grown to make bread, plus corn and rye. The assessment did not distinguish between grain for animal feed and grain kept to produce seeds for the next year's planting.

According to the valuation in 1771, William Prescott's farm had an Annual Worth of Whole Real Estate equal to eight pounds, meaning this was the estimated value of the property if it were placed for sale at the time.[6] This put his farm in the top 10 percent of taxpayer properties in Pepperell. The Bancroft property, belonging to Captain Edmund Bancroft, a militia captain in Pepperell who fought in Colonel Prescott's regiment at the battle of Bunker Hill, was valued at 15 pounds, which made it far and away the most valuable in town.

The valuation gives us good insight into the nature and probable workings of Prescott's farm. For instance, the valuation noted that Prescott's property consisted of the following buildings and structures:

William Prescott—Massachusetts Valuation of 1771

Buildings and Boats	Items	Number
	Dwelling Houses	1
	Shops Adjoining, Tanhouses, Stillhouses, Warehouses, Gristmills	0
	Ironworks	2

Prescott's home was the sole dwelling on the property. The only other structures were two ironworks, which was not surprising given the ore deposits that were found in that region and his ancestors' experience in smelting iron.

Armed with this information, Jonathan concluded that Prescott seems to have had the knowledge, foresight, and inventiveness to be a "modern" farmer, something he underscored repeatedly to me.[7] The ironworks would have allowed Prescott to forge his own tools and implements. As an example, he could have made iron bands to wrap around his wagons' wheels to extend their life. He could have made saws for cutting down trees, which was extremely important for clearing land as well as producing firewood. He also could have made chains, another important implement for uprooting tree stumps, dragging felled trees, and pulling other equipment.

The report does not mention a barn, but it is hard to imagine that Prescott, as a cutting-edge farmer, did not have a barn to house his animals, store equipment, and stockpile foodstuffs. Given the size of his farm, a barn would have been a necessity. So, the absence of a barn in the report is puzzling. However, in a real estate transaction dealing with Prescott's farm right before he died, the legal document mentions his property having a "Dwelling and Barn."[8]

Prescott did not own many animals or livestock. He reported having 21 adult farm animals, of which 14 were goats and sheep. He also had a horse and a team of oxen, which might have been sufficient for Prescott to do many chores around the farm. In addition, Prescott must have had a riding horse to get him from place to place, although this horse was probably not included as a farm animal. Prescott also reported having three cows and one swine. The cows were likely milking cows and probably served the family needs. As Jonathan pointed out, Prescott might have killed one cow a year and replaced it with another or raised a new one born from his existing cows. Normally a fattened cow that was slaughtered would produce anywhere from 400 to 500 pounds of meat. The meat would have been preserved through salting and could feed the family for the year. Any excess, Prescott might have sold or traded to his neighbors. The same was probably true with Prescott's swine.

William Prescott—Massachusetts Valuation of 1771

Farm Animals and Livestock	Type	Number
	Horses	1
	Oxen	2
	Cows	3
	Goats and Sheep	14
	Swine	1

Prescott's goats would have been useful for providing milk, cheese, and meat. Goats are relatively easy to maintain and will survive even the harshest conditions. As Jonathan said, they eat almost anything and may have been used to help clear fields of brush and weeds. Goats also provide good skins, which could have been fashioned into needed clothing items. Likewise, sheep would have been extremely useful to Prescott. In particular, his sheep would have been a source of wool, which was used to make or line clothes, produce knitted hats and sweaters, and create other textiles, rugs, and upholstery.

Sheep, like goats, would also have served Prescott as a source of meat, milk, and cheese—dietary staples. Sheepskin would have been another useful output, and sheep droppings could have been used to make parchment. In addition, all farmers typically raised chickens for eggs and meat, so we can assume that Prescott kept a flock of chickens on the farm.

In general, the towns of Groton and Pepperell did not employ many oxen in their agriculture. Prescott reported having two oxen in the 1771 valuation. Oxen were hard workers and they ate a lot, which meant they cost a lot to maintain. Consequently, farmers tended to share their oxen with each other, which kept down expenses. In fact, there are notes in Prescott's paybook that refer to the lending of oxen.[9] He could have lent or rented out the team to neighbors and friends from time to time in an effort to support food production in the town. Such cooperation was not uncommon according to Jonathan, as a community had to work together to promote its survival.

As part of his inventory, Prescott reported that approximately 20 percent of his acreage was dedicated to productive, agricultural use. He had 20 acres of pasture, which, Jonathan suggested, was enough to support about 10 cows. He had 12 acres of tillage, seven acres of what's called English and Upland Mowing Land, and 10 acres of fresh meadow.

William Prescott—Massachusetts Valuation of 1771

Land and Agriculture	Item	Number
	Acres of Pasture	20
	Cows the Pasture Will Keep	10
	Acres of Tillage	12
	Bushels of Grain Produced per Year	20
	Barrels of Cider per Year	10
	Acres of Salt Marsh	0

(Continued)

(Continued)

Land and Agriculture	Item	Number
	Tons of Salt Marsh Hay per Year	0
	Acres of English and Upland Mowing Land	7
	Tons of English and Upland Hay per Year	5
	Acres of Fresh Meadow	10
	Tons of Fresh Meadow Hay per Year	8

While cattle, swine, flax, and butter were major products in Middlesex County, grass was the largest local crop, and farmers produced far more bushels of grain than was necessary for self-sufficiency and much more than many other towns on a per capita basis.[10] Prescott produced five tons of English and Upland hay per year, or nearly one ton per acre, which was a respectable output. He also produced eight tons of fresh meadow hay per year.

Jonathan explained that to generate grain, the grasses, once reaped, had to be threshed. This meant it had to be beaten with a tool called a flail in order to separate the edible part of the grain from the straw. Bread has been a staple of all civilizations dating back to antiquity, so a major effort would have been put into producing grain on Prescott's farm. After the grain was beaten out, the straw was carefully removed by using a rake or tossed into the air with a pitchfork to be blown away by the wind. Again, this entire process required hard, physical labor.

At roughly 20 bushels of grain per year, Prescott was a modest producer of grain relative to his Pepperell neighbors, but he produced more cider than most. In fact, the many hillsides in the region were highly amenable to the development of orchards, and a fair amount of Prescott's time and effort seems to have gone into the cultivation of fruits. Jonathan was particularly animated when talking about the fruit on Prescott's farm, as his own farm largely produces fruit and berries. He noted that apples and apple cider were major products that farmers cultivated and manufactured across the state. Indeed, Prescott's paybook frequently references apples and pears, even noting where some of the trees were sourced, including overseas, and using numbered locations to indicate where grafts had been applied. The paybook also indicates that Prescott grew many varieties of apples on his farm, which was not uncommon in the region.[11] Thus, apples may have been Prescott's largest crop, and he would have had seasonal, hired hands pick the apples and deliver them to a press.

The initial output of Prescott's apple crop would have been sweet cider, which was commonly stored in 30-gallon kegs. No synthetic chemicals were available to protect a farmer's orchards in those days, but luckily the farmer also did not have to deal with as many diseases as they do today. The cider that was not used at first may have been allowed to ferment into hard cider, which was an alternative or substitute for other forms of hard alcohol. Farmers like Prescott did not want to waste any output. They had to put food on the table for their family and typically also fed their workers. They tried to find as many uses for their crops as they could, and anything leftover was sold or traded.

Prescott's paybook also references transactions involving Indian (his term) or colored corn used for meal, oats, and beans, which might have been kidney or harder beans. These were also popular products in this part of the state. So, overall, it is safe to say that Prescott managed a diverse and active farm that was nearly unsurpassed in Pepperell. A lot of credit should go to Abigail, as well, as she must have had a large role in running the operation while William was away fighting or involved in other local and regional matters of significance.

Prescott's brothers also had substantial farms in neighboring Groton. His brother James's property was worth 24 pounds annually—three times as much as William's—and produced sizable quantities of grain (100 bushels/yr.) and cider (100 barrels/yr.). James also had more than four times as much acreage dedicated to pasture, three times as many acres committed to English and Upland Mowing Land, and twice as many acres of fresh meadow as William did. Oliver's property was also evaluated at 24 pounds annually, with more than twice as many acres dedicated to pasture and 50 percent more acres of tillage than William owned. The discrepancies in farm value might be partially explained by the fact that William Prescott was periodically away from his farm fighting in the war, and his brothers weren't.

Slave Ownership

Among the citizens of Pepperell and Groton, few owned as much land as the Prescotts. They were a well-established family with deep roots in the area. They received large land grants, particularly when the border with New Hampshire was established, and they managed their properties very well. However, one surprising aspect of their property profiles in the 1771 valuation is that Oliver is listed as being a "Servant Owner," a term that was a euphemism for slaveholder.

In this report slaves were referred to as "Servants for Life." The slave history of Groton has recently been examined by Joshua Vollmar, a lifelong Groton resident, who has also worked for the Groton History Center and is a member of the Groton Historical Commission. Joshua says there is clear evidence of slavery there dating to the town's founding in 1655.[12]

To underscore the point, a 1760 document in Pepperell's Town Hall describes a transaction between two men from the towns of Uxbridge and Wrentham (it is not clear why this document was in Pepperell) that says in summary:

> I John Hazeltine of Uxbridge…have received…eighty-three pounds Lawful money in sale of three Negroes…I have sold him [Samuel King of Wrentham] being one man and one woman and one child…now at the breast, all being slaves…and do now sell them to the Said Samuel King his heirs and assigns…[13]

The document reminds us of the horror that was slavery. How people accepted this abhorrent practice, including someone as educated as Oliver Prescott, is beyond comprehension. As Joshua has pointed out, in that era, the exploitation of slaves infiltrated the colonies, including Massachusetts, and Groton's history with slavery was unfortunately a microcosm of the country's.

The Tax Valuation of 1771 indicated that four taxpayers in Groton were Servant Owners, Oliver Prescott being one. While James Prescott was not listed as a Servant Owner in that report, at some point he also owned a slave through his wife's side of the family, the Lawrences. Meanwhile, none of Pepperell's 166 taxpayers, including William Prescott, were designated Servant Owners. For context, in 1771, there were 1,343 Servants for Life across Massachusetts, with Suffolk (325), Middlesex (254), and Essex (217) counties—the major population centers—responsible for 796 or roughly 60 percent of the total. The valuation only recorded slaves who were between the ages of 14 and 45, so it is virtually certain that there were more slaves in the colony than those recorded for tax purposes.

As a result of his examination, Joshua also noted that in a probate document describing the holdings of Benjamin Prescott, the brothers' father, there is a listing of "One Negro Wench," who is referred to as Peg. This would imply that even though there is no record of William Prescott ever owning slaves, until he moved out of the household, he most likely grew up around Peg, a female slave. So, even though Groton and Pepperell later became staunchly abolitionist, there is no escaping its—and the Prescotts'—erstwhile entanglements with slavery.

Thankfully, the Revolutionary War led to a turning point in Massachusetts's slave history when a slave woman from Sheffield found an abolitionist lawyer to represent her in a case. She was seeking freedom based on the new Massachusetts Constitution in 1780. She won her case and took the name Elizabeth Freeman in recognition of her momentous victory. Massachusetts formally abolished slavery in 1783.

Long-Term Financial Concerns

Like other farmers at the time, William Prescott would also have had to think about his long-term financial situation and hopefully tried to put some of his farm's revenue away for his retirement years. Unfortunately, another reality for the colonial farmer was that he couldn't always count on a steady income. Jonathan Nourse explained that bad weather, insect infestations, and other natural calamities could wipe out a year's crop, depleting a farmer's income. Experiments in the field, such as attempts to make the land more productive or to try new crops, could fail and set back the farmer for years. Changes in economic conditions, which were beyond the control of the farmer—falling demand, rising inflation—might also undermine any gains in the farm's output.

Consequently, Prescott could not take anything for granted. He was a very active man and was away from the farm for long stretches while serving in the military. On top of this, he seems to have suffered a severe injury on the farm in his later years, which may have not only curtailed any later military duty but limited what he could do physically.[14] Farm injuries were fairly common at the time. Clear-cutting trees was dangerous business, for example, as was handling large saws and equipment. Financial security would likely have been a constant worry for Prescott. One wonders how even a family as well-established as his could have kept things together without unbearable stress.

Still curious about William Prescott's property holdings, I consulted Brian Donahue, Professor Emeritus in American Environmental Studies at Brandeis University and an agriculture and forest ecology expert. Brian is the author of several books, including *The Great Meadow: Farmers and the Land in Colonial Concord*. Like a number of resources I drew upon, Brian has an interesting link to the colonial era. Brian is a descendant of Samuel Hartwell, who built the famous Revolutionary War-era house and associated tavern in Concord that bear his name and were backdrops to the fighting in Concord in April 1775.

Brian gave me some very useful information about how towns were formed and farms maintained, and suggested I visit the Massachusetts Registry of Deeds to see whether Prescott owned any other land or was involved in any real estate deals that could have improved his landholdings and financial position. Much to my relief, the land records for Pepperell are kept in the

Middlesex South Office of the State Registry, which is located in Cambridge, only a little over a mile from where I lived at the time.

Massachusetts is divided into 21 registry districts, each with an elected Registrar of Deeds. These offices maintain all documents about real estate ownership within their respective district. Brian warned me, however, that tracing land records to the 1700s, moving back and forth across a few generations, and looking for transactions involving neighbors, is where "it [research] can get arduous." As I would find out, this was a gross understatement.

Despite this portentous message, I decided to visit the registry right away, hoping I'd defy the odds and come upon the exact records I was looking for. The Middlesex South Office is housed in an imposing, albeit scruffy-looking, red brick building on highly trafficked Cambridge Street, a couple of miles east of Harvard Square. The façade, with four enormous Ionic columns and a classic entablature with triangular pediment, sits atop 23 granite steps. It's not an inviting-looking building. The reception desk is located on the second floor and sits on the edge of a large, stained-glass-domed atrium. The room, which is circular, has one of those decorative, mini-tiled floors that recall another era. It's the kind of place where, if you are wearing shoes with leather heels and soles, your footsteps reverberate loudly off the walls and your voice seems to carry well beyond where you intend.

One of the first things I noticed was that there weren't many people working in this cavernous building (perhaps due to the lingering impact of Covid-19), so finding help was a bit challenging. Finally, a pleasant, white-haired woman named Sue Karen appeared at the front desk and directed me upstairs to where the hardcover index volumes reside on rows of metal shelving. Minutes later, Mike Ducrow, the registry's microfilm supervisor, stopped by where I had seated myself (Sue sent him) and instructed me on how to use the complicated online reference system. "I heard you needed some help," said Mike as he approached me. I was sitting in front of a computer screen trying to figure out how to locate the relevant land documents associated with William Prescott. "It can be very hard if you aren't familiar with the system," Mike added. I quickly agreed.

Mike, trim and youthful, is a 10-plus-year veteran of the registry, and he was only too eager to help. He showed me the stacks where the reference books are arrayed and pulled out *Grantee Book: Volume 6* from 1639 to 1799. I discovered 13 entries for William Prescott, with him as either the grantee or the grantor in assorted land transactions. Often these references included one or more of his brothers, sometimes as a co-grantee and sometimes on the opposite end of a transaction with William. These entries date from

December 13, 1738, when William was 12 years old (the year his father died), to August 14, 1794, roughly a year before his death.

The reference numbers for each entry (i.e., Book and Page) pertain to a scanned, digital copy of the original real estate document that you can pull up on one of the two desktop computers located nearby, or at home if you prefer. To demonstrate, Mike took control of one of the computers, began typing keywords, and pulled down various windows. Ancient records began appearing on the computer screen. Each of these typically hard-to-read, handwritten records provides basic details about the transaction—essentially, the names of the parties, the amount of land exchanged, and the monetary cost. Two hundred pounds for 120 acres here, 500 pounds for 130 acres there. These entries were, for my purposes, mildly interesting, nothing blockbuster. The main takeaway was that William Prescott was not frequently involved in real estate transactions. His 13 transactions over almost 60 years was not terribly impressive. More research was needed, and I was reminded of Brian Donohue's admonition. This was going to be harder than I had hoped.

However, on a second trip to the registry, I again teamed up with Mike and we tried to hunt down several transactions involving the Prescott brothers and a person named A. Williard, whom I presumed was the loyalist husband of Elizabeth Prescott, Abijah. I found myself raising an eyebrow at the last of a series of three entries between these parties. The entry, dated June 1788, between Willard as grantor and the three Prescott brothers as grantees, was well after Elizabeth's death in 1752 and of course well after the battle of Bunker Hill and the war itself.

Unfortunately, when I searched the digital record file to learn more, this document was missing. I found this puzzling, but Mike assured me that it happens from time to time. Mike, now as engaged as I was in the investigation, raced off to see if he could locate the wayward document in the bowels of the registry somewhere. Unfortunately, Mike returned 20 minutes later shaking his head. No luck.

What did this transaction signify? Was Willard selling property back to the Prescott brothers that once belonged to him and Elizabeth? Did this transaction mean that Willard and the Prescotts had reconciled after fighting on opposite sides of the war? It's impossible to know. But what I did learn in a parallel search was that Willard, who had been temporarily imprisoned in Connecticut on the eve of the revolution and was evacuated twice with the British to Nova Scotia during the war, died in Saint John, New Brunswick, in 1789. So, whether there was a reconciliation or not, it seems Willard never returned to Massachusetts after the war and his association with the Prescotts probably ended with this land transaction.

Despite the frustrations of trying to delve into Prescott's property-owning past, one of the things I had learned by this point was that William was a significant presence in his hometown of Pepperell for many years. He worked on numerous town committees, headed assorted posts, and participated in key civic activities. The next logical step in my search, then, was to go to Pepperell to see what I could turn up about its most famous resident.

CHAPTER 4

Civic Leader

William Prescott was a colossal presence in Pepperell and is unquestionably the town's most favorite son. It wasn't surprising then, that when I contacted people in this small community about my project, I received a very warm welcome and more assistance than I could have imagined. Before I even drove out to Pepperell, several folks in town said I needed to speak with Franek Kiluk and Tony Saboliauskas, two residents and die-hard Prescott enthusiasts. When I reached each of them by phone, they were excited to hear about my project and regaled me with stories of Prescott's life before, during, and after the war.

"You should read everything that Frothingham wrote about Bunker Hill and Colonel Prescott," urged Franek. "He's the best source of information and will cover the key parts of the Charlestown fight." I told him I appreciated the lead and welcomed any other books, speeches, or other material that might be useful. Franek mentioned he had compiled some notes in a folder he'd left in the town's Lawrence Library, including a presentation that he gave at the Bunker Hill Museum. He also told me about his efforts, as yet unsuccessful, to promote the building of a Prescott statue in Pepperell.

Sometime later when I spoke with Tony, he echoed Franek's remarks and provided details regarding Bunker Hill Day in Pepperell.

"The celebration has been a longtime tradition, but it has started to fade in recent years," said Tony with regret.

"Oh, that's too bad," I replied. "Maybe the upcoming 250th anniversary of the Bunker Hill battle will revitalize the festivities."

"That would be good," Tony offered. "There was a time when the kids in town really got into it."

It was nice to connect with two local Prescott devotees, but the biggest breakthrough was learning that the town's Lawrence Library held original documents of town proceedings dating back to the 18th century. The classically designed Lawrence Library was built in 1902 and sits on Main Street only a few steps from Town Hall. Wasting no time, I made an appointment to see the library's sharp and very capable Senior Research Librarian, Debra Spratt. Debra has been at the library for nearly 20 years and was immediately helpful in arranging for me to examine the historical town records.

On my first visit, Debra quickly got me situated at a long wooden table in a small, upstairs reading room.[1] No one else was in the room; I'd have complete privacy to do my work. From an adjacent locked storeroom, Debra then retrieved a large, red-covered, bound volume labeled Pepperell Town Records 1742–1809 Volume 1 and placed it in front of me on the table. Debra also outfitted me with a magnifying glass and a pair of white cloth gloves.[2] I would soon discover that the magnifying glass was indispensable, but it was the white gloves that spoke to the reverential nature of these records. These are much-valued artifacts from the early years of the town and are guarded with great care. So, with great anticipation—but also with nervous trepidation lest I do something wrong—I started to go through the ancient documents. Each page, some more than 200 years old, was delicate and fragile. I turned them over in slow motion. Handling these papers was, to me, the equivalent of dealing with the Dead Sea Scrolls or the *Book of Kells*.

Here, I hoped, was the key to Prescott's non-military life, as well as his relationship to the great events of the era. No doubt there was a lot here. But deciphering the contents was going to be a chore. The notes are written in every imaginable form of penmanship; some are very flowery, with curlicues and exaggerated flourishes, while others can best be described as chicken scratch. Very quickly, I rued the fact that the typewriter had not been invented until the early 1800s. After about an hour, my eyes began to ache. I resorted to photographing some of the pages with my iPhone in order to read them later at home. Three hours into my session, I needed to call it a day. I wasn't totally satisfied, but I wasn't disappointed, either. I hadn't gotten very far into the volume, but based on what I was uncovering I knew I would be back.

It took multiple visits to the Lawrence Library to make headway in the town records, but, on the positive side, it was thoroughly amazing to read these old town meeting notes in the varying hands of the committee members. Luckily for me, William Prescott is highly present in these pages, except for when he was away fighting in the French and Indian War and, of course, in the Revolutionary War. Prescott was listed as the moderator at various town meetings, and he was assigned to assorted committees that addressed key issues in Pepperell. His name appears as a signatory on important town pronouncements and directives to its representative on the General Court.

The information presented in these town meeting notes provided a substantial timeline of Prescott's Pepperell activities as he moved from loyal British subject in the mid-1700s, to growing revolutionary in the 1760s and 1770s, to town elder in the 1780s and early 1790s.

In contrast to today's constant digital data collection, old town records and meeting notes are obviously not as comprehensive or voluminous. That also makes each entry a potentially precious snapshot in time regarding what was being discussed and debated by the leaders in town. What struck me as I turned through the pages was how casual most of these notes are. Unlike on today's social media, they weren't written in all caps, don't have a string of exclamation points to at the end of a sentence, or are dotted with emojis. In this way, they're almost matter of fact. Whether talking about the battle at Bunker Hill, the Declaration of Independence, or the new United States Constitution, to pick a few examples, the entries don't scream off the page. They look like all the other collected notes and essentially just report the facts of the meetings, without color commentary. I suppose I should have expected this, but I regretted that there weren't more copious remarks fully describing what various participants in the meetings said, what positions each took, or revealed whose opinion carried the day.

I coupled my trips to the Lawrence Library with sit-down conversations with local historians and revolutionary era buffs. One of the first people I contacted was Ron Karr. Ron has been a member of the Pepperell Historical Society for 35 years, and he was extraordinarily helpful, fielding my questions about Colonel Prescott and pointing out the prevailing conditions that served as the backdrop to his actions. Ron is an academically trained historian, librarian, and teacher (31 years at UMASS/Lowell), who has written both academic and popular historical books largely focused on New England. He is retired, yet even now leaps at the chance to discuss Pepperell's history, of which he is an authority. Ron is amiable, smiles easily, and has the light, relaxed air of a college professor. His studied appreciation of local views held in the latter half of the 1770s immediately grounded my thinking. For instance, Ron said that local leaders like Prescott were much more concerned with parochial conditions than they were with heady, national issues and not likely to be following the famous social philosophers of the day. He also cautioned that I be careful not to succumb to the trap of accepting at face value every tidbit of information that might present itself, but instead try to find corroborating evidence before I accept some "fact" as, well, fact.

Wendy Cummings was another Pepperell resident who quickly responded to my outreach and informed me on some of the local lore regarding William

Prescott and other revolutionary era figures. Wendy is the Chapter Historian of the Daughters of the American Revolution and also a member of the Pepperell Historical Society. Wendy was also very generous with her time, and, when we first met, gave me a guided tour of the main historical sites in town. Delightfully pleasant, Wendy is unabashedly proud of Pepperell's origins and the role it played in the heady days of revolution and war.

Naturally, based on my success unearthing an abundance of information on Prescott in Pepperell, I decided to venture over to neighboring Groton—Pepperell's birthplace—to see what I could discover there. Checking in with the Groton Public Library (libraries really are the hub of information), I was directed to reach out to Kara Fossey at Boutwell House, the home of the Groton Historical Society. Kara suggested I come by so I could examine a collection of books by local, late-19th-century historian Samuel A. Green, who wrote extensively on Groton's history. A couple of trips later, I walked away with a new set of details about the Prescotts, the town that they'd helped build, and other extraordinary facts about Groton's role in an incandescent, post-Revolutionary War controversy (more on this later).

Although my project had gotten off to an uneven start, I now felt I was making real progress. As a wise person once said, it takes a village. Actually, my efforts were showing that, in some cases, it takes two or three villages. I finally felt like I was zeroing in on Prescott and a side of his life that the glorious accounts of his actions at Bunker Hill did not touch upon. The portrait of Prescott was becoming more comprehensive, nuanced, and interesting.

A Leader in Town Government

Having learned what life was like for William Prescott as a colonial farmer, I wondered how he had the time and energy to devote to local civic matters. Given the seriousness of some of the events he was involved in, it seemed like farming was actually the least of his concerns. In addition to the time-consuming and dangerous military experiences, the Pepperell town records show another highly active and less known side of Prescott—at least outside of Middlesex County.

Starting when he was in his early 20s and shortly after moving to Groton's West Parish in the 1740s, Prescott became extremely active in town government. As the family's genealogical history reveals, such civic activity was a longstanding tradition in the Prescott hereditary line. Generally, positions in local government brought notoriety and respect, as towns held special status in colonial New England and residents took particular pride in their communities.

Until midway through the 19th century, whenever most Americans reflected upon government, they thought first about their town and about their state, which they routinely referred to as their "country." For the most part, colonists established small, structured towns built around a central meetinghouse that served as both a church and town hall. Religion was a primary element of colonial life, as it gave the colonists a common purpose that shaped the way they ruled themselves and led their daily lives.[3]

In the 1600s, the Pilgrims and the Puritans were the first English settlers in the northern colonies, and they shared a Calvinist faith that was based on the concept of predestination—meaning that it was preordained whether a person went to heaven or hell. Consequently, Puritans were constantly looking for signs that they were among the chosen ones. According to Calvinism, wealth and the accumulation of material possessions were indications of God's favor. This philosophy kept citizens in line and working very hard. While industriousness was essential for pleasing God, it was also absolutely required to maintain life in a climate that was cold and uninviting for roughly half the year.

By the mid-1700s, however, the influence of the church in Massachusetts Bay had waned measurably. The clergy still set the moral tone for the community, yet as important as they remained, ministers were prohibited from holding political office. That privilege was reserved only for church members, the so-called "visible saints." Nonetheless, although there was a desire to keep church and state separate, ministers controlled who could become a member of the church, and therefore they had a meaningful, indirect influence on who held public office.

Out of this convoluted environment, a new and unique mechanism for conducting a town's business emerged—the town hall meeting. This form of governing was not the vision of John Winthrop, the first governor of the Bay Colony, but it became what the new immigrants favored. In early America, most people lived their entire lives in the towns of their birth, and they wanted a large, democratically administered hand in running their communities. Hovering over these independent town governments was the General Court, the original ruling assembly in Massachusetts. In 1632, shortly after Boston was founded, citizens were given the right to elect two people from each plantation to confer with the General Court. Representatives were elected annually; there were no extended terms and certainly no lifetime positions. This allowed the possibility of turning over government representatives on a regular basis.

The very first town hall in America was held in 1633 in Dorchester, a fishing community of English settlers adjacent to Boston. According to court records, every Monday at eight o'clock in the morning, townspeople in Dorchester held a meeting to settle and establish "such orders as may tend to the general good aforesayd."[4] The decisions that were approved at these meetings were considered law and "every man to be bound thereby, without gaynesaying or resistance."

The proceedings of town meetings were open and public; anyone could attend. Citizens could listen to how arguments were being made and could participate in the discussion by being recognized by the moderator. In this way, town meetings were highly inclusive. But voting at town hall was a different matter. To vote in town elections, a person had to be male, at least 21 years of age, a resident of the town for the past year, and own property of a minimum, specified value.[5] This cut down the election population substantially. But all male taxpayers, regardless of land ownership, could vote on propositions that were brought to the floor. Women could attend, but they could not vote, a practice that, of course, extended for nearly 300 years in America. Indeed, women had few rights and were expected to submit to their husband's wishes and give up their own economic and property rights once married. Women were expected to hold the family together and oversaw much of the work that went into not only maintaining the household but also the farm and any small businesses the family ran.[6]

At early town meetings, attendees did a wide variety of things. They elected town officials, awarded grants of land, approved infrastructure projects, set up schools, determined land usage, voted on taxes and tax rates, fixed the town minister's annual salary, established bounties for wolves and other predatory animals, and decided other community issues, such as caring for the poor. However, it wasn't long before all these items on the town meeting agenda overwhelmed the ability of attendees to get through them all. So, for practical reasons, topics were eventually limited to taxes, appropriations, and other recurring matters.

Initially, attendance at town meetings was mandatory and citizens were fined if they did not show up. That was one surefire rule to instill participatory democracy.[7] In Puritan towns, "seaters" were elected to determine the relative rank and dignity of the seats in the meetinghouse. Where you sat conveyed prestige and importance. High-ranking officials, like the governor and the wealthiest families, got the best seats up front.

The practice of town halls soon spread throughout New England, as it appeared to be an effective way for citizens to decide important matters of the day. This informal, out-in-the-open, majority-rules approach to conducting business represented an early foundation of democracy in the country that is still used today in some quarters. The longest continuously functioning town hall is held in Pelham, Massachusetts, and has been run out of the same two-story wooden structure since 1743.[8]

William Prescott was more than just a regular attendee at the Pepperell Town Hall meetings; he was one of the few participants who, for years, drove the process. Town meeting notes from March 1747 indicate that Prescott, at just 21 years old, was chosen to be on a committee of selectmen who repeatedly made decisions about items such as funds for the local school, the development and repair of roads and bridges, the salary of the local minister, and other important tax-related and spending issues. He was also named part of a three-man group of town assessors, a powerful position that kept its eye on the future needs of the town. In addition, over the next few years, Prescott moderated many town meetings and was part of a core group of men who were involved in all the major activities of the town. The names Shattuck, Lawrence, Spaulding, Hobart, Farnsworth, and others also appeared regularly on these committees. As I suspected, Prescott's activities in Pepperell government were very similar to his brothers' in neighboring Groton.

In March 1754, Prescott, still not yet 30 years old, was voted Treasurer of the district in addition to his other posts as town assessor and Clerk of Weights and Measures. Given all the hats that Prescott wore, he was clearly one of the indispensable individuals in town. Seven years into his residency in the West Parish, Prescott was deeply ensconced in town matters (except for those periods when he was away performing military duties), holding about every position there was—selectman, treasurer, town clerk, auditor, tax assessor, town hall moderator, ad hoc committee member, representative to the General Court, and judicial magistrate.

One of Prescott's keen interests, and one that he continually pressed for in town meetings, was education. Education was considered extremely important throughout Massachusetts, and children there were relatively well-educated. There was an especially large focus on literacy, as the Puritans believed that everyone should be able to read the Bible by themselves. Although William Prescott did not have a formal schooling, he and his wife, Abigail, greatly valued education and pushed for more money to be allocated to the local school to accommodate the growing population. They not only impressed this upon their son, William Jr., but they were also strong advocates for widespread access to education. Not surprisingly, William Jr., and his son, William Hickling Prescott, became highly respected, scholarly individuals who climbed to the heights of their respective professions as a lawyer and a historian, respectively.

Looking more broadly at the governing structure in America, each colony existed under an individual charter given by the Crown in England. These charters were viewed by the people as inviolable constitutions. They specified the form of government and the level of citizen participation in the government. In America, the rights granted to the colonists were greater than those given to citizens in England, as well as almost anywhere else in the Western world.[9] For a long stretch, there was a lot for Americans to like about their circumstances. Into the early 1760s, Pepperell town records report little derogatory talk about the Parliament in London or the monarch, King George, and certainly there was no talk of independence.

As historian Gordon Wood has written, "The white American colonists were not an oppressed people; they had no crushing imperial chains to throw off... they knew they were freer, more equal, more prosperous, and less burdened with cumbersome feudal and monarchical restraints than any other part of mankind in the 18th century."[10] As proof, the Massachusetts colony was growing, it was largely self-run, most people were happy, and the king and ministry were an ocean away.

Because of this there was growing anxiety in London that many years of indulgence in America had led to a dangerous degree of colonial autonomy. Moreover, the fact that about 20 percent of the free population in the colonies had non-English backgrounds, and consequently harbored no deep affections for Great Britain, was a cause for concern. As a result, many in Parliament urged caution in handling the American colonists. This concern continued to be debated with strident views on both sides for more than the next decade, right up to the outbreak of war. Nothing in the town records indicates that William Prescott was dissatisfied with the political situation in Massachusetts through the 1750s, but that was soon to change.

CHAPTER 5

Embracing the Cause of Liberty

One of the more intriguing issues in my research was learning when and how William Prescott began to trade his devotion to England for his public support for "the cause." Here again the Pepperell town records and other primary materials would be instrumental in making this determination.

Given Prescott's elevated status as a citizen of the Commonwealth, it would have been easy for him to remain a loyalist, as his brother-in-law and others who held comfortable posts in the Bay Colony did. But, as the records show, Prescott's political attitudes took a turn, and that set him off on a new and riskier course.

Changing Attitudes

Despite the advantages they had, by mid-century, many colonists were beginning to be frustrated with Great Britain's commercial policies, and growing numbers were dissatisfied with the constant warfare that beset their parent country. The imperial interests of the Crown kept Great Britain at war for roughly half of the 75 years preceding 1763, the year the French and Indian War ended.[1] These conflicts caused multiple strains. The financial burdens of these wars, principally those with Spain and France, were crushing for the Massachusetts colony and nearly drove it into insolvency. During this time, commerce in the Bay Colony had been severely disrupted, and labor shortages forced many businesses into bankruptcy. Also, thousands of citizens had been enlisted in the military. By the end of the French and Indian War, an estimated 75,000 colonists had been combatants and thousands had died. William Prescott and the soldiers he recruited in and around Pepperell were part of those statistics. Prescott went off to war willingly, but having participated in two wars since the 1740s, he must have been eager for calmer days.

The Treaty of Paris in 1763 officially ended the fighting with the French, but in the aftermath the bonds between Great Britain and its colonies began to break down. After all the hardships they had to endure, the citizens of Massachusetts were wondering what was in it for them. As historian John Ferling, who has written extensively on colonial America, has declared, "Empires exist for the parent state, something the American colonists eventually came to realize… and goes a long way toward explaining the American Revolution."[2]

Around this time, it was estimated that one-third of England's trade, including both imports and exports, was with the colonies. This prompted some to say that the American colonies were more important to England than its European allies. It is certainly hard to argue with that opinion. The end of the war also brought into power a new ministry in Parliament, led by George Grenville, a member of an influential political family with expertise in finance, who wanted to enforce the existing trade laws with the colonies more rigorously. Great Britain's national debt had nearly doubled in the prior seven years, and Grenville had to find revenue. To help offset the costs of the war and the continued presence of the British troops in the colonies, the British Parliament, at Grenville's direction, passed a series of laws that levied new restrictions and eventually taxes on the American citizenry. These included the Sugar Act of 1764 and the Stamp Act of 1765, the first acts to levy a direct tax on the colonies.[3]

Boston was particularly hard hit by Grenville's measures. For example, Britain's termination of lucrative military contracts in the region left many colonial laborers without work. Accelerating rates of taxation also put a crimp on colonists' finances, at the exact moment they were coping with the needs of an unprecedented number of war widows and their children, as well as a swelling poor population. In response, Boston merchants hired a team of lawyers to fight the application of writs of assistance, which were used to enforce the new laws and regulations. This group of advocates was led by James Otis, a 35-year-old Harvard graduate, who was an expert on common, civil, and admiralty law. Besides being a superb lawyer, Otis was an accomplished orator and pamphleteer writer. These skills were now quickly put to use.

Otis immediately asserted that the "Parliament of Great Britain is circumscribed by certain bounds" that it could not exceed. Otis argued that Parliament could not act against the fundamental principles of the British constitution, nor overrun the natural rights of life, liberty, and property. He declared that the sanctity of "natural rights" was a rule of law that was superior to parliamentary sovereignty. What this boiled down to was, as Otis claimed, "No parts of his Majesty's dominions can be taxed without their consent."[4]

There it was—no taxation without representation. Or, as Otis famously said, "Taxation without representation is tyranny." Otis also warned Parliament that they were playing with fire. Years later, when John Adams reflected on the coming of the American Revolution, he concluded that Otis's courtroom presentations and pamphleteering had been so pivotal that "Then and there the child Independence was born."[5]

Parallel to this, Pennsylvanian lawyer, political leader, and eventual Founding Father John Dickinson wrote that acquiescing to the Stamp Act could lead the colonists into a trap, for "the smaller the taxes [like those in the Stamp Act], the more dangerous they were, since they would be more easily found acceptable by the incautious, with the result that a precedent would be established for making still greater inroads on liberty and property."[6]

Hundreds of miles to the north in Pepperell, members of the town committee were making the same point as Dickinson. In town meeting notes from October 21, 1765, the governing town selectmen, with William Prescott presiding, voted "to give their Representative Instructions for his conduct at the General Court at this Important Crisis."[7] A group including William Prescott, Captain Edmund Bancroft, Josiah Fisk, Nehemiah Hobart, and Ephraim Lawrence was selected to prepare a statement to make sure that Pepperell's representative on the colony's governing body would not do anything that would support the execution of the Stamp Act measures. The statement said:

> ...taking into Consideration the measures that have been adopted by the British ministry and acts of Parlement [sic] made which press hard upon our Invaluable Rights and Previlages [sic] by the Royal Charter Granted for the first settlers of this province the Power of making Laws and Levying Taxes is vested in the General Assembly it is Certain we were not represented in Parlement [sic] neither was the Remonstrance sent by this Province admitted there when the Late act called the Stamp Act by which an insupportable and unconstitutional tax is Laid on the Colonies was made we think that if this act be carried into Execution it will afford a precedent for the Parlement [sic] to futer [sic] times to tax us without our Consent wee [sic] therefore think it our indispensable Duty to Desire you by no means to join in any measures for Countenancing or assisting in the Execution of the said Stamp act furthermore as the trade of this Province is greatly obstructed and the people Labour [sic] under allmost [sic] an unsupportable Debt wee [sic] Expect you will use your utmost Endevors [sic] in the General Assembly that the monies of the Province Drawn from the individuals may not be applied to any other uses under any pretense whatfor or than what is Evidently intended in the act for supplying the Province Treasury.[8]

While the language of the statement is awkward and verbose, it is clear that the leaders of the town were adamantly opposed to the taxes that would be raised by the Stamp Act and were also concerned that, if accepted, it would form a precedent for additional taxes on other yet-to-be-named goods or services.[9] This was a growing concern in the colony, and Prescott was part of the group chosen by Pepperell to lodge their disapproval. Consequentially, in the aftermath of the Stamp Act crisis, Pepperell became increasingly involved in anti-British activities.

Then, in 1766, the British Parliament exerted their power over the colonies by enacting the Declaratory Act, which held that Parliament could "make laws for America…in all cases whatsoever." This was a provocative statement of governmental authority that would be consistently maintained by those in power in Great Britain, and it was never abandoned, right up to and through the outbreak of war.

In the autumn of 1768, a day of fasting was set aside in Pepperell to seek divine guidance for political action and planning. Later, the district passed more resolutions censuring the British policies and repeatedly sent delegates to the colonial congresses with instructions to voice opposition. The town's history declares that the district was so "patriotic" that a Tory could not be found within its borders.

Angered by Britain's taxing policies, Samuel Adams, the older cousin of John Adams and a representative in the Massachusetts Assembly, organized a boycott of the goods that Parliament had taxed, including lead, paint, glass, and other items. In this way, a strategy of "nonimportation" became the successor of the colony's Stamp Act resistance. An example of this tactic was the Boston Non-Importation Agreement, drafted in March 1768, which called on merchants to sign an oath forswearing certain English goods.[10] About 60 merchants signed the agreement on August 1, 1768. Then, in October, two regiments of British soldiers, approximately 2,000 men, arrived in Boston to guard against an escalation of troubles, further incensing the citizenry.

Pepperell's growing disapproval of Parliament's actions was also evidenced in 1770 when the district voted unanimously to join the boycott of British goods. The town did not express any animosity toward the king, however, which shows it was still far from contemplating separation from England. It appears from his participation in Pepperell's activities that Prescott, who had loyally fought with the British in the late war with France, was now becoming more radicalized and falling closer in line with reactionary Boston leaders.

The person who may have had the most relevant perspective on the state of affairs in the colonies was British General Thomas Gage, commander in chief of all land forces in North America from 1763 to 1775, who was, as mentioned earlier, in charge of the troops who fought at Bunker Hill. Gage said the general outcry about the imposition of the new taxes was not limited to one or two states but spanned the continent. He astutely suggested that the colonists' objections had not emerged from their inability to pay the tax but rather from the belief that the tax was unconstitutional. This led Gage to conclude that the colonies ultimately wished for independence from the legislative power of Great Britain.

Then, in 1766, William Pitt, the first Earl of Chatham, agreed to become Prime Minister, and he brought in Charles Townshend as Chancellor of the Exchequer. It was an inauspicious choice. While Pitt was somewhat sympathetic toward the colonists, Townshend thought the upheaval stimulated by the Stamp Act showed that Britain needed to be stricter with them. He also believed the Americans should share the costs of maintaining the British Army in the country. The resulting Townshend Acts were passed in 1767 and 1768 and laid even heavier burdens on the colonists.[11]

Not surprisingly, Americans were enraged by Townshend's onerous measures. Their disdain became clearly evident with the publication of *Letters from a Farmer in Pennsylvania* in late 1767, a series of essays by John Dickinson.[12] Dickinson assailed the Townshend Duties as unconstitutional, insisting that Parliament had no legal authority to impose any tax on the colonies.[13] Dickinson's pamphlet struck a powerful chord among Americans.

Resistance Turns Violent

The mounting strains in Massachusetts culminated in a disastrous, and perhaps predictable, calamity in early March 1770 when British troops opened fire on a raucous mob of colonists, killing five in an event subsequently referred to as the Boston Massacre.[14] A young John Adams agreed to defend the British soldiers in court, even after being warned by friends that he would be throwing away his budding legal career. In the trial's final verdict, six soldiers were fully acquitted while two were found guilty not of murder but of the lesser charge of manslaughter. To prevent the men from being hanged, Adams pleaded with the judge to give them the "benefit of the clergy," a practice of the day typically afforded clergymen, which would be a more lenient sentence involving branding the thumbs of the two men and thereby permanently indicating their guilt in a serious crime.[15] Prescott's reaction to the shooting, the trial, and its verdict is not recorded in any notes or correspondence. Like most colonists, though, he might have been swept up in the anti-British feelings that rose to a fever pitch.

The issue of Parliament's authority again came to the fore in Massachusetts when, in January 1773, presiding British Governor Thomas Hutchinson—who served from August 1769 to May 1774—gave a confrontational speech in front of the colony's General Court. Hutchinson started by praising the British constitution for its spirit of liberty. Then he took a swipe at activists like Samuel Adams, John Hancock, Joseph Warren, James Otis, and others, by decrying the fact that some colonists in the province had been moving toward denying the authority of Parliament for years. Hutchinson's remarks, along with his disreputable patronage practices, were, to John Adams and the others, a straightforward and serious threat to liberty.[16] In reaction, Samuel Adams then proposed that Boston form a committee, with representation across the colony, to keep the citizenry politically informed, and he recommended that other towns do likewise to form a network that would disseminate timely information.[17] The newly formed Committee of Correspondence produced a report called the Boston Pamphlet that outlined the rights of British Americans and stated, in bold and unvarnished terms, how British policies were violating those rights.

William Prescott was no doubt aware of this commotion and invective, as his brother James was active in the provincial government and would have been well-versed in the prevailing arguments. At a town hall gathering on January 11, 1773, the citizens of Pepperell discussed the town's response to the Boston Pamphlet. Town records indicate that the district "voted unanimously that the pamphlet sent by the town of Boston should be read at this meeting, which it was by the moderator." At the same meeting, nine men were chosen to form a committee to consider what was proper for the district to do "at this alarming time respecting the encroachments which have been made upon our civil priviliges [sic]..." A week later, on January 18, a letter was sent from Pepperell to the Committee of Correspondence at Boston stating:

> Gentlemen, you will be so good as to inform the town of Boston that we have received their letter, together with the pamphlet setting forth our liberties as men, as Christians, as Subjects, with the infringements which have been made upon them...
>
> Desire them [citizens of Boston] to accept of our hearty acknowledgement for their vigilance over our dominion Interests
>
> We are greatly alarmed at the large strides, which have been made by the enemies of our excellent constitution, towards enslaving a people [the colonists]
>
> We tremble at the thought of Slavery, either civil or ecclesiastical, and are fully sensible of the mean connection there is between civil and religious Liberty, if we lose the former the latter will not remain
>
> [We] stand ready to cooperate with them in all measures warranted by the constitution[18]

Many other Massachusetts towns sent similar letters, letting the leaders in Boston know that they backed the Boston Pamphlet and all it implied. Pepperell's town leaders, including William Prescott, also sent the following statement to James Prescott, William's older brother, who was a representative to the General Assembly for the town of Groton and of the districts of Pepperell and Shirley:

> Sir, we his majesty's most loyal and dutiful subjects, the freeholders and other inhabitants of the District of Pepperell legally assembled January 18, 1773, Being ever ready to give due assistance and encouragement to government in a constitutional way; at the same time concerned that the rights and priviliges [sic] of British subjects, (our birth-right and the noblest inheritance left us by our fathers) may be securely enjoyed by us, and transmitted to our posterity, cannot but be greatly affected at the frequent innovations which have been made on our happy constitution...We therefore, who are no small part of your constituency do desire and expect that you assert yourself in the great and general assembly, to the utmost of your ability for the regaining of such priviliges [sic] as have been unjustly wrestled from us... Directions that you be led into the path of truth and equity, and never be driven aside from seeking the welfare of your country. The above respectfully is offered to the consideration of the District by your humble servants." [Signed by Capt. William Prescott and eight others.][19]

Again, it is clear that William Prescott and the other prominent leaders of Pepperell were very concerned about the real and potential loss of their long-held rights and privileges as British Americans. Nonetheless, despite their strong tone, they continued to express their loyalty to King George, declaring they were "dutiful subjects." Thus, even nearly 10 years after the passage of the Sugar Act, they did not sound like revolutionaries hellbent on separating from the Crown. They valued their British birthright and eagerly looked for the benefits of it to accrue to their descendants.

At this time, William Prescott was chosen to represent Pepperell in a regional Committee of Safety. Pepperell's participation in the committee network indicated that the district was firmly opposed to the severe current British policies. The district also established a Committee of Correspondence, with William Prescott and Nehemiah Hobart as members, in order to stay apprised of all information and actions flowing through the central Committee of Correspondence in Boston.[20] Clearly, Pepperell fervently wanted to stay plugged in to the latest political developments.

Unfortunately, the turmoil of the early 1770s did not end there, but instead took a rather escalatory turn. On December 16, 1773, an explosive incident occurred that had tremendous ramifications for the citizens of Boston. The event stemmed from the British government's desire to aid the East India Company, the second largest commercial institution in Great Britain after the Bank of England, which was facing bankruptcy.[21] The company, which received 90 percent of its profits from tea, was in serious financial trouble due to a glut of tea on the global market. Boycotts in America and illegal trade of Dutch tea also reduced sales, so that by 1772 only about 15 percent of the tea sold in the colonies was East India Company tea. In response, Parliament passed the Tea Act in May 1773 to buck up the company's balance sheet by forcing Bostonians to buy their cherished tea only from English ships, which would be consigned to a limited number of designated merchants.[22] Bostonians also learned that they would have to pay a tax on the tea, a way for Parliament to support the English merchants whose excess stocks of tea were growing.[23]

After negotiations with Governor Hutchinson failed to resolve the situation, Samuel Adams and other plotters put a daring plan into effect. A select group of men, many disguised as Native Americans, boarded three British tea ships in Boston harbor—the *Dartmouth*, *Eleanor*, and *Beaver*—and tossed an entire shipment of English tea overboard. It consisted of 342 crates containing 90,000 pounds of tea valued at 9,659 pounds sterling (around several million dollars in today's currency).[24] The action was swift and no one was hurt. The Boston Tea Party was a dramatic demonstration of Boston defiance. Other ports along the east coast similarly rejected the British tea, but the Boston event stood out because of the city's leading opposition to British policies and the growing violence that accompanied it.

Following the Tea Party, the anti-British leaders in Boston heard from the people in the backcountry, many of whom were not happy with the destruction of the tea. Some towns even went so far as to sever their ties with Boston's Committee of Correspondence. In Pepperell, William Prescott, in his role as District Clerk, issued a statement on December 20, 1773 to the townspeople that read: "In his Majesty's Name, you are required to assemble...to see what the District wil [*sic*] act Relating to a Letter Sent by the Committee of Correspondence at Boston to the Committee of Correspondence in Pepperell in Reference to tea Sent by the East India Company to America in order to raise a Revenue against our consent."[25] So the town, ever aware of what was going on in Boston, clearly intended to discuss the issue and determine what position it wanted to take.

Overseas, outrage over the Tea Party swept England. Moreover, for the first time, Parliament seriously discussed the use of force in the colonies.[26] Few in Prime Minister Lord North's cabinet (North held office from 1770 to 1782) imagined that defeating the colonists would be very hard, and they wanted to retaliate strongly. There were some dissenting voices, however. Edmund Burke, a member of the House of Commons, as well as a respected economist and philosopher, warned presciently that strident measures could lead to war and the loss of the colonies. But only about 20 percent of Parliament sided with him. So, in the end, the ministers coalesced around a series of bills that became known as the Coercive Acts in England and the Intolerable Acts in America. The bills closed the port of Boston, abrogated the Massachusetts charter, enabled criminal trials to be moved to Great Britain, expanded the quartering of British soldiers, and installed Thomas Gage as Military Governor.

As noted earlier, Gage was born into an aristocratic family in England and fought in the French and Indian War along with George Washington, most notably at the disastrous battle of the Monongahela in 1755. He arrived in Boston in May 1774 and, regrettably for him, governed over the most contentious time in Massachusetts. Although he was initially somewhat sympathetic to the colonists, in a relatively short time, Gage would come to despise his stay in the Bay Colony.

The reaction in Pepperell was swift and firm. On June 27, 1774, a Pepperell town meeting passed a resolution regarding the increasingly heavy hand of the Crown. The statement read:

> Resolved, it is the opinion of this District, that we have a just and lawful Right to meet together, when and so often as we shall have occasion to cultivate harmony, and to transact our Town affairs, and that we shall hold, use, and improve that privilege, and never give up, or quit the usual practice of meeting together on any mandate whatsoever...and that lord north nor any other British minister, or person whatever hath any Right, to trample America, under his feet nor to invade its privileges, either civil or religious
>
> We are resolved: to do all in our Power, by abstainence [sic], and every other Lawful and Proper way, to recover and preserve, our charter rights and privileges, and that we will not tamely submit to the yoke of bondage...and we will not have any hand in the consumption of (East India tea) British goods...or merchandise, imported after the last day of August.[27]

Simultaneously, the Bay Colony's leaders formed the Massachusetts Provincial Congress, a conditional government that controlled all of the Commonwealth outside of British-controlled Boston. Importantly, the Congress possessed all power to govern the colony, collect taxes, purchase supplies, and raise a militia. John Hancock was chosen to be the Congress's initial president, and he sent Paul Revere to Philadelphia to announce to the First Continental Congress that Massachusetts had established regionally the inaugural autonomous government in the colonies. This was clearly a momentous step.

Much to the delight of those pushing for a more extreme backlash against the British, letters of sympathy and supplies of provisions poured into Boston's Committee of Correspondence. One of the earliest of these letters was written by William Prescott, dated from Pepperell on July 4, 1774.[28] Prescott's letter is short and to the point, supporting opposition to the British, stating, "by order of the committee of that always patriotic town [Pepperell], sending at once 40 bushels of grain, promising further assistance with provisions and men." Prescott went on to tell the Committee of Correspondence to "stand firm in the common cause," which was not only uniting the citizens of eastern Massachusetts, but also citizens from around the colonies.

In case there was any doubt of Prescott's stance toward the British, a second letter of his—written afterward to the "men of Boston" and discovered years later by historian and politician George Bancroft—eliminated any ambiguity.[29] Bancroft, whose own family arrived in Boston in 1632, came into possession of this second letter in which Prescott, on behalf of his fellow Pepperell farmers and townspeople, wrote:

> Be not dismayed or disheartened in this great day of trials. We heartily sympathize with you, and are always ready to do all in our power for your support, comfort, and relief; knowing that Providence has placed you where you must stand the first shocks, we consider that we are all embarked in one bottom, and must sink or swim together. We think if we submit to those regulations, all is gone. Our forefathers past the vast Atlantic, spent their blood and treasure, that they might enjoy their liberties, both civil and religious, and transmit them to their posterity. Their children have waded through seas of difficulty, to leave us free and happy in the enjoyment of English privileges. Now, if we should give them up, can our children rise up and call us blessed? Is not a glorious death in defense of our liberties better than a short, infamous life, and our memory to be had in detestation to the latest posterity? Let us all be of one heart, and stand fast in the liberties wherewith Christ has made us free; and may be of his infinite mercy grant us deliverance out of all of our troubles.[30]

The ardent revolutionary, Samuel Adams, could not have written a more supportive letter. With it, Prescott indicated his solidarity with his eastern neighbors and showed that he was all in with the goal of independence. Moreover, the references to Providence and Jesus Christ illustrate Prescott's firm religious grounding, which might have been influenced or reinforced by the beliefs of his wife, Abigail. Here we have the revolutionary Prescott, someone who has become comfortable with his decision to oppose the king and fight, if necessary, for personal freedom.

During the year, as the political climate heated up, Prescott was sent as a delegate to the Provincial Congress at Concord and appointed colonel of a regiment of minutemen that spanned the contiguous communities of Pepperell, Groton, and Hollis in New Hampshire.[31] Prescott was a neighbor and friend of Captain Reuben Dow, Lieutenant John Goss, and many others in the Hollis company. Moreover, his brother-in-law, Colonel John Hale, was one of the leading patriots of Hollis. These connections most likely explain why the Hollis company joined Prescott's regiment rather than one from the state of New Hampshire.

More colonist anger was stoked when, on August 9, General Gage announced the creation of a new provincial council in Massachusetts, with hand-picked members who supported the Crown.[32] Crowds gathered in many towns to pressure the new council members to resign. In Pepperell, town documents from August 29, 1774 record the raising of the Liberty Pole and one of the first American flags that was flown in defiance of the Crown.

While the traditional Massachusetts government was replaced by a makeshift council whose members were appointed by Gage, the colonists had their own Massachusetts Provincial Congress. This organization, headed by Dr. Joseph Warren (he succeeded John Hancock), met as a shadow government and formulated distinct policies for the colony. Dr. Warren was one of the more spirited activists in Boston and a strong anti-British proponent.[33]

Warren was an extraordinarily popular figure in Boston. He was born in Roxbury, Massachusetts, came from modest means, but had a sharp intellect and was educated at the prestigious Roxbury Latin school and Harvard College, where he decided to pursue a career in medicine.[34] He established a large practice in Boston and in the 1760s was instrumental in inoculating the citizens of Boston against smallpox. Warren also led one of the largest Masonic groups in Boston, St. Andrew's Grand Lodge of Freemasons. In addition, Warren was the head of the vitally important Committees of Correspondence and Safety. He wrote newspaper essays, gave speeches, and was twice the main orator during anniversary ceremonies marking the Boston Massacre. He also plotted opposition strategy with Samuel Adams and other radicals, and argued for military preparations.[35]

Still, even up to late 1774, the major provincial agitators and pamphleteers were only willing to aim their ire at Parliament—not at King George. That would begin to change, however, when the young Virginian, Thomas Jefferson, released his pamphlet *A Summary View of the Rights of British Americans*, which focused directly on the harmful actions of the monarch.[36] Jefferson's delineation of grievances against the king was a precursor to his monumental Declaration of Independence, penned two years later. Jefferson's pamphlet was meant to animate the discussions at the upcoming First Continental Congress, which was held in September and October of 1774. In addition to complaining about the king, Jefferson's opinion piece bore right into the heart of the matter, going so far to say Parliament had no right to govern the colonies.

Concomitantly with Jefferson, Joseph Warren collaborated with Samuel Adams on the Suffolk Resolves, an anti-British polemic that came out of the Suffolk County Convention of Committees of Correspondence in Massachusetts on September 9, 1774.[37] The resolves were carried to Philadelphia by Warren's good friend, Paul Revere, and presented to the First Continental Congress. The Congress condemned the attempts of "a wicked administration [Parliament] to enslave America."[38] On September 17, when the Congress unanimously endorsed the Suffolk Resolves, John Adams declared it was one of the happiest days of his life, saying, "In Congress we had generous, noble sentiments, and manly eloquence. This day convinced me that America will support Massachusetts or perish with her."[39]

If William Prescott was following the political stances of James Otis, Samuel Adams, John Dickinson, and Joseph Warren, and it's highly likely he was fully aware of at least the Massachusetts leaders, it was probably then that his views regarding the British presence in Boston and the Crown's increasingly draconian policies would have been fully radicalized. While elite colonial leaders were delving into the treatises of philosophers like John Locke, John Stuart Mill, David Hume, and Thomas Hobbes, the more common folk, such as farmers like Prescott, were turning to the Bible and church ministers for guidance on the principal issues of the day.[40] The most ardent religious followers believed that even before the first governments were established, God had bestowed universal rights on mankind. Either way, the colonists were beginning to think very deeply about their rights and the limitations of government.[41]

With these moves and pronouncements, Military Governor Thomas Gage was extremely concerned about the situation in America, and his letters to the ministry in England revealed growing desperation and fear. He asked for more troops, maybe ultimately as many as 100,000 men he said, and he recommended that the Coercive Acts be suspended. Moreover, to rebut those in Parliament who thought this was an isolated Massachusetts problem, one of Gage's messages said, "The Flames of Sedition have spread universally throughout the Country," and all New Englanders were "as furious as they are in Massachusetts."[42] Gage pointedly told the king that Massachusetts was in "actual rebellion and must be subdued." The king agreed with Gage that the growing unrest must be quieted, but thought Gage's recommendation to suspend the Coercive Acts "was the most absurd that can be suggested."

Events moved quickly as 1774 turned into 1775. The situation in Massachusetts was getting more dangerous and the possibility of war was now a distinct possibility. Prescott must have been weighing the odds that a wider and more dangerous conflict might soon erupt. He didn't know it at the start of the new year, but the confrontation in Charlestown eventually known as the battle of Bunker Hill, that would forever mark his life, was only six months away. I needed to know what actions Prescott was involved in immediately before that fateful confrontation. As even casual history buffs know, the big event during that period was the fighting in mid-April at Lexington and Concord. Citizens in Massachusetts began celebrating this notable event as "Patriot's Day" in 1894, and still mark it with dramatic, annual reenactments.

So, it was more than a curiosity to discover if William Prescott was involved in April 19, 1775 and the fast-moving events for two months afterward.

To investigate if Prescott had any association with the historic fighting, I reached out to National Park Service ranger Jim Hollister, who is stationed at Minute Man National Park in Concord. Jim was not aware of any involvement by Prescott, who was about 20 miles away in Pepperell when the fighting started. Jim told me in no uncertain terms that confrontations that day should not be referred to as skirmishes, as some observers do, due to the heavy casualty totals. He also emphasized that several thousand militia flooded to Concord and conceded it is possible that Prescott and his troops were among them.

I then got in touch with local Concord resident and eminent historian Dr. Robert (Bob) Gross, who has written about the events in April 1775, and invited him to lunch. We met at the historic Colonial Inn in the center of town and sat in a quiet spot in the oak-darkened pub room. When I told Bob about the dearth of any documents by or about William Prescott during the period, he said he was not surprised given the practices of the day. Bob advised me to do what I could to track Prescott's behavior and the choices he made in order to make inferences about his posture with respect to the growing anti-British movement. It was clear Bob didn't envy my predicament, but he tried not to be discouraging. I leaned in to the positive advice and tried to convince myself something would turn up.

I then caught that break when Pepperell's Wendy Cummings alerted me to a compilation of historical essays called *The Pepperell Reader*, originally compiled in 1975, which provided valuable information about Prescott's activity shortly before Bunker Hill that I had not found elsewhere, and, yes, Prescott responded to the Concord Alarm.

CHAPTER 6

War Begins

As William Prescott moved closer to the views of the more active anti-British leaders in Massachusetts, the situation in the state was rapidly escalating to a war footing. Late in January 1775, Thomas Gage, feeling vulnerable in Boston and cut off from the local food sources, started to look for roadways that would provide opportunities to march inland. His spies traveled to Concord and Worcester to map the roads and topography, to monitor the political pulse of the countryside, and to learn what they could about the provincials' munitions and supply depots.[1] However, Gage's forays did not go undetected—despite his men wearing disguises—and the spies' actions were reported to the Committee of Safety. One of the patriot men documenting these movements was Paul Revere, the local silversmith and night rider, who typically sent word of British maneuvers to his friend, Joseph Warren.[2]

On April 14, Gage received a letter from Lord Dartmouth, the Secretary of State for America, which summed up the ministry's disappointment with Gage's dire reports and informed him that his immediate request for 20,000 additional troops would not be fulfilled. It noted that they were probably not necessary to put down "the rude Rabble" that couldn't possibly resist the British Army.[3] Dartmouth told Gage that Massachusetts was in open rebellion and not to delay his moves any further. Dartmouth also issued orders to arrest the principal rabble-rousers, even if that should spark greater hostilities.

Stung by Dartmouth's words, Gage decided to act quickly against the insurgents, even though his concerns about the size of his force had not been rectified. Gage's new plan was to send troops out from Boston to capture the guns and ammunition that he had learned the provincials had hidden in Concord, about 20 miles northwest of Boston. Along the way, he also hoped to round up John Hancock and Samuel Adams, who were believed to be in the nearby town of Lexington, roughly 5 miles closer to the city. The strike was to be secret and quick, so that the troops could be back in Boston before the provincial militias could respond.[4] Not surprisingly, given how freely soldiers and citizens discussed matters on the street, these plans were quickly discovered by the colonists and counteractions were set in motion to thwart Gage's aims.[5]

During all of this, Gage was kept aware of Revere's movements, and so he had an inkling that the provincials were onto his plans. That they were, and on April 17, the Committees of Safety and Supplies voted to move four six-pounders, certain ammunition, and other materiel from Concord to Groton.[6] Ordnance in Stow was also moved to Groton. All of this materiel was stored in the Groton powder-house and placed under the supervision of Oliver Prescott, who was a member of the committees and, as previously noted, William Prescott's younger brother. While Gage was told the colonists had relocated some of the armaments they'd housed in Concord, he was assured that there were still large stockpiles there worth capturing. So, on Tuesday, April 18, Gage sent out a mounted patrol of 20 men—10 officers and 10 sergeants—with orders to intercept all American messengers in the countryside and keep them from spreading the alarm.[7] Gage also informed his brigadier, Hugh Percy, that no townspeople were to leave Boston that night.[8]

Gage then told Lieutenant Colonel Francis Smith of the 10th Infantry that he would be leading an expeditionary force, but he didn't tell him where he was sending him until later that evening. This information began to leak out mostly through indiscreet comments made by British soldiers in Boston. Informed of these reports, Joseph Warren enlisted Paul Revere and William Dawes to carry a warning out to the countryside. Warren met with Revere at his home and ordered him to "immediately set off for Lexington where Hancock and Adams were, and acquaint them with the [British] movement."[9] The only bits of information they were lacking were the time of the British departure and their route.[10]

Revere then set up a signaling system with Colonel William Conant of the Committee of Safety to let him know which route the British were going to take. One lantern hung in the steeple of the North Church in Boston meant that the British were taking a land route via the Boston Neck; two lanterns meant a water route across the Charles River and westward through Menotomy.[11] When, on the evening of the 18th, Revere saw two lit lanterns, he knew it was the water route.

Quickly, Revere was rowed across the Charles River, evading detection from the British man-of-war, the HMS *Somerset*—which was there to keep Boston harbor closed—and landed a short distance away in Charlestown around 11:00 p.m. Exiting the boat, Revere was given a fast steed, Brown Beauty, by local Deacon John Larkin, who had borrowed the horse from his father, Samuel. By prearrangement, Revere's compatriot Dawes headed out of Boston via the Boston Neck on the city's south side, where he'd have to pass the British guards. Dawes frequently crossed the Neck, and on this evening one of the guards was a soldier he had befriended, who let him pass despite Gage's orders not to allow anyone to leave town.[12] Other night riders also fanned out to spread the word in other parts of eastern Massachusetts.

Revere arrived in Lexington around 12:30 a.m., the precise time the British troops were being rowed across the Charles River. Revere went straight to the house of Reverend Jonas Clark, where Hancock and Adams were staying temporarily.[13] At the Clark house, Revere was told that the household asked not to be disturbed by any noise.[14] "Noise!" exclaimed Revere. "You'll have noise enough before long. The Regulars are coming out!"

As word spread and alarm bells sounded, militiamen grabbed their flintlocks and rushed to Lexington Green in the center of town. One of the first individuals informed of the British action was Captain John Parker, the 45-year-old head of the Lexington militia. Parker then had his young drummer boy, William Diamond, beat a call to arms to summon local minutemen to the Green to await the British.[15] Initially, about 130 men turned out, muskets in hand, and waited in the chilly April air for the arrival of the British regulars.

His work in Lexington done, Revere and the soon-arriving Dawes rode west toward Concord, where they were quickly joined by a 23-year-old doctor from Concord named Samuel Prescott, who was returning from a date with Lydia Mulliken of Lexington. Samuel was a fifth-generation descendant of John Prescott—the earliest Prescott to arrive in America—making him a not-too-distant relative of Colonel William Prescott.[16]

Dr. Prescott knew the people of Concord well and would be instrumental in spreading the word.[17] As the three riders, still shrouded in darkness, approached Hartwell Tavern on the way to Concord, they were accosted by four British officers who patrolled the area. Revere was captured outright, while Dawes was able to spur his horse and elude the British. However, in his furious effort to escape, Dawes lost his mount in the woods and ended up walking back to Lexington.[18] Fortunately, Dr. Prescott escaped cleanly by jumping a nearby stone wall, and he sped to Concord to deliver the warning.

There is a small, almost innocuous stone structure on the west-bound side of the Concord Road, about 10 yards off the roadway, that marks the spot where Revere was captured. Motorists whiz by this spot every day on their way to and from work or in the course of doing their chores, and I'd venture many do not know the significance of the memorial. It is about halfway between Lexington and Concord, which reminds us how close the three night riders were to their destination.

Interrogated by the British, Revere concocted a story to sow doubt in the minds of the enemy soldiers. He told them that the Americans knew the regulars were marching out to Concord and that hundreds of militia men were there waiting for them. In his most convincing voice, Revere tried to persuade his captors that the regulars were marching into a trap and would be advised to turn around and go back to Boston. The British weren't sure what to make of Revere's story, but ultimately, they were not convinced enough to follow Revere's suggestion. Instead, they took Revere's horse and let him go, forcing him to walk back to Lexington as well.

At one o'clock, the bell atop the Concord town house began to peal; Samuel Prescott had arrived with the alarm.[19] It wasn't long before minutemen and militia were pouring into Concord center from every direction. The soldiers gathered at Wright Tavern, the designated rendezvous spot, under the command of Major John Buttrick. At 4:00 a.m., another company of minutemen from the neighboring town of Lincoln filed into Concord to wait in the cold for the British.

Lexington Green

Knowing the British were in the area and fearing capture, Hancock and Adams gathered their belongings and headed east to the town of Woburn before eventually traveling south to the Second Continental Congress that was soon to meet in Philadelphia.[20] In the meantime, Captain Parker led the Lexington militia onto the Green and waited for the British to arrive. However, after a while, when the British failed to appear and there was no word from any of Parker's scouts about their approach, some of the minutemen went home. The rest—maybe a few dozen—filed into Buckman's Tavern just off the Green. There, the men rested and tried to stay warm with a glass of rum.

At 4:30 in the morning, the last scout dispatched by Captain Parker, Thaddeus Bowman, brought word that the British were indeed approaching Lexington.[21] So, the provincial troops left the warmth of the tavern and headed back onto the Green.[22] At this point, Revere was still in Lexington and, from an upstairs room in Buckman's Tavern, he could see the regulars nearing the town and decided it was time to take his leave. Revere passed through the militia on the Green, lugging a trunk with Hancock's important papers, and never saw the confrontation that was about to occur.

Church bells tolled in a slow, dirge-like manner, and more men rushed out to meet the British troops. Ultimately, 77 men—about half the males in town—huddled together on the dewy grass and peered down the road to the east, not sure what they were likely to confront. Concerned they would be badly outnumbered, Parker had his men spread out a bit on the Green so they would appear more numerous.

At daybreak, a British advance guard of 200 soldiers, led by Major John Pitcairn, marched into Lexington Green. The expedition's commander, the portly General Smith, was lagging behind, in no particular hurry. Parker related to his men the Committee of Safety order, saying that if a confrontation occurred, not to fire first. He told his men, "Stand your ground. Don't fire unless fired upon, but if they [the British] mean to have a war, let it begin here." For very savvy political reasons, the committee wanted to induce sympathy for the Americans by painting the British as the aggressor. However, the vulnerability of the minutemen was not lost on at least one American soldier, who remarked, "There are so few of us, it is folly to stand here."[23] To which Parker reputedly replied, "The first man who offers to run will be shot down." Nearby, just off the Green, stood about 40 spectators anxious to see what was about to happen.

As the Americans and British opposed each other, Major Pitcairn, with his pistol in hand, rode into the space between the two opposing lines of troops—a gap of about 25 yards—and ordered the Americans to disarm. "Lay down your arms and disperse, you damn rebels!" he shouted.[24] The Americans stood their ground and did not obey Pitcairn's repeated command. The situation was very tense, and the riled-up British troops made menacing taunts and leveled their guns toward the Americans.

For a moment, nothing happened. Then, a shot rang out. Later, neither side took credit for the initial firing, and instead blamed the other. In fact, to this day, who fired the first shot on Lexington Green has not been resolved. It could have even been unintentional. At the sound of the gunshot, the British troops reacted spontaneously and opened up on the militiamen, charging toward them on the Green. Most of Parker's men began to disperse quickly, while a few turned to fire on the British. Pitcairn and the other officers tried to get their unruly troops to stop shooting, but the firing kept up for a few minutes. The Americans retreated from the field, but not before eight of their comrades lay dead and nine were wounded. Most of the American victims were shot in the back as they withdrew. Two British soldiers were injured, but not seriously.

Soon afterward, the rest of Lieutenant Colonel Smith's troops caught up with Pitcairn's men in Lexington.[25] Now, with the element of surprise definitely lost, some officers wanted Smith to call off the expedition and head back to Boston, but Smith was not deterred.[26] About 30 minutes after the confrontation on Lexington Green, the British troops fired off a traditional victory salute into the air and resumed their march toward Concord, while townspeople retrieved the bodies of the dead and wounded.[27]

Prescott Responds

As word continued to spread in the morning about the action at Lexington and the British objective up the road, additional militias made their way to Concord. At about nine o'clock, a messenger from Concord arrived in Pepperell with word about the earlier fighting. They added that the regulars were on their way to, or were possibly already in, the town. Upon getting the message from Concord, William Prescott strapped on his sword, said goodbye to his wife and his son, and immediately gave the order for the Pepperell company—as well as the company in neighboring Hollis, New Hampshire—to march southeast to nearby Groton.[28]

The militias in these three towns were under Prescott's captaincy, and he had prepared them for just such a contingency.[29] So well-prepared were Prescott's minutemen that when the summons arrived to gather, they hastened from what they were doing to assemble in rapid fashion. In one instance, Edmund Bancroft, a sergeant in Captain John Nutting's company, had just started out to Maine when the Concord messenger got to Pepperell. Edmund's father, who headed the household, said, "Perhaps he is not out of hearing yet." He ran out in the field, mounted a high rock, and called out to his son. Edmund heard his father's voice and returned home. He took his gun and lit out toward Concord.[30] In another case, Abel Parker, also a captain in Nutting's company, was plowing his farm about three miles away when he heard the alarm. Immediately, he left his plow—not even stopping to unyoke his oxen—ran to his house, and grabbed his coat in one hand and his gun in the other. He set out on a run and did not stop until he overtook his comrades about three miles below Groton.

To save time, William Prescott rode off ahead of his troops to check on the Groton company. When Prescott got to Groton, about five miles away, its militia was not ready to move out. So, after a short rest, he directed his Pepperell and Hollis men to begin the march to Concord, some 20 miles away, without waiting for the Groton troops. This was much to the chagrin of Oliver Prescott, who did not enjoy seeing his own men from Groton outdone by his brother's from Pepperell.

The long march from Groton would take at least five or six hours, even if they were able to move at a sustained clip. This would put them in Concord in the mid-afternoon. While Prescott was likely on horseback, his men had to trudge along on foot, carrying their guns and ammunition, plus whatever victuals and other supplies they needed.[31]

Lieutenant Colonel Smith's column of British regulars had arrived in Concord at around eight o'clock. It was still early in the morning, but there was already a buzz of activity throughout the town. Smith broke his troops into two groups and began to search for the store of munitions. To get to Colonel James Barrett's farm—where the British thought much of the ammunition was hidden—the British had to march past a group of buildings, including a meetinghouse, a few taverns, and 20 or 30 houses. The road headed to the right and climbed across a ridge before cutting to the left at the North Bridge, a roughly 25-yard span that gently arched over the Concord River about a half mile from the town's center. Overlooking the North Bridge on the western side was Punkatasset Hill, which rose to a height of 200 feet. This is where the local militias were assembling.

Smith placed seven of his 10 companies under the command of Captain Lawrence Parsons, at the narrow North Bridge. Parsons, with 196 men, had two assignments: first, to secure the North Bridge, and, second, to search Barrett's Farm. Parsons had been given a lot of responsibility despite his limited experience. In hindsight, too much responsibility. Smith had the remaining troops, including his elite grenadiers, with him in the town. The British knew exactly where to look for the stores, as a spy had furnished them with maps of the hiding places.[32]

By now, there were about 400 minutemen and militia in Concord. These men were mainly from Concord and from nearby Acton, Bedford, Carlisle, and Lincoln.[33] The largest contingent of troops amassed on the west side of the Concord River on Punkatasset Hill above Parsons's men at the North Bridge. As the British spread out around town, some of the militia urged Colonel Barrett to do something, but he was reluctant to take any action.[34] However, from their elevated position, they could keep their force united and monitor the British activity, especially the actions of a company of 35 men that Captain Parsons had left under Captain Walter Laurie—also on the west side of the North Bridge.

At 11 o'clock, about two hours since they left Pepperell, Prescott and his troops had gone roughly seven miles. They still had a long way to go. It was then that the provincials on Punkatasset Hill saw smoke rising from the direction of Concord Center, and the situation rapidly changed.

Joseph Hosmer, a lieutenant in one of the Concord minutemen companies, thought the British had set fire to the town. (They were merely burning some wooden crates and the like.) Hosmer was fed up and gave a speech mocking his comrades for not taking action, shouting, "Will you let them burn the town down?"[35] At this, the men started marching from their heights down the Groton Road toward the North Bridge. Colonel Barrett told his men to load their guns but not to fire them until the British did. This was the first time an American military unit under a unified commander ever intentionally advanced on the British Army.[36]

British Captain Walter Laurie quickly pulled his company back across to the east side of the Concord River and joined two other companies in defending the bridge. His men began tearing up planks on the bridge to keep the militia from crossing as well, but it was too late. Six companies of minutemen, with Captain Isaac Davis of Acton and Major Buttrick of Concord at the head, got to roughly 50 yards of the bridge before halting in a standoff with the British. Buttrick yelled to the British to stop pulling up the bridge's planks. Then a shot was fired, accompanied by several more. As was the case at Lexington, it hasn't been definitely determined who fired the first shot, but Captain Laurie—who never gave the order to fire—reported afterward, "I imagine myself that a man of my company (afterward killed) did first fire his piece." The first British bullets went into the Concord River and may have been meant as warning shots. The jittery British soldiers then unleashed a volley at the Americans, after which Acton's Captain Davis shouted, "God damn it, they are firing ball!"

Davis and another man from Acton were hit and killed, and a young fifer was wounded. Major Buttrick immediately gave the order to return fire, shouting "Fire, fellow soldiers, for God's sake fire!" This was another first—the first time an American military officer ordered troops to fire on British soldiers. The American volley killed three British soldiers and wounded nine others.[37] The exchange was immortalized in Ralph Waldo Emerson's 1837 poem "Concord Hymn," written for the dedication of a battle memorial. The opening stanza reads:

> By the rude bridge that arched the flood,
> Their flag to April's breeze unfurled,
> Here once embattled farmers stood,
> And fired the shot heard round the world.

The outbreak of fighting and the growing number of militias descending on Concord convinced the British it was time they departed for Boston.

Only now there were somewhere between 3,000 and 4,000 militia waiting for them along the Concord Road, which subsequently came to be called Battle Road. This time there was no British victory salute and their march was not accompanied with fife and drum.

A 20-Mile Gauntlet

At first, the British retreat in April 1775 was uneventful. But when they got to Meriam's Corner, a mile or so outside of Concord, where the road forked between Bedford on the left and Lexington on the right, they were attacked by a large group of minutemen shooting from hidden positions. To the British, who were accustomed to open-field fighting, it was the action of "rascals" and "concealed villains." Or, as one soldier put it, "Making the cowardly disposition…to murder us all."[38] The British returned fire and quickened their pace on the right fork toward Lexington. At this point, Prescott and his men were about 10 miles into their trek from Groton, leaving another 10 miles to go to reach Concord.[39]

When Lieutenant Colonel Smith's troops got to Lexington at two-thirty in the afternoon, they were met by a group of reinforcements sent by General Gage. This group of about 1,000 men was led by Brigadier Lord Hugh Percy. At about the same time, American Major General William Heath arrived in Lexington as well. Heath was a 38-year-old farmer with a strong interest in military theory. He had been appointed a general by the Continental Congress despite his lack of military experience. Heath was joined by Joseph Warren, who was eager to get involved in the fighting. Heath and Warren participated in the action along the Concord Road and were so close to the shooting that a British musket ball knocked a pin out of Warren's hair. After this brush with death, Warren wrote, "I can with truth assure you, I heard bulletts [sic] whistle and believe me there is something charming in the sound."[40]

William Prescott and his troops were now in Concord, only to find that the British had already left. But he was scarcely five miles behind them now, as the British had been slowed by the near constant fighting they encountered. Prescott wasted little time and continued his pursuit, hoping they could close the gap and get involved in the fighting. Meanwhile, the British retreat from Concord turned into a 15-mile gauntlet that at times narrowed to less than 50 yards in width. The entire way, the Americans harassed the British and poured deadly fire on them from behind trees, buildings, stone walls, and other obstacles.[41]

The march to Boston was as harrowing as it was exhausting. Eventually, the British made their way to Cambridge, but rather than press on to the Boston Neck some distance away, they crossed another nearby "Neck" to Charlestown and safety. As one British officer ironically noted, they found refuge at a place called Bunker Hill.[42] There, they bivouacked for the night. The British troops were transported by boat back to Boston several days later, a move they would shortly come to regret.

On one of my visits to Concord to view the North Bridge and learn what Concord Center looked like to William Prescott as he responded to the news of the fighting there, I decided to walk east on the Concord Road to replicate Prescott's pursuit of the retreating British. About a quarter mile or so from Concord Center, I came to a commemorative plaque embedded in a stone wall in front of a colonial-style house. The plaque indicated it had been placed by the Old Concord Chapter DAR on April 19, 1965. It said:

> Beyond This Stone Wall Is The Site Of The Home Of
> DOCTOR SAMUEL PRESCOTT
> A Citizen of Concord and
> A High Son of Liberty
> Who at Lexington on the morning of April 19, 1775,
> Joined Paul Revere and William Dawes and
> When intercepted by a British Patrol in Lincoln
> He alone got through and brought the alarm to Concord.
> In 1776 he was in Ticonderoga and later he served on
> A privateer that was captured by the British.
> He was taken to Halifax, Nova Scotia and imprisoned
> And there he died.

I snapped a photo using my phone and sent it off to Jon Feltner, Prescott descendant, telling him this was the location where his distant, heroic ancestor had his home.

In the excursion to Concord and back, the British took 273 casualties, with 73 killed, 174 wounded, and 26 missing, a casualty rate of 20 percent.[43] Lord Percy, who had rescued Lieutenant Colonel Smith's troops, remarked, "Whoever looks upon [the rebels] as 'an irregular mob' will find himself much mistaken."[44] In addition, in a harbinger of things to come two months later in Charlestown, 33 of the 74 British officers who had marched to Lexington and Concord were either killed or severely wounded—an astounding figure.[45] The Americans also suffered a sizable number of casualties, with 49 killed, 39 wounded, and 5 missing, for a total of 93 men or about three percent of their forces. As the Americans, including Joseph Warren, were still technically subjects of the king, they were all guilty of high crimes for attacking the king's troops.

William Prescott and his men never did catch up with the British, only getting to Cambridge when the British were secure in Charlestown. Prescott's experience was very typical for the militia troops who were alerted on April 19 and the two subsequent days. Muster rolls indicate that roughly 20,000 militia responded to the call, some from distant towns, but only about 4,000 actually participated in any fighting. Still, Prescott's troops were prepared and willing to fight. They now became part of the growing number of forces who enveloped Boston and laid siege to the city. There, they would stay until they were called into action to defend the Heights of Charlestown, which the British were so kind to relinquish.

Soldiers were gathering in large numbers in Cambridge, and Warren got right to work getting them organized. He held a Council of War that was attended by William Heath, John Whitcomb, Artemas Ward, and William Prescott. Warren also urged a recruitment effort of thousands of new soldiers in order to put the Boston-based British under siege.

Prescott and most of his men enlisted in the Provincial Army for a term of eight months, by which time the prevailing opinion was that the war would be over.[46] Prescott, considered a good soldier and known for his staunch political views, was promoted to colonel.[47] It isn't known exactly when the Committee of Safety voted to give Prescott his "beating orders" because the draft minutes of the committee's meetings before April 26 are missing, and these votes were not included in the printed minutes.[48] Although Prescott's troops, now called the 9th Regiment of the Provincial Army, were not on hand for the fighting in Concord, it wouldn't be too long before their mettle was tested, as the die was cast and war seemed inevitable.

Back in Pepperell, the District Clerk's notes from the April 19 town meeting document the tragic news of the fighting at Lexington and Concord. These notes signaled that a momentous, and perhaps irrevocable, shift had occurred in the relationship between Britain and Massachusetts—and likely the entire set of American colonies. The same could be said about the British viewpoint. Military Governor Thomas Gage declared the Massachusetts colony to be in open rebellion. Moreover, the king, perturbed by the colonists, was now committed to using significant military force to quash any further disturbances. Indeed, it seemed there was no going back. Meanwhile, safely back in Boston, the British troops were angry and humiliated by what had happened on their return trip from Concord. Those emotions, still acute, would boil over two months later on the same ground in Charlestown that had been their refuge in mid-April. William Prescott, of course, would be at the center of that monumental clash.[49]

As if to make it official, U.S. Army records later recorded, in rather understated prose, that "America's Revolutionary War began on 19 April 1775 with exchanges of musketry between British regulars and Massachusetts militiamen at Lexington and Concord." To those Americans who stuck with the British, the rebellion seemed incomprehensible given the amount of autonomy the colonists enjoyed relative to their contemporaries in England. It was, according to Peter Oliver, a loyalist entrepreneur and Boston jurist, "the most wanton and unnatural rebellion that ever existed."[50] Referring to the disruptive citizens of Massachusetts, Oliver wrote, "The Annals of No Country can produce an Instance of so virulent a Rebellion, of such implacable madness and Fury, originating from such trivial Causes, as those alleged by these unhappy People."

Gage underscored the problem in Massachusetts when he wrote to Lord Dartmouth, saying, "We are threatened with great multitudes. The people called friends of government are few."[51] As for Joseph Warren, on May 2 he was elected president of Massachusetts's Second Provincial Congress, while retaining the chairmanship of the Committee of Safety.[52] Soon, Warren and Prescott would find themselves together in a battle that would shape American history.

CHAPTER 7

Bunker Hill: The Ferocious Fight

After months of delving into William Prescott's past, seeing how he came to embrace the drive for liberty, and learning his response to the Concord Alarm, I arrived back on the cusp of Bunker Hill. This fight was where I first became acquainted with Prescott, but what I had subsequently learned about him was so much greater. As for the battle itself, I knew the basic outlines of the story, the key actors, and the toll that was incurred. Now I had to fill in the gaps and resurrect the forgotten details. This took me back to the Massachusetts Archives and various libraries, including the flagship building of the Boston Public Library, where I scanned microfilm reels, read contemporary newspaper reports from June 1775, and dug up firsthand accounts of the battle from soldiers on both sides of the conflict.

A Major Battle Approaches

In late April 1775, a few weeks after the fighting in Lexington and Concord, it was discovered through military intelligence that the British intended to take the Heights at Charlestown, north of Boston, and at Dorchester, south of Boston.[1] It was no surprise that both the British and the Americans used informants to learn what the opposing side was doing. This wasn't necessarily high-level espionage, as often the information that was obtained was simply picked up from loose conversations or chatter on the street. It could be difficult to tell who was a potential bad actor since a lot of the population was from Great Britain, or were descendants of the same, and therefore looked and spoke alike. For years, there had been a great deal of interaction between those loyal to the Crown and those now looking for independence, and personal preferences were not always obvious. A lot of the time you could characterize the intelligence under the practice of "hear something or see something, say something."[2] Still, as rudimentary as this might have been, the information that was gathered was often of immense value.

Though the fighting in Lexington and Concord was not planned by the Americans, it marked the beginning of the Revolutionary War. As for the British, after returning to their barracks in Boston following a largely unsuccessful search and destroy mission (the British didn't find the large cache of the provincials' armaments they thought was there), they were eager for revenge. The gathering of provincials on top of Breed's Hill in mid-June gave them that opportunity.

Now, with fighting out in the open, the British wanted to secure the heights around Boston in order to protect their position on the tenuously connected, bulbous peninsula that defined the city. They also wished to guard incoming and outgoing ship traffic—their lifeline for supplies and troop reinforcement. In fact, Thomas Gage had learned through his own informant that the Americans had their eyes on the high ground in Dorchester and Charlestown as well.[3] The provincials were tightening the noose around the city, and the British knew they could not outlast a siege without command of the high ground. As author Samuel Adams Drake noted, Dorchester had the more important bearing to the British, as it commanded the inner harbor, and of course their vital shipping, while Charlestown was more important to the Americans because it was more accessible from the center of their operations in Cambridge.[4]

At the time of the battle in Charlestown, the British had about 6,000 effective fighting men in Boston. And while not all the troops were seasoned soldiers—as many of those men had left the colony after the French and Indian War—some of the remaining men belonged to the elite corps of the army. The British also had seven frigates in the Charles River, as well as at Boston's Long Wharf.[5] These were the *Falcon, Lively, Somerset, Cerberus, Glasgow, Symmetry,* and *Spitfire*—a formidable arsenal of firepower that faced no opposition from the Americans.

Ten years earlier, when the British had defeated the French in the French and Indian War and taken control of America and parts of Canada, their armed forces had been one of the strongest in the world. In that war, the British were assisted by thousands of Americans, including some men who were now standing on Breed's Hill. Not the least of these was William Prescott, whose reputation was burnished by his fighting prowess. Now Prescott had been given responsibility for the defense of the Charlestown peninsula against the British.

Had Parliament been more lenient and reasonable with the colonists, it is quite possible that Prescott would have reconciled his feelings with the mother country and have been satisfied to continue to be ruled by the king.

Other patriotic leaders held these views. Benjamin Franklin had tried to soothe tempers between the British government and American opposition forces while he was stationed in London.[6] Even Joseph Warren had not spoken out about breaking from the monarchy for a long time.[7] The major complaint the colonies had was that they did not control their government and had no representation in Parliament through which they could have aired their grievances.

Unfortunately, the Boston Massacre and the imposition of the Coercive Acts probably pushed Prescott beyond his tolerances. It can be argued that Prescott did not think the relationship between Great Britain and the colonies could be repaired. Prescott was ready to die for his beliefs, as he told his brother-in-law, Abijah Willard, which means he was all in with respect to the fight for liberty.

Once hearing about the British plans to capture the high ground around Boston, Prescott, who would be commissioned a colonel of the Massachusetts Army by Joseph Warren on May 27, and General Israel Putnam of Connecticut, wanted to take immediate action. Prescott's regiment now had 10 companies, numbering about 425 men.[8] His staff officers were Lieutenant Colonel John Robinson of Westford, as well as Major Henry Woods and Adjutant William Green of Pepperell. General Putnam, 57 years old and affectionately known as "Old Put," was a tavern keeper, accomplished farmer, and celebrated soldier. He had signed up as a private in the Connecticut militia during the French and Indian War, became a captain in the fabled Rogers' Rangers, and eventually was promoted to general by the time the battle of Bunker Hill took place.

Putnam was very active politically, objecting to the stringent British policies of the mid-1760s. He was elected to the Connecticut General Assembly and was one of the founders of the state's chapter of the Sons of Liberty.[9] Various accounts describe Putnam as "a cherubic bulldog mounted on a jaw cut like a block of wood, strongly made, no fat, all bones and muscles."[10] Putnam was barely literate, with little of the elite education of other famous patriots of the era, yet he was a gregarious man despite also having a lisp.[11] He was considered an expert in bush warfare and seemed to have boundless energy. He was exceedingly aggressive as a soldier, advocating strong action against the British, and he "dared to lead wherever any dared to follow."[12] As such, Putnam's bravery was unquestioned.[13] Furthermore, as one observer has noted, Putnam was "the provincial army's most beloved officer."[14]

Both Prescott and Putnam hoped to draw the British out of Boston for a fight on the Americans' terms. Although no action was ordered, Putnam nevertheless took the initiative and led 2,000 troops in Cambridge to the hills of Charlestown on May 13 in a flagrant affront to the British.[15] The enemy observed the maneuver but, not respecting the fighting capabilities of the American soldier, did not pay Putnam and his troops any attention. The incident was all for naught as, in the end, the rumors about imminent British attacks never materialized.

At this time, Major General Artemas Ward was commanding American forces in the region. Ward was 47 years old and had two degrees from Harvard.[16] A teacher and a farmer, Ward was from the town of Shrewsbury near Worcester and a respected veteran of the French and Indian War, in which he served as a major in the Massachusetts militia.[17] He was promoted to colonel in 1758, a few years into the war. While on Massachusetts's Court of Common Pleas in 1762, he spoke out strongly against British taxes alongside Samuel Adams and John Hancock, who were members of the Committee on Taxation. Then, in October 1774, Ward's 3rd Regiment resigned en masse from British service and elected him as their leader. After the fighting at Lexington and Concord, the provisional governments of neighboring New Hampshire and Connecticut named Ward commander of their forces as well, making him the leading military figure in New England.[18]

Weeks after Putnam's Charlestown theatrics, Ward again learned through an informant—described as a "gentleman of undoubted veracity"—that the British were going to attack the two critical local heights. This time they were planning it on Sunday morning, June 18, when they thought citizens would be sleeping or at church.[19] This intelligence seemed credible, so the Committee of Safety decided to meet at Hastings House near the Cambridge Commons on June 15 to decide what, if anything, to do.[20] There were divided opinions about the course of action. Israel Putnam wanted to entrench on Bunker's Hill and set up a defensive barrier to block a British effort to attack Cambridge. Artemas Ward and Joseph Warren were uneasy about Putnam's plan. They thought if the provincials were to occupy the heights in Charlestown, they would likely face a heavy cannonade and perhaps even an assault, for which they did not feel they were prepared. Putnam explained his plan to Ward and Warren:

> We will risk only two thousand men. We will go on with these, and defend ourselves as long as possible; and if driven to retreat, we are more active than the enemy, and every stone wall shall be lined with their dead. And at the worst, suppose us surrounded, and no retreat, we will set our country an example, of which it shall not be ashamed, and teach mercenaries what men can do, who are determined to live or die free.[21]

William Prescott and Northampton's distinguished veteran of the French and Indian War, Seth Pomeroy, supported Putnam's proposal.

According to one account, Warren then walked the floor of the room, paused, leaned on his chair, and addressed Putnam, saying, "Almost thou persuaded me, General Putnam, but I must still think the project rash; if you execute it, however, you will not be surprised to find me at your side."[22] "I hope not," replied Putnam, "you are young, and your country has much to hope from you, in council and in the field. Let us, who are old, and can be spared, begin the fray. There will be time enough for you thereafter for it will not soon be over."

The discussion was settled when the Committee of Safety voted, in secret and unanimously, to man both Bunker's Hill and Dorchester Heights.[23] The issue was now Ward's. However, despite his military experience 20 years earlier, Ward had never commanded an army before. According to one historian, this "lack of experience may have led to a caution that approached timidity."[24] He concluded that Ward "hated to act, preferring to prepare, to husband resources, to dig in; he seems never to have felt ready for the bold stroke or the daring operation." Now the Committee of Safety gave him no choice. So, Ward sent Lieutenant General John Thomas and about 1,000 men to protect Dorchester Heights. He also gave orders to William Prescott on Friday, June 16, to assemble a detachment of Massachusetts troops in order to "take possession of, and fortify, Bunker's Hill."[25] This included troops from his and Frye's regiments, who would be joined with soldiers from Putnam's Connecticut regiment and an artillery company from fellow Massachusetts native Richard Gridley's command, for a total of about 1,100 men.

Why General Ward selected Prescott to lead the defense of Charlestown isn't entirely clear. Ward could have reasonably chosen General Israel Putnam instead, as Putnam outranked Prescott and had more military leadership experience. But, since this action was in Massachusetts, it is understandable that Ward would have opted for someone from Massachusetts for the assignment. General Ward also might have assigned General William Heath, another more senior commander, to defend Bunker's Hill, but Heath clearly lacked adequate military experience.

Interestingly, there is no indication that Ward knew Prescott personally, but it is possible that Ward, whose wife, Sarah Trowbridge, was from Groton, held favorable views of that town's militia and may have learned about Prescott's capabilities and experience from that group. James Prescott, the Colonel's older brother, was the region's representative in the Massachusetts General Assembly and likely would have had interactions with the Committee of Safety, and thus Ward may have also learned of Colonel Prescott from him.[26]

Certainly, Colonel Prescott's involvement in King George's War and later the French and Indian War gave him valuable warfare experience. So, although

Prescott was not a professionally trained soldier, he brought critical skills to the battlefield. He seemed also to have natural leadership abilities, which were likewise evident in his ancestors. Ward and others might also have been aware that years earlier the British had offered Prescott a commission in their military ranks. Prescott was from a distinguished family and, being tall and athletically built, had a strong personal appearance—like George Washington—which likely amplified his perceived capabilities and inspired confidence in those who would serve under him.

One historian has suggested why Prescott might have been Ward's choice, saying, "Prescott rarely acted rashly; he exuded a quiet air that made men listen to him and heed his counsel."[27] There is also speculation that Prescott's approval of the Charlestown defensive plan may have weighed heavily with Ward. So, Prescott was Ward's choice and there is no evidence that Ward considered anyone else for the assignment. Prescott accepted the job without reservation. While it is hard to conceive that Prescott knew fully what was in store for him over the next 24 hours, he certainly understood the seriousness of the moment and had at least an inkling of the danger he might confront.

While the troops that Prescott and his men would face were not the cream of the crop of the British Army—many of those men had already returned to England after the French and Indian War and were substituted with greener replacements—they were nonetheless trained soldiers. More importantly, they had experienced leaders who had previously led men in battle. The same could not be said for the American forces.

Heading to Charlestown

On Friday evening, June 16, Reverend Samuel Langdon, the president of Harvard, gave an address to a gathering of provincial troops led by Prescott near the prestigious college before they headed out for Charlestown. Reverend Joseph Emerson of Pepperell was also on hand, visiting his parishioners in Prescott's regiment. According to reports, Emerson offered the first prayer that was made in the American camp.[28]

When the American troops departed that night, Prescott led the way eastward out of Cambridge, wearing a blue overcoat with a single row of buttons and a tricorn hat. There was purpose to his step and, as one of his troops said about him, "He [Prescott] was a bold man and he gave his orders like a bold man."[29]

On the three-and-a-half-mile trek, Prescott had with him three Massachusetts regiments. Nine regiments had originally been ordered to Charlestown, but only five eventually reached their destination.[30] The others, apparently, were misinformed or, not having a map, got lost on the unfamiliar roads. As one officer wrote later, troop discipline was "extremely irregular…each regiment advancing according to the opinion, feelings, or caprice of its commander." This lack of unity was a consequence of not having a central command structure. Then, at the Charlestown Neck, Prescott met Putnam, who had with him some wagons loaded with gabions (wicker baskets filled with dirt) and fascines (tightly bundled brushwood and sticks), both of which could be used to create fortifications. Prescott took the soldiers across the Neck and up the steep slope of Bunker's Hill—the promontory named after George Bunker, an early landowner in Charlestown.[31]

According to Ward's orders, it was only after the men crossed the Neck that Prescott was to inform the troops of the expedition's object. Not expecting a protracted encampment, the American forces carried with them provisions for only one day, blankets, and a small amount of gunpowder and bullets. They also had entrenching tools—shovels and axes—to help them dig into the rocky terrain to construct their fort. The understanding was that replacements and reinforcements would arrive in the morning. They did not know exactly how long they might be in Charlestown, or precisely how the British might react to them, so there was likely some concern among the troops as they marched along in the dark. Meanwhile, General Ward remained at Hastings House, which served as his headquarters. Once the troops had left for Charlestown, Ward would have little communication with them. Decision-making was now in the hands of Prescott, Putnam, and Gridley.

Charlestown was a unique piece of ground to mount a defense. It may best be envisioned from this description, written in 1850, when it most likely looked much like it did in 1775:

> The peninsula of Charlestown is a mile and one-eighth in length, from east to west, and two-thirds of a mile across, from north to south. The Mystic River forms its northern, and the Charles River its southern, border—the distance between them at the Neck, being only one hundred and thirty yards. A narrow channel separates it from Boston on the east. Bunker's Hill commences at the Neck, and rises abruptly to the height of one hundred and thirteen feet, and then, falling off in a gentle slope towards the east, stretches, in a low ridge, for a considerable distance along the shores of the Mystic, and parallel with Breed's Hill. Breed's Hill, which is eighty-seven feet high, commences near the southern extremity of Bunker's Hill, and extends towards the south and east, the two summits being distant from each other one hundred and thirty rods [approximately a third of a mile].
>
> The grounds on the east of Breed's Hill, as well as on the north, between that and the village…is low and marshy, constituting what was called *the slough*. The village of Charlestown was on the south side of the hill, and had begun already to extend itself a little upon its slope. Morton's Point [also called Moulton's Point], where the ground was also somewhat elevated,

the hill being thirty-five feet above the level of the water, forms the north-eastern extremity of the peninsula, with a narrow channel between that and Noodle Island.[32]

Prescott and the troops arrived on the Charlestown Heights around midnight. As noted, these were not professional soldiers but rather patriotic volunteers, mostly with limited military training. In their everyday lives, they were farmers, merchants, artisans, fishermen, traders, and the like. Part of a makeshift army, the troops wore plain, homespun clothing (there were no uniforms) and sported muskets of all types and variety.[33] They were mainly white, Anglo-Saxon Protestants, and, of course, subjects of the king. Notably, though, among them were an estimated 160 "patriots of color," according to researcher George Quintal, including African Americans (both free and enslaved) and Native Americans, who also opposed the British and in many cases were prepared to fight for their freedom and rights.

Prescott was worried about the British discovering the Americans, especially once the fort's construction started, so he sent a contingent down to the village of Charlestown and the waterfront to keep an eye on the enemy.[34] This included his Pepperell neighbor, Captain John Nutting, as well as Captain Hugh Maxwell, Major John Brooks, and Private Amos Farnsworth, along with several dozen men. Farnsworth described the scene this way in his diary: "about Dusk Marched for Bunkers-Hill; [at] Charlestown we was halted; And about Sixty men was taken out of our battalions to go into Charlestown; I being one of them: Capt Nutten [Nutting] heeded us Down to ye town house; we Sot our Centres by ye waterside; the most of us got in the town But had orders not to Shut our eyes."[35]

Prescott also made a couple of trips down to the shoreline with Major Brooks during the night to check on the situation in person. The Americans were so close to the British ships in the Charles River that they could hear the sailors talking to one another. Happily, their fears were allayed when they distinctly heard the call "All's well" onboard the ships. Interestingly, while reports later indicated that sentries had indeed perceived the construction racket on Breed's Hill (even General Henry Clinton claimed he'd heard the noise), the British showed no concern and did nothing about it. Satisfied that his troops' movements into Charlestown were undetected, Prescott focused his attention on the placement of the redoubt.

Siting the Redoubt

The three principal commanders—Prescott, Putnam, and Gridley—discussed whether to build a redoubt on the top of Bunker's Hill or on another spot closer to the Charlestown waterfront and Boston. The commanders and some of their men quietly reconnoitered the rest of the peninsula, including an elevation about a half mile to the east of Bunker's Hill, which was only beginning to be called Breed's Hill—similarly named after a local resident. At the time, the area was primarily used by landowners for pasturage and was intersected by many fences that separated the properties.

Reports are not definitive, but tradition has it that it was first the aggressive Putnam who insisted the fort be built on Breed's Hill rather than Bunker's Hill.[36] Putnam's argument was that entrenchments on Bunker's Hill would have little value unless a more forward post on Breed's Hill was secured first. Richard Gridley, the Boston engineer who would design the fort, objected, wanting to build on Bunker's Hill, which he felt were Ward's orders.[37] Gridley had gained wartime experience helping the British storm Louisbourg in 1745, and was one of the few provincials to go back there in 1758 to retake the fortress that, in the interim, had been returned to the French. He had also fought at Crown Point and had seen British General James Wolfe fall on the Plains of Abraham. So, his opinion on this night carried some weight.

The advantage of locating the fort on the much lower Breed's Hill (62 feet above sea level versus 110 feet for Bunker's Hill) was that, being closer to Boston, it would enable the Americans to see more easily what the British were doing. Another advantage of Breed's Hill was that the village of Charlestown, which contained about 300 houses, a church, and a few public buildings, was close by on its eastern side, where provincial troops could be ensconced and fire on the advancing British from concealed positions.[38] In addition, the slopes of Breed's Hill were encumbered with an array of obstacles—stone walls, rail fences, brick kilns, orchards, and other natural impediments—which would hamper a British advance. Breed's Hill also put the Americans in range of firing on the British, if they had the right heavy cannon. Of course, the reverse was true as well and the British had the guns. Prescott, who may have also suggested building on Bunker's Hill initially, eventually accepted Breed's Hill as the site, and that ended the discussion. However, the group decided to build a second barricade on Bunker's Hill as well. This would be a place where the provincials could retreat if they were forced off Breed's Hill. It has been speculated that putting the fort atop Breed's Hill, in plain view of British forces in Boston, was also meant as a not-so-subtle provocation.[39]

Much has been made of the decision to build the redoubt on Breed's Hill instead of Bunker's Hill. Since it seems the location of the redoubt on the lower promontory, nearer to Boston, was not yet routinely referred to as Breed's Hill until after the battle, one credible explanation is that the entire elevation from Bunker's Hill to Breed's Hill was all considered a part of "Charlestown Heights" and that the commanders were merely using their discretion as to where the defensive fortifications would be placed.[40] They felt the lower promontory was a better location for the fort, and so the redoubt was erected there. More critical observers, including professional military observers, have felt the commanders clearly disobeyed the strict letter of Ward's orders. What will never be known is: Would the outcome of the day have been different if the redoubt had been built on Bunker's Hill? It seems the British were intent on assaulting Charlestown regardless of where the fort was, but would the battle's consequences have been different? Would either force have benefited more from the fort being on Bunker's Hill instead of Breed's Hill? The answers rest in the land of speculation.

A lot of time was consumed deliberating on the choice for the fort, until Gridley warned that any further delay would defeat their plans altogether since they would run out of time.[41] Resigned to the group's decision, Gridley laid out the specifications for the Breed's Hill redoubt, which would be a long rectangle, measuring about 10 rods by eight rods (140 feet by 120 feet) and six to seven feet high, with a redan (a V-shaped salient) jutting out on the southwestern side. Since it was the beginning of summer, when there were only about seven hours of darkness, Prescott quickly got the men into action, furiously digging a deep trench and using the dirt to build the fort's walls. The combination of a trench and wall would offer great protection and make it difficult for the British to get into the fort.

It took the provincials all night and into the day to construct the redoubt and breastwork on Breed's Hill. This was tough physical labor. Selecting a spot for the fort in the dead of night had not been the best idea, and it showed a lack of preparation on the part of the Americans. Prescott was surprised to see how exposed and vulnerable his fortifications were when the sun rose on Saturday June 17, which belies any suggestion that he intended to provoke the British. He was not known to be a rash man, and it is difficult to conceive that he would have intentionally placed his troops, which included his friends and neighbors, in an untenable position.

Prescott must have known that his men would be tired, hungry, and thirsty by daybreak, and thus not in good shape to fight. Moreover, if he were looking for an engagement with the British, he would have wanted more munitions at the outset and more assurances that replacement troops would relieve his initial party of men in the morning. On the other hand, Putnam seemed to have been in favor of provoking the British, given his showy, if inconsequential, parading of troops in Charlestown in May. Prescott may have been taken in by Putnam's desire to do this until he saw what a precarious position he and his men were in on Breed's Hill when dawn broke and the British warships opened fire on the redoubt.

Throughout the morning and into the afternoon, the Americans went about constructing their fort and taking their places on the summit of Breed's Hill, along the northern slopes descending to the Mystic River, and in various structures in Charlestown village. Everyone there knew a battle was coming. The cannon barrages from British warships, which continued largely unabated, were an undeniable signal that the British meant business in objecting to the Americans' position on the heights. Richard Frothingham cites a British writer as saying, "The Americans bore this severe fire [from the ships, floating batteries, and Copp's Hill] with wonderful firmness, and seemed to go on with their business as if no enemy had been near."[42] Now, in the early afternoon, with hundreds of British troops making preparations along the Charlestown waterfront, there was simply no doubt that a major confrontation was about to take place.

The Americans' dirt fort did not amount to much, but as General Putnam had said at a recent war council, "The Americans are not at all afraid of their heads, though very much afraid of their legs. If you cover those, they will fight forever."[43] Although it had been decided to place a second entrenchment on Bunker's Hill, because the work on Breed's Hill got off to a slow start, the work on Bunker's Hill in the rear was never properly completed. Nonetheless, Putnam kept a good number of troops there during the fighting.

The Battle is Joined

By three o'clock in the afternoon, Howe had his men ready. They were just awaiting the order to begin the assault. Meanwhile, citizens around Boston thronged to every elevated point that gave them a view of the scene: to Copp's Hill, to rooftops, to church steeples, and to the masts of vessels anchored in the harbor. So many had assembled that, according to one who was there, the area appeared "like unto an amphitheater in which the battle was being staged."[44] So ominous was the scene that all the spectators seemed to understand that it was not only a battle that was about to be waged, but that this was the beginning of a war.

Prophetically, from a hilltop far to the south in Quincy, Abigail Adams, John Adams's wife, looked toward Charlestown and held the hand of their young son, John Quincy. She would note, "The day—perhaps the decisive day—is come, on which the fate of America depends."[45] Abigail was not being hyperbolic and may well have been right. If the British made quick work of the Americans in Charlestown, the nascent idea of independence might have given way to the improbability of the task. Maybe the citizens of Boston would have agreed finally to pay for the British tea they had unceremoniously dumped in December 1773, which precipitated the closing of the harbor and a series of other harsh consequences. Maybe they would have agreed it was foolish to think they could expel the powerful British Army, throw off the yoke of monarchy, and govern themselves.

However, despite the obvious danger, at no point on Saturday did Prescott seem surprised by the British reaction to the presence of the provincials on Breed's Hill. Clearly, their actions at Lexington and Concord should have indicated to Prescott that the British would react strongly to the fort they were building. The warships in the harbor were certainly a worry, particularly if they sailed up the Charles and Mystic Rivers to the Charlestown Neck to block an escape route, should it be needed. The British had, indeed, discussed this strategy, but it was rejected by General Gage. With about 5,000 to 6,000 troops in Boston and more out in the harbor, the British were well-equipped to send a sizable force against Prescott, supported by naval power, and thus were capable of seriously outgunning the provincials. Prescott would have known this was a possibility. He recognized he'd be in for a real fight if the British objected strenuously to the provincials' presence on Breed's Hill, and yet he seemed quite willing to take on the challenge.

Although the men about to oppose each other in Charlestown may not have known it at the time, the course of history hung in the balance. And there on Breed's Hill and along its slopes stood Prescott's soldiers, most of whom were lightly trained militarily and who had never experienced a major battle. Some may have been working in their fields and shops days ahead of the battle, unaware that they would now be standing where they were, facing a force not only larger and better equipped but much more experienced. It was very likely that few of those men had ever shot a weapon at another human being.

The focal point of the provincials' defense was that unconcealed redoubt on Breed's Hill, boldly erected in the face of the British. The British commanders did not respect the American fighters, which likely lowered the perceived expectation of the upcoming confrontation. As the historian Paul Lockhart put it, Generals Gage and Howe "dismissed the American fighting man as being beneath contempt, bereft of any and all military value. Any exercise of diligence or careful planning or anything that smacked of effort would be wasted on such rabble. It would accord the rebels too much respect."[46] Indeed, Howe expected to knock the "rabble" off the hill in short order.

Despite their fierce spirit, one can only imagine the fear that must have coursed through the minds of the provincial soldiers as they awaited the British. From their perch on the hill, they saw the enemy in their smart, red uniforms, lining up with their bayonets glistening in the sunlight, about to attack. They saw that they were outnumbered, too. They had also been under naval bombardment for much of the day. So, surely they must have known that many of them would die on this day. The American commanders had to hold the line as best they could. When General Putnam saw one of his officers arguing with an unwilling soldier, he did not mince words and growled, "Run him through if he won't fight."[47]

At this point, many Americans could have fled the field. It would have been totally understandable and was precisely what the British expected. The provincials went to Charlestown to erect a defensive position. That was Ward's intention—to prevent the British from establishing a presence in Charlestown from which they could attack his troops in Cambridge. The Americans knew they lacked the experience and training for a traditional fight with the British, much less a major battle. In fact, some troops thought their stand was suicidal.[48] Yet, there they stood in their hodgepodge of homespun clothes and looking very much like the rabble the British accused them of being.

It is not unfair to say that one of the main reasons the soldiers stayed was because of their commander, Colonel Prescott. While men from Bridge's and Frye's Massachusetts regiments began to leave when the British cannon started firing, Prescott's men remained with him. They admired him and had confidence in him. As one veteran of the battle said later, "Had it not been for Prescott there would have been no fight."[49]

But more to the point, what were Prescott and the others on that hill willing to risk their lives for? It wasn't as if the prize of victory was clearly spelled out for them. Their reward was not immediately awaiting them in the offing. It would be another year before the Declaration of Independence was written and more than 12 years before the Constitutional Convention in Philadelphia drew up the United States Constitution that would establish the enduring republic that Americans cherish today. Ideals such as personal liberty, independence, self-governance, and the rule of law were concepts yet to be roundly embraced. The divine right of kings had not been universally rejected. Representative government had not been adopted. However, as Prescott stood there in the redoubt, he, either consciously or unconsciously, embodied these goals. Conceivably, he may have already felt the tug of history, been willing to pursue it, and consented to put his life quite literally on the line for it. Without them knowing it, the hopes of the colonial leaders were also now resting squarely on Prescott's shoulders.

Certainly, Prescott was the pivotal person in this coming battle. He had been given the orders to defend Charlestown Heights. He commanded the redoubt, the primary point of the American defense. While Prescott did not supersede Putnam and Stark in rank, they would have to coordinate their activities with him for success. But Stark was with his men along the stone wall down by the Mystic River. Putnam was moving about the area somewhat frantically on his horse. Without any convenient means of relaying messages, Prescott's commands only went as far as his voice would carry or as quickly as a message could be carried to its recipient. As has been pointed out, there was no overall, coordinated American battle plan. In fact, they had no plan at all other than to oppose the British and keep them from taking the Charlestown Heights.[50]

Significantly, just before the fighting began, Joseph Warren arrived at the battlefield. He had heard about the British action while in Cambridge and had started toward Charlestown on foot. Along the route, he'd borrowed a horse and rode the rest of the way to the heights. Warren first came upon Putnam, who beseeched him to leave the field, knowing how dangerous the action would be. But Warren insisted he wanted to fight, so Putnam urged him to go on to Breed's Hill, where he might enjoy the protection of the redoubt.

At the time of the battle, Warren was 34 years old, the widowed father of four children, and the current president of the Massachusetts Provincial Government, having succeeded John Hancock, who was away at the Second Continental Congress in Philadelphia. Three days before the battle, on June 14, Warren had been voted by the Third Provincial Congress to be Major General of the American forces in the region, and so, on the day of the battle, would have outranked Prescott. When Warren appeared at the redoubt at about one o'clock, Prescott immediately offered him command, knowing his superior rank.[51] However, Warren declined Prescott's offer, pointing out that he had not been officially commissioned and was therefore still a civilian. Warren assured Prescott he did not want to interfere, but he added that he wanted to fight as a volunteer.[52] Knowing he was a novice in comparison to Prescott, Warren said, "I shall take no command here," adding he "was happy to learn service from a soldier of experience."[53] Warren then shouldered his musket and filed into the redoubt, to the cheers of the other soldiers.

So, here was Warren exactly where he'd told Putnam days earlier he would be, willing to risk his life if the fortification of Charlestown Heights sparked a confrontation. Incensed by the British disregard for the American soldier, Warren had memorably said, "These fellows [the British] say we won't fight: by heavens, I hope I shall die up to my knees in blood."[54] Warren certainly was committed to the revolutionary cause, having written earlier to Samuel Adams, in a sentiment famously echoed by Virginian Patrick Henry in March 1775: "The mistress we court is LIBERTY; and it is better to die than not to obtain her."[55]

Warren was dressed in his finest clothes, which included a "light colored coat, with white satin waistcoat, laced with silver, and white breeches, with silver loops, and his wig."[56] As historian Christian DiSpigna has pointed out, what Warren lacked in battlefield tactics, he compensated for with sheer nerve and bravery. A similar opinion was advanced by others, who noted that Warren animated the Americans in the redoubt with new courage.[57]

Now, as they peered down at the British, the provincials had nothing to do but wait. The day had grown warm, and sunlight drenched the field. A light wind rustled the thigh-high, uncut grass below them. It was eerily quiet, as the British cannonade had stopped so as not to hit their own men, who would soon be marching up toward the Americans. The task of removing the provincials would be left to the infantry. The stage was set.

In the calm interlude, the provincials looked anxiously on the foe that would soon start advancing toward them. No doubt they were scared and uncertain of their fate. Most likely the men shifted about nervously, their palms sweaty, their throats dry, their pulses quickening. Probably there was not much chatter, save for those who needed to bolster their courage with braggadocio. One soldier poignantly called the moment "the awful pause."[58] Certainly many on the heights must have felt it shocking to find themselves in such perilous circumstances. Some of their comrades had left the field—having not bargained to be in a major fight—but those who remained surely wanted to conduct themselves honorably, even as frightened as they were. Prescott would have talked up this point, encouraging the soldiers, telling them they were in a strong position, fortifying them for the horror they would shortly experience. He told the men that, if they followed his instructions, the enemy would not be able to take the fort.[59]

Moments before the British assault began, Prescott's adversary in the coming battle, General William Howe, addressed his officers and troops with these words:

> Gentlemen, I am very happy in having the honor of commanding so fine a body of men. I do not in the least doubt but that you will behave like Englishmen, and as becometh good soldiers. If the enemy will not come from their intrenchments, we must drive them out at all events, otherwise the town of Boston will be set on fire by them. I shall not desire one of you to go a step farther than where I go myself at your head. Remember, gentlemen, we have no recourse to any resources if we lose Boston but to go board our ships, which will be very disagreeable to us all.[60]

The British attack then proceeded as drawn up, even though Howe, once in Charlestown, had observed previously unseen American activity along a newly formed front extending to the Mystic River. These were Stark's troops. Howe thought the fighting would be tougher because of it, but he didn't realize how tough. When the order to advance was given, the light infantry headed out on the British right along the Mystic River beach. They would attack the Americans' far left, intent on flanking them and clearing the ground behind the barricades. The grenadiers, with Howe supervising, marched directly toward the rail fence to enable the light infantry's actions. All of the other regiments to the left advanced in a line along the American front from the breastwork to the redoubt. Howe expected to break through the American left and attack the Americans in the redoubt and behind the breastwork from their rear, while also cutting off their potential retreat.

While the British were readying themselves, Prescott was giving last-minute instructions to his men in the redoubt. They were to hold their fire until the command was given. Because of the relatively short effective range of the musket—less than 100 yards—this order would not happen until the British were in close. Stark relayed a similar message to his troops, going so far as to hammer wooden stakes across the field, about 50 yards out from the rail fence, to serve as markers for the firing zone.[61]

Historians are unsure who, if anyone, might have uttered the famous line, "Don't fire until you see the whites of their eyes."[62] These words, or something very much like them, have mostly been attributed to Prescott (as an etched plaque next to the Bunker Hill Monument states), but some say it was Stark and others point to Putnam. Regardless, it is highly likely that the various commanders would have made the same point. Powder and musket balls were not in abundance, so every shot had to count. Each of the American troops had somewhere between 15 and 30 balls and a limited amount of powder. For a nonprofessional force with limited battle experience, this paucity of ammunition was their Achilles' heel. Without sufficient ammunition and if forced to fight hand-to-hand, the Americans would be no match for the British, who, by comparison, carried 60 rounds and were trained in how to use the bayonet—a fearsome weapon the Americans lacked.[63]

The untried provincials were told their tendency would be to fire too high and so they should aim at British waistlines and below.[64] They should also try to pick off officers, whom they could identify as those wearing the more vivid and attractive uniforms. In truth, aiming a musket was difficult as the gun did not have a rear sight. By some estimates, it might take dozens of rounds to kill or wound one soldier. Consequently, the most effective way to shoot was for everyone to level their muskets and send a volley in the direction of the target. If the soldiers shot in unison, the result would be a devastating sheet of fire. As evidence of this, many British soldiers in the line of fire were hit with multiple rounds, maybe as many as six or eight.

Ten minutes into their march, the advancing British were now within 200 yards of the Americans. Their approach was impeded, however, as they had to climb over sturdy fences in the field, push through the tall grass, and deal with rocks, holes, and other obstacles.[65] Moreover, the grenadiers had a difficult time moving the cannon through the swampy areas they had to pass through on the north side of the hill.[66] The going was not easy, and the British lines flexed and broke up into inconsistent units.

In addition to wearing their bright red woolen coats on this warm day, the British hauled backpacks weighing upwards of 100 pounds, containing enough gear, blankets, and provisions for a three-day occupation. They also toted the popular 10-pound Brown Bess musket (affectionately called the King's Arm), equipped with a 17-inch bayonet.[67] The Brown Bess was a flintlock musket, which had been around since the beginning of the 1700s and was used globally.[68] It was a smooth bore, muzzle-loading weapon that fired a 69-caliber lead ball (about three-quarters of an inch in circumference) and weighed about an ounce. The musket's length was roughly five feet, which, given that most men were a little over five-and-a-half feet tall, meant it was unwieldy and a challenge to hoist, aim, and fire. While the musket shot was highly inaccurate (only good to roughly 50–75 yards), the weapon facilitated the use of the bayonet. Soldiers in formation would traditionally discharge a volley and then commence a bayonet charge, which often was the thing that induced their enemy to flee.

On Breed's Hill, the British planned on using this tactic, and they fully expected the Americans to abandon their defenses and flee as fast as their legs would carry them. This straightforward battlefield tactic was common in the day, especially if your side held numerical superiority, as the charging soldiers could terrorize and overwhelm the enemy before they could effectively reload their own muskets and shoot at the advancing troops.[69] The complicated nature of reloading the musket made the bayonet charge that much more effective. To get off a single shot required a series of steps that had to be done quickly under often frantic battlefield conditions. The soldier first had to pull a paper cartridge from a leather cartridge box slung over his shoulder, bite off the end, and then pour one-third of its powder into the musket's flash pan. The remaining powder from the packet—nearly half an ounce—was then poured down the muzzle. Next, the soldier inserted a musket ball and the cartridge wadding into the muzzle and forced the items down the barrel using a steel ramrod that was attached beneath the gun's barrel. Once the ramrod was extracted and returned to its place, the soldier was ready to fire. This action typically took an experienced soldier about 20 seconds, a not insignificant time when the enemy was bearing down on him with a shaft of cold steel extended toward his torso.

To shoot, the soldier hoisted the musket straight up to eye level, cocked the musket, aimed, and pulled the trigger. As described by author David Price, the flint on the falling hammer struck a glancing blow against the gun's steel frizzen—an L-shaped piece of steel hinged at the front and held in one of two positions, open or closed, by a leaf spring.[70] This caused a burst of sparks to ignite the powder in the flash pan, which set off the main charge through a touchhole in the side of the breech or back part of the musket. The explosion sent a yellow-orange flame out the muzzle, accompanied by a loud bang and expulsion of white smoke. The exiting lead musket ball was propelled at a speed of 1,000 feet per second or nearly 700 miles per hour. That meant the musket ball would hit its target nearly a quarter mile away in about the time it takes to snap one's fingers twice. Given the speed of sound, if a soldier at the receiving end of the shot heard the report of the musket it was already too late for him to avoid being struck.

Human bones, organs, and tissue were no match for the size and speed of the musket ball.[71] A direct hit, or even a lateral blow, almost assuredly meant either instantaneous death or bleeding out of a large wound on the battlefield. Unlike a small bullet that might pass through the body, a musket ball frequently remained lodged inside the body, perhaps for the remainder of the person's life if they survived the shot. Although firing at targets beyond 100 yards was considered a waste of ammunition, the shot was capable of killing or injuring an enemy at distances of up to 300 yards.[72] Indeed, the musket was even powerful enough to bring down a large animal, such as a galloping horse.

As devastating as musket fire could be, however, the soldier still had to contend with a flawed weapon that might not fire in the rain or damp conditions. Since the musket barrel was not rifled, it was only with some skill and lots of luck that the bullet would head in the direction it was intended. Variables such as imperfect barrels, imperfect balls, defective powder, wind, and lack of sights also made hitting an intended target very difficult.

I was given a primer on the musket by Patrick Boyce, a National Park Service ranger in Boston who leads the musket-firing-demonstration program at Bunker Hill National Historical Park. Patrick throws himself into his period work (which occurs on Saturdays in the summer), dressing in full colonial soldier regalia. One time Patrick even replicated the British march to Concord with his father, a 40-mile round trip, to feel for himself what it was like for the regulars in April 1775.

Patrick's musket-firing demonstration certainly seemed to me to be as complicated as the manuals indicate. There was a lot of room for error caused by things like spilled powder; powder in the pan blown away by the wind; faulty or damaged flint; warping of an overheated barrel; fouling due to powder residue; tired, shaky arms; and so on. Plus, if you were left-handed, you had to learn how to fire from your right side. Patrick, an experienced shooter, also pointed out that the musket fired correctly only about three-quarters of the time. That's not a great percentage when in the heat of a battle or facing a bayonet charge.

Howe's plan called for a coordinated movement, with the main attack coming from the far right along the Mystic River and delivered by 11 companies of light infantry.[73] Because of the narrowness of the land there, the light infantry would have to advance in a column of fours. To the left and above them Howe had another 26 companies in two lines, led, as was the custom, by the grenadiers—an elite force that contained the tallest and finest-looking fighters of each regiment.[74] Behind them were the supporting infantry. On the far left, Howe gave Brigadier Robert Pigot 38 companies, about the same amount he had on the right. These troops, which included three companies of grenadiers and light infantry, were arrayed in three lines just like the troops that Howe led.

So convinced was Howe of his troops' superiority that he disregarded conventional wisdom and placed his own troops between two enemy forces.[75] Moreover, he ignored standard military doctrine, which said that elevated, fortified positions should be attacked in columns. Instead, he had his men in line formation, spread across the field shoulder to shoulder. This force was to attack the rail fence. As fine as they looked, they were an inviting target.

Howe's grenadiers and infantry would be met by Thomas Knowlton and his Connecticut men along their line. Standing with Knowlton was the septuagenarian General Seth Pomeroy, who took a position along the rail fence.[76] Meanwhile, Stark's troops further down on the American left would face the famed Royal Welch Fusiliers, a distinguished force of light infantry. It is likely that neither British group knew what, in a few minutes, they were about to encounter. Stark delivered a brief oration to his men, urging them to prove their mettle and instilling in them a sense of patriotic purpose.[77] This speech was met by three cheers from the troops.

Despite the hindrances that the British encountered on the Charlestown hillside, they came on with determination etched in their faces. Finally, only a hundred yards separated the two sides. After the battle, Americans who were there said the discipline and order the British displayed was an impressive sight. Many of the British soldiers were itching for combat, still angry over the significant casualties they'd suffered on their return trip from Concord two months earlier. Their blood was up, and they were seeking retribution. And leading his troops along the Mystic River on his horse was the supremely confident General Howe, who was accompanied by an aide walking alongside him and carrying a silver tray with a decanter of wine.[78]

However, Howe's plan, which relied on timing and coordination, was disrupted right from the start. Because of the impediments in the field, as well as the snipers shooting from Charlestown village, Pigot's men could not maintain their synchronicity with Howe's troops on the right and their lines became disordered. Down along the beach, the Royal Welch Fusiliers did not encounter the same obstacles as Pigot's men heading toward the redoubt, but they became bunched together in the narrow lane they were traversing. The fusiliers were instructed not to fire their weapons but simply to overrun the Americans using their bayonets and then turn their left flank.[79]

On the American side, except for a few stray shots here and there that they were angrily reprimanded for, the soldiers adhered to their officers' orders. Colonel Prescott was incensed by the premature discharge and vowed severe consequences to anyone who should repeat it, reinforcing to the soldiers that he would give the command to fire at the proper moment.[80]

The British advance did not slow. Moments later, they were in the effective firing range—about 50–100 yards out. The provincials could see the faces of the enemy. The time had come, and Prescott shouted the order to commence firing. A thunderous volley was unleashed and poured into Pigot's troops. Pigot's men were also subjected to a crossfire from provincials on his left who had taken up positions in and around the buildings in Charlestown village. White smoke from the muzzles of hundreds of muskets blanketed the field below the redoubt. From the sound and billowing smoke, the spectators across the water and on elevated vantage points knew the battle was on.

Down along the northern slopes of Breed's Hill and along the Mystic River, a similar action played out. John Stark waited until the lead troop of British grenadiers and light infantry had drawn close before giving his men the command to fire. According to both American and British commentators, the troops at the rail fence did not start shooting until the firing started at the redoubt a few minutes earlier.[81] The American salvo, sporadic at first, exploded into a loud, rolling, and sustained roar.[82] An acrid, white cloud enveloped the men. The pungent smell of gunpowder from hundreds of muskets hung in the air across the battlefield. All along the American defenses, British soldiers were hit with unusually deadly frequency. The fusiliers, who were about to begin their charge, were easy targets in their bunched columns. The ferocity of the American volley decimated their front ranks. Across the field, the British front lines were staggered and, as one of their survivors noted afterward, appeared to just melt away.[83]

In Stark's line, the Americans had arrayed themselves three-deep to maintain a constant fusillade, a tactic Stark picked up while fighting with Rogers' Rangers.[84] After the lead row of soldiers fired their muskets, they would kneel and let the men behind them step up and shoot. Then it was the third row's turn. In the 20 seconds or so it took to reload their muskets, the first row of men was back up and ready to fire again.[85] Thus, the American shooting was unrelenting and just too hot for the British to keep up their advance. Even the highly disciplined fusiliers could not withstand the slaughterous fire, and in a few minutes, they ceased moving forward and eventually withdrew their attack.[86]

The cacophony of the musketry drowned out all other sounds, and the smoke from the exploding powder drastically reduced visibility. Casualties mounted rapidly, with the Americans pouring round after round into the British left as they attempted to reach the redoubt and break through the defenses at the rail fence. Author Samuel Adams Drake described the action in his 1875 account of the fighting at the redoubt:

> Arriving within musket-shot of the American works, the [British] troops commenced firing, receiving in return only a few scattered shots, until they came within about seventy-five yards. The provincials had been ordered all along their line to reserve their fire until they could see the whites of their enemies' eyes. The troops, though doubting what this ominous silence might mean, continued to sweep the ramparts with their musketry, and to advance. When the English battle-line crossed the fatal boundary, already determined, a sonorous voice within the redoubt cried out, "Fire!"
>
> Then began that terrible fusillade, which so many have in vain attempted to describe. A blaze ran along the whole line; the hill shook. Like the leap of a pent-up wave of fire from out of a burning building, it rolled and surged down upon the English line, bursting through and eliminating it,— flashing with deadly gleams, and crested with battle smoke. Whole companies withered away. Standards sunk out of sight, and ranks of muskets fell from nerveless hands. When it had passed, a broken line of bewildered men, unable to advance, unwilling to fly, stood where the heaps of the dead and dying were more than the groups of the living. Then the bugles sounded recall, and they retreated to the shore, where the Americans' exultant hurrah followed them.[87]

In fact, the Americans did not let up along any of their defenses until the British recoiled from the intensity of the barrage and fled back down the hill—despite their officers pleading that they keep moving forward. But it was virtually impossible for the British troops to hear their instructions. Some men were advancing while others were retreating. It was total chaos and confusion, though there was no doubt that the British assault had been thwarted. The American defenders, who had been gripped with trepidation just a few moments earlier, let out triumphant shouts from behind their fortifications as they watched the British turn and run.

The Americans did not flee as the British commanders had predicted. One British officer later described the assault from their perspective. He wrote that both columns advanced initially "with great confidence, expecting an easy victory," until at roughly 40 yards from the American defenses they were suddenly staggered then ripped apart by "an incessant stream of fire poured from the rebel lines...Most of the Grenadiers and light infantry the moment of presenting themselves lost three-quarters, and many nine-tenths of their men. Some had only eight or nine men in a company left, some only three, four, and five."[88] This description was echoed by an American soldier who said, "So precise and fatal was our fire that in...a short time, they [the British] gave way and retired leaving many wounded and killed."[89]

Richard Frothingham wrote that after the British retreat from the first assault, "Colonel Prescott mingled freely among his troops, praised their good conduct, and congratulated them on their success. He felt confident that another assault would soon be made, and he renewed his caution to reserve the fire until he gave the command."[90]

As historian Christian DiSpigna points out, it is very likely that "Warren's presence bolstered morale and almost certainly helped prevent a premature mass retreat by the provincials."[91] The American resistance was so successful that it led Stark to declare, "The [British] dead lay as thick as sheep in a fold."[92] Nonetheless, both Prescott and Stark knew that there would be more action to come and that the British would attack more forcefully the next time. So, they walked along the lines encouraging their men, lauding their efforts, and reminding them that they needed to be ready for another attempt.[93] In the heat of the fighting, a messenger alerted Stark that Caleb, his son, had been killed somewhere along the line in Breed's pasture.[94] Stark reprimanded the messenger for bringing him this horrible news at such a sensitive time.

At this point, as some Americans had abandoned the field and others were casualties, Prescott had only about 150 men in the redoubt, another 200 behind the breastwork, and about 400–500 along the American far left.[95] Thus, the British still had the numerical advantage, even considering their sizable casualties from the first assault. But, to the Americans, the British regulars were no longer seen as invincible.

To put down the sniper fire from the buildings in Charlestown, Admiral Graves got permission to fire incendiary bombs, which set the town ablaze.[96] According to George Washington Warren's history of the battle, the church, the courthouse, four other public buildings, and some 400 houses and 200 stores, warehouses, and shops were burned to the ground.[97] He noted that "the fast moving flames, the clouds of smoke, and the alarms and shrieks of the homeless, added to the terror of the bloody scene."

The Second Assault

A few minutes after their retreat, the British reformed their lines and attacked a second time. On they came, more determined this time to finish their job. But to the consternation of their officers, they met a similar fate. This time, both Prescott and Stark allowed the British to get even closer before ordering their men to fire. Their troops kept their heads down, out of sight of the British, and waited for the order to recommence firing. Afterward, some of the British survivors said that since they got so close to the redoubt and rail fence, they'd thought the Americans had abandoned the field.

William Prescott Jr., Colonel Prescott's son, wrote of the second assault based on his father's retelling: "The discharge was simultaneous the whole length of the line, and though more destructive, as Colonel Prescott thought, than on the former assault, the enemy stood the first shock, and continued to advance and fire with great spirit; but before reaching the redoubt the continuous, well-directed fire of the Americans compelled them to give way, and they retreated a second time, in great disorder than before…"[98]

Likewise, here's how Colonel Prescott described the second assault on the redoubt in his own words: "The enemy advanced and fired very hotly on the fort, and meeting a warm reception, there was a very smart firing on both sides. After a considerable time, finding our ammunition was almost spent, I commanded a cessation till the enemy advanced to within 30 yards when we gave them such a hot fire that they were obliged to retire nearly 150 yards."[99]

Once again, the roar of muskets was deafening. The provincials were loading and firing as quickly as they could, clearly cognizant that since they were outnumbered, they needed to hit their targets as often as possible. Unfortunately, despite Prescott's best efforts to conserve ammunition, the second assault consumed most of the Americans' remaining powder and bullets.[100] It was also reported by one source that General Putnam, who generally was not involved in the direct fighting, performed heroic service along the rail fence, encouraging the (Connecticut) troops and directing their fire.[101]

The British were firing in response, but many of their shots were sailing high over the Americans' heads. The trees behind the American defenses were riddled with musket balls, and branches were splintered and severed off. Like before, the British could not maintain their advance. More men fell in the field, and the ground, now streaked with British blood, was again surrendered. As the British retreated a second time, another rousing cheer went up from the Americans. General Burgoyne, who watched the battle from Copp's Hill, spoke of the second assault as "the most incessant discharge of guns that ever was heard by mortal ears."[102]

From the redoubt, Prescott saw Howe standing almost alone in the field, looking bewildered among the dead and wounded.[103] Howe was stunned, and he would later admit that the American resistance was much stronger than he expected, noting that the firing along the rail fence was as hot as he had ever encountered. Though Howe's and Pigot's assaults failed for a second time, Howe later wrote of the gallantry of his officers in the face of what one of them described as "an incessant stream of fire."[104] Perhaps Samuel Adams Drake had it right when he wrote that the British troops were "more dispirited at their want of success, more shaken by the appalling slaughter. This was not fighting, but downright butchery."[105] Reflecting on the inability of the grenadiers and light infantry to break through the American line, Howe, to his everlasting dismay, admitted, "It was a moment that I have never felt before."[106]

At this point in the battle, Howe received troop reinforcements from Boston—estimates range from 400 to 600 men—and General Henry Clinton, who had watched the early action unfold from Copp's Hill, was rowed to Charlestown to assist.[107] In the third assault, the British ditched the heavy backpacks they were carrying and many removed their woolen coats.[108] This time, Howe decided to avoid the rail fence, where so many of his soldiers had been killed or wounded, and focus instead on the redoubt. Howe's men would make for the glaring gap between the rail fence and the breastwork in order to then fire across the fort. They would also advance in column formation rather than across the field where they were more easily hit. Although some of Howe's officers urged him not to make a third assault, Howe was resolute and would not accede to their wishes.

During the comparatively long interval between the second and third assaults, vigorous strides were made by the Americans to rush fresh soldiers up to the front lines, and it was reported that General Putnam was exceedingly active in this effort.[109] In all the confusion, casualties, and mayhem, it was hard to know exactly how many American troops were still standing along the fortifications.

When the British were at last ready, Clinton and Pigot led their columns against the redoubt. Their soldiers were ordered to move quickly, refrain from firing their muskets, and use the bayonet only.[110] On the British right, the artillery was directed to take a position to enfilade the vulnerable gap between the rail fence and the breastwork. Howe, still on the field, would march against the breastwork with the remainder of his grenadiers and light infantry.[111]

Prescott knew the Americans' powder was nearly spent.[112] But rather than evacuate their positions, the defiant Colonel broke open a cartridge box or two that had been left behind by the artillery and passed out the small amount of powder to his men.[113] He was not about to cede the field to an enemy he felt he was getting the better of, even though the troops he had left in the redoubt—between 100 and 200 men—were exhausted by the fighting and the hard work they had done overnight.[114]

Prescott strode along the line, exhorting his men to hold their positions one more time. He told his remaining troops, "If we can drive them back again, they cannot rally."[115] The worn-out soldiers accepted Prescott's words, and even though the British were getting closer to the redoubt with each assault, they stayed behind the ramparts and prepared for the next surge. Realistically, though, there wasn't enough ammunition to stave off the British if they came hard on a third assault. Some provincials had only one ball left. Those without ammunition rammed nails and other materials down their barrels in order to be able to keep firing and hurt the enemy.[116]

In Frothingham's account of the battle, reported by Keith Brough, he says that "Colonel Prescott remained at his post, determined in his purpose, undaunted in his bearing, inspiring his men with hope and confidence, and yet chagrined, that, in this hour of peril and glory, adequate support had not reached him."[117] Nearly two hours into the battle, Prescott recognized that reinforcements were probably not on the way and he would have to fight it out with only the men he had. It could not have been a comforting thought.

The Third Assault

The British did come a third time. There was really no doubt this would happen. Howe needed to emerge victorious after suffering so many casualties. All focus was on the redoubt. As planned, the final assault was largely a bayonet charge, which would reduce the time needed for the British troops to get to the redoubt. Howe was going for broke.

Inside the redoubt, it was desperation time for the provincials, their early euphoria replaced with blatant fear. Prescott recalled, "We having very few bayonets could make no resistance." The best he could do was station those soldiers who had bayonets at the points of the redoubt that were most likely to be scaled.[118] As the sweaty, bloodstained British soldiers closed in on the redoubt, screaming a range of guttural sounds and indiscernible epithets, Prescott ordered any man who still had loaded muskets to fire. And once again, the last American troops mounted their firing steps in the fort's walls and let loose a point-blank volley that staggered the British troops.[119]

In his telling, Frothingham relates an account of the Americans' final defense provided by William Prescott, Jr.:

> I heard my father say that when he saw the British approaching the works on two sides with artillery to enfilade the breastwork, their whole fire concentrated on their position, and advancing without firing a gun he well understood their intention, and considered that the post must inevitably be carried; but he [Prescott] thought his duty and honor and the interest of the country required that it should be defended to the last extremity, although at a certain sacrifice of many lives. He gave direction to place the few men who had bayonets at the points where he considered the wall most likely to be scaled, and as most of them had a charge of ammunition, and many two or three left, and a few perhaps more, he waited until the enemy had advanced to within about twenty yards before he gave the order to fire.[120]

But would it be enough to break the British soldiers? Given the expected ferocity of the charge, even Prescott must have had his doubts. In a display of extraordinary courage, Prescott faced down the British charge and did not waver. The odds of surviving the assault were somewhere between slim and none.

The British finally turned the tide of the battle on the third assault, due in large measure to the field artillery, which had been brought around to the right side of the redoubt where the guns "enfiladed the line of the breastwork and drove the remaining Americans there into the redoubt."[121] The Americans did what they could to repulse the enemy, but with their ammunition almost spent and their muskets fouling, the numerically superior British were able to scale the parapet and get inside the fort. The initial side that they breached was the south wall, and Major Pigot was one of the first to scale the works.[122] British Major John Pitcairn, a leading participant at Lexington and Concord and part of Pigot's frontal assault, was also one of the first to try to get into the redoubt.[123] He was less lucky than Pigot and was shot down, falling back into the arms of his 19-year-old son, Lieutenant Thomas Pitcairn, who carried him from the field. It was later recorded that "a negro man belonging to Groton took aim at Major Pitcairn, as he was rallying the dispersed British troops, & shot him thro the head, he was brought over to Boston and died as he was landing on the ferry ways."[124] As it turned out, the provincials were very good at spotting and hitting British officers. The final toll would be shocking.

Mayhem and desperation reigned inside the redoubt as the fighting moved to hand-to-hand combat. The Americans used their muskets as clubs and hurled rocks, but the British bayonets were deadly in close quarters. In this calamitous moment, Prescott continued to give orders coolly.[125] He directed those without bayonets to move to the rear of the redoubt and fire on the British as they came across the parapet. However, because there was only a single narrow exit at its rear, the redoubt, which had protected the men up to now, became a death trap for the Americans inside. At least 30 men caught in the redoubt were bayoneted by the British, who were eager to exact their revenge.[126] The bravery of the Americans did not go unnoticed. One British officer recalled, "There are few instances of regular troops defending a redoubt till the enemy were in the very ditch of it, and [yet] I saw several pop their heads up and fire even after some of our men were upon the berm."[127]

Prescott had vowed not to be taken alive by the British, and true to his word and the command he was given, he remained in the fort until all hope was lost. With the fighting still going on, Prescott parried the thrusts of the British bayonets aimed at him, and although his long coat was pierced multiple times, he escaped unscathed. How Prescott was not wounded, killed, or captured is something of a miracle. His men were now trying to evacuate the redoubt any way they could as the tall Prescott moved toward the exit with his sword raised above his head, the signal for retreat.[128] Amos Farnsworth was also in the redoubt at the bitter end, and he described the general fighting this way:

> Notwithstanding we within the entrenchment and at a breastwork within sustained the enemy's attacks with real bravery and resolution. Killed and wounded great numbers, and repulsed them several times; and after bearing for about two hours as severe and heavy a fire as perhaps ever was known, and many having fired away all their ammunition, and having no reinforcement although there was a great body of men nie by [nearby], we were overpowered by numbers and obliged to leave the intrenchment, retreating about sunset to a small distance until the enemy had got in. I then retreated about ten or fifteen rods. Then I received a wound in my right arm, the ball going through a little below the elbow, breaking the little shell bone. Another ball struck my back, taking off a piece of skin about as big as a penny; but I got to Cambridge that night.[129]

The American retreat from the redoubt was not completely orderly, but how could it be? With their bayonets, the British were making quick work of the remaining provincial soldiers in the fort. With no chance of saving the fort, it was every man for himself. As the redoubt's rear exit became congested, the men simply, and of necessity, hurled themselves over the wall and raced away as fast as they could. Stark's and Knowlton's men, still arrayed far down the slope to the left, were not engaged during the final assault and, in retrospect, could have assisted the men in the fort.[130] But in the confusion and without any means of communication, they stayed where they were. Their presence was not wasted, however, as they provided strong cover for the provincials retreating from the redoubt and no doubt saved many lives.

The British did not pursue the Americans, but they fired at them as they disappeared into the distance. Some of the retreating soldiers later told of hearing the bullets whizzing by them as they moved out of the effective range of the British muskets. The provincials fled to Cambridge, Prospect Hill, and Winter Hill.[131] Putnam left, cradling an armful of entrenching tools while on his white horse, and his men guarding Bunker's Hill also fled the scene. Of the battle, Putnam would say, "I never saw such a carnage of the human race."[132]

While on the retreat from the battlefield, Prescott came to a house on a Charlestown street close to the Neck where three or four men had just prepared a bowl of punch. Before tasting it themselves, they offered it to Prescott. This was a generous offer for a man suffering enormous fatigue and parched with thirst. But before he could imbibe from the bowl, a British cannonball passed through the house. The other soldiers fled immediately, leaving Prescott to drain the bowl by himself and at his leisure.[133]

It was during this last bit of frantic fighting and terror that Joseph Warren, who had tried to rally the men one last time, was shot in the head when he finally attempted to flee the scene.[134] He was no more than 60 yards from the redoubt when a musket ball hit Warren's face below his left eye and exited through the back of his head, killing him instantly.[135]

When the fort had been taken and Howe was told that Warren had been killed, he was incredulous. Howe and the other senior officers couldn't believe that Warren was involved in the fight, feeling he was too important to the provincials' cause to be a part of such fraught action.[136] So, Howe thought the report was erroneous until a British physician he sent from the field identified the body definitively. Howe, who considered Warren to be perhaps the leading incendiary in Boston, said Warren's death was worth the loss of 500 of his men.[137] Warren's body was left on the battlefield, where it was savagely desecrated by the British. His lifeless form was bayoneted multiple times, and he was decapitated then tossed in a mass grave.[138]

Leaving behind the battle, Prescott made his way back to Cambridge and reported to General Ward that he had executed his orders, made the best fight in his power, and yielded only when he was overwhelmed by a superior force.[139] Yet, despite relinquishing the field, the fight was not out of him.

He asked Ward for three regiments (about 1,000 men) well equipped with ammunition and bayonets, so he could immediately try to recapture the hill.[140] Observers noted that Prescott said he was even willing to perish in the bid. Ward refused his request, knowing the day was lost and thus the battle was ended. As one commentator noted, "He [Prescott] had not done enough to satisfy himself, though he had done enough to satisfy his country. He had not, indeed, secured final victory, but he had secured a glorious immortality."[141]

There was one more tragedy for the provincials. With many wounded Americans in retreat, Major Andrew McClary of New Hampshire mounted a horse and rode five miles north to Medford to obtain bandages and other supplies. His son and other men cautioned him not to go back across the Charlestown Neck to aid the wounded. McClary went anyway, saying, "The ball is not yet cast that will kill me."[142] McClary was struck in the back by a shot from the British frigate HMS *Glasgow* while walking across the Neck back toward Cambridge. "He leaped two to three feet from the ground, pitched forward, and fell dead upon his face," reported one of the officers.[143] McClary was the highest-ranking officer—and the last American—to die in the battle. John Stark was grief-stricken when he learned that his close friend had been shot and killed, but this was tempered by the news that his son, Caleb, had not been killed as previously reported and was very much alive and well.[144]

As the American fighters slinked back to Cambridge, Warren was unaccounted for, and for a while, no one was sure if he was dead, captured, or in hiding. Concern spread through both the commanders and the ranks, as everyone worried about the fate of their great leader. Some thought Warren must have gotten separated from the men but would turn up soon enough. Others who were there on Breed's Hill at the end weren't so sure, as they knew the intensity of the last fighting. They tried to hold out hope, but dread filled their hearts. Adding to the confusion, *The Boston Gazette* newspaper, a weekly, ran a short article on Monday, June 19, two days after the battle, under the byline of Joseph Warren that read in large part:

> Whereas the Enemies of America are multiplying their Cruelties towards the Inhabitants of the New England Colonies by seizing Provision Vessels, either the Property of, or intended to supply them; and also by plundering the Stock of Cattle, Sheep, etc. on their Sea Coasts,
>
> Resolved, That it be, and it hereby is recommended to the Inhabitants of the Towns and Districts of this Colony, that they forthwith exert themselves to prevent the Exportation of Fish, and all other Kinds of Provisions, except only as shall be intended to supply the Colonies aforesaid...And it is strongly recommended to the Select Men, Committees of Correspondence, and the Committee of Safety throughout the Colony, that they cause this Resolve to be strictly executed.[145]

Joseph Warren seemed to be issuing post-battle orders to the citizens of Massachusetts. This must have confused people. Was he still alive? Had he once again slipped the clutches of the British? Would he turn up any minute, reunite with his family, and resume his duties? The answer was no. The loss was a severe blow to the cause and to the community who loved him.

Although they did not realize it at the time, the provincials were lucky they had evacuated the peninsula when they did. If the British had followed Clinton's plan from the beginning or resorted to it when the Americans had stubbornly clung to the Charlestown Heights, they might all have been captured with the closure of the Charlestown Neck.[146] Decades later, General Charles Francis Adams also remarked on the Americans' luck at Bunker Hill, saying, "They [the Americans] had chanced on the right man [William Prescott] in the right place—and it was one chance in a thousand."[147]

After the battle, Abigail Adams would write to her husband, John, to tell him, "Charlestown is laid in ashes…Tis expected they [the British] will come out over the Neck tonight, and a dreadful battle must ensue…The constant roar of cannon is so distressing that we cannot eat, drink, or sleep."[148] However, night fell and the British did not come out to extend the battle. Meanwhile, on June 23, General Gage ordered an attack on Dorchester Heights—his other original objective—but he then canceled the assault, deciding that he could command the heights with his artillery if necessary and avert another possible bloodbath.[149]

When I tell the story of the battle of Bunker Hill, Park visitors are struck by the slaughter that occurred on both sides. The most horrified of them ask: How could this have happened? The idea that opponents would simply stand within yards of each other and blast away the way they did seems incomprehensible. Frankly, I have to agree with them. So to come up with some answers I felt the need to examine the decisions that were made by the opposing leaders and explore their rationality. In other words, I had to do a postmortem of the postmortem. One of the analysts I wanted to turn to was the United States Army, which I figured must have made judgments about this battle.

CHAPTER 8

Bunker Hill: The Aftermath

In retrospect, and with the advantage of time and perspective, it is clear that mistakes were made at Bunker Hill. How much of this might be attributable to William Prescott or others is debatable. It is far easier to look back and spot errors than to avoid them in the moment when chaos and confusion abound, when bloody death dominates the scene, when the action is fast and thinking is reduced to instinct.

Since many accounts of the battle came years later, including Prescott's thoughts, it has left a large hole in the historical record. Only a small number of anecdotes about the battle were handed down by his family members. One brief but insightful communication did survive, however. A couple of months after the battle, Prescott wrote a short account of the conflict in a letter to John Adams, dated August 25, 1775.[1] It certainly appears that Prescott did not feel chastened by his actions, and his account did not settle one of the key questions that most observers have had. Prescott begins apologetically by telling Adams he is unable to give a full accounting of the battle at the current moment: "I have recd. a Line from my Brother [James] which informs me of your desire of a particular Account at Charlestown, it is not in my Power at present to give you so minute an Account as I should choose being ordered to decamp and march to another station."[2] Prescott was still on active duty, and he let Adams know that he was in the middle of a military movement. At this time, Prescott would have been involved in the siege of Boston, and it appears he had been ordered to move his troops to another area. A more belligerent General Gage was still in control in Boston, but only because his recall orders, issued by Lord Dartmouth in England in mid-summer, did not arrive in Boston until September. General Howe would be his replacement. And the British Army, despite the heavy losses in Charlestown, was still a present threat.

Bunker Hill had proved that the British were willing and able to take massive actions against the provincials. The complexion of the war was entirely different after Bunker Hill, and anyone now within range of British firepower was not safe. In other words, Prescott had little time for detailed reporting. So, in the end, Prescott did not give a full accounting of the battle but said just enough to try to satisfy Adams. In his letter, Prescott goes on to say, "On the 16 June in the Evening I recd. Orders to march to *Breed's Hill* [italics added] in Charlestown with a party of about one thousand men…" Here it seems Prescott is either confusing Breed's Hill with Bunker's Hill, or perhaps is indicating that he regarded Breed's Hill as part of the Charlestown Heights that he felt his orders directed him to defend. More mischievously, it is also possible that Prescott was trying to cover up his failure to follow orders regarding where to establish his defensive fortifications, replacing Bunker's Hill in his account with Breed's Hill.

Prescott then proceeds to describe the work on the redoubt: "We arrived at the Spot, the lines were drawn by the Engineer [Colonel Gridley] and we began the entrenchment about 12, o Clock and plying the Work with all possible Expodition [*sic*] till Just before sun rising…" Prescott does not mention that Gridley disagreed with Putnam and himself regarding the placement of the redoubt. Again, he may have wanted to downplay that fact or else felt that Adams did not need to know it. Certainly, making the decision on the fort's placement in the middle of the night was not ideal. And, if it were true that, when the sun rose on Saturday morning, Prescott was alarmed by how dangerous their position was, he may have regretted placing the fort on Breed's Hill in the first place. Thus, Prescott does not settle the burning question of whether he disobeyed orders regarding the siting of the fort.

Artemas Ward did not want, or expect, to be involved in a major battle on June 17. He did not supply his troops with enough ammunition or provisions for a sustained, hot fight. Ward's aim was to block the British, whom he knew were planning to come to Charlestown, from being able to cross Charlestown Neck easily and potentially attack his troops in Cambridge. There is no record of Ward blaming any of the officers for the fight. Nonetheless, the Committee of Safety evidently ascribed the defeat to the commanders' [Putnam, Prescott, Gridley] mistake in proceeding "beyond their lines to Breed's Hill." The committee did not single anyone out in particular for this error. However, in looking for someone to blame, at least one commentator put the onus on Putnam, not Prescott or Gridley, describing Putnam's military decision-making derogatorily:

> General Putnam appears to have been a nervously active man, with plenty of personal courage, one to whom constant motion was almost a necessity; and whose self-confidence inclined him to meddle with whatever was afoot in the army, but of little military skill. If, as it is

likely, it was his [Putnam's] urgent advice that induced Prescott to deviate from his orders, he must have felt a peculiar responsibility for the result, and he evidently did what he could to rectify the error; but it was too late.[3]

Near the end of his August letter to Adams, Prescott describes—in a simple sentence—the provincials' dire situation with respect to their ammunition as the British made their third, and finally successful, assault: "Our Ammunition being nearly exhausted we could keep up only a scattering fire." Prescott admits that the American troops were not equipped to withstand a third assault from the British. This calls into question his judgment about whether he should have allowed his troops to remain on the field. However, Prescott told his troops that if they could hold off the British one more time, the British would give up their attack. Unfortunately, it isn't known how he thought they could do this if their ammunition was almost exhausted. Perhaps Prescott was hoping reinforcements from Cambridge would arrive, or that Stark's and Knowlton's men were in better shape and would be able to support him. He might have also hoped that Putnam's men would come forward from their position on Bunker's Hill in the rear. Of course, none of these things occurred. But, on that day, Prescott was not one to back down. He was ready to die if necessary, and to push his men to the limit. These factors may have kept any thoughts of leaving the field after the second assault from entering his mind. More simply, Prescott may have thought that his orders required him to stay on the hill until the battle was over, one way or the other.

There is another, more remarkable aspect of the decision to stay and fight. Prescott and the others were battling for certain lofty, but as yet vaguely defined, concepts—freedom, liberty, independence, the right to self-government. This was presumably also true for Stark and McClary, as well as Putnam and Knowlton, and the hundreds of troops of their militias. And, not to be forgotten, Dr. Joseph Warren in his finest clothes. Quite simply, they were willing to stake their lives on a set of ideals.

There is no evidence that Adams replied to Prescott's letter or asked him for more information, or that Prescott gave a more detailed account to Adams later. The Americans went to Charlestown to defend Bunker Hill, but they ended up losing the entire peninsula. For this reason, some authorities were furious that a battle had even taken place.[4] In addition, Warren, one of the principal figures on the colonists' side, was now dead. Some of the American fighters also felt like the battle was a defeat, and many were angry at what a Connecticut captain called "a shameful and scandalous retreat."[5]

The artillery companies performed badly and provided no value to the fight, retreating and leaving their field pieces at the scene. Several officers faced court-martial and dismissal from the service for their cowardly performance, and one senior officer criticized the higher ups by saying that American generalship had been confused and hesitant, leaving the force "commanded without order and God knows by whom."[6] A large amount of the blame was directed toward Artemas Ward, who, in the view of the new president of the Provincial Congress, James Warren (no relation to Joseph Warren), was "a general destitute of all military ability."[7]

Even in the days and weeks that immediately followed the historic fight, the consequences of the battle—including the basic details regarding what actually happened—emerged slowly. It took time for the battle's importance to sink in. As Robert Winthrop said in a memorial speech given years later, the outcome of the battle "was regarded at first not without disappointment, and even some indignation; and some of the contemporary American accounts, private and official, are said to have been rather in the tone of apology, or even censure, than of exaltation."[8] He noted that Richard Frothingham, an authority on the battle of Bunker Hill, also remarked that for years no one came forward to take credit for having directed the battle, such was the critical ambiguity surrounding the event.[9]

It took time to assess Bunker Hill, since the battle took the Americans by surprise. As Winthrop explained in his address:

> No wonder that a cloud of uncertainty so long rested on the exact course and conduct of this eventful action. Everyone was wholly occupied in making history; there was no leisure for writing history. It was a sudden movement. It was a secret movement. It was designed only to get the start of the British by an advance of our line of intrenchments [*sic*]. No one imagined that it would involve a battle, and no adequate provision was made for such an unexpected contingency.[10]

However, the Provincial Congress and the Committee of Safety refrained from prosecuting any of the commanders. A possible reason for this is that much of the citizenry was actually thrilled by the battle. If there had been doubt about taking on the British beforehand, the battle showed that the Americans would not only fight but could hold their own under the right circumstances. This was evident in Prescott's credible remark that, if he had more ammunition, he could have held off the British all day. Other assessments were also positive. James Knowles of Chester's Connecticut company wrote a day after the battle, "I think yesterday was a Glorious Day."[11] John Stark, whose role at the battle was so critical, said, "We remain in good spirits yet, being well satisfied that where we have lost one, they have lost three."[12]

Stark's assessment may have been an exaggeration, as the Americans also incurred significant casualties, but those inflicted on the British were horrifying. For a war where casualty rates were typically in the 5–15 percent range, Bunker Hill was a bloodbath. The British suffered roughly 45 percent casualties, with 226 dead and 828 wounded, including 92 officers.[13] All 12 of Howe's immediate direct reports were casualties, as well as his aide carrying the tray of wine.[14] The toll on British officers was enormous. By some estimates, roughly 12–15 percent of all the British officers who died in the eight years of the Revolutionary War died in approximately two hours at the battle of Bunker Hill.[15]

One of the British officers who perished was Colonel James Abercrombie. As he lay fatally wounded on the battlefield, he said of his American friend from the French and Indian War now turned Bunker Hill adversary, "If you take General Putnam alive, do not hang him for he is a brave man."[16] This sentiment is a reminder that many of the British and American officers knew each other from the earlier wars with the French when they were compatriots. After all, they had been British subjects together before circumstances put them on opposite sides of the looming war.

American casualties were also high at Bunker Hill, with 139 dead and 278 wounded, or roughly 25–30 percent of the men who took the field in Charlestown.[17] Another 31 Americans were captured by the British, which, given how prisoners were treated, was almost a death sentence. Even though the Americans had less than half the total of the British casualties, these were staggering numbers.

The largest number of casualties was from the town of Groton, with one officer and 10 enlisted men either killed or mortally wounded.[18] This total included Sergeant Benjamin Prescott, the son of James Prescott and nephew of Colonel Prescott. Of the Pepperell soldiers who fought in the battle, eight were killed—Jeremiah Shattuck, aged 30; Nathaniel Parker, 33; William Warren, 20; Wainwright Fisk, 24; Ebeneezer Laughton, 27; Joseph Spaulding, 37; Benjamin Wood, 20; and Edmund Peirce, 44. A similar number were wounded as well—Jonathan Stevens, Moses Blood, Simon Green, Adjutant William Green, John Adams, Thomas Lawrence, Abel Parker, and William Spaulding.

For two relatively small towns out on the frontier, these casualties were significant, as they represented a sizable portion of the fighting-age, male population in the towns. However, the whole conflict frankly could have been worse. Fortunately, the Americans' retreat was ably covered by the New Hampshire and Connecticut troops behind the rail fence, and it was even admired by the victorious British, who were gaining a grudging respect for the American soldiers. Another belated casualty of the battle was Reverend Joseph Emerson of Pepperell, who developed a fever while administering to the physical and spiritual needs of the soldiers after the fight, which led to his death on October 29, 1775 at the age of 51.[19]

So, while the British won the day, it was a pyrrhic victory of stunning proportions. The extensive British battlefield statistics caused the young and emerging commander, Nathanael Greene of Rhode Island, to quip, "I wish we could Sell them another Hill at the same Price as we did Bunker's Hill."[20] Certainly a lot more blood would be shed in this conflict, but it would not be restricted to just one side. The British would be victorious on the field in numerous instances down the road, but in this first major clash they bore the brunt of the carnage.

Despite the intense interest in knowing what had occurred at Bunker Hill, the citizens were left in the dark for days, as indicated by a report in *The Boston Gazette* on June 19, two days after the battle. And even then, this report did not lead off the paper but was buried behind a number of other stories and articles. The author of the report even apologized to his readers for the paucity of information:

> Friday Night last, a number of the Provincials Intrenched on Bunker-Hill in Charlestown; and on Saturday about Noon a large Number of Regulars from Boston came across Charles' River, and landed a little below the Battery near the point, when a bloody battle commenced, (many being killed and wounded on both sides). The very heavy firing from the Shipping, the Battery on Cop's-Hill, Boston, together with the Train of the Enemy, obliged the Provincials to retreat a little this side of Charlestown Neck about Sunset, when the Enemy took Possession of our Entrenchment, after which they set the Town of Charlestown on Fire, beginning with the Meeting house, and we hear they have not left one Building unconsumed. The Engagement continues at this Publication, 9 o'Clock, with Intermissions. The Confusion of the Times render it impracticable to give a particular Account of what has already occur'd, but hope to give a good one in our next. The Provincials are in high spirits.[21]

How exasperating it must have been for the citizens of Boston and eventually the rest of the colony—not to mention the other New England states—knowing that a large battle had taken place but they were still uncertain of the outcome. Those within sight of Charlestown saw clearly with their own eyes the columns of smoke rising from the British heavy guns and over the town, which only got worse when it was set ablaze. They also heard the thunderous roar of the cannons and, if near enough, the cacophonous discharges from thousands of muskets. To use a contemporary term, the "shock and awe" of that spectacle must have shaken the citizens to their core.

After such a horrific slugfest, which was characterized by close combat, it is natural to wonder how the soldiers felt about the decisions to build a redoubt in tantalizing view of the British, to take on the British forces that held an obvious lopsided advantage, and to stay on the field when the troops were physically exhausted and their ammunition was nearly expended. The answer, which only the survivors could provide, was probably mixed. No doubt, some men had not bargained for a major fight with the British and they left the field before the fighting started or during the battle itself. They probably felt this stance was a fool's errand, and they wanted no part of it. Those who stayed throughout the fight may have also broken into camps. One camp might have agreed with those who left early that this was an unmitigated mistake, particularly as they witnessed the horrific carnage and watched their friends, family, and neighbors fall around them. The other camp may have been as dedicated as Prescott and supported the idea of confronting the British and standing their ground until the bitter end. There isn't very much evidence that the troops who carried the fight on Bunker Hill felt that Prescott, or the other commanders for that matter, had made the wrong choices and failed them as leaders.

Similarly, there is no evidence that Putnam, Stark, Knowlton, and Gridley felt Prescott had been reckless or cavalier with the lives of the troops. Frankly, it is difficult to believe, for example, that Putnam would have spoken critically of Prescott after the battle since he himself had been pushing for a confrontation with the British. Putnam was also in favor of placing the redoubt on Breed's Hill; he may have instigated that decision and so would have been just as culpable as Prescott. On the other hand, Gridley did oppose setting up on Breed's Hill, and he did not stay around for the entire battle. Gridley was older and perhaps didn't have the stamina for a difficult fight. There is also a report that he had been injured early in the confrontation. It is entirely conceivable that he would have voiced his objections to the move, if, after the fight, Ward had pressed him on the issue. But nothing appears documented to this effect.

As for Stark and Knowlton, they may have only had limited contact with Prescott before the battle. They did all they could to support the American commander and stayed in the fight until the men on Breed's Hill made their retreat and prudence warranted their own withdrawal. Of all these commanders, we know that Stark thought the engagement was a glorious event. With the exception perhaps of Gridley, it is likely that these commanders would have closed ranks and chosen not to criticize Prescott.

On the other hand, there is an account of Prescott's disparaging feelings toward Putnam. Prescott's nephew, Dr. Oliver Prescott Jr., heard his uncle tell various stories and anecdotes about his experiences in the army. Several excerpts from sketches he wrote about Colonel Prescott are quite revealing.[22] In one of these sketches, Dr. Prescott says:

> The command of the detachment sent to Bunker Hill has by some writers been stated to have been given to General Putnam, but it appears General Putnam was not in the redoubt

during any part of the action. He came in the morning before the action and ordered a division of the men to carry away the entrenching tools that they might not be taken by the enemy, and at the same time engaged to send these men back with a reinforcement. But these men did not return nor was a reinforcement sent.

Colonel Prescott met Putman after the action, near Charlestown Neck, and inquired the cause of this failing to fulfill his engagement. General Putnam replied, "I could not make the dogs go." Colonel Prescott then stated, "If you had said to them come, you would have found men enough."[23]

Prescott reputedly never forgave Putnam for this breach of his promise. Several other officers who were in the battle gave the same account of Putnam's less than stellar conduct on that day, while Colonel John Stark simply called Putnam a poltroon.

There is no doubt, however, that Ward was upset that the redoubt was built on Breed's Hill rather than Bunker's Hill as he had ordered. He was also upset that, because that move instigated the British attack, Prescott needed to urgently call for reinforcements, along with additional food and water for his overworked men. These were requests that Ward felt he was not in a position to grant, at least initially. Ward was not expecting a major battle that day. He was in a bad position, because he did not know exactly what British intentions were. So, he split his forces between Charlestown and Dorchester. He clearly didn't feel he had extra resources to spare for Prescott. Consequently, it is probable—although the evidence is lacking—that he would have held harsh views of Prescott and Putnam.

Given the magnitude of the battle and its potential consequences, it is fair to ask if Prescott's precipitous actions in Charlestown nearly undermined the cause of liberty and independence. For instance, if the provincials had been quickly routed from the field—or worse, annihilated on Breed's Hill—the broad population might very well have concluded that it was foolish to oppose the British Army and throw off the yolk of British oppression. There certainly was no uniform opinion among the colonists regarding their relationship with respect to the king and their own subjugation.

Despite the bad decisions, loss of life, and forfeiture of territory, there was little opprobrium hurled at Prescott or the other provincial commanders following Bunker Hill—perhaps because the public was too enthralled by the emotional impact of the battle. Rather than evoke anger and revulsion, Bunker Hill seemed to have reinforced the colonists' determination to continue their resistance. Their soldiers fought a good fight. They acquitted themselves very well against a larger and feared opponent. Even the death of Joseph Warren, which was a devastating blow, stoked rather than diminished the flames of independence through his martyrdom. In this respect, Prescott was fortunate that his troops were not totally decimated, as that certainly would have triggered a different reaction.

On the British side, there was a distinct effort to glorify the victory and explain away the difficulty the troops had in taking the redoubt and forcing the Americans to retreat. Much was made of the obstacles in the field, as well as the American defensive structures. But there was also a repeated claim that the Americans far outnumbered the British. A record of the 52nd Oxfordshire Light Infantry stated it this way: "The approach to the hill was covered with grass reaching to the knees, and intersected with walls and fences of various enclosures. The difficult ascent, the heat of the weather, and the superior numbers of the enemy, together with their accurate and incessant fire, made the enterprise particularly arduous."[24] An account by Adjutant Waller of the Royal Marines was more specific with respect to the erroneous discrepancy in the number of combatants, reporting that "the rebels had five thousand to seven thousand men…the number of the corps under General Howe (who performed this gallant business) did not amount to fifteen hundred."[25] And in another general summary by the Royal Marines, which echoes the claim of over 5,000 rebels, the report speculates that "their [the Americans'] loss must have been considerable."

This type of accounting extended up the British chain of command. In the aftermath of the battle, General John Burgoyne, who witnessed the battle from Copp's Hill, sent a letter to Lord Stanley. While he clearly recognized the battle's toll, he also tried to glorify the British action. Burgoyne's letter describes the scene in part:

> Howe's disposition was extremely soldier-like: in my opinion, it was perfect. As his first arm advanced up, they met with a thousand impediments from strong fences, and were much exposed. They were also very much hurt by the musketry from Charlestown, although [General] Clinton and I did not perceive it, till Howe sent us word by a boat, and a desire for us to set fire to the town, which was immediately done. We threw a parcel of shells, and the whole was instantly in flames. Our battery afterwards kept an incessant fire on the heights; it was seconded by a number of frigates, floating batteries, and one ship of the line. *And now ensued one of the greatest scenes of war that can be conceived* [italics added], if we look to the heights.[26]

After an additional description of the battle in which Burgoyne also regrets that his nephew, a young soldier, was not there to see the action, he finishes his missive acknowledging the battle's toll: "The day ended in glory, and the success was most important considering the ascendancy it gives the regular troops; but the loss was uncommon among the officers, considering the number engaged."[27]

However, despite Burgoyne's attempts to salvage some respectability from the fight, King George and other officials in England were shocked by the casualty toll. Although Howe was not held accountable, General Gage was eventually relieved of his duties and recalled to Britain. Howe's role at Bunker Hill solidified his reputation for personal courage, but, as historian Joseph Ellis has noted, also added a new dimension of fatalism to his military mentality.[28] General Howe was so shaken by the outcome that he was reluctant to challenge the Americans again in a frontal assault on an entrenched and elevated position. About Bunker Hill, Howe, who had experienced many ferocious battles in his career, wrote, "He never knew nor heard of such a Carnage in so short a time," adding that the Americans fought "more like devils than men."[29] Writing to another officer, Howe referred to the battle as "this unhappy day."[30] Howe was clearly shocked by the battle's toll, saying, "I freely confess to you when I look at the consequences of it [the battle] and the loss of so many brave officers I do it with horror."

Reporting on the battle to Lord Dartmouth, a stunned and forthright Gage said, "The rebels are not the despicable rabble too many have supposed them to be…The number killed and wounded is greater than our forces can afford to bear…The conquest of this country is not easy…I think it is my duty to let your lordship know the true situation of affairs."[31] Gage now knew that it would take many thousands of troops to maintain control in America. General Clinton's note after the battle echoed Gage's comment, saying, "A dear bought victory, another such would have ruined us."[32] Gage wrote separately to Secretary of War William Barrington on June 26, in which he said, "These people…are now spirited up by a rage and enthusiasm as great as ever people were possessed of," adding, "You must proceed in earnest or give the business up. The loss we have sustained is greater than we can bear. Small armies can't afford such losses…I wish this cursed place was burned."[33]

General Thomas Clark, King George's military aide, had once said that with 5,000 troops he could "march the length of the American continent and along the way, geld all the Males, partly by force and partly by a little coaxing."[34] But Bunker Hill showed just how wildly inaccurate that assessment was. This was another important consequence of the battle. It awakened the British to the realization that this would be a real fight that would be very expensive in terms of lives and treasure and would probably last a number of years. Before the war was in full swing, there had been skeptics in London who said it wouldn't be easy to quell the American uprising. After Bunker Hill, that number increased dramatically.

In the House of Lords, William Pitt condemned the decision to militarize the conflict with the Americans.[35] Pitt argued that the American colonies were too valuable to lose and suggested that the government give them whatever they were asking for. Edmund Burke also made many of the same points, stating, "The Americans had the better part of the argument, and if war were to ensue, they were likely to win."[36] Bunker Hill had verified their fears and underscored the validity of their arguments.

Decision-Making

Clearly, the battle of Bunker Hill was not a planned event; it did not fit in some well-reasoned, strategic decision-making process. Was one side, the British or the Americans, more rational in their decision-making? What about the decisions made by William Prescott, the principal American leader on the field? And ultimately, in the end, was there a clear-cut winner in the engagement? I also wondered what the U.S. Army thought, since I figured they would most likely study such things. So, I sent an email to Mike Johnson, an old high school friend who had attended West Point in the early 1970s and who had a memorable career in the service. I had caught up with Mike at our 45th high school reunion in 2015, where I found out he had been working in the Pentagon when a hijacked commercial jet was flown into the massive structure on September 11, 2001. Mike was fairly close to the impact zone, but unharmed.

Mike quickly responded to my email and directed me to a colleague of his, Dr. James Scudieri, telling me that he was the guy who could help. Jim, a retired colonel, is a Senior Research Historian and Associate Professor at the U.S. Army War College's Strategic Studies Institute. Jim has extensive military education credentials and owns a host of military awards and decorations, including the Distinguished Service Medal, the Legion of Merit, a Bronze Star, and more. Fortunately but not surprisingly, when I reached out to Jim, he replied right way.

Garrulous and enthusiastic, Jim offered very cogent views of Bunker Hill and provided several links to archival Army files that document the history of the U.S. Army, knowing that they touched upon Bunker Hill. "The American commanders disobeyed orders by placing the fort on Breed's Hill," Jim claimed succinctly. "They shouldn't have made that decision in the dark, which in the morning light showed their exposure to British firepower." Still, Jim acknowledged the bravery of the American troops during the fighting and talked about the importance of Bunker Hill psychologically, while not holding any strategic significance. "Possession of Charlestown was not critical to either side."

Jim and I also discussed war-planning and the use of decision-analysis and game theory in today's Army versus decision-making practices back in the mid-1770s.[37] Without getting too nerdy, Jim and I wondered what game theory, with its statistical underpinning, would say about the decisions made at Bunker Hill. He suggested that maybe the Army should conduct an analysis using the battle as the subject.[38] (Okay, maybe we were getting a bit nerdy.) However, while game theory provides a more strategic way to make decisions—where the potential choices of the opponents are explicitly considered—neither of us could envision the framework being used in the later 18th century.

As Jim reminded me, there wasn't much planning before the battle of Bunker Hill; each side had its own objective, and events took on a life of their own, for better or worse. Jim pointed out that Major General Artemas Ward was not expecting a significant fight and did not make arrangements for one. Once Ward sent Prescott to Charlestown, Prescott was essentially on his own to decide what to do before, during, and at the end of the battle. He didn't rely on extensive analysis; he didn't really analyze the situation quantitatively at all. He simply made his decisions intuitively on the fly—like any other commander would have.

So, how did the decision-makers at Bunker Hill—including Prescott—actually do in the moment? From my perspective, the core decision that each side had to make as June 17 unfolded was whether to fight or not to fight. Once the British spotted the Americans on Breed's Hill, General Gage had to decide what, if anything, to do about it. Then, after he moved to attack Charlestown, William Prescott and the other commanders on the field had to decide whether to stay and fight the British or to withdraw. Similarly, once the battle was underway, the opposing field commanders—William Prescott and William Howe—continuously needed to decide if they wanted to carry on the battle or pull back off the field.

Of course, Gage did not call off or postpone the attack, as he thought his troops would easily outclass the American "rabble" and take the heights without much of a fight. The British doubted if the Americans would stay at all, since prior experience led them to hold the American fighting soldier in low regard. On the contrary, Gage accelerated his attack plan, assembling an expedition force to send to Charlestown on Saturday rather than wait until Sunday, which was his initial plan. Gage may have had good reason to think the Americans would retreat if attacked, but this notion should have been discounted when his aide, Abijah Willard, told Gage that his American brother-in-law (William Prescott) would fight until his last drop of blood. However, Gage had no doubt that his troops would easily take the heights and so, for him, attacking Breed's Hill seemed to be a rational decision.

We obviously know what took place next. A major battle that no one envisioned, or even wanted, ensued. None of the actors, either on the British side or the American side, seemingly contemplated this possibility. Consequently, without forethought, the momentum that led to the battle gathered steam until there was no turning back. William Howe, the British decision-maker on the battlefield, pressed the fight rather than withdraw, and his troops, while ultimately capturing the ground, suffered tremendous losses.

On the American side, William Prescott was sent to Charlestown to secure the heights and, once the British attacked, the idea of retreating without a fight was, most likely in his view, not a viable option. As Jim Scudieri noted, "Prescott had to stay and defend the heights; those were his orders." Unfortunately, the heights were eventually lost to the British, leaving open a clear avenue for the British to attack General Ward's army in Cambridge—the very thing Ward had been trying to prevent by sending Prescott to Charlestown in the first place. Prescott also suffered significant casualties, among them Joseph Warren, the beloved doctor and newly appointed major general of the provincial forces in New England. There were no tangible benefits to the Americans from the fight, aside from the psychological benefits of having stood their ground.

Bottom line, it seems that given the day's carnage, all the key decision makers—Gage, Howe, and Prescott—made bad decisions. Both sides vastly underestimated the potential casualties from a fight and miscalculated the value of possessing the territory itself. Of course, Bunker Hill was the first major battle of the nascent war, and apparently neither side conceived that such a slaughter was a possibility. But, clearly, and in hindsight, both sides should have at least thought through this potentiality. If they had, perhaps the battle would never have occurred. And who knows how this would have affected the prosecution of the war? In true game theory fashion, all of these decisions would have needed to be thought out in advance to have any benefit for anyone. But that was not how things were done at the time.

With respect to what the U.S. Army thinks about Bunker Hill, Jim Scudieri told me that since the battle occurred before the U.S. Army was established, it has not been scrutinized like the battles in more recent wars, especially those during World War II and onward. Perhaps the Army's best description of the battle of Bunker Hill is that it was "a tale of great blunders heroically redeemed."[39] Jim reinforced this opinion, saying, "It is not surprising that many errors occurred at Bunker Hill because the American forces were not a trained and disciplined army, with well-understood practices and procedures, but rather a loosely organized, volunteer militia that had little experience in warfare. There was no real command structure, which no doubt led to poor decisions being made before the battle, as well as lots of confusion on the battlefield once the fighting commenced." For instance, the U.S. Army calls the construction of the works on Breed's Hill, "A tactical blunder, for these exposed works could much more easily be cut off by a British landing on the Neck in their rear."[40] This was precisely the plan that General Henry Clinton put forth, but that was rejected by Generals Gage and Howe. Of course, it was Putnam and Prescott who decided to locate the redoubt on Breed's Hill, placing their forces in extreme jeopardy, which Prescott realized when the sun started to rise and he could take better stock of the situation.

General Ward did not want to alert the British regarding their actions, so he sent Prescott and his men over to Charlestown at night. But the decision that Prescott and Putnam made in darkness to build the redoubt on Breed's Hill was ill-advised, to say the least. Putnam may have been more familiar with Charlestown and its heights because he had marched a large number of troops there the month before the battle as a show of force. It is not clear how familiar Prescott was. Prescott and a party of his men reconnoitered the area in the darkness around midnight, but that was a catastrophically bad decision, as Jim heartily declared.

In its archives, the U.S. Army states the obvious: "The American command structure violated the principle of unity of command from the start, and in moving to Breed's Hill the patriots exposed an important part of their force in an indefensible position, violating the principles of concentration of force, mass, and maneuver."[41] Gage and Howe were also not immune from the U.S. Army's criticism when it added: "Gage and Howe, for their parts, sacrificed all the advantages the American blunders gave them, violating the principles of maneuver and surprise by undertaking a suicidal attack on a fortified position."[42]

Despite owning the field and expelling the Americans from Charlestown, the British gained no advantage and remained besieged in Boston. Samuel Adams Drake called the battle, "The dearest bought and barrenest victory of the war, perhaps of any war."[43] In its history of the American Revolution, and despite its criticisms of the battle, the U.S. Army offered this succinct and more positive opinion about the ramifications of Bunker Hill:

> Bunker Hill was a pyrrhic victory, its strategic effect practically nil since the two armies remained in virtually the same position they had held before. Its consequences, nevertheless, cannot be ignored. A force of farmers and townspeople, fresh from their fields and shops, with

hardly a semblance of orthodox military organization, had met and fought on equal terms with a professional British Army. On the British, this astonishing feat had a sobering effect, for it taught them that American resistance was not to be easily overcome; never again would British commanders lightly attempt such an assault on Americans in fortified positions. On the Americans, the effect was hardly sobering, and in the long run was perhaps not salutary. Bunker Hill, along with Lexington and Concord, went far to create the American tradition that the citizen soldier when aroused is more than a match for the trained professional, a tradition that was to be reflected in American military policy for generations afterward.[44]

Bunker Hill became a rallying cry for Americans. And Joseph Warren became a legitimate martyr for the cause. Once the dust settled from the battle and all the details of its aftermath were considered, Americans were proud of how their soldiers acquitted themselves and reinforced their resolve to oppose the British. In this respect, Bunker Hill can be viewed as a "win" for the Americans. For the British, they too could claim a "win," but at an exorbitant price. As for Prescott, he was fortunate that public opinion broke his way. He may have been lucky that that was the ultimate verdict, but luck often plays a part in the emergence of heroes.

By any assessment, no one could question Prescott's coolness under fire or not see his heroism. He was the only commander who was on the battlefield the entire time—from Friday night through Saturday afternoon. He displayed extraordinary courage, tenacity, and steadfastness. He could claim he did the best he could under the circumstances, and it is not clear if anyone could have done better. As someone who penned a note to Samuel Adams after the battle said: "To be plain it appears to me [about the battle] there never was more confusion and less command. No one appeared to have any but Col. Prescott whose bravery can never be enough acknowledged and applauded."[45]

The ferocity of the battle signaled that the war that was breaking out would not be short or perfunctory. The battle catapulted the American drive for independence forward and showed all of America that the emerging fight for freedom was real. Pushing back after the battle became a moral imperative for Americans, who saw British actions leading up to the battle as unjust and the fighting on June 17—and the desecration of American dead—as particularly brutal. In truth, the Americans were becoming more and more belligerent, and the recent toll on the British in various encounters certainly justified a strong response. Still, the sting of Bunker Hill, and other subsequent battles, would sustain the Americans' determination through the long years of struggle until their quest for independence was eventually fulfilled.

On the very day of the battle, the Continental Congress in Philadelphia said that Great Britain had already declared war on the United Colonies and ratified a commission for George Washington as commander in chief of all the Continental forces. This was indeed the case, as King George had declared the colonists "to be in open and avowed rebellion, by arraying themselves in a hostile manner, to withstand the execution of the law, and traitorously preparing, ordering and levying war against us [Great Britain]."[46]

Washington, upon hearing about Bunker Hill somewhere near Trenton, New Jersey, as he traveled toward Massachusetts, expressed confidently that the liberties of America were now safe, as its citizens would take up arms and the British would not win. Moreover, the ever-prescient Benjamin Franklin, who heard about the battle in France, wrote to his friends in London to say, "America will fight; England has lost her colonies forever."[47]

CHAPTER 9

The Boston Siege, New York Campaign, and Saratoga

What most people know about William Prescott begins and ends with the battle of Bunker Hill. That was my starting point as well. However, through my early research I learned a great deal about Prescott's life prior to the battle—his ancestry, his participation in the French and English wars of the 1740s through the early 1760s, his reaction to Parliament's taxes and Coercive Acts, his response to the Concord Alarm. Now I had to turn my attention to his activities after Bunker Hill.

A number of popular books on 1776, the siege of Boston, and the battle for New York City retell the enormous military buildup in the two northeastern cities (especially New York City), focusing on the behavior of George Washington and William Howe. After all, they were the principal commanders who engaged each other in both of these high-stakes standoffs. These events were followed by the extremely consequential fight in the Hudson Valley in the fall of 1777. But what of William Prescott? What role, if any, did he play? Was he even at these places? The historians I spoke with had little familiarity with Prescott's actions after June 1775. One said: "All I know about William Prescott is in my book on Bunker Hill." Once again, I'd have to go to the Massachusetts Archives and the MHS to pursue my detective work.

What Came After Bunker Hill

On July 3, less than a month after the Bunker Hill battle, George Washington came to Boston with orders from the Continental Congress proclaiming him overall commander of the new Army of the United Colonies. To Washington's great surprise, the New England army that he thought he was now committed to command was really no army at all. Once Washington got a chance to see the regional troops up close and personal, he was decidedly unimpressed. He thought they were undisciplined, dirty, devoid of any military training, and, to top it off, they drank too much. Incredulously, he found there to be no central command structure or hierarchy to the forces, just a loose collection of town-based militias. This meant he had to start from the basics and create an army rather than take over an army. The work would be long and frustrating—especially because he was pining to confront General Howe, who was hunkered down in Boston where his troops were kept comfortable by loyalists.

Washington wasted no time in warning his newly acquired troops regarding wanton behavior and dereliction of duty. In one of his first pronouncements, issued on July 7, he threatened to court-martial any officer for cowardice, "a crime of all others the most infamous in a soldier, the most infamous to an army and the last to be forgiven in as much as it may Prove the Destruction of the whole army."[1]

Once settled in his Cambridge headquarters, at the former home of loyalist John Vassall (and future home of poet Henry Wadsworth Longfellow) on Brattle Street near Harvard Square, Washington would no doubt have wanted a complete debriefing on Bunker Hill, including a review of the decisions made by William Prescott and the other commanders. Similarly, Ward most likely would have told Washington about his opposition to the placement of the redoubt on Breed's Hill and the unintended confrontation with the British. However, if Ward did have harsh words regarding Prescott and the other commanders, they did not lead to Prescott's demotion or any other effects. To the contrary, as part of the reorganization of the troops, Prescott retained command of his Massachusetts company, which became the 10th Regiment in the new army and then the 7th Regiment of the renamed Continental Army in January 1776.[2]

As a result, Prescott followed the same path into the new army as, notably, Putnam, Stark, and Knowlton. Like them, Prescott chose to stay the course, putting aside his busy life in Pepperell and once again potentially risking his own demise in fighting the British. That decision spoke volumes about his commitment to the American cause.

Based on orders dated July 22, Prescott's regiment was assigned to a brigade commanded by General William Heath. Along with another brigade and a reserve corps, they were designated to defend several posts north of Roxbury and west of Boston.[3] Then, on November 12, Colonel Prescott's regiment was ordered to "furnish the gard [sic] at Leachmors [Lechmere's] Point, on the Boston side of the Charles River, close to Charlestown." Later, Prescott's peripatetic regiment was reassigned to Cambridge, followed by orders on January 3, 1776 to relocate to Sewall's Point, an area that would become Kenmore Square just a mile or so west of Boston Common and beside the tidal marsh that ran along the Charles River.[4]

Yet, despite the escalating fighting in Massachusetts from April through June 1775, the Second Continental Congress was still not ready for a complete break from England. Even with the sting of Bunker Hill still fresh, the Congress's delegates decided to make one last-ditch effort to come to terms with the Crown. On July 5, 1775, Congress adopted the Olive Branch Petition, a peace offering initially drafted by Thomas Jefferson and then modified by John Dickinson. In this final effort to avoid war, the delegates extended a conciliatory hand to the king by expressing loyalty to the Crown while also rejecting Parliament's authority over the colonies. However, the logic of the peace offering was clearly flawed, and the colonists' effort proved futile as the king did not even deign to receive the document.

As Washington, with William Prescott's help, was busy organizing and training an army in Boston, the drive for independence sped up dramatically. By this time, discussions regarding personal freedom in the colonies shifted considerably, moving away from referring to their rights as Englishmen—as delineated in the Magna Carta and the Declaration of Rights of 1768—and toward their "natural-born rights." These were rights that existed in nature and that did not have to be enumerated in formal documents, rights that they possessed inherently as humans. This altered perspective formed the basis of the next great argument that came to an explosive head with the January 1776 publication of Thomas Paine's pamphlet, *Common Sense*.[5]

In his powerful tract, Paine called for a "Continental Conference," which "being empowered by the people would have the legal authority to draw up a charter answering to what is called the Magna Carta in England."[6] Paine went on to say that the document would outline a new form of government and secure "freedom and property to all men, especially the rights of conscience and such other matters as necessary for a charter to contain." Paine then added a flourish, saying, "Where is the King of America? [Tell them] in America, THE LAW IS KING."

Common Sense fanned the flames of revolution among the colonies. Paine argued that, at that time, Americans were participating in something much bigger than a fight over taxes and parliamentary authority. He said their fight was an epic event for the survival of liberty. He claimed they were involved in a world-altering historical happening that had far-reaching implications for all of humanity. Paine said what might have been on many colonial leaders' minds: "For God's sake, let us come to a final separation. The birth of a new world is at hand." The cause of America, he stated, "is the cause of all mankind."[7] Paine directly addressed the issue of possible reconciliation with the Crown, arguing that, under Britain's jurisdiction, the colonists' trade would be limited to serve England's benefit. "TIS TIME TO PART," said Paine.[8] And, in one of the most moving passages that has been referenced over the years, Paine intoned:

> I have never met with a man, either in England or America, who hath not confessed this opinion, that a separation between the countries, would take place one time or other: And there is no instance, in which we have shewn less judgment, than in endeavoring to describe, what we call the ripeness or fitness of the Continent for independence.
>
> As all men allow the measure, and vary only in their opinion of the time, let us, in order to remove mistakes, take a general survey of things, and endeavor, if possible, to find out the very time. But we need not go far, the inquiry ceases at once, for, the time hath found us.[9]

George Washington immediately expressed his enthusiasm upon reading *Common Sense*. He endorsed Paine's "unanswerable reasoning," as he called it, and predicted the pamphlet would hasten the arguments for a declaration of independence.[10]

Given the widespread distribution of *Common Sense* and its notoriety, it is highly likely that William Prescott would have been familiar with the pamphlet and no doubt discussed it with his family, friends, and other members of his community. It was, plainly and simply, the hottest topic in the colonies. As a leading citizen of Pepperell, Prescott's views would have been sought after and taken note of. Disappointingly, there is no record of his opinion regarding Paine's bombshell, but one can reasonably assume, given his anti-Parliament stance and desire for liberty, that he was aligned with its core message.

In the background of these political arguments and the growing radicalization of the colonists, Washington was still eager to bring the fight to General Howe—who was now in charge of the Massachusetts colony after Military Governor Thomas Gage was recalled to England. Howe's force had grown to roughly 10,000 troops, and they were well fortified in Boston. Howe was content to hole up in the city, to avoid any precipitous fighting with the Americans—even with the presence of Washington on the scene—and to enjoy himself as much as he could. There were three things that Howe openly and enthusiastically indulged in: gambling, theater, and the charms of Elizabeth Lloyd Loring, although not necessarily prioritized in that order.[11]

Several times over the months since he'd arrived, Washington had proposed striking Howe in Boston, but despite a three-to-one superiority in manpower, his generals voted against the plan each time.[12] The inchoate army was too green and undisciplined, they felt. It still lacked the firepower to conduct a credible attack. Then, in November, Henry Knox, a little-known, 25-year-old bookseller in Boston, came to Washington with a proposition to lead an expedition to Fort Ticonderoga on Lake Champlain in upstate New York to retrieve the dozens of cannons that had been captured when the fort fell into American hands in May 1775. Washington quickly gave his approval, and Knox and his 19-year-old brother, William, set off on horseback from Cambridge in mid-November on a challenging trek just as winter was arriving.[13]

The brothers headed to New York City first where they made arrangements to send military supplies to Boston. They then traveled up the Hudson Valley, covering as many as 40 miles a day. On December 5, they arrived at Fort Ticonderoga—at the southern tip of Lake Champlain where it meets Lake George—and were joined by dozens of men to transport the desired armaments back to Boston, a 300-mile march. George Washington had notified General Philip Schuyler (Alexander Hamilton's future father-in-law) of Knox's expedition so that he could help arrange the needed men and supplies.

Knox reviewed the stockpile of weapons, mostly French guns that had been captured by the British in the French and Indian War in 1759. He placed 59 mortars and cannons on sleds and began the long journey back to Boston.[14] The trip down Lake George took the expedition eight days and required four crossings of the Hudson before they reached Albany. On January 9, the caravan headed east over the Berkshire Mountains, with 100 miles across the width of Massachusetts still to go. The trip was not easy as Knox and his men faced snow, ice, and bitter cold. At Springfield, with roughly 50 miles left, Knox switched the sleds from oxen to horses to quicken their pace. He delivered his arsenal to the town of Framingham, about 15 miles west of Boston, at the end of January. Not one military piece was lost.

Around the time that Knox left Boston for Fort Ticonderoga, Congress had issued enlistment papers throughout the colonies to recruit an army of 30,000 men, who would serve until December 1776.[15] However, only about 3,500 of the 16,000 troops around Boston signed on, William Prescott being one of them.[16] Prescott's close aide in Boston was Lieutenant Colonel Johnson Moulton, a native of Maine, which was still part of Massachusetts at that time.[17] Notes and orders in Moulton's orderly book describe the activities of Prescott's regiment both in Boston during the siege, as well as later during the New York campaign. This gives us an idea as to Prescott's movements in the early months of 1776.

These entries, many of which come from Washington's headquarters in Cambridge, are fairly mundane, aiming to tighten up routines for guard duty and barracks inspection.[18] They also deal with precautions against smallpox, which was a feared and deadly disease that could ravage troops in a hurry. The orders also instruct the troops to strengthen their fortifications against a potential surprise attack by the British who, at the time, still had ships hovering in the area.

In an entry dated January 24, 1776 from Headquarters, Moulton lays out the organization of the American regiments in Washington's developing Continental Army. The post reads:

> Head Quarters, 24th January 1776
>
> The Regiments are to Brigade in the following Manner
>
> Brigadier General John Thomas—Col. Leonard's, Col. Reed's, Col. Whitmore's, Col. Ward's, Col. Bayle's
>
> General William Heath—Col. Prescott's, Col. Sergeant's, Col. Phinney's, Col. Greaton's, Col. Baldwin's

So, Prescott received a coveted regimental assignment, and he reported to General Heath, who had been a military mentor to Joseph Warren. With no fighting going on at the time, a number of Moulton's entries deal with ordinary disciplinary matters, such as this pair from early February. The first of these entries reads:

> Head Quarters, February 2, 1776
>
> William Prescott, as commanding officer, approves of the court martial and orders the Punishment [lashes on the bare-back with cat-o-nine tails] to be inflicted on the Prisoners Sergt Graham and Loudon accordingly.

That entry was followed by this order a few days later:

> Head Quarters, February 8, 1776
>
> Regimental Order
>
> Any Non-Commissioned Officer or Soldier belonging to Col. Prescott's Reg. who is found on [illegible]…any Part between this and Boston without leave in writing from the Commanding officer will be immediately confined and tried at a Court Martial for Disobedience of Orders on Suspicion of Deserting to the Enemy.

Of course, maintaining troop levels was a major concern for Washington, and Prescott made sure the soldiers in his regiment knew the consequences of walking away from their commitments. Military discipline had to be instilled in the new recruits. Commitments were commitments, and the troops had to understand that they could not simply leave their regiments at will. This behavior and the relatively short enlistment terms were a headache for Washington, who, for a long time, was never quite sure how many fit and able-bodied troops he had under his command.

Other orders and pronouncements in Moulton's orderly book also refer to Prescott's need to deal with some of the inevitable rowdiness that occurred when large groups of troops were placed together for extended periods of time without much serious business to attend to. An example is this entry from early March:

Head Quarters, 7th March 1776

> This is to notify the many Grog Sellers or any other Liquors in my Regiment not to exert themselves in so doing any more by Reason I had many Complaints made about it which in Reason ought to be for it has been the Cause of a great Many unbecoming Practices, with the Lavishing their Interest of Support of the Families at home therefore I desire that there shall not be no more such doings in my Regt by no means whatsoever: If this order be found in the least to be Disobey'd you may expect to be Dealt with to the utmost Exactness: Likewise your Liquor shall be spill'd about or upon the Ground; this by me
>   N.B. Not one shall be allowed only the Sutler [a person who followed an army and sold provisions to the soldiers] that belongs to my Regt called by the Name of Johnathan Frezendon

Wm Prescott Col.

Just prior to this notice, George Washington, now armed with the heavy guns from Fort Ticonderoga, knew he could confront the luxuriating William Howe in Boston. So, once again, he called a council of war. This time, Washington's plan was approved. The critical aspect of this action was apparent in Washington's orders to his troops when he said, "Every man's conduct will be marked and rewarded or punished accordingly, and cowardice in a most exemplary manner."[19]

Ahead of daybreak on Tuesday, March 5, an additional 3,000 American troops hiked up Dorchester Heights to man the fortifications and relieve the exhausted men who had worked there through the night. The Americans had clearly learned their lesson from Bunker Hill and had replacement troops ready this time. In addition, stationed up the Charles River were two floating batteries and 45 bateaux, each able to transport 80 men.[20] Four thousand troops under General Israel Putnam were also stationed in Cambridge, including his highly valued commander, Thomas Knowlton, ready to strike Boston with an amphibious assault if called on. New Hampshire's John Stark was situated in Medford, north of Cambridge, while William Prescott was still at Sewall's Point.

When the sun rose on March 5, British sentries could see that they were now under a formidable array of heavy guns and therefore vulnerable to attack. British officers climbed to the rooftops and were stunned by what they saw through their spy glasses. "A most astonishing night's work," one engineer confided to his diary. He also wildly overestimated the American forces: "Must have employed 15,000 to 20,000 men."[21] Another officer colorfully wrote, "[The rebels] raised the forts with an expedition equal to that of the genie belonging to Aladdin's wonderful lamp." General Howe was summoned, and when he saw what had been done, he exclaimed, "My God, what their men have done in one night I could not get my men to do in three months."

Washington was present on the heights, and he addressed his troops. He told his soldiers that they were going to be in a large battle on this day, and he pointedly reminded them that this was the anniversary of the Boston Massacre—a hallowed date in colonial Boston. "Remember the fifth of March," Washington beseeched them, "and avenge the death of your brethren."[22] Word spread through the line and bolstered the spirits of the men who might have been worried about another Bunker Hill. Did Washington select this date specifically for this reason? It seems probable, as without a doubt he knew this would have a positive psychological effect on his troops.

Howe's initial reaction was to mount an assault on the heights. He ordered General Hugh Percy—who had rescued General Smith on his retreat from Concord in April 1775—to attack with a force of 2,400 men, essentially the equivalent number thrown against Bunker Hill. Gun ports on the British men-of-war in the harbor also snapped open, and British shore batteries rotated toward Dorchester.[23] Immediately, there followed a massive cannonade that was easily the loudest ever heard in Boston. Fortunately, as at Bunker Hill, the British cannonballs fell harmlessly on the slopes of the heights and did nothing to deter the Americans, who were now taking aim at them.

However, after prolonged preparations and weather delays, Howe's determination to battle Washington began to soften, as the extra time to contemplate the situation—along with his likely remembrance of Bunker Hill—may have convinced him that such a move was not favorable. There was also the matter of British supplies, which were low. With only about six weeks of food on hand, the British could not have held on too much longer.[24] So, instead, Howe offered Washington a proposition. He told the general that if the Americans did not attack the city, he would not burn it down. He also indicated that he and his army would leave the city. Despite Washington's desire for a major confrontation, he saw the wisdom in Howe's offer and took the deal.[25]

Although there was some postponement, on March 17, General Howe took his 10,000 troops and approximately 1,100 loyalists and boarded roughly 110 ships that were anchored in Boston harbor. They set sail for Halifax, Nova Scotia. As he was sailing away, Howe penned a note (reminiscent of General Gage's previously expressed weariness), stating his own frustrations and warning about what lay ahead:

> All my struggles to supply the army with provisions had come to naught. A thousand difficulties are arose and the rebels forced his hand exposing the army to the greatest distresses by remaining in Boston or of withdrawing from it under such straitened circumstances. The scene here at present wears a lowering aspect, there not being the least prospect of conciliating this continent until its armies have been thoroughly dealt with…Such an event will not be readily brought about.[26]

Boston had been liberated. And Bostonians were eager to cheer their conquering savior. But then Washington made a magnanimous gesture that also evinced his political savvy. Washington suggested that General Artemas Ward, his predecessor in Boston, lead the troops into the city. He noted that, after all, the New England troops were Ward's men.[27] This was a shrewd move on Washington's part, as he knew he would need Ward's allegiance, as well as that of the New Englanders, in the battles that clearly lay ahead.

In Cambridge, General John Sullivan, observing that the British sentries who had occupied Charlestown were unusually quiet, crossed the Charlestown Neck and rode up the heights. Here, he found uniformed dummies wearing horseshoe gorgets and shirt ruffles made of paper, but not a British soldier in sight. The one-square-mile peninsula where so many soldiers from both sides were killed and wounded was once again in American hands.

In the days and weeks afterward, the provincials fortified the Charlestown Heights, not knowing if the British had any intentions of returning. They also unearthed the mass graves that contained the decomposed bodies of their deceased brethren-in-arms. Of great interest was the whereabouts of Joseph Warren's body. In one particular grave, a small distance from the site of the redoubt, Warren's remains were unearthed. His body was identified by his brothers, John and Ebenezer, who recognized in Warren's skull two artificial teeth that had been "fastened in with a gold wire" by Paul Revere.[28]

William Prescott had done his duty during the siege, but, like his comrades in arms, he didn't actually have to fight the British. Nonetheless, he had his regiment ready in case a confrontation ensued, and when the siege ended, he was intent on carrying out his enlistment. It wasn't long before he knew his new assignment.

The New York Campaign

Although Howe had evacuated Boston, Washington knew their paths would cross again. Congress learned that, undeniably, Howe was next headed for New York City, and so Washington quickly made arrangements to take his New England troops there.

On March 18, the day after the British evacuation, George Washington ordered General Heath to march to New York City with five regiments, including Prescott's, and a supply of artillery.[29] General Orders on March 23 from Colonel L. Baldwin's orderly book indicate that Prescott's regiment was "first to march under General Sullivan...at a moment's notice." Then, on March 28, Prescott was given more specific orders "to march his regiment at sunrise."[30] Prescott had his instructions; he was to get to New York City before the British.

The trek to New York would be roughly 200 miles—a significant undertaking that would probably take the troops about two weeks. For Prescott and his men, it likely was the furthest south most of the men had ever ventured. None of them knew exactly what to expect in the bustling city, though they knew they would likely have to face off against General Howe and his formidable troops again. Prescott had been on long marches before, such as during the King George and French and Indian Wars, but this experience must have provoked great anxiety among his men, and maybe even Prescott himself. Prescott was leaving behind his family in Pepperell, where they would have to manage for themselves. Abigail was 44 years old at the time, and William Jr. only 14. There were other family and friends in the area to support them, but Prescott's departure must have been a significant hardship at a critical time.

The Massachusetts Archives record a letter dated April 6, 1776 "from said Prescott, Colonel, to Colonel Bowlding [Baldwin?]" stating that "he [Prescott] had received orders from the General to march his division, as soon as possible, to New Haven, that he intended to march his regiment there that night and would be glad if said Bowlding would make his way thither as soon as possible."[31] Prescott had gone about 135 miles or two-thirds of the way to Manhattan.

By the second week of April, all of Washington's key commanders were in the city, including Generals William Heath, John Sullivan, and Nathanael Greene with each of their supporting regiments.[32] Israel Putnam was also there, replacing General Charles Lee as head of the city's defense. Thomas Knowlton, now a lieutenant colonel, was also in New York. John Stark, Prescott's other top-ranking compatriot at Bunker Hill, did not go to New York. Instead, in the spring of 1776, he was directed north with his men as reinforcements to the Continental Army during an ill-fated invasion of Canada.

For his part, George Washington left Cambridge on April 4 and arrived in New York City on April 13. He had 10 brigades, split evenly between General William Heath and General John Thomas. As a regiment commander in Heath's brigade, Prescott brought valuable experience and fighting prowess to the less-experienced Heath. Prescott's orderly, Lieutenant Colonel Johnson Moulton, resumes recording entries of Prescott's activities. One of the first—undated, but most likely recorded in the first week of April—indicates that the soldiers in Prescott's regiment were "to be informed they are to march to the Grand Battery in lower Manhattan in case of an Alarm." The British were not in New York harbor yet, but this entry shows how concerned Washington was that they might be caught flatfooted by the British. Everyone was to know what to do if the alarm was sounded.

A separate entry in Moulton's orderly book illustrates another significant concern for Prescott and other commanders. Written on April 14, the entry says, "All persons infected with the Small Pox are to be immediately Removed to Secure Places to be provided by the Quarter Master." There were constant concerns about smallpox, and it was not clear how many soldiers had been inoculated. The new army was deathly afraid of an outbreak, and so there was close monitoring of emerging cases. Prescott was doing what he could to maintain order and keep track of the health of his troops. He wanted his men to be in fighting order, as Washington could ill afford to have significant numbers of troops laid up and be a risk to the remaining troops.

Since the British had not arrived in New York in the first half of 1776, the American troops had no enemy to fight, except maybe boredom. The Continental Army might have been glad the British had not yet made their presence felt in New York. Few were probably eager for a battle, but they needed to stay mentally sharp in addition to physically fit. The extended weeks of calm would have enabled the troops to advance their military training and given commanders like Prescott the chance to turn these mostly green men into a worthy fighting force.

The real problem for the American commanders in early April was how to defend the city. Washington had a difficult task since the British could invade the city from literally any direction. He certainly knew the size of General William Howe's troop strength, but he would not know for a few more months just how many troops and how much British firepower he would have to confront. With deep-water access around Manhattan Island, there simply was no way to predict where the British were most likely to attack or if they would attack from multiple directions.

General Putnam, now in charge of the defense of New York, did not waste any time, and he continued to execute General Lee's previously sketched-out plans. Putnam also was eager to take possession of Governors Island, a 172-acre parcel of land about a half mile off the southern tip of Manhattan.[33] Putnam saw this small island as a linchpin to protecting the city. Sitting below the mouth of the East River between lower Manhattan and Red Hook in Brooklyn, it had the potential to keep the British ships out of that critical waterway. Blocking the British navy would serve to protect the eastern side of Manhattan, as well as Brooklyn Heights on the opposite side of the river. "Should the enemy arrive here, and get a post there [on Governors Island] it will not be possible to save the city, nor could we dislodge them [the British] without great loss," said Putnam.

Prescott's Strategic Posting

On April 7, General Putnam ordered Colonel Prescott to proceed to Governors Island and erect breastworks there.[34] The following night a force of 1,000 men took control of the outpost and were dug in before the sun was up.[35] On April 9, Colonel Silliman of Connecticut wrote to his wife:

> Last night draughts were made from a number of Regiments here, mine amongst the rest, to the number of 1100 men. With these and a proper number of officers General Putnam at candle lighting embarked on Board of a number of vessels with a large Number of entrenching tools and went directly on Nutten Island [also known as Governors Island] where they have been intrenching all night…and have got a good Breast work there raised which will cover them from the fire of the Ships.[36]

Without British troops in the area, there was no opposition to this move.[37] General Orders of April 16 then read: "Colonel Prescott's Regiment is to encamp on Governors Island…They are to give every assistance in their power to the works erected thereon."[38] Prescott was put in charge of a regiment of roughly 400 soldiers—referred to as the famous Bunker Hill Regiment—which were later joined by the 4th Continental Infantry under Colonel Nixon's command. Putnam also placed a gun battery on Red Hook, a jut of land projecting from southern Brooklyn that was directly across the small channel from Governors Island. He also sank various obstructions in the waters there, which would have made it more difficult for the British to pass through the gap and sail up the East River.

Based on his placement, Prescott was now quite literally isolated from the mainland and the other American troops. Had the British attacked Manhattan from the southwest, rather than eventually from Long Island to the east, Prescott would likely have been involved in some of the first fighting. His troops could have been subject to merciless bombardment from the many British warships that would eventually operate freely in the harbor. Prescott's nemesis, William Howe, could easily coordinate with his soon-to-be-arriving brother, Admiral Richard Howe, and use his fleet of warships to pulverize Prescott and his troops on Governors Island with relative ease. Stuck out in the middle of the harbor, Prescott's circumstances looked eerily like Bunker Hill, which may be why he was given that precarious assignment in the first place.[39]

To get a sense of Prescott's predicament and for what he might have felt, my wife and I took a trip out to Governors Island in the summer of 2024 so I could take in the panoramic view for myself. You can get there via a short ferry ride from one of several wharfs in lower Manhattan and Brooklyn.[40] We took the ferry from Battery Park, sharing the ride with dozens of young campers, elderly tourists, and others who had arranged to do some glamping (yes, glamping) on the southern tip of the recently renovated island.

As we rode out, I was immediately struck by the potential importance of the island for the American forces. Properly equipped, the island could make it hard for the British to attack the southern tip of Manhattan or to get into the East River. But "properly equipped" is the operative phrase here. In 1776, the Americans fortified Governors Island as best they could; however, their artillery was clearly overmatched against the large number of British warships. So, instead of being a bastion of the American defense, the island was an easy target for the enemy and an exceedingly vulnerable position for Prescott and the troops who were stationed there. I had envisioned that I would find some structures still standing from 1776—hopefully with "William Prescott was here" scratched into the wall of one—but that was just a fantasy, as no structures exist there from that time. Prescott's men were housed in tents and other temporary shelters. There was no luxuriating; they had work to do.

From a moderate rise on Governors Island, Prescott and his men had a 360-degree view of the large harbor. Prescott would have been able to see the fortifications at the southern end of Manhattan. The battery was a couple of hundred yards further away then, and lower Manhattan was narrower on the east and west. This was before grading took place that reduced the local hills and the excess dirt was used as landfill on the perimeter. Prescott could have seen the British ships, one after the other, sail in and dock at Staten Island.

He could have taken in the shoreline of Red Hook in Brooklyn, all the way up to Brooklyn Heights, where the iconic bridge that unites Brooklyn with its famous borough to the west was opened in 1883. It must have registered to Prescott that he and his men could easily be cut off from the security of either borough. He likely felt the isolation, the peril, and, to a certain measure, the helplessness.

We don't know Prescott's views about being stationed on Governors Island (though stranded might be a more apt description), but he took on his assignment without issue. The island was considered a strategically important post, but it certainly could not have been comforting to know that escape from the island would be very problematic, especially once a massive British fleet occupied the harbor. But as Washington would soon attest, Prescott's regiment—and the others that were there as well—got down to business and quickly erected formidable defenses on the tiny island.

Unable to squander any time, Washington had to assess the situation in New York City to determine how to deploy his forces while waiting for the British to arrive. Washington was in constant fear of where Howe might land his troops, with the base of Manhattan one possible landing site and others being Long Island, the west side of Manhattan, or northern Manhattan. Washington understood that he needed to keep the British off Brooklyn Heights and out of the East River. If they placed their cannons on Brooklyn Heights, the British would dominate the lower part of Manhattan and its all-important wharfs. They would also provide cover for British warships sailing in the East River after entering from Long Island Sound through Hell's Gate or from New York harbor just beyond Governors Island.

When he got the chance to inspect Governors Island, Washington liked what he saw there. Redoubts and gun placements were being erected, which would stand directly in the path of the East River between Brooklyn Heights and Red Hook at the southern end of Brooklyn.[41] "We have done a great deal of work at this place. In a fortnight more I think the city will be in a very respectable posture of defense," said a satisfied Washington, writing to General Lee.[42] "Governors Island has a large and strong work erected…the point below (called Red Hook) has a small, but very exceedingly strong barbette (mounted) battery—and several new works are constructed and many of them alone executed at other places." In June, the works on Governors Island boasted four 18-pounders and four 32-pounders.[43] Prescott could certainly take much of the credit for the military readiness of Governors Island.

The British delay in getting to New York had enabled the Americans to put together a solid plan for its defense. Some did have their doubts about the efficacy of these preparations in the face of such overwhelming enemy forces and firepower, but this was the hand Washington had been dealt. The New York campaign was sizing up to be a significant battle with the British. The operation in the city would be the largest assemblage of troops in the entire war. There, General William Howe would be joined by his older brother, Admiral Richard Howe, who had been sent by King George to put down the insurrection once and for all. General Henry Clinton would also bring his troops up from South Carolina to assist in the capture of this pivotal port city. Altogether, counting British and Hessian soldiers as well as British sailors and support personnel, approximately 42,000 enemy troops would descend on New York City.[44] The British also had 1,200 cannons and had assembled an astronomical 427 ships in and around the New York harbor. Against this force, George Washington had amassed in the vicinity of 20,000 troops, although a sizable portion of that number were inexperienced and some did not even have guns.[45]

Unfortunately, entries in Johnson Moulton's orderly book, which I found in the Massachusetts Historical Society, ended in May 1776. Consequently, knowledge of Prescott's actions and directives is limited during the British buildup in the summer months. However, Keith Brough's account, titled *General Ward's Colonial Army*, includes a letter that provides some insight. The letter, sent by William Prescott in early July to his brigadier general, William Heath, states:

May it please your Honour, Governors Island, July 3, 1776

We the Officer's [sic] of the Seventh Regiment, stationed on Gouvernour's [sic] Island, are determined to fight in the defense of our country to the last; yet we think too much for America to risk such an important post as this with seven or eight hundred men, especially considering the extensiveness of the lines we have to defend, and the difficulty which will attend our immediate supplies, when most probably in case of an attack wind and tide will be against them; whereas, should a sufficient number be on the spot to withstand any force that could be sent against them, they would have the same advantage of wind and tide with the enemy, should they aim at any other part. We think it likewise very necessary to have some field-pieces and reinforcement of the train, in order to secure the retreat, should it be thought proper, from the out works to the citadel.

We therefore, pray your Honour to represent the affair to his Excellency [George Washington] and solicit a proper reinforcement, which in our opinion cannot be less than two thousand men. We are, as in duty bound, your Honour's most obedient humble servants.

William Prescott, Colonel
Johnson Moulton, Lieutenant Colonel
Henry Woods, Major
In behalf [sic] of ourselves and Officers, to the Honourable Brigadier General Heath.

Clearly, Prescott thought Governors Island was undermanned and vulnerable to British assault. He could see firsthand the enormity of the British forces that were assembled below Manhattan. It must have astonished him and, no doubt, frightened him and his troops, who were in close proximity of such lethality. It seems his request was approved, as, in Edmund Banks Smith's history of Governors Island, he reports the requested 2,000 troops were at the outpost as of August 1776.[46]

Declaring Independence

In parallel with the developments in New York City, and as the year moved into spring, one thing was clear: there was more talk among colonial political leaders about the prospect of independence. On May 10, 1776, as the Second Congress was entering its second year, it appointed a committee that included John Adams, Richard Henry Lee, and Edward Rutledge of South Carolina to prepare a preface for an independence resolution. Three days later, a draft was produced and, after rancorous debate, approved by the Congress in a split vote. Truth be told, those who were reluctant to back independence had good reason to oppose a republican form of government. Until to 1776, there had been no successful examples of republican governments of the sort Thomas Paine advocated, in which all authority rested on popular choice and none on hereditary procedures.[47] The best-known republics, like Athens, Rome, and even England in the 1650s, had all failed. In the newly approved independence resolution, an important bridge was crossed. For the first time, Congress publicly placed responsibility for American grievances with King George.

It was fast becoming decision time for Congress's delegates regarding the momentous step of declaring independence. Once taken, there would be no going back. A declaration of independence would be viewed as a treasonous act, and those signing the declaration would have put their personal freedom, if not their very lives, at risk.[48]

On July 1, Congress debated the resolution, and on July 2, the delegates voted to accept the Declaration of Independence.[49] Two days later, on July 4, the delegates assembled in the Pennsylvania State House, now called Independence Hall, to sign the monumental document. Notably, while many of the framers of the declaration signed the document on July 4, it was many weeks before all members had done so, including the New York delegates who were finally allowed to vote on the measure on July 19. By signing their names, they were publicly admitting their action—which from the British perspective was nothing short of sedition.

It was John Hancock's responsibility, as president of the Continental Congress, to distribute the Declaration of Independence throughout the states.[50] He sent letters to each one, as well as to George Washington in New York City, informing them of the Congress's action and asking that the declaration be communicated to as many people as possible.[51] The most common method of announcing the declaration was to read the document before large groups of people, which is what Washington did. Hancock had advised Washington to proclaim the declaration "at the Head of the Army."

Consequently, on July 9, Washington ordered several Continental Army brigades stationed in New York City to pick up copies of the declaration and to read the document to the troops "with an audible voice."[52] Prescott's regiment would have been part of this ceremony, and we can guess what that meant for him and his men who had been through so much already. The document was also read to large civilian gatherings, with the appropriate pomp and circumstance. In Boston, John Adams recalled that, "Battalions paraded on the Common, and gave Us the Feu de Joie, notwithstanding the Scarcity of Powder. The Bells rang all Day and almost all night."[53]

In Pepperell, the Declaration of Independence was written into the town record, and it was noted that the document was "Publicly read in this town [on the] Lord's Day September 15, 1776 by Mr. Joseph Emerson of this place…" Town records do not indicate what the reaction was to the declaration, but it may be safely assumed that the overwhelmingly patriotic people of the town would have been very much in favor of the pronouncement. As its records show, the town had come gradually to independence, holding off criticizing the king until it was no longer possible to do so.[54] But by a certain point, the status quo was not satisfactory; they were now in favor of liberty. With the Declaration, the country had decided, as Thomas Paine said, the time had come.

The Contest for New York

Across the ocean, King George had hoped that the decisive battle for New York City would begin in June, but various setbacks and obstacles delayed the arrival of the massive British force until the end of the summer.[55] There were some actions in July, however, that presaged the difficulties ahead for Washington. In the journal of British Lieutenant Colonel Stephen Kemble, there is an entry on July 6 that states: "Observe the Rebels have fortified Governors Island very strongly."[56] This entry is followed by another on July 12, saying: "About half after three in the Afternoon His Majesty's Ship *Phoenix* and the *Rose*, with the *Tryal* Schooner and two tenders got under sail to pass the Town of New York…They received the Whole of the Rebel fire from Red Hook, Governors Island, the Battery, and from some guns in the Town [Manhattan]…At half past four the ships were all past all the Batteries. Number of Shots fired by the Rebels, 196."

In August, William Alexander, also known as Lord Stirling, wrote in a report (possibly to Congress) that "The General [Washington] bids me to say that in our present situation Governor's [sic] Island is more strong and better guarded than any other post in the army."[57] That may have stopped the British Army from attacking the island, but it appears that Governors Island did receive the attention of the Royal Navy at some time during the summer. It was reported that before the final land-attack plans at the end of August, Admiral Richard Howe anchored four ships roughly two miles below Governors Island and kept up a "most tremendous fire against the rebel fortifications there."[58] So ferocious was the bombardment that, even into the 20th century, British cannonballs were occasionally dug up on the island.

As at Bunker Hill, Prescott had to keep his men calm through this terrible cannonade. He and his troops might also have felt that the British were now preparing to assault their island defenses, where their prospects would likely be grim. Again, the situation called on him to display unwavering physical courage and resolve to maintain morale. While I did not find any detailed reports on the engagement, nor any reports of casualties, everyone there must have been fearful given the enormous British flotilla of warships and troops that were so terrifyingly close. Prescott excelled in these situations and his acknowledged coolness under fire and personal fortitude would have had a settling effect on the troops.

As British activity was ratcheting up, Washington still had to deal with the issue of where General William Howe's troops would attack, and there was now a growing sense that an attack was imminent. The British possessed overwhelming naval and infantry power, and nothing the Americans had done defensively had affected Howe's options. Curiously, just as General Henry Clinton had suggested landing on the Charlestown Neck at the start of the battle of Bunker Hill, in this case he argued the troops should land at the top of Manhattan to cut off Washington's escape route. The army could then methodically march down toward Battery Park to confront the Americans. But for a second time in a major operation, Howe ignored Clinton's advice.

Unsure of Howe's plans, Washington divided his troops between lower Manhattan and Brooklyn, feeling those locations were the most likely to see action. Indeed, General Howe ultimately decided that he would land his attack force on Long Island, and on August 22 put ashore 15,000 troops and 5,000 Hessians at Gravesend Bay. Meanwhile, on August 23 Richard Howe's navy traded cannon fire with the American battery at Red Hook as a number of British ships tried to pass through the channel between Governors Island and the Brooklyn shore in order to bombard the American forts at Brooklyn Heights.

Prescott and his men on Governors Island had a front row seat to this exchange and may have wondered once more if the British bombardment would soon turn on them. They were at the mercy of the British warships and had no practical means of escape. One imagines the American soldiers on the island rallying to their posts and ducking behind cover from what could have been, if the British elected, a petrifying rain of bombs.

Unfortunately for the British, and as a precursor of things to come, the wind was blowing in the wrong direction, thwarting their efforts to move their ships into the East River. Instead, they could have focused their warships' attention on Governors Island, sitting exposed in the harbor, and taken the opportunity to rake the outpost with its prodigious firepower. Prescott most likely had to use his powers of persuasion to keep his men steady and prepared for a possible invasion. Luckily for them, the British opted not to bother with Governors Island, and they sailed away without inflicting any harm on the American troops there.

However, in a series of sizable skirmishes that ensued over the next week, the British gained significant ground on Long Island that applied enormous pressure on Washington's army. It appeared the moment had finally arrived where the king would have his decisive battle for New York City, and perhaps snuff out the incipient insurrection.[59] Howe's forces made strong advances westward toward Brooklyn and were clearly in control of the situation. It seemed only a matter of time before the remaining American troops would either be captured or crushed by Howe's superior army.

About a mile from Manhattan and with their backs to the East River, the American troops were nearly out of options. So, Howe laid siege to the Americans, hoping to avoid a bloody battle and provide time to convince Washington that he had no choice but to surrender. But Washington stubbornly hung on, feeling that to retreat on the field of battle would be a stain on his honor. To a gentleman in that age, death was preferable to suffering the disgrace of retreat.

Then, in a war council on August 29 at his headquarters in Brooklyn Heights, Washington was finally convinced that evacuating Brooklyn was the best thing to do.[60] The daring plan was aided by two fortuitous events—first, strong winds out of the north once again prevented British ships from sailing up the East River, and, second, a dense fog in the evening reduced visibility to roughly six yards, shrouding the evacuation until the morning sun on August 30 burned off the haze. Governors Island also shielded the British forces' view of the lower part of the East River. In a miraculous feat of coordination and stealth, Washington got all of his roughly 10,000 troops back to Manhattan, save for three stragglers. And only when Washington was assured that the evacuation was complete did he step into the last boat and depart Brooklyn.

Shortly thereafter, at 7:00 a.m., as the fog began to lift, the last American soldiers—William Prescott's unit on Governors Island—departed their garrison for the safety of lower Manhattan.[61] It was then that the flight of the American troops from Governors Island was discovered. In a letter to his wife on August 31, Colonel William Douglas wrote, "We have evacuated Governors Island where we have lost some cannon. They [the British] fired smartly from Fort Stirling yesterday at our boats passing from Governor's [sic] Island." Another report made clear how close the troops from Governors Island came to meeting a disastrous fate. The report reads: "Lord Howe sailed up the Bay and anchored near the Island, whereupon our troops withdrew to the mainland, sustaining only one injury, a soldier wounded as he was embarking, by a ball from the British man-of-war."[62] Somewhat miraculously, Prescott and the American soldiers had escaped unscathed.

As they sailed away, the Americans could see the British troops occupying the abandoned forts on Brooklyn Heights.[63] Prescott must have been glad to reach the Manhattan shore without incident or distress, but that defiant streak in him, last seen on Breed's Hill, might have revealed itself once again. Perhaps he regretted the missed opportunity to confront his old adversary, William Howe, in another spirited confrontation.

Of the daring escape of the Continental Army, Thomas Jones, a justice of the peace in New York and a dedicated loyalist, wrote in September: "The rebels in their hurry upon leaving Long Island left the Garrison on Nutten Island consisting of 2,000 men, 40 pieces of heavy cannon, military stores and provisions in abundance without the least means of quitting the island...the Royal Army consisted of near 30,000 men...yet no steps were taken to make prisoners of the garrison and get possession of the forts, stores, artillery, and provisions."[64] In short, the British had missed a big opportunity.

Edmond Bancroft of the 7th Regiment also cited the precariousness of Prescott's evacuation from Governors Island. He wrote, "For the time Washington could only hope to keep at bay the great army opposed to him. The dilatoriness of his [Washington's] antagonist left him leisure to withdraw the garrison from Governors Island, where Prescott ran almost as great a risk of captivity as at Bunker Hill."[65]

When Washington decided retreat was the best and most expedient thing to do, Prescott ensured the orderly withdrawal of his regiment from the southern tip of Manhattan to the safety of the new line of defense up island.[66] Washington publicly acknowledged Prescott's leadership in the transfer of his troops, who could have easily been trapped in the lower reaches of Manhattan if they had been tardy in their withdrawal.[67] Israel Putnam was also nearly ensnared by British forces in southern Manhattan. It was the guidance of New York resident and Continental soldier Aaron Burr who led Putnam's men up the west side of the island past the enemy and to safety.

General Howe waited several weeks before crossing from Brooklyn to Manhattan, coming ashore at Kips Bay. He then proceeded to move his army methodically up Manhattan where Washington's troops had set up a defensive line. There was a spirited clash at Harlem Heights on September 16, where Thomas Knowlton was unfortunately killed. George Washington took the news very hard as he had grown very fond of the Connecticut soldier.

Howe continued to push northward, forcing Washington to retreat further up the island. Then, after some debate regarding whether he had the authority to relinquish the city, Washington moved the army off Manhattan and camped at Kingsbridge in the northwest part of the Bronx, near the Hudson River. In accordance with this movement, service records, dated September 27, 28, and 30, place William Prescott in that location. Like the rest of the Continental Army, Prescott's regiment was in a safer spot, but Manhattan had been surrendered.

There has been continued speculation and acrimony about why William Howe did not act more quickly to capture Washington and his army in New York. In Edmund Banks Smith's account, he writes, "Had Lord Howe taken his fleet up the East River on the day of the action on Long Island and the River been lined with the Ships from Governor's Island to Hellgate, not a rebel would have escaped from Long Island. But this was not done, and why it was not done, let the Howe brothers tell."[68]

In the end, despite the massive military buildup, the New York campaign—which was waged from August to November 1776—produced relatively few casualties. For instance, despite being a focal point of the fighting, the battle on Long Island had only 576 casualties on both sides, less than 40 percent of the total at Bunker Hill.[69] The Americans did suffer other losses, though, as more than 1,000 troops were captured by the British. Major bloodshed had been averted, however, and due to incredible maneuvering, Washington's army survived to fight another day. New York City and Governors Island were occupied by the British, who used the metropolis as their North American military headquarters for the remainder of the Revolutionary War.[70]

Interestingly, after the war, Prescott told an anecdote about an incident that occurred while he was in New York City that was recorded in the family's genealogical history.[71] According to the story, while Prescott's regiment was stationed in Manhattan, the perimeter guards brought in a British deserter. As the group approached the camp, the deserter observed to the guards, "That officer yonder is Colonel Prescott."

One of the guards promptly informed Prescott, who said to the deserter, "How come you to know me?"

The soldier replied, "I saw you on Bunker Hill, and recollected you immediately."

"Why did you not kill me at the time?" asked Prescott.

"I tried my best," said the soldier. "I took deliberate aim at you more than once when I thought it was impossible for you to escape. I also pushed at you several times with my bayonet when I was as near to you as I could have wished, and after several of us had taken possession of your works."

"You are a brave fellow," said Prescott. "Come into my tent and I will treat you." The story epitomizes Prescott's empathy for the ordinary soldier—here even an enemy—and helps explain why his troops felt so fond of him.

Another event from Prescott's time in New York City is also noteworthy. In September, while Prescott was still in the city, Nathan Hale, a 21-year-old former Yale student and member of Thomas Knowlton's unit, was caught in New York while on an intelligence-gathering mission. On September 22, Hale was hanged as a spy.[72] Of course, it was Nathan Hale who unforgettably said as he was about to meet his fate, "I only regret that I have but one life to lose for my country." According to U.S. Congressman William Everett's later telling, Nathan Hale may have been a blood relative of Prescott's wife, Abigail Hale. The odds of two people with the same last name and from the same general region being related was much greater in the early, less populous days of the colonies, so this was not out of the realm of possibility. Ironically, the British general who had Hale hanged was none other than William Howe, Prescott's familiar foe. However, although it makes a good story, there is no tangible evidence that the two Hales—Nathan and Abigail—were, indeed, related.

Heading Home

While fighting in Manhattan was now over, another engagement with Howe's army took place in mid-October in Pelham, just north of the Bronx. That was followed by a fight nearby in White Plains on October 28. There is an entry in another orderly book, written by Lt. Colonel Johnson Moulton, titled Camp at White Plains, dated October 20, 1776, so it is possible that Prescott was at least in the vicinity, if not part of the confrontation.[73] Moulton does not record any other entries in his orderly book dealing with this fighting, so it is not clear if Prescott was directly involved in either of these events.

Washington had resorted to a war of posts strategy in which he took repeated stands while retreating to thwart the enemy's progress. But while the British drive was temporarily slowed, it was not eliminated. Washington simply could not hold back their advance on him. Then, in early November, Washington learned that General Howe was planning "an expedition to the Jerseys," so he began making arrangements to counter Howe's thrust.[74] On November 9, Washington started to move his army across the Hudson at Peekskill, an area in Westchester County about 50 miles north of Manhattan, in order to respond to Howe's anticipated attack.[75]

The next entry in Prescott's orderly's book is dated December 7, about a month after Washington began moving his troops across the Hudson, and is titled Highlands Near Pigskill.[76] That Prescott appears to have still been at Peekskill seems to indicate that he did not accompany the Continental Army to the western side of the Hudson and into New Jersey. Additional entries in Moulton's orderly book, dated January 2 and January 3, 1777, again from Camp Highlands, indicate that Prescott was still in Westchester County, New York, at the start of the new year.

As Washington headed west into New Jersey, Prescott relinquished his command and retired from the service. Departures from the army were not unusual during this part of the war. Enlistments were relatively short, as the men often needed to get back to their families, farms, and businesses. The near constant turnover made Washington's job much harder, as he was continually breaking in new troops and never exactly sure how many soldiers he could count on at a particular point in time.

A service record ledger card summarizes Prescott's final tour with the Continental Army as follows: "the ledger of the Commissioners for the War Department, Revolutionary War, containing a debit and credit account with the person named above [William Prescott, Colonel, 7th Regiment], the earliest entry in said account being dated March 16, 1776 and the latest January 11, 1777."[77] The long and varied term of Prescott's multiple enlistments documented the evolution of the American Revolutionary War forces. After Lexington and Concord, where Prescott was the captain of a militia unit, he had signed up with the Provincial Army for eight months or to the end of 1775. In May of that year, he became a colonel. His 9th Regiment of that force became the 10th Regiment of the Army of the United Colonies from July 1775 through December 1775. Prescott then re-upped with what was then the Continental Army, commanding the 7th Continental Regiment from January 1776 throughout the New York campaign and into the first week of 1777, for a period of another 12 months. In total, that was a span of 20 months. It had indeed been a long journey.

By the time the ledger card recorded Prescott's final tour of duty, he may have already been on his way back to Massachusetts and into retirement.[78] There is a note dated January 11, 1777 in Prescott's personal paybook, in which he logged various and sundry financial transactions, pertaining to the rental of one pair of oxen. This would suggest Prescott was back in Pepperell tending to his farm at that time.[79]

There is no evidence that Prescott resigned from the army out of pique. By all indications, he supported the war and did not express any grievances with how it was being prosecuted. He did not have harsh words for his commanders or for the army's commander in chief. More likely, Prescott felt compelled to return to his family and to keep his farm operating effectively. He had done his part with his enlistment—more than was asked for—and now he was leaving the fighting to those whose enlistments were not up or who were situated where the war was migrating, namely to the west and the south.

When William Prescott returned from the New York campaign, he applied his energies to the usual town issues engulfing Pepperell. But, when the outlook appeared fairly bleak for Washington's army as he continued to try to elude the British in New Jersey and Pennsylvania, Prescott made sure that Pepperell was still very much aligned with the needs of the war. In the words of town records, he voted that "Militia Officers in Conjunction with the Selectmen and Committee complete our quota of Men for the Continental Army at their own discretion."[80] Prescott knew firsthand the precariousness of the army, and he used his influence to make sure that Pepperell was not shirking its conscription responsibilities, even though the war was now hundreds of miles away.

Saratoga

As 1776 drew to a close, Washington abandoned his war of posts strategy in favor of a Fabian strategy. Named after the Roman general Quintus Fabius Maximus, this approach was based on a guerilla-war style of fighting that never risked a straight up confrontation, but only engaged when there was a clear tactical advantage. The goal was to wear down the enemy in a long war of attrition. However, facing mounting pressures for a victory after being forced out of New York City, Washington finally took a bold stroke and got the better of the British at battles in Trenton and Princeton, New Jersey. Stung by these losses, the British commanders looked to recapture momentum, and they devised a strategy to separate the New England colonies from the rest of the country. The plan called for General John Burgoyne, one of the three generals under Military Governor Thomas Gates's command in Boston at the time of Bunker Hill, to lead his army down from Canada along the Hudson River corridor. They would join up with Howe's army, who would march north from New York to meet him.

Burgoyne soon began to make his presence felt in the Hudson Valley, making quick work of American resistance at Fort Ticonderoga on the shore of Lake Champlain and at other smaller forts nearby. Unfortunately, Burgoyne's bravado, miscalculation, and miscommunication eventually undermined his aggressive efforts and undid the British plan to isolate the New England colonies.

Burgoyne was executing his orders to meet Howe who, Burgoyne believed, was coming up from the south, when Howe suddenly changed his plans. Instead of marching up the Hudson Valley, Howe decided to head south and attack Philadelphia, the seat of the American government. It was nine months after Trenton and Princeton, and General Howe was determined to turn the tables on a more confident Washington. Howe scored consecutive wins of his own in Pennsylvania at Brandywine Creek in early September 1777 and at Germantown in early October. These battles enabled the British Army to capture Philadelphia, causing the members of Congress to flee on the morning of September 19 to the city of York, 100 miles away.

Despite the British misalignment, Burgoyne's advance in upstate New York signaled large-scale fighting was likely. And so, word went out across the northeast for militia to support the American Northern Army under General Horatio Gates. Like many others in New England, William Prescott in Pepperell heard the call and responded. He decided to quit his retirement and rejoin the military, not as an officer as he had been, but as an ordinary soldier, a private. He was 51 years old.

Documents at the Massachusetts Archives indicate that Prescott joined the company of Captain James Hosley, a part of Jonathan Reed's regiment drawn from Middlesex County. An entry in the Massachusetts Muster and Payrolls indicates that Prescott was engaged on September 26, "Serving as a Volunteer" in a unit raised from the abutting towns of Ashby, Townshend, and Pepperell.[81] Prescott is listed as a private soldier, but the muster roll also recognizes him as a former colonel.

William Prescott wasn't sure what kind of a situation he was heading into, but as before he was willing to risk physical harm for the goal in which he believed. Displaying the courage of his convictions, think of the example Prescott was setting, at 51 years of age, for the others from Middlesex County that volunteered with him. At least some of that courage must have rubbed off on his fellow troops and reinforced their determination as they prepared to support General Gates' forces in New York.

The ensuing trek from Pepperell to Saratoga was a long one, roughly 140 miles. The distant town, soon to be the center of one of the most momentous battles in American history, was about 35 miles north of Albany and already a draw for new settlers due to the region's rolling, forested landscape and pristine waters. It was fall, and while the days were relatively warm, the nights were getting darker and cooler. Frost was possible overnight, and Prescott certainly wanted to get to his destination as quickly as possible.

I needed to find out more about Prescott's activities associated with this campaign, so I emailed National Park Service ranger and military historian, Eric Schnitzer, whom I had been referred to by historian John Ferling. John described Eric as very knowledgeable on the Saratoga battle, adding he would likely be a valuable resource. To my good fortune, Eric responded immediately to my outreach.

After our first interaction, I found Ferling's assessment of Eric to be dead on the mark. Eric reminded me of all the National Park Service rangers I've met; he was responsive, knowledgeable, and dedicated to his work. "Prescott was indeed at Saratoga," Eric confirmed, "but he was not part of any of the fighting, as he arrived too late." Eric told me, however, that Prescott was there for the American siege of Burgoyne's army, as well as the surrender ceremony.

To make the long journey to Saratoga, I wondered how Prescott would have gotten there, by horse or on foot. Eric said that, although he couldn't be sure, Prescott most likely would have marched to Saratoga with his unit as opposed to riding his horse. Walking 140 miles is no mean feat, particularly for someone Prescott's age. Eric explained, "The Army did not pay for the upkeep of horses owned by individuals, and those who did ride to Saratoga were given orders to have their horse sent back home." So, middle-aged Prescott seems to have plodded along, day after day, up and down declivitous summits like the rest of the New Englanders in his regiment.

Traveling at a consistent pace of 20 miles per day, and allotting for rest, it would have taken Prescott and the other 66 volunteers from Middlesex

County more than a week to complete the journey. The troops might have stayed in roadside inns where they could have had hot meals and been able to refresh themselves with a bath. If such accommodations were not available, they would have had to camp out along the road and tough it out. This was not an unknown experience for Prescott, but one that I'm sure he wouldn't have relished. It is fair to say that the aging Prescott's experience as a common private in the army was not pleasant. At Saratoga, the lower-level soldiers slept in tents—if they were lucky enough to be assigned to one. If they weren't among the lucky ones, some soldiers coped by making brush shelters, while others fashioned hovels out of plank boards. The cold nights gave way to damp, bone-chilling mornings. Prescott weathered these conditions, and there is no sign that he regretted coming out of retirement to endure this ordeal.

When Prescott got to Saratoga, the jig was already up for the commander of the British forces. Burgoyne, who never got word of Howe's change of direction until it was too late for him, was in dire straits even before Prescott left for Saratoga. On September 19, Burgoyne's army battled General Horatio Gates's troops at Freeman's Farm and then again at nearby Bemis Heights on October 7. As their names suggest, the area was a combination of farmlands and rolling hills. Thick forests surrounded the battlefields. The Americans and British squared off in two hot fights, with the still-loyal Benedict Arnold rallying the Americans in a famous charge, before the British began to retreat. Burgoyne's embattled troops were then aggressively pursued north by the Americans to the village of Saratoga. At this point, Gates's soldiers far outnumbered Burgoyne's army, and the fight settled into a siege. Besides being outnumbered, Burgoyne's troops were also short of supplies, having moved far from their base of support, and so they were not in an effective form to turn the tide.

Wishing to know more about Prescott's actions at Saratoga and to see the terrain for myself, I suggested to my wife, Mary, that we take a trip to Saratoga National Park. Mary was less interested than I was, but in the end she consented. As a result, on a rainy April Saturday in Boston, I set the car's GPS to the Saratoga National Historical Park in Stillwater, and Mary and I got underway. The three-hour journey through exceedingly wet conditions did not dampen my spirits, and a smile creased my face when we turned onto the driveway to the historic battlefield. The 3,400-acre Saratoga National Park spans the woods, trails, and camps of the respective armies, and boasts of a winding, 10-mile paved road that is enjoyed by cyclists as well as those interested in the battle. The site of Burgoyne's surrender and the commemorative Saratoga Monument are farther north, close to the Philip Schuyler Country House.

Mary and I pulled up to the Visitor Center, an attractive facility with a splendid view of a portion of the battlefield, and we bounded inside. Well, one of us bounded. Being the only visitors that day, probably due to the rain, we were met by the small staff who gave us their full attention. We watched a short movie about the battle (something I always do at these facilities), examined the displayed memorabilia, and chatted with staff about the two important battles.

As I learned from Eric Schnitzer, foot soldier William Prescott had no major role at Saratoga. He did not oversee strategy; he did not lead troops; he may not have even shot his gun. However, it was the case that the majority of Horatio Gates's Northern Army present at Saratoga did not fight in the battles; they just stayed behind their defensive lines. So, even if Prescott had been there in time, he still may not have confronted the British on the battlefield.

On October 17, with his discouraged troops in severe distress, Burgoyne was forced to surrender his army of approximately 5,900 British and Hessian soldiers in order to avoid a slaughter.[82] It was a momentous occasion, as it was the first time the British Army had ever surrendered on the field of battle. Burgoyne was disgraced, and his capitulation sent shock waves through England. The ignominy of losing an entire army was a startling blow to his colleagues, the Parliament, and the king. With this, the war took another monumental turn; in fact, it has been proclaimed the turning point of the war. Prescott must have been overjoyed when Burgoyne raised the white flag. In his last major military confrontation, Prescott had fled headlong up Manhattan Island to avoid capture or worse. He must have known the significance of this event a year later and been glad he was there to participate in it.

The surrender took place on a bluff overlooking a sweeping meadow surrounded by old-growth forest. It would take a second trip to the park for me, under sunny skies this time, to walk the battlefields and the more distant site of the siege and surrender of Burgoyne's army. There is a memorial marking the historic surrender spot, with granite engravings, a field cannon, and a plaque quoting General Horatio Gates to the president of Congress, dated October 18, 1777, that says: "I have the Satisfaction to present Your Excellency with the Convention of Saratoga, By Which His Excellency Lieutenant General Burgoyne, has Surrendered Himself, & his whole Army into my Hands."

It isn't clear where Prescott and his fellow Massachusetts soldiers were standing while the surrender ceremony took place, but I hoped he would have been able to see the moment Burgoyne handed over his sword. Burgoyne had watched the besieged Prescott from Copp's Hill during the battle of Bunker Hill; now it was Prescott's turn to witness Burgoyne's stinging defeat.

Shortly after the surrender ceremony, on November 9, Prescott was dismissed from the army—along with others in Hosley's company—and he made the long return journey back to his Pepperell farm, leaving behind the Continental Army permanently.[83] He was reimbursed three pounds and 15 shillings for his month and a half of service. No doubt Prescott's return to Pepperell must have pleased his wife and son, as well as other friends and relatives in the greater Groton–Pepperell area. If Prescott entertained any thoughts of getting back in the action again, a serious injury on his farm seems to have assured his lasting retirement from the war.[84]

While William Prescott was done with fighting in the Revolutionary War, I suspected that he was probably not done with the cause itself. After all, nothing had really been achieved yet. The British were still a formidable foe and held significant territory both in the North and the South. Although the French were now coming to the Americans' aid, the contest was definitely still in doubt. I did not see Prescott stepping off the stage yet. So I headed back to Pepperell and several research libraries to find out if Prescott had any further role in the continuing drama regarding independence and nationhood.

Undated photo of the home of William Prescott, Pepperell, MA. (Wikimedia Commons)

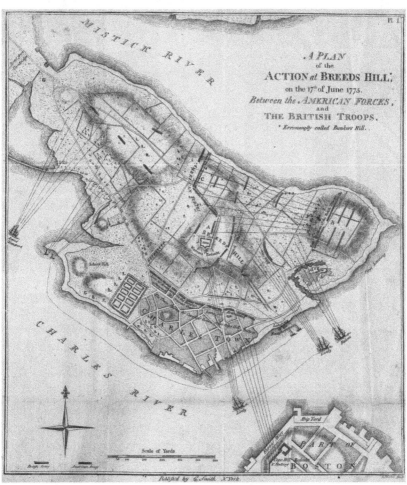

Map depicting Charlestown, site of the battle of Bunker Hill, June 17, 1775. (Normal B. Leventhal Map & Education Center, Boston Public Library)

Artemas Ward, Major General of the New England Army during the outbreak of the Revolutionary War. (Wikimedia Commons/Harvard Art Museums)

Portrait of Joseph Warren, by John Singleton Copley. (Wikimedia Commons/Museum of Fine Arts Boston)

Statue of William Prescott in Bunker Hill National Historical Park, Charlestown, MA, dedicated June 17, 1881. (Wikimedia Commons)

General Israel Putnam, leader of Connecticut troops at the battle of Bunker Hill. (Library of Congress)

John Stark, Colonel of New Hampshire troops at the battle of Bunker Hill. (Wikimedia Commons)

Thomas Knowlton of Connecticut fought at Bunker Hill and was killed in action at the battle of Harlem Heights, New York City, 1776. (Wikimedia Commons)

General Thomas Gage, British Military Governor of Massachusetts 1774–75. (Wikimedia Commons/ Yale Center for British Art)

General William Howe, British field commander at the battle of Bunker Hill. (Wikimedia Commons)

General Henry Clinton, participated in the battle of Bunker Hill and later succeeded William Howe as leader of British troops in North America. (Wikimedia Commons)

General John Burgoyne was in Boston during the battle of Bunker Hill and surrendered his army at the battle of Saratoga, October 17, 1777. (Wikimedia Commons/The Frick Collection)

The Death of General Warren at the battle of Bunker's Hill, 17 June, 1775, by John Trumbull. (Wikimedia Commons/Museum of Fine Arts Boston)

William Prescott statue and Bunker Hill Monument at Bunker Hill National Historical Park, Charlestown, MA. (Wikimedia Commons)

Statue of Joseph Warren in the Lodge building at Bunker Hill National Historical Park, Charlestown, MA. (Wikimedia Commons)

The Surrender of General Burgoyne at Saratoga, by John Trumbull. (Wikimedia Commons/United States Capitol)

CHAPTER 10

The War Ends, Then Rebellion

As 1776 was turning into 1777 and George Washington was improvising a strategy to keep his army alive, new governments were being created at the state level. The colonial charters had been abolished, and, even though the outcome of the war was very much in doubt, the Declaration of Independence insisted that America had broken free from monarchical rule. New state governments had to be formed and new constitutions had to be written to codify how the individual states would govern themselves. And so, the work began.

Establishing New Governments

Starting shortly after the publication of the Declaration of Independence, each state took the opportunity to consider putting in place a new governing constitution, and most availed themselves of it fairly quickly. This work garnered as much attention as anything that was going on with the war itself and, although the states did not know it at the time, it represented the first steps toward a new, national government.

By the end of 1776, six states had written new constitutions, including Virginia, North Carolina, Maryland, New Jersey, Delaware, and Pennsylvania. New York and Georgia wrote their new constitutions in 1777, and South Carolina approved its in 1778. However, the process for the rest of the former colonies took time. It wasn't until June 1780 that Massachusetts ratified its new constitution, while New Hampshire didn't institute its own until 1784. Remarkably, Rhode Island and Connecticut, whose original constitutions were written in 1633 and 1639 respectively, decided not to rewrite theirs either during or in the aftermath of the war. This might have been because in neither of these two longstanding state constitutions were there any references to the Crown. Connecticut eventually altered its state constitution in 1818, and Rhode Island did the same in 1842.

In parallel with the earliest state efforts, the Continental Congress decided it needed a national government to manage the new nation and, especially, the complex and critical war effort, while hostilities still existed between the United States and Great Britain. After lengthy deliberations, the Continental Congress finally reached an agreement on the form of government that it wanted to put in place in November 1777. This agreement, aimed to unify the states, was known as the Articles of Confederation. However, it wasn't until February 1781, more than three years later, that the Articles were finally ratified by all 13 states. They became effective a month later. The protracted nature of this process presaged how hard it would ultimately be to form a permanent, single national government with broad powers.

Though the Articles would only last for a little over six years, it was the first step in joining the 13 states in a common bond. As historian Gordon Wood has pointed out, a continental republic with a single government coalescing all the states was as nearly impossible in 1776 as erecting a monarchy.[1] In actuality, few Americans who lived through the process would have believed that the 13 states were forming a unified nation.

Since the Articles of Confederation were put together during wartime, they did not cause the comprehensive and contentious public discussion that the United States Constitution did later in the decade after the war had concluded.[2] To make it easier for the states to come together, Congress approved an article guaranteeing each state equal voting power. This arrangement showed that a confederation was being formed—an *alliance* of independent states, not a single, all-encompassing nation. Tellingly, once the articles were ratified by the 13 states, the Continental Congress became known as the "Confederation Congress," and the word *United* was not used.[3]

Although the articles had obvious deficiencies, they did confer important military powers on Congress that allowed it to raise an army, appoint a commander in chief, and negotiate treaties with foreign nations. The articles would get the states through the war, but it seemed unlikely that they would forge a strong, centralized structure that could govern in the aftermath. For one, the requirement of unanimity was simply too tough a criterion for many actions.

William Prescott was home in Pepperell at the start of 1777, back from the New York campaign, and he had a front row seat as the discussions for a new state constitution, as well as the Articles of Confederation, were underway. Something had to be done to put the state and the nation on solid governmental footing. A war needed to be won and mechanisms were needed to guarantee national security and financial solvency. The road ahead was not easy.

Amazingly, it took about as long for Massachusetts to institute a new state constitution as it did for the 13 states to reach agreement on the Articles of Confederation. Stoughton, Bellingham, and Pittsfield were the initial Massachusetts towns to argue for a new constitution.[4] In Massachusetts in 1776, towns elected representatives to a Provincial Congress. But that body did not have the legal authority to make or enforce laws. There was no governor; the state Congress was headed by a president.[5] Courts convened in some towns but not in others. The non-uniform situation was a prescription for disaster.

Dismayingly for a state so integral to the drive for self-governance, an initial attempt to put forth a new Massachusetts state covenant failed in 1778. Massachusetts citizens looked at what had been proposed and simply rejected the initial offering. Three reasons have been given for this.[6] First, voters objected to provisions that limited some citizens the right to vote. Second, it was feared that the newly proposed state constitution gave too much power to the governor. There was still a wariness regarding anything resembling monarchical power. And third, the new document did not provide a Bill of Rights, which many felt was necessary to guarantee certain liberties. The Massachusetts General Court then ordered that a selection of delegates from every town gather at a convention in September 1779 to try again to write a new constitution.

In Pepperell, the town assembled a public meeting in May 1779 "to see whether this Town chooseth at this time to have a new Constitution or form of Government made or not. And wither they will Impower the Representatives for the next year to vote for the Calling of a State Convention for the sole purpose of forming a new Constitution or to give any other Institution as shall be thought proper."[7]

William Prescott was right in the midst of these discussions, and, following the dictum of a more recent Massachusetts politician that "all politics is local," he would likely have favored a rigorous debate on the rights of Massachusetts citizens and what form of government would best ensure the state's future.[8] But again the lack of definitive documentation in the historical record prevents us from knowing what positions Prescott took as the work on the Massachusetts constitution played itself out. Did he actively engage in the debate, or was he more passive? On which side of the vote did Prescott stand? How did he react to the failure to pass the first proposed draft? I ached to find out, but nothing in the Pepperell town meeting records or anywhere else shed light on these queries and, unfortunately, Prescott did not leave any writings to explain his views.

One can imagine that he was at least pleased that stability was preserved in the state, which he most likely would have felt essential, particularly as a substantial landowner and prominent town administrator.

As the decade of the 1770s was ending and with Prescott once again sitting on an assortment of town committees and posts—including the vital Committees of Correspondence, Inspection, and Safety—he added one more position to his roster. In March 1779, Prescott was elected to a "committee to take care of the families of Continental Soldiers."[9] As various observers have attested, Prescott was sensitive to the war's veterans and their families, understanding only too well the tremendous hardships they had endured over the years-long struggle against Great Britain. So this assignment made logical sense, and Prescott poured his energies into it.

The War Drags On

While the states were forming new constitutions and a national confederation was taking shape, the war continued apace. In December 1777, Washington chose Valley Forge, about 18 miles northwest of Philadelphia, to put his weary and bedraggled army into winter quarters. However, the trek to Valley Forge was brutal, as it took the troops a week to travel just 13 miles through snow, sleet, and icy rain, only to arrive at a desolate destination.[10] Washington later wrote of the march to Valley Forge:

> To see men without clothes to cover their nakedness, without blankets to lay [sic] on, without shoes by which their marches might be traced by the blood from their feet, and almost as often without provisions as with; marching through frost and snow and at Christmas taking up their winter quarters within a day's march of the enemy, without a house or hut to cover them till they could be built, and submitting to it without a murmur is a mark of patience and obedience which in my opinion can scarcely be paralleled.[11]

Immediately, the army went to work erecting housing and other structures. In all, an estimated 1,500–2,000 structures were built to house and manage Washington's 12,000 troops and support personnel.[12] Valley Forge thus became the first large-scale encampment of the Continental Army.[13] Washington saw the dreariness of his troops and told his men, "I will share in your hardships and partake of every inconvenience," and to a great extent he did.[14]

According to hospital records, at any point in time, only about one quarter of the troops—or about 3,000–4,000 men—were fit for duty.[15] The troops stayed at Valley Forge for six months, from December 19, 1777 to June 19, 1778. Estimates are that 1,700–2,000 men died of disease, exacerbated by malnutrition and exposure to the cold.[16]

News of Valley Forge had a sobering effect on the populace, and the camp became the quintessential symbol of stoic survival amidst punishing circumstances. The very existence of the Continental Army was in doubt.

With his deep well of empathy for the soldiers, there's no doubt that Prescott would have been devastated by the news of Valley Forge. Like everyone else, he must have wondered if the army could hold on. This was the nadir of the war. Yet historian Joseph Ellis saw something else in Valley Forge. To him, the real meaning of Valley Forge was that "the character of the War for Independence changed from a clash of armies to a competition for the control of the countryside."[17] It was generally believed that if the war was a conventional contest between British and American military might, the Americans could not win. But if the war was a protracted conflict for the hearts and minds of American citizens, the British would almost certainly lose.

Then, just when it seemed like the situation couldn't get worse, General Benedict Arnold—who was widely thought to be the best field commander the Americans, having distinguished himself in several battles including at Valcour, Bemis Heights, Freeman's Farm, and Saratoga—had defected to the British.[18] When Washington learned of Arnold's treachery, he turned to his aide, the Marquis de Lafayette, and dispiritedly asked, "Whom can we trust now?" To Prescott, such treachery was diabolical.

At the start of 1781, the war was approaching its sixth year, and there seemed to be no end in sight. Looking to break the stalemate, the British turned their attention to the southern states, where they thought the prospects for gain were brighter. But General Charles Cornwallis, now leading the British forces in the region, became convinced that southern Tories were not rushing to join the British Army as expected. Furthermore, roughly half of Cornwallis's 8,500 troops had been lost in the fighting in Charleston, Camden, King's Mountain, Cowpens, and Guilford Courthouse. Growing short of men, Cornwallis made a fateful decision to march his army to Yorktown, Virginia, looking for a safe site for a naval base that would enable General Henry Clinton, who had succeeded William Howe as overall commander of British forces, to provide him reinforcements or evacuate him.[19]

Washington ordered the Marquis de Lafayette to do everything in his power to prevent Cornwallis from escaping the Yorktown peninsula.[20] American and French land and sea forces laid siege to the area and began pounding away at the British fortifications. In a penultimate action, Alexander Hamilton, who had hankered for a field command for years, volunteered for a dangerous mission in which he captured one of the British lines of defense. Then, after heavy American artillery bombardment on October 16 and 17, Cornwallis raised a flag of truce. At 2:00 p.m. on October 19, Cornwallis surrendered his army. More than 8,000 prisoners were taken. It was precisely six and a half years since the first shots of the war were fired on Lexington Green in Massachusetts.

A humbled Cornwallis claimed illness and did not attend the surrender ceremony. Instead, he sent a stand-in, Brigadier General Charles O'Hara. In response, and sensing a slight, Washington sent his second-in-command, General Benjamin Lincoln, to accept O'Hara's sword. It was another display of honor on Washington's part; he would not take the sword from a commander below his rank, even though he must have relished that moment for a long time. When Lord North in Downing Street was informed of Cornwallis's surrender, he exclaimed, "Oh God, it is all over."

Joy swept through the colonies. Far from the battlefield, but, with his heart still with the American troops carrying on the fight, William Prescott must have rejoiced at the unbelievable news. While the war did not officially end until 1783, this was a great relief to a war-weary nation. Soon Prescott could truly set aside any more military concerns as the British war effort was effectively done. Prescott could direct all of his attention to issues associated with the new form of governance in Massachusetts, along with his civic responsibilities in Pepperell.

The World Turned Upside Down

By late 1782, neither side in the war was eager to see any more effusion of blood. An American delegation that included John Adams, John Jay, Henry Laurens, Benjamin Franklin, and William Temple Franklin was sent to Paris to negotiate a final peace accord.[21] The American Congress had indicated several terms: British recognition of American independence, the removal of the British Army from the United States, Nova Scotia was to be ceded to the United States, and all territory extending west to the Mississippi River was to be recognized as part of the United States. In addition, Congress wanted American fishing rights in and around Newfoundland to be recognized, and they wanted navigation rights on the Mississippi River to the 31st parallel.[22] The treaty also specified that Canada would remain a British property and Britain was to return East and West Florida to Spain.[23]

On November 30, 1782, the proposed peace treaty was signed in Paris. The preliminary agreement was then carried to Philadelphia on March 12, 1783 for final approval. For dramatic effect, George Washington promptly sat on the news for more than a month, waiting to announce it on April 19, 1783, the eighth anniversary of shots fired at Lexington and Concord. The treaty was adopted by Congress, formally ending the Revolutionary War. Towns across the country began to address the internationally accepted reality: American self-rule.

In May, William Prescott, now closing on 60 years of age, was chosen to represent Pepperell in the Massachusetts General Court. This was a high honor.[24] In the report publicizing the news, it was also announced that the town had unanimously voted that:

> …it is the opinion of this Town [Pepperell] that those persons known by the name of Tories and Absentees ought never to be suffered to Return to this or any other of the United States…
>
> Also unanimously voted the following Instructions that the Representative [William Prescott] use his utmost Endeavor to prevent from returning to this Commonwealth all those persons Commonly known by the names of the Absentees Refugees and Tories…
>
> Also voted that the Representative use his influence that neither officers or soldiers of the Continental Army have any further allowances for their services than Justice Requires and that no pensions be allowed to able Bodies Efective [sic] officers nor Soldiers.[25]

There was to be no tolerance in Pepperell for anyone who had not been part of the patriotic cause. As in any war—but especially in one that persisted for so long and produced such hardship—there were deep resentments that were hard to overcome. The Pepperell townspeople were tired of the sacrifices they had to make and the interruptions to their daily lives, and thus were not going to let bygones be bygones, at least not in the short term. William Prescott was designated to help make sure that enemies of the Commonwealth would not return and escape accountability.

The war was over, but it had severely hurt average Americans economically and, like most citizens, those in Pepperell were eager to move on with their lives. They were fed up with the amount of money spent on the war, and they did not want to be compelled to contribute any more funds than they deemed reasonable. They felt that they needed to husband their financial resources, so they decided to cut off funding of the army and its veterans, aside from those who had suffered permanent injuries. Not surprisingly, though, Prescott continued to be supportive of aid to veterans and their families, which endeared him to those who bore the heaviest burdens of the protracted conflict.

William Prescott's military career was truly done with the conclusion of the war, but I had learned he participated in yet another event that had significant consequences for the ultimate development of the United States. This time, the issue was purely a domestic controversy known as Shays's Rebellion.

Confronting Insurrection

In the early 1780s, in order to pay for war debts, most states had raised taxes to levels several times higher than they were before 1776. This relied largely on unpopular regressive taxes on both persons and property. New York and

Pennsylvania, which received substantial revenue from taxes on imports, were the exceptions. By mid-decade, the economy in Massachusetts was in terrible shape, and individual debts were expected to be paid in specie (i.e., coins, not notes), which was in very short supply. If they did not have the money to pay their debts, then farmers, in particular, were forced by the courts to sell their farms to obtain the required money, and those who could not meet their obligations were put in jail.

In the backcountry of Massachusetts, hostility toward state authority, which had been festering for some time, resurfaced again. This was much to the dismay of Governor James Bowdoin.[26] Revolutionary veterans, who should have been basking in the glow of their victory, held the most fervent negative feelings. Particularly annoying to many old soldiers, and more generally to citizens living in the central and western parts of the state, were new powers that the state legislature granted to the governor and the governor's council.[27]

The intensifying anger turned into a strident rebellion in the late months of 1786. Protests in rural Massachusetts led to the organization of a sizable insurgent group that called themselves "Regulators," a reference to a movement in the late 1760s in North Carolina that had sought to reform corrupt government practices. Then, on August 29, 1786, a band of protesters gathered in Northampton in western Massachusetts and prevented the county court from sitting. A Revolutionary War veteran named Daniel Shays, who had fought at Lexington, Concord, Bunker Hill, and Saratoga, took part in this action and assumed a major role in the burgeoning insurgent movement. Because of his significant involvement, the insurrection that would emerge would bear the name Shays's Rebellion.

To the east, several other key insurgents came from Middlesex County, and Groton in particular, such as another former soldier, Job Shattuck. When I learned this, my thoughts immediately went to William Prescott, and it didn't take long to find him associated with this momentous event—although the more prominent Prescott involved in trying to quell the rebellion was his younger brother, Oliver.

To bone up on the revolt, I contacted Leonard Richards, a now-retired University of Massachusetts history professor and author of a respected book on Shays's Rebellion, asking what he knew about William Prescott's involvement in the conflict. Professor Richards, fully settled in his retirement, suggested I contact Tom Callahan of Groton, who had impressed him with his knowledge of the insurrection from work he had done in the early 1990s. This was another unexpected lead, and, as I had learned, sometimes you can uncover valuable information by stepping off the beaten path to follow a new or unforeseen avenue of inquiry. Based on Professor Richards's recommendation, I went about tracking down Tom.

The Groton Historical Society knew Tom quite well and gave me his contact information straight away. I'm pretty certain Tom was surprised that someone had reached out to him about work he had done roughly 30 years prior. Tom, who is in his early 70s and also retired like me, has done meaningful historical research into the town of Groton in the late 1770s. Tom sports a trim beard, now more salt than pepper, and the friendly countenance of a former high school teacher, which is what he is. What I swiftly learned when we started communicating is that Tom is a clear-eyed lover of history who is quite willing to call things as they are—or were, in the case of Shays's Rebellion.

In our initial conversation, I quickly sensed Tom's passion for the work he had done, which was extremely helpful in describing the political climate of the era. He provided insight into the split in the town between the two major early American families, the Prescotts and the Shattucks, over the Shays uprising. "I'm not a big fan of Oliver Prescott," Tom informed me right away. "Lots of people were hurting in the region after the war, and Oliver Prescott did not seem to be very sympathetic." In a subsequent face-to-face meeting with Tom in Groton, he enthusiastically took me on a meandering bike tour of the town, pointing out various historical sites and expounding on the Prescotts (especially Oliver) and the Shattucks (especially Job) while we stopped at a roadside coffee shop.

Tom also passed along a copy of the book *Artful and Designing Men: The Trials of Job Shattuck and the Regulation of 1786–1787*, by Gary Shattuck, a half-nephew of Job Shattuck many generations removed. Like the cautions regarding the Prescott genealogical history, the information provided in this descendant's account of Job Shattuck's involvement in Shays's Rebellion, while deemed accurate, should be carefully considered.

In order for me to get an even fuller picture of what happened, though, Tom said, "You ought to go to the American Antiquarian Society (AAS) in Worcester; it has a great collection of historical information and you'll probably find useful material there." It was a good recommendation. Like the other research libraries and repositories I had visited, the AAS is a deeply respected and rich storehouse of early American documents. It was founded in 1812 by Revolutionary War patriot and printer Isaiah Thomas, and currently describes itself as "a national research library and community of learners dedicated to discovering and sharing a deep understanding of the American past."[28] When dating my future wife, Mary, a proud native of Worcester, I had frequently driven by this stately building with nary a notice of it. Frankly, I didn't even know what the building was at the time. Now I was hoping the AAS would unlock additional clues to William Prescott's past.

The red-brick, Doric-columned AAS building on Salisbury Street is a short walk from the Worcester Polytechnic Institute and the city's distinguished Art Museum, making the area an impressive amalgam of art, culture, and education. With a white dome hovering behind the AAS's elegant façade, the building might remind you of Jefferson's Monticello. I visited mid-week when I hoped it would not be crowded and I could buttonhole a staffer or two to help my investigation.

Checking in, I received a membership card and deposited my shoulder bag containing pens, notebooks, and other verboten items in a small locker off the vestibule. I was getting to be a pro at these procedures and quickly secured a spot at an oak table near the first-floor reference desk. I was given a brief introduction to the collection and learned how to access materials, then set free to begin my work. I perused the online catalog and submitted a number of requests.

Fortunately, I found a number of documents about Prescott that I had not come across in the other repositories I had accessed. Some of these were about his life in Groton, while others addressed Shays's Rebellion. Together with additional books and papers, I set out to determine what Prescott had done as the famous insurrection took shape and expanded across Massachusetts.

Friends Now Enemies

In September and October 1786, rebellious protests took place in a number of towns across the state, including Great Barrington, Worcester, Concord, and Taunton. Notably, one of the main insurgents in Middlesex County in Central Massachusetts was Job Shattuck of Groton. As a 19-year-old, Job Shattuck was a member of William Prescott's militia regiment that took part in the expedition to expel the French from Nova Scotia during the French and Indian War in 1755. In fact, Shattuck was a longtime captain in Groton's militia and had also distinguished himself in the Revolutionary War.[29] His patriotic bona fides were unquestioned. Now, 31 years later, he was opposing the Massachusetts government and coming up against his longtime neighbors and associates—the Prescott brothers—both in thought and deed.

While Oliver Prescott got deeply involved in rebuffing Shays's Rebellion, older brother William did not sit back idly while the local insurrection played itself out. As a rural farmer, Prescott could easily have been sympathetic to the rebellious cause, like many of his fellow Pepperell citizens. However, William did not align himself in that way. Instead, he stayed committed to the state government and its new taxing and judicial policies, as controversial as they were.

The Prescott and Shattuck families were two of the most notable and prominent families in the neighboring Middlesex towns of Groton and Pepperell. These abutting communities were listed as separate towns in the Massachusetts Property Valuation of 1771, even though Pepperell was a district of Groton at the time and not incorporated separately until 1775. The two small towns shared a longtime, common heritage, and the citizens knew each other quite well. In 1771, Job Shattuck was the only Shattuck taxpayer in Groton, but there were 22 Shattuck taxpayers in Pepperell. Conversely, while William Prescott was the only Prescott taxpayer in Pepperell at that time, there were five Prescott taxpayers in Groton, led by William's brothers, James and Oliver.

In terms of outlook, the Prescotts and the Shattucks held different views regarding how they thought the economy should be developed and the role of the state government in managing the Commonwealth. Job Shattuck, and most likely other Shattucks, favored an agricultural-oriented economy, while the Prescotts backed a more diversified, multi-dimensional economy that also emphasized manufacturing and trade. These divergent economic views could explain how each family reacted to Shays's movement.

The Prescotts' domination in Groton dated back to Jonas Prescott's settlement there in the late 1600s. The baton was passed from generation to generation without controversy or interruption. For nearly 30 years during the revolutionary era, the Prescotts held a tight grip on the management of Groton.[30] In the period from 1760 to 1786, one or the other (or both) of William Prescott's brothers, James and Oliver, held the position of selectman for 25 of those 27 years. Oliver was a selectman for 22 years and James for 17. Only three other Groton men served as selectmen 10 or more years during that period. Moreover, Oliver and James overlapped 14 of those years, 12 consecutively. Oliver served eight years by himself and James three years by himself. Given that the Groton selectmen committee only had five members, the Prescott influence was unsurpassed.

By contrast, Job Shattuck was selectman in Groton for only three years—1778, 1779, and 1781. In Groton, the average tenure of the 10 selectmen not named Prescott between 1760 and 1786 was six years, while the two Prescotts' average tenure was 19 and a half years. This was a remarkable record and illustrated the esteem in which each man was held and the reluctance of the town to alter its slate of selectmen very much. It is fair to say that the

Prescott family held a strong grip on the direction of Groton for a very long time. It is quite possible that this may have caused some resentment or jealousy among some of the citizenry, including Job Shattuck. William Prescott also had a long tenure as a Pepperell selectman, and was involved in Pepperell government for large portions of the 1750s to the 1780s, with the exception of those years when he was in active military duty.

Despite the longstanding, admired status of the Shattucks in Groton, by 1786, Oliver Prescott and Governor James Bowdoin considered Job Shattuck to be one of the area's most pronounced troublemakers. Job had been an irritant to state government for years. As early as October 1781, while Job was a Groton selectman alongside Oliver Prescott, he had already exhibited his contempt for the new state government and its taxing policies, convincing the town to oppose the tax the state had imposed on it. But when that failed to stop the collection of the tax, Shattuck, along with Oliver Parker, led a mob of 17 Groton citizens against the town's two constables who had the responsibility to collect it. This tax conflict spurred on by Job Shattuck was followed up, two years later, in October 1783, when he led another mob with "staves and clubs" against other local tax collectors.[31]

Then, in September 1786, Shattuck, aged 50, took a major role in leading the Shaysite insurgents in Middlesex County. Following protests at the Worcester County courts in late summer, Shattuck next set his sights on the judicial courts in Concord—about 20 miles down the road from Groton—which were scheduled to open on September 12. The demonstrations focused on the Court of Common Pleas and the Court of General Sessions of the Peace, of which James and Oliver Prescott were judges. At that time, the Concord Courthouse sat in the center of town, very near the currently still-operating, historic Colonial Inn, which was established in 1716. The Colonial Inn was one of the larger places that stored arms and provisions before the April 19, 1775 confrontation with the British. The courthouse was also just about a half mile from the famous North Bridge. Standing at the site on a visit I paid the town in March 2024, I could not help but envision the tense, chaotic, and rebellious scene from September 1786.

As the court's opening date approached that year, Governor Bowdoin was under pressure to come up with a solution to the protests that were gaining steam in the state. Between September 7 and September 11, Bowdoin met with a group of government officials, including Samuel Adams, to discuss the situation.[32] Adams supported using military force against the protestors, along with inflicting harsh punishments. Bowdoin also consulted with two judges scheduled to sit in Concord—Oliver Prescott and Samuel Philips

Savage—who, although concerned, advised Bowdoin not to call out the militia so that "some lenient measures might be adopted."[33]

A group of roughly 80–100 insurrectionists from Groton and led by Job Shattuck were joined by a similar number of supporters from Worcester County. They all descended on Concord. The majority of these men were in their 20s, with the average age being 26. Assisting Shattuck were Oliver Parker of Groton, Nathan Smith and John Kelsey from Shirley, and Peter Butterfield from Townshend. Three other Shattucks came to Concord from Groton as well, along with 12 others from Pepperell. This was fairly typical. Of the 74 Groton men who were involved in the action, 48 were brothers, fathers, or brothers-in-law to at least one other participant.[34]

By 5:00 p.m. on Monday, September 11, the insurrectionists had taken possession of the courthouse in Concord without any opposition. The judges were not there, since they were not due to sit until the following day. So as not to be involved in a direct confrontation with the contingent from their hometown of Groton, James and Oliver Prescott stayed away from the area, which was the prudent decision.[35]

The next day, a Tuesday, broke with cloudy and threatening skies. The Concord judges gathered at Jones' Tavern, while many citizens from the surrounding towns assembled in the Concord meetinghouse. As tension mounted and with rain pelting down, insurrectionist Nathan Smith marched through town and came back with about 90 armed men, including groups from Hampshire and Worcester counties. Another group from Westford also descended on Concord, led by Colonel John Robinson, who had participated in the fighting at Concord and Bunker Hill in 1775 and who was Job Shattuck's superior during the Boston Siege.[36] This put the protestors' strength at 250–300 men. Job Shattuck, surrounded by this mob at the courthouse, released a one-page statement that read:

> Court of the general sessions of the peace and Court of common pleas, shall not enter this Court House until such time as the people shall have a redress of grievances they labor under at present, which will be set forth in a petition of remonstrance to the next General Court.[37]
>
> Concord Sep. 12, 1786 Job Shattuck

It has been noted that Shattuck's statement, which essentially sealed his fate as an insurrectionist, was very reminiscent of the one that the Prescott brothers had patriotically issued regarding the same courts in the aftermath of the Intolerable Acts of 1774.[38] The difference now was that Shattuck's position was against the existing government of Massachusetts and therefore was deemed a treasonous act.

In response to this pronouncement, a committee was formed consisting of concerned leaders from several local towns to negotiate with the insurrectionists. This group was headed by Doctor Josiah Bartlett and included Colonel John Buttrick, who had acted so memorably during the Concord Alarm, and, as I was not surprised to learn, William Prescott. Although Pepperell had not sent a delegation to Concord, William was in attendance as an "interested person" and, no doubt, to support his brothers.[39] It had been nearly a decade after Prescott had retired from the Continental Army and 21 years since Bunker Hill. He was now 60 years old. Even so, William was willing to step into an explosive situation once again to see that stability would be restored in the state.

This action by Prescott was a clear-cut example of civil courage. Unlike the bravery Prescott demonstrated on the battlefield, here he was taking a non-violent stance to intervene in an escalating civil matter that was threatening to upend governmental harmony in the state. Momentum was on the side of the insurrectionists, at least away from Boston, and it was difficult to see how the circumstances could be defused. The possibility of widespread violence was also a distinct possibility, since neither side in the conflict seemed willing to compromise. County-by-county, town-by-town, proverbial dividing lines were being drawn in the sand.

In a region that was decidedly pro-Shays, where individuals were very aware on which side their neighbors stood, William Prescott took a contrarian stance. He was not supporting the Shaysites. In doing so, he was willing to suffer the likelihood of being ostracized by those in his community and throughout the region. No doubt, he knew this locally unpopular position could potentially damage his reputation, perhaps irreparably. He did it anyway. Of course, if the confrontation with the rebels escalated, Prescott could also suddenly find himself in physical danger as well. The men around Job Shattuck carried guns and clubs, and were in an excited state.

It is altogether fitting, given his moral character, that William Prescott took this courageous posture. His brothers, especially Oliver, strongly opposed the rebels, and as judges in Concord were personally more affected by the insurrection. The Prescotts thought they were on the right side of the legal and political argument, and so they aligned themselves with the General Court and the governor. While the Prescotts might have been trying to preserve the status quo of a system in which they were excelling, for William, it would also have been a patriotic decision and in accord with his support for a new, more effective governing apparatus. By traveling to Concord, Prescott's aim was to quell the spread of the rebellion, which he viewed as dangerous to the state.[40] The newly formed negotiating committee then issued the following order: "Voted that Doc. Josiah Bartlett, the Honorable Joseph Hosmer, Col. William Prescott, Mr. Sam White, and Col. John Buttrick be a Committee to confer with a body of armed men paraded before the Court House and to know their views and designs in their assembling."[41]

How incredible it must have been for William Prescott to come face-to-face with his well-known neighbor and former captain to try to convince him not to go down this dangerous path. Prescott had personally recruited Shattuck in 1755 for the Nova Scotia expedition, attested to his good behavior during the Concord Alarm, and endorsed his promotion to captain in the militia.[42] Now, the insurgency had created a severe and potentially permanent rift between the two men and their two families.

After receiving this new Committee in Concord, Job Shattuck then wrote another note on the reverse side of his first, saying:

1/4 past three o'clock [September 12, 1786]

Since writing the within, it is agreed that the Court of Sessions may open and adjoin till thee last Tuesday in November next without going to the Court House.

William Prescott and the other committee members went back to the meetinghouse with Shattuck's amended statement, and around four o'clock they sent word to the awaiting judges that they would meet with them shortly. When the committee convened with the judges, they explained what had happened and told the judges, "The only method we could take, all circumstances taken into consideration, was to return to our respective homes without attempting anything."[43] The committee clearly wanted to avoid an armed confrontation. In this delicate balancing act, the judges then asked the committee to go back to the meetinghouse and "procure, if possible, the opinion of the whole body."

The committee returned to the assembly, got the people to vote on the resolution, and visited the judges again with a note, saying:

That it be recommended to the Honorable Judges of the Court of Common Pleas and Court of Sessions to suspend for the present term the execution of all public business on account of an armed force now paraded to oppose their proceedings.[44]

Concord September 12, 1786
Order of the Committee
Josiah Bartlett, Chairman

The committee said that the vote reflected, "The opinion of ¾ if not ⅞ of all the Gentlemen from the several towns." The judges then adjourned their meeting and left Concord. William Prescott must have been very happy that no blood was shed, and he headed back to Pepperell.

Thus, the conflict ended and violence was averted, but the primary issue presented by the insurrectionists—the crushing taxing policies leading to farm liquidations—was not resolved. Protests continued around the state, with the court in Great Barrington prevented from sitting by roughly 800 farmers, and the court in Taunton similarly interrupted by around 500 men.[45]

These sizable demonstrations prompted James Warren, head of the Massachusetts Provincial Congress, to write to John Adams on October 22, saying, "We are now in a state of Anarchy and Confusion bordering on Civil War." Meanwhile, Governor Bowdoin was able to keep the courts open in larger towns by calling out the state militia. Oliver Prescott responded to the crisis by riding with the militia to Cambridge to oppose the court there closing.

The rebellion was getting bigger and was at its most widespread in the western part of the state where Daniel Shays resided. Overall, Hampshire County produced roughly half of all the insurgents. The region had twice as many rebels as Worcester County to its east and five times as many as Berkshire County to its west. In Middlesex County, closer to Boston, where Job Shattuck was a leading figure, nearly all of the insurgents came from just four contiguous towns—Shirley, Townshend, Groton, and Pepperell.

These repeated disturbances involving Job Shattuck seem to have exhausted the patience of Oliver Prescott, who then persuaded Governor Bowdoin to arrest Shattuck and his allies—although the governor may not have needed much convincing. Using the authority granted to him in 1781 to arrest anyone he deemed dangerous to the Commonwealth, Oliver Prescott released the following pronouncement on November 28: ·

> To the Governor and Council of Massachusetts
>   I hereby certify that Job Shattuck and Oliver Parker, Gentlemen, and Benjamin Page, Yeoman, all of Groton and Nathan Smith and John Kelsey of Shirley, Gentlemen,...have been active in the late rebellion and stirring up the people to oppose government, are therefore dangerous persons and pray a warrant may be issued to restrain them of their personal liberty.[46]
> Oliver Prescott
> Boston, November 28, 1786

Governor Bowdoin subsequently issued warrants for the arrest of the five men, all of whom were veterans of the revolution. As a result, early on the morning of November 29, 300 horsemen raised by the governor and led by Boston attorney Benjamin Hichborn and his Harvard classmate John Warren struck out in search of the primary rebel leaders: Shattuck, Parker, and Page.[47] They were joined by Sheriff Laommi Baldwin and Colonel Henry Woods of Pepperell and about 100 additional men.

The next day, a group of 12 men were able to track down Shattuck and pursued him as he tried to get away. Shattuck resisted arrest and struggled with Samson Reed, the leader of the militia. During the tussle, one of the pursuing horsemen, John Rand, rode up and slashed Shattuck across his knee with his sword, opening a 12-inch gash and capturing him.[48] Parker and Page were also apprehended, and the three men were summarily whisked off to jail in Boston, where they remained incommunicado for the rest of the winter, through the spring, and into the summer.[49]

The suspension of habeas corpus and the jailing of the three rebels in a "distant county" unleashed a storm of angry reactions. More than 30 towns formally protested the state's move. With the fortunes of the three men still hovering in the air, another rebel group of approximately 300 men marched on Springfield, 90 miles to the west, and forced another court closure. Back in Boston, a more contrite Job Shattuck met with Judge Edmund Quincy on December 18, who then wrote to Governor Bowdoin that Shattuck was remorseful, saying, "Shattuck had subscribed the oath of allegiance prescribed in the Constitution of this Commonwealth."[50]

At this point, Governor Bowdoin, worried that he did not have enough pro-government troops to stop the rebellion, decided to hire a private army. On January 4, 1787, a call went out for 4,400 men to put down the rebellion. This unit was recruited almost exclusively from eastern towns, backed by wealthy merchants who were concerned about the economic impacts of the revolt on their businesses. This dramatic step was done without legislative authorization, and the pop-up army was put under the command of General Benjamin Lincoln, George Washington's Revolutionary War friend and the person who stood in for him at the surrender of Cornwallis in Yorktown.[51] This force then marched to Worcester on January 19 to confront the insurrectionists there.

Around the same time, Job Shattuck Jr. had been trying to gain access to his father, who had spent the prior six weeks in jail. He approached Oliver Prescott for help. Sympathetic to Job Jr.'s plea, Oliver agreed to assist, and on January 9, he wrote to the governor, saying, "I desire he [Job Shattuck] may be allowed to return to his family and business."[52] This gesture, on behalf of someone Oliver had considered a danger to the Commonwealth, may have truly been high-minded and perhaps reflected the empathy they were all feeling during this very trying time. It could also have reflected Oliver's desire to regain some of his lost reputation in Groton for pursuing Job so ardently.

As this was transpiring, Daniel Shays was busy assembling a force of roughly 1,200 men—mostly war veterans—in the middle of the state, where they intended to take action against the state government. These rebels were not all down-on-their-luck farmers as they have generally been depicted, nor were they people deep in debt. Indeed, while the insurrectionists did oppose the newly administered taxes, their broader dispute was with what they thought were a tyrannical group of elites who were in charge of the state.[53]

In response, Continental soldiers were quickly called out to confront Shays's men. However, as an example of the strength of Shays's movement, of the 637 veterans from Northampton and other towns near Springfield, only 23 volunteered to oppose the rebels. Furthermore, the captain and senior lieutenant of the Continentals who responded to the state's call had only 14 days of Revolutionary War experience between them; the rebel captains in contrast had over three years' experience.[54]

Meanwhile, the situation continued to heat up in Springfield, where the insurgents set their sights on the federal arsenal. Three groups intended to surround the arsenal and capture its stockpile of arms. These were led by Daniel Shays in Palmer to the east, Luke Day in West Springfield, and Eli Parsons in Chicopee to the north. General Benjamin Lincoln's troops were intent on stopping these rebels, and they headed west from Worcester. Fortunately for the government's soldiers, miscommunication spoiled the insurgents' plan, leading Shays and Parsons unknowingly to attack the arsenal without Day on January 25, 1787. The rebels were quickly and decisively overwhelmed by militia troops headed by General William Shepard. The well-prepared militia fired on the attacking insurgents, who were headed by James White, killing and wounding 20. The uprising was put down, and Shays and the others fled north to New Hampshire and Vermont.[55]

By February 1787, the rebellion was over. Ultimately, about 4,000 people confessed to the revolt in exchange for amnesty while several hundred others were charged with insurrection. Oliver's efforts to have Job Shattuck released did not change Job's fortunes, and his tribulations dragged on for another seven months. In May, Shattuck was put on trial, convicted, and sentenced to hang. He was one of only 14 insurrectionists out of the thousands who had participated in the revolt to be sentenced to death.[56] There is no indication that either James or William Prescott disagreed with Oliver's plea for leniency.

A document held in Pepperell's Town Hall shows that William Prescott was involved in the amnesty process. I uncovered the document while perusing a collection of records and deeds held in a room just off the town clerk's office. Joan Ladik, a spirited, part-time worker in Town Hall—who is spearheading an effort to restore Prescott Hall on the top floor of the building to its original elegance—opened a stout vault and extracted several volumes of records from the late 18th century for me to review. In a folder labeled Valuable Old Special Papers, there was a single, unadorned sheet of paper in William Prescott's hand, dated March 23, 1787, that stated the following: "This may certify that the persons whose names are above written have delivered up their arms and taken the oath of allegiance according to Law before me Wm Prescott Justice of the Peace."[57] There were 36 names listed in two columns on the page, including seven Shattucks. On another document, dated the same day, Oliver Prescott, Justice of the Peace in Groton, recorded that three additional Shattucks had also taken the oath.

In order to reunite the Commonwealth, John Hancock, the popular former governor, decided to run again for the office in April. Hancock showed compassion toward the insurrectionists and was reelected convincingly. In keeping with his desire to patch things up, Hancock restored the voting rights that had been taken from many of the insurgents, if they had, like the Shattucks in March, sworn an oath of allegiance. In addition to this move, when Oliver Prescott contacted Hancock about a pardon for Job Shattuck, whose hanging had been postponed until June 28, Hancock placed the matter before the State Council on June 19.[58] However, Hancock did not suggest pardoning Daniel Shays and eight other rebel leaders, as well as anyone who shot at government supporters, had reneged on their oath of allegiance, or had been indicted. Somewhat surprisingly, the council did not move in the direction of the governor regarding Shattuck and denied the petition to pardon him. Shattuck's execution remained set for the end of the month.

Petitions supporting Shattuck continued to come to Hancock from the countryside. Even Thomas Jefferson, who, as an agrarian, was sympathetic to the insurrectionists' plight, urged leniency. Because of these appeals, momentum built for a reprieve for the rioters. As a result, the council granted one to Shattuck until the end of September, although he remained in lockup.[59] By this time, the council's anger at the insurrection may have subsided and its members may have grown more sympathetic to the Shays–Shattuck views. Most of their neighbors were hurting, and they most likely would have wanted an agreeable resolution to the conflict.

The council was also busy addressing some of the protestors' concerns, enacting legislation to end lawsuits for debts, and substantially reducing the tax burden on citizens to 10 percent of what it had been. The council also took away the advantages bondholders were granted when they were directly receiving tax revenues as returns on their investments. This caused a significant reduction in poll taxes. In this way, the protestors finally saw some benefits from their dramatic actions.

Finally, on September 13, 1787, after being incarcerated for about 10 months, Shattuck was pardoned by Hancock a week before his scheduled execution. The permanently crippled Shattuck returned to Groton where he was welcomed back by sympathetic supporters. Even James and Oliver Prescott were cordial about Shattuck's return home, not wanting to further upset their own status in the community. However, they could not escape the scorn of the town completely, as neither was ever reelected as a selectman after the rebellion. Later, when the economic fortunes of Groton boomed, Job Shattuck faded into the background and the reputations of the Prescotts recovered. Job Shattuck died on January 13, 1819, over 30 years after the rebellion.

As for Daniel Shays, he was also pardoned by the state of Massachusetts. After abandoning his farm and fleeing the Commonwealth to the independent Vermont Republic when the insurrection collapsed, he returned briefly before relocating to New York State. Shays died largely in obscurity on September 29, 1825, and is buried in Union Cemetery in Scottsburg, New York.[60] He was 78 years old. However, Shays was not forgotten entirely, as the eponymous Daniel Shays Highway in Massachusetts is a part of the 638-mile Route 202 roadway that stretches from Maine to Delaware. It isn't often that insurrectionists are awarded such tributes.

In September, the same month that Shattuck was finally pardoned, the delegates at a constitutional convention in Philadelphia would craft the finishing touches on a dramatically new governmental structure for the country. Their proposed scheme would be put to the test in state-by-state debates, the outcomes of which were still very much up in the air. Here too, William Prescott would be involved in a critical affair that would shape the country—the last in his eventful career.

CHAPTER 11

Instituting a New Constitution

The importance of Shays's Rebellion, despite it being short and unsuccessful, was that it dramatically pointed out the fragility of the United States government under the Articles of Confederation. Fear of even wider spread insurrections thus spurred discussion for a new, strong national replacement. For instance, it prompted Richard Henry Lee of Virginia to remark to his friend George Washington that the insurrection proved that "Mankind left to themselves are unfit for their own government."[1] James Madison was also convinced that the Articles needed to be exchanged for a potent national government. Madison smartly allied himself with Washington, who he knew would be a vital advocate to have, and the two worked together to recommend a constitutional convention to take up the heady matter.[2]

Madison and Washington had another ardent supporter for a constitutional convention, and that was the indomitable Alexander Hamilton. It didn't take much convincing to get Hamilton on board. The visionary New Yorker had already written about the need for a strong government in a letter to a friend in 1780. These three leaders felt the states had too much power and wanted not merely to amend the articles, but, controversially, to replace them entirely with a new form of government.[3]

A New National Government

Seventy-four delegates across the 13 states were chosen for the Constitutional Convention, set to begin in May 1787, though only 55 actually attended at least one day. It was not until May 25 that a quorum of seven states was obtained. For such a momentous undertaking, the delegates were mostly a precocious group, with few members over the age of 40.[4] It is also safe to say that not every delegate came to the convention with a common understanding of why they were meeting. Ostensibly, the convention was called for "the sole and express purpose of revising the Articles of Confederation," but once the convention was underway, it would not take long for everyone to be disabused of that notion. Throughout the months of intense discussion, the specter of Shays's Rebellion—which was a prime example of how close the country could be to losing the goal of national government—hung over the convention like a pall.

Two rules that governed the convention would ensure that this assembly of learned and experienced men would drag on throughout the long, hot summer in Philadelphia. First, the convention followed the existing practice of the Articles of Confederation in granting one vote for each state delegation. This obviously magnified the power of the states with smaller populations, putting them on an equal footing with the larger states. Second, the convention allowed every decision that was reached to be reconsidered, at any time, on the recommendation of any single delegate, which opened the door for lengthy and repetitive argumentation.[5]

A number of the delegates were renowned men such as Washington, Madison, Franklin, Dickinson, and Hamilton (who was not a delegate but attended anyway). Well-regarded men such as John and Samuel Adams, Jefferson, and Hancock could not or did not want to attend. Still others would become famous, or more famous, by their participation, such as Mason, Randolph, Sherman, Gouverneur and Robert Morris, and the Pinckneys.

The Massachusetts delegates were Elbridge Gerry, Nathaniel Gorham, Rufus King, and Caleb Strong. They were, respectively, a merchant, a businessman, and two lawyers. And they were mostly seasoned gentlemen, with three in their mid- to late 40s and only one, Rufus King, in his early 30s. These were all distinguished men—like all the delegates there—who traveled to Philadelphia to conduct very serious business.

On May 29, Virginia's Edmund Randolph presented to the convention the Virginia Plan, a straw man for the delegates to consider and debate. This structure was largely formulated by Madison and Washington. The plan contained 15 resolves and outlined an entirely new national government with a national executive, a bicameral legislature, and a national judiciary. This plan did not "correct and enlarge" the Articles as was expected, but instead replaced them in full, and it caused much consternation with many of the delegates.[6]

Over the next three months, the delegates discussed, debated, and refined the various parts of the Virginia Plan, which survived an alternative plan offered by William Paterson of New Jersey—the New Jersey Plan—proposed on June 15. Paterson's offering kept the sovereignty of the states, making it a federal plan, not a national plan. The New Jersey Plan also argued for a unicameral Congress within which each state would vote equally, as in the Articles of Confederation. There was still a lot of skepticism about a national plan, with a single, strong national leader, after eight years of fighting the British monarchy. In contrast, the New Jersey Plan preferred multiple executives.

Repeatedly, the delegates discussed how to handle a host of issues, including: representation in the House and Senate, how slaves would count toward state populations, presidential election procedures, executive power, terms of office, impeachment, and other major items.[7] All the while, back in Massachusetts, many citizens—Prescott among them—were left to wonder what was going on at the convention. Due to a strict policy of confidentiality, in which delegates were not permitted to speak about the deliberations externally, information was not forthcoming. So, Massachusetts citizens, as well as the rest of the nation, just had to wait for the convention to conclude to see what form the proposed new government would take.[8] Prescott certainly was as much in the dark as anyone else. This might have made him nervous, as he was already on edge because of the revolt that had recently taken place in Massachusetts. Who knows what a diverse group of men from across the colonies might consider as a worthy and effective form of government to rule the fledgling nation? Prescott had experienced directly the power of the agricultural interests in his state. Might this power be amplified in the many southern states, and what would this ultimately mean for the citizens of Massachusetts?

The convention delegates held a series of votes in the Committee of the Whole to decide what was in and what was out; the outcomes of these votes frequently flipflopped as members changed positions and state delegations reversed themselves. The Committee of Detail then compiled all the approved elements of the proposed Constitution and a draft was passed along to the Committee of Style, whose members were William Samuel Johnson of Connecticut (Chairman), James Madison, Rufus King, Alexander Hamilton, and Gouverneur Morris. Morris, a New Yorker turned Pennsylvanian, was given the responsibility of producing a clean draft for the delegates to consider and vote upon.[9] The time for consensus had arrived.

Gouverneur Morris began his masterful final draft with, "We the People of the United States…" In this way, he did not have to enumerate all the states and, in keeping with his desire, he could present a straightforward, plain, and uncomplicated document.[10] Morris's beginning also underscored that the power of the government emanated from the people, not the states. This was an important distinction, and not something that all the delegates would have said they believed. Morris also used his pen like pruning shears, trimming and condensing the 23 articles that had been discussed into just seven, with various subsections tucked underneath. The final product contained only 4,543 words, much shorter than every state constitution today. Most have at least 8,000 words, topped by Alabama's Constitution, which has approximately 345,000 words. Controversially, the draft did not include a Bill of Rights, which upset a number of the delegates. These would be added later as the first 10 amendments to the Constitution.

On September 17, 1787, 39 of the 55 participating delegates were present, and all but five signed the document. Although he did not officially belong to the New York delegation, Alexander Hamilton signed the document as well. Franklin, whose opinion would carry much weight, spoke in favor of the Constitution "with all its faults, if they are such."[11] The dissenters who did not sign were Edmund Randolph and George Mason of Virginia, Elbridge Gerry of Massachusetts, and the two delegates from New York: Robert Yates and John Lansing.

William Prescott was unaware of what stances were taken by the Massachusetts delegation. It was only later that he would learn that Elbridge Gerry, who would eventually be elected as a member of the U.S. House of Representatives, Governor of Massachusetts, and fifth Vice President of the United States, was one of the five non-signing delegates. Gerry explained he did not sign the Constitution because it did not contain a Bill of Rights, but he had other concerns as well. He thought the Constitution threatened the liberties of the people and the rights of the states. He did not want too much power embedded in one person, group, or branch of government. At the convention, he spoke on limiting military power, the manner of electing the president, checking the power of the chief executive, and against having a vice president, particularly one who was the president of the Senate.

Unfortunately, we do not know what Prescott thought of Gerry's objections, nor do we know definitively if he himself would have signed the Constitution as it stood in September 1787, if given the chance. It is entirely possible that Prescott was more consumed with life in Pepperell and Massachusetts in general than focusing on what was happening in Philadelphia. But Prescott would soon get more engaged when the issue of the Constitution's ratification came to the fore. It was a critical time for the nation.

Ratification

After the draft of the Constitution had been approved by the Convention, the individual states needed to ratify the new governmental structure.

Passage would require nine of the 13 states to assent.[12] And so the process began, and 13 separate battles took place, with some moving along more quickly than others. The first state to ratify was tiny Delaware on December 7, an achievement it has been proud of ever since (just look at its license plate). It voted 30–0 for ratification. Pennsylvania and New Jersey quickly followed with affirming votes on December 12 and December 18, respectively. While New Jersey and Georgia—which ratified on January 2, 1788—also produced unanimous votes, Pennsylvania's passing vote of 46–23, with 33 percent against, illustrated that there could be strong headwinds against the Constitution down the line. Connecticut, up next, presented no problem becoming the fifth state to ratify with an overwhelming vote of 128–40 on January 9. The pro-Constitution forces were now halfway toward their goal of nine states. It was only about a month since Delaware got things rolling.

William Prescott must have been keeping score on the ratification process. There wasn't a bigger headline in the country. But even though all five of the first states to vote had approved the Constitution, tension was building and each subsequent state debate from there on out was pressure-packed and momentous. Roughly four weeks after Connecticut's vote, Massachusetts was wrapping up its hotly contested debate and was about to vote.[13]

As historian Pauline Maier has pointed out, the idea that the government received its authority from the people was not new.[14] It came from 17th-century English radical thought and was familiar to people in America. In fact, the preamble to the 1780 Massachusetts Constitution starts, "We...the people of Massachusetts," which the federal Constitution echoed seven years later. Consequently, feeling empowered, the citizens of Massachusetts expected to be able to criticize the federal Constitution and did so heartily. Condemnation appeared liberally in the Boston newspapers, and the citizens of the state gave the Constitution a thorough review.[15]

The process started on October 25, 1787, when the Massachusetts state legislature called on towns and districts to select qualified representatives to convene at the State House in Boston in early January 1788 for the purpose of "assenting to and ratifying" the proposed federal Constitution.[16] Towns could send as many delegates as they had representatives to the lower house of the legislature. To fulfill their duties, the separate towns chose a moderator for their local meetings and then sometimes read aloud the Constitution before discussing it. The towns first voted on whether or not to send delegates to the ratifying convention and how many to send. They also discussed whether or not to instruct the delegates on how to vote or to leave that decision up to each delegate.

In all, Massachusetts towns elected 370 delegates, of whom 364 attended the convention at some point. Ironically, at least 29 communities selected well-known Shays rebels to represent them at the ratifying convention. It was an inauspicious omen. The town of Groton chose as its delegates Benjamin Morse, a 57-year-old wheelwright and erstwhile compatriot of Job Shattuck, and Joseph Sheple, a lawyer.[17] Understandably, James and Oliver Prescott were not pleased with these choices.

On November 26, 1787, Pepperell gathered a town assembly "to choose a Delegate to Represent said Town in [the] Convention to be held at the State House in Boston on the second Wednesday of January next for the purpose of Ratifying the Constitution agreed upon by the State General Convention agreeable to a Resolve of Congress of September 28, 1787 and the Recommendation of the Legislature of this Commonwealth."[18] In a follow-up meeting on December 18, 1787, with William Prescott presiding, Pepperell chose Daniel Fisk to be its delegate at the convention in Boston. There is no indication why Fisk was chosen or if other potential delegates were discussed. Nor was there any indication in advance about how Fisk would vote. Pepperell did not give any instructions to Fisk regarding how he should respond to the call of the roll in Boston.

Prescott certainly knew Deacon Fisk well and, without other evidence, it appears he did not oppose this selection to represent the town. It does not seem Prescott pressed his own views on Fisk, unless this occurred privately. Prescott might have been confident that Fisk would perform his duties well, or he simply had no control of the situation and had to let Fisk decide on his own how the town should react to the draft Constitution.

As the Massachusetts Convention got underway, it was clear right away that some towns were for adoption while others were staunchly against it. A sizable number of towns also fell in an in-between category, willing to support the measure provided there were some amendments to the Constitution. For example, the town of Harvard in Worcester County simply wanted to have amendments that would strengthen the Articles of Confederation, but go no further. Across the state, a heated debate ensued, which gripped the public for weeks.[19] In the view of Pauline Maier, if Massachusetts did not ratify, other states like Virginia, New York, and New Hampshire probably wouldn't either.[20] This was what James Madison and George Washington feared. On the other hand, if Massachusetts did ratify, then the Constitution was likely to be adopted.

The objections to the Constitution were fairly similar across Massachusetts towns. Some were concerned that there would be an inadequate number of members in the House of Representatives; others thought the terms of senators (six years) and the president (four years) were too lengthy. Terms of office in Massachusetts were for only one year at a time, so the Constitution's longer terms seemed extraordinary and dangerous. In addition, some objected to Congress's power to override state laws, as well as having unlimited authority to collect taxes, duties, imports, and excises. Provisions that allowed the president and the Senate to decide certain items, like treaties and particular judicial matters, without involving the House of Representatives, were also opposed.

The contentious debate left the decision in doubt, but on February 6, 1788, Massachusetts finally assembled to vote. The ultimate tally was relatively close: 187–168 in favor. A swing of only 10 votes, or less than 3 percent, would have changed the outcome. That was a remarkably narrow victory for a state that could claim it was the birthplace of the revolution.

The tightness of the tally surprised me, so back I went to the Massachusetts Archives to find out who voted for and who voted against ratification. Two of my impromptu team of helpers at the Archives—Caitlin Ramos and Conor Snow—were at the front desk when I arrived. "I need your assistance again," I said meekly, worried that I had already worn out my welcome on prior visits. But they were as enthusiastic as ever.

"What's the issue?" asked Conor. I explained I wanted to find out how each of the Massachusetts ratification convention delegates had voted. After a quick review of online resources proved empty, Caitlin and Conor went off to see if they could find anything useful in other areas of the repository. After about 15 minutes, I was presented with a copy of a document titled Massachusetts Ratification Project, "The Great Debate of '88."[21] This was precisely what I wanted—a county-by-county, delegate-by-delegate listing of all 355 votes.

On the first page, just following the entries for Suffolk and Essex counties, was the listing for the County of Middlesex, which voted 17 for, 25 against, with one abstaining. My eyes scanned down the listing until I reached Daniel Fisk of the self-proclaimed patriotic town of Pepperell. Next to his name, it said nay. I'd like to say I wasn't surprised, but I was. Pepperell was no doubt patriotic, but it was also part of the very region that had supported Shays's Rebellion. Since William Prescott opposed the insurrection, what did Deacon Fisk's vote say about Prescott's influence on this matter? If he supported ratification, which I suspect he did, then Deacon Fisk's nay vote was an affront to Prescott's stance.

I then checked the two delegates from Groton, home of Job Shattuck. The outcome seemed evident and, indeed, Dr. Benjamin Morse and Joseph Sheple voted nay as well. The 17 delegates of Middlesex County who voted for ratification were from Cambridge, Charlestown, Concord, Newton, Framingham, Lexington, Sherburne, Sudbury, Malden, Weston, Medford,

Stow, Waltham, Dracut, Dunstable, and Lincoln. With a few exceptions, most of these towns were relatively close to Boston, where anti-rebellion feelings were high. As for the other 22 delegates who voted nay, they came from communities both close to, as well as distant from, Boston.[22]

Other Massachusetts counties voting largely against ratification were Berkshire (seven yay, 15 nay), Hampshire (19 yay, 33 nay), Worcester (seven yay, 43 nay), and York (six yay, 11 nay). These were all central to western Massachusetts counties, with the exception of York in southern Maine. The counties that were largely in favor of ratification were Cumberland, Maine (10 yay, three nay), and the eastern Massachusetts counties of Essex (38 yay, six nay), Suffolk (34 yay, three nay), Plymouth (21 yay, six nay), and Barnstable (seven yay, two nay). The remaining—Bristol, Dukes, and Lincoln—cast few votes and were relatively evenly split. Interestingly, an account of the convention was written by Justus Dwight, delegate from Belchertown in Hampshire County, who voted nay along with the majority of his local colleagues. In Dwight's account, he mentioned that a "good number [of the delegates] voted contrary to their constituents."[23] Why was this the case? Had they gone to the convention with this in mind, or were they swayed by the arguments made at the convention? We may never find out.

Unfortunately, it isn't known how William Prescott felt about the debate at the convention and Fisk's decision, or other votes of the delegates from Groton, Shirley, and other neighboring towns. Nonetheless, it is likely that he would have been pleased with ratification. Prescott was not a vocal opponent of a republican form of government; he didn't object to strong authority as long as the citizens were treated fairly and opportunity was not stifled. It might be correct to say that Prescott simply wanted what was best for Massachusetts. However, it can also be argued that what was best for Massachusetts was a strong national government whose united strength would look out for and ensure as much prosperity as possible for each of the states.

In the end, the crisis that Madison worried about in Massachusetts had been averted. The Constitution now had six votes in favor. But it then took three and half additional months to garner the next two states' approval—Maryland on April 28 and South Carolina on May 23. Clearly momentum had slowed appreciably. In those three months, the issue also suffered its first defeat when, in a popular referendum, Rhode Island rejected the Constitution with a stinging vote of 237 for versus 2,708 against.[24] All eyes turned toward the three next most likely states to vote, including Virginia, New York, and New Hampshire. Would one of them put the issue over the top with the ninth affirmative vote?

Naturally, there were strong feelings in the Old Dominion, from where the idea of a national convention and a new government had sprung, and which had been represented at the Constitutional Convention by prominent delegates such as Washington, Madison, Randolph, Mason, and George Wythe. Simultaneously, there was a fierce battle being waged in New York, where Hamilton was pouring his considerable energies behind ratification, including writing the bulk of 85 anonymous essays, later called the Federalist Papers. In the end, however, it was New Hampshire that got the Constitution over the top, ratifying it on June 21 with a vote of 57–47. Virginia followed on June 25, voting 89–79. And New York squeaked by on July 26 with an affirmative vote of 30–27. All three of these states had tight votes.

Four more months would then transpire until North Carolina approved the Constitution on November 21. Finally, tardy Rhode Island, which had lagged behind the other states throughout the entire constitutional process, reversed its earlier stance and voted for ratification on May 29, 1790, with the slimmest possible margin of 34–32 from a much smaller population of delegates. It was almost exactly three years since the Constitutional Convention of 1787 had kicked off in Philadelphia.[25]

Eager to get the new government in place, Congress wasted little time in electing the new President of the United States. Between December 15, 1788 and January 10, 1789, presidential electors were chosen in each state.[26] To no one's surprise, George Washington was the unanimous selection, receiving the votes of all 69 electors. In fact, many delegates at the convention thought of Washington as the model when they were considering the role and powers of the president. Citizens were likewise overwhelmingly pleased with the presidential choice, and William Prescott must have been one of them, seeing his old commander elevated to the country's highest office.

With the election for the executive branch and Congress over, it was now time to put the new government into practice. James Madison was less sanguine, admitting at the time, "We are in a wilderness without a single footstep to guide us."[27] Although the path forward was uncertain, the new government was now looking like a plausible, functioning entity.

A lot of history had occurred since young William Prescott had set out on his own and built a life in Groton's West Parish. Although I now felt a culmination of my gumshoe work approaching, I couldn't really be sure. Prescott surprised me when, at 51 years of age, he volunteered for potentially dangerous military duty at Saratoga and when he stepped into the breach in Concord during Shays's Rebellion about 10 years later. So I've kept the file open, in case I have missed something.

CHAPTER 12

Twilight of a Life Well-Lived

William Prescott spent a good deal of his life working for the country's independence and his belief in liberty and personal freedom. He had taken up arms when his colony needed defending, and he'd fought in the ensuing war, even coming out of retirement as a volunteer at a most critical stage of the conflict. As few others could say, Prescott was present at three of the most important military actions in the war: Bunker Hill, the New York campaign, and the siege and surrender of Burgoyne's army at Saratoga.

After these immense wartime events, Prescott remained active civically and was enormously interested in what the war and the creation of a new government might achieve. While stability and national unity remained uncertain, he responded when Shays's Rebellion threatened the fragile new order. Like his ancestors before him, throughout his life he continued to be an important figure in his community. He held many posts, and his devotion to civic duty only bolstered his reputation as a citizen of high integrity. Moreover, his dedication to his long-held support of education was underscored in a document I came across in Pepperell Town Hall on one of my last visits. The document says that, on the 10th day of February 1792, William Prescott created the following deed, which reads in part:

> …that Wm Prescott hath hereby leased demnified and firmly [unintelligible] to the Selectmen of said Pepperell or their successors in office the ground where the school house now stands… so long as there shall be a house for the use of a school and put to another use…that myself, my heirs, executor and administrators shall have no right nor claim to said land so long as there shall be a house appropriated for the use of a school…[1]

Spared an early death in the wars in which he fought, Prescott emerged from his military life physically unscathed and unhindered. He avoided being bayoneted, shot, or otherwise dispatched on the battlefield, even as destruction and death closed upon him. He escaped the infectious diseases and other ailments that felled so many soldiers. He didn't perish as a British prisoner-of-war. And, as he predicted, the Tories never had the satisfaction of seeing him hang.

There is no indication that, in his last years, Prescott suffered any particular grave medical conditions. As a result, it may have been a shock to his family and neighbors when the end came. Prescott died on October 13, 1795, in the house in which he'd lived for most of his life. He was 69 years old. The cause of death was referred to at the time as dropsy of the heart, or what we today would call congestive heart failure. This means he probably had been experiencing shortness of breath, fatigue, and some swelling of his legs for a while—certainly for weeks, if not months or longer. It was a little more than 21 years after Bunker Hill.

Prescott was buried with full military honors in Pepperell's rolling and peaceful Walton Cemetery near the old town church. He was placed in a simple, above-ground tomb built of four upright granite slabs, forming a rectangular enclosure about two and a half feet high. On top of the tomb rests a slate stone bearing the following inscription:

> This stone is erected
> in memory of
> Col. William Prescott,
> of Pepperell,
> who died on the 13th day
> of October, Anno Domini 1795
> in the seventieth year
> of his age

Prescott's grave is in a part of the cemetery that is very close to the main roads that intersect the town. In this regard, the citizens of Pepperell are never very far from their native hero. Prescott's burial was reported by Captain Thomas Lawrence, who pleasingly wrote the following:

> Col. William Prescott was buried under arms and my company turned out volunterly and Capt. Lee Parker's company. They was commanded by Major Bancroft. The men was all in uniform. William Ferguson played the fife. Major Samuel Sarles beat the drum. Their music was good and the men was behaved themselves exceeding well. We marched very slow time to the grave about thirty steps in a minute. There was three platoons was find at the grave. This was a warlike meloncolly scene.[2]

As for the simple and unpretentious tomb, Lorenzo Blood, a Pepperell historian, said years later that the "Pepperell farmer who commanded the yeomanry of Middlesex at the battle of Bunker Hill needs no costlier or more imposing mausoleum. His epitaph might well be, *Exegi monimentum aere perennius* (I have reared a monument more enduring than bronze)."[3]

The Years After

Throughout his life, Prescott held the land on which his house sat under the original Native American deed and this remained so for his son, William Jr. and his grandson, William Hickling (W. H.) Prescott. The house still stands today on the corner of Prescott and Hollis Streets.[4] Over the years, the Prescott farm dwindled in size, and 250 acres now number only 15 according to town records. Prescott left his estate in arrears, but his son, William Jr., settled his father's debts and saved the family home from sale or creditors. William Prescott was survived by his wife, Abigail, who lived another 25 years. She passed away on October 19, 1821 at the advanced age of 89. A twin tomb containing her remains stands alongside her husband's in Walton Cemetery.

In time, the Prescott house was expanded to accommodate the needs of William Hickling Prescott, who lived there after the Colonel passed away. W. H. wrote a number of his esteemed historical works in the family home and entertained many distinguished visitors from other parts of the United States, as well as abroad. The home was graced by family heirlooms, including Colonel Prescott's Continental Army commission, signed by John Hancock, as well as two cannonballs that had been fired at the redoubt atop Breed's Hill in 1775. The house remained in the family for a total of seven generations before transferring into the hands of non-Prescotts.[5]

In the year William Prescott passed away, the country was about to enact a new treaty with Great Britain. This had been negotiated by John Jay, who at the time was the Chief Justice of the United States Supreme Court. The Jay Treaty was signed on November 19, 1794, but would not become active until February 29, 1796. The pact, which had been designed by Alexander Hamilton and supported by President George Washington, intended to settle several outstanding issues between the two countries that had been left unresolved since American independence. Most prominently, it also called for the withdrawal of British Army units from the Northwest Territory that it had refused to give up at the conclusion of the Revolutionary War. It also settled an argument over the collection of debts owed to Great Britain stemming from the confiscation of loyalist estates during the war.

Despite these efforts, many contentious issues with Great Britain remained unresolved. William Prescott might have thought that the hard-fought victory over the British and the peace signed in 1783 would have enabled the citizens of the new United States of America to pursue their lives unimpeded by foreign influence. He also might have felt that the lives and treasure that were lost over the eight years of war would have been paid out with freedom, peace, and personal liberty. But he would have been mistaken.

More than he was able to, his wife—who lived longer—saw the new country grow and stabilize, then endure some very dangerous shocks. Longstanding issues with England led to another war in 1812, and included significant naval battles this time around. In August 1814, The Capitol in Washington, D.C. and the White House were burned, before a string of American military victories culminating in the battle of New Orleans ended the fighting.

The seven years of peace and common cause that Prescott witnessed from 1788 to 1795 might have given him a false sense of hope, but the realist in him—formed by his participation in three wars during his early life—might have dissuaded him of the notion of perpetual tranquility. After all, the French and Indian War was not the war to end all wars, as some called it. America would not be protected from attack by a wide ocean. The Revolutionary War had proven that armies could, and would, cross the sea to engage in protracted conflicts at high cost in lives and treasure. Thus, vigilance would be required, military preparedness would be necessary, and national unity would need to be maintained.

Abigail also witnessed a strenuous and inevitable internal fight over slavery, prompted by whether the horrid practice could be banned in the admission of new states. The argument ended temporarily and unsatisfactorily with the Missouri Compromise of 1820. That agreement simultaneously admitted Missouri as a slave state and Maine as a free state, and it barred slavery only in the remaining Louisiana Purchase territories north of the 36th parallel. Of course, the abolition of slavery was not accomplished with the Missouri Compromise, only postponed some 45 years until the Civil War settled the issue.

Although Prescott's father and brothers possessed slaves, I believe he and Abigail would have seen the perpetuation of slavery as a repugnant blight on America. Dozens of African Americans stood with Prescott in Charlestown on June 17, 1775. Their heroic action was not lost on him. Afterward, Prescott praised African American soldier Salem Poor, who fought bravely at Bunker Hill, and he co-signed a letter recognizing Poor's service, urging the General Court of Massachusetts, apparently unsuccessfully, to reward him for those actions.

Massachusetts banned slavery in 1783, one of the first states to do so. Still, the proposition to extend slavery into new territories after the Constitution was adopted, rather than to bar the practice, likely would have chilled him. While slavery, that original sin of the republic, would finally be totally abolished, its vile companion, bigotry, would remain a stubborn obstacle to human rights for decades on end until modern times.

It is highly likely that William Prescott would have been severely disappointed had he lived to experience these national traumas. Perhaps fortunately for him, we'll never know for sure.

Leadership

William Prescott had been a leader his whole life. As commander of his local militia, Prescott's responsibility was to recruit, train, and prepare the men of this unit, as well as guide them when in battle.[6] Like other militiamen, Prescott was never a professional soldier. He was first and foremost a farmer who enlisted for military service when the situation called for it. As the author George Hillard described Prescott on the centennial of his death: "We see a man summoned from the plough, and by the accident of war called upon to perform an important military service, and in the exercise of his duty we find him displaying that calm courage and sagacious judgment which a life in the camp is supposed to be necessary to bestow."[7] Historian John Ferling, in explaining how Prescott might have been elected to lead the local militia, also said of the Pepperell commander, "[William] Prescott looked like a soldier and was very much a warrior."[8]

Beyond his martial appearance, it is easy to see why Prescott was the choice of his townsmen to be their leader. Prescott was certainly a prominent figure in Pepperell, a significant landowner, wealthier than most men, with a formidable carriage, and experienced in war. For these reasons, and the fact that his ancestors also took up arms when their communities needed support, the townsmen naturally gravitated to Prescott. It was a mark of his leadership that so many men in his company stayed on the Bunker Hill battlefield when it became evident that a major confrontation was going to take place, and who, by doing so, clearly trusted his judgment and believed in him.

Historians and organizational scholars have analyzed the attributes of leaders to understand what truly separates the good leaders from the bad, and the great leaders from the good. While many of these observers note that leadership is mostly an acquired trait, there are undoubtedly some natural elements involved as well. Great leaders have strategic vision, can motivate those around them, and are imbued with integrity, empathy, compassion, resilience, self-awareness, humility, prudence, and courage. Leaders also have the proper expertise for the job they are being asked to do, and they back this up with a sufficient level of experience in the real world. These are characteristics that engender trust and make followers believe that their leader can get the job done.

Beyond this, leaders are decisive, share credit appropriately, and are willing to admit their mistakes. The real test of leadership is most evident in times of crisis, when a leader must utilize all of their natural and acquired skills to find the right path forward and guide everyone through difficult times. According to Nancy Koehn—a contemporary Harvard scholar on the subject of leadership—courage and crisis have a symbiotic relationship.[9] She says, "Crises make serious leaders better and courageous, emotionally intelligent leaders become indispensable in crises."

William Prescott had all the ingredients to make him a strong and effective commander. When Prescott was tapped to lead the provincial soldiers to Charlestown in June 1775, he was eight months shy of his 50th birthday. Whatever opinions he had once held about the British, by this time he fully supported the notion of opposing them. He thought the British actions had gone beyond the pale, and he was ready to lead like-minded citizen-soldiers into battle. On the eve of the Bunker Hill fight, it is fair to say that he did not foresee what would transpire the following day. But he was willing to absorb the risks and do what he thought was right.

Despite the many accolades Prescott received, there has lingered some dispute regarding who was actually in charge of the provincial forces during the battle of Bunker Hill. Despite the preponderance of evidence to the contrary, some historians refer to Israel Putnam as a "hero" of Bunker Hill and cite his "bravery" during the battle.[10] These generous declarations may have been influenced by Putnam's prior exploits, particularly in the French and Indian War, since certainly in comparison to Prescott, Stark, and Knowlton, his actions on the battlefield were relatively minor.

Francis Jewett Parker, who wrote a tribute to Prescott in 1785, clearly intended to settle this dispute when he stated, "Colonel Prescott was no doubt selected to command the expedition as being one who favored it in the council, who was mature in years and judgment, and who, in the campaign at Cape Breton (referring to Prescott's actions in King George's War), had proved himself to be not only courageous but cautious."[11]

Bunker Hill authority Richard Frothingham also weighed in on this subject, saying, "General Putnam's conduct was that of a patriot, ardent volunteer, rather than of a commander-in-chief on the day of and during the perilous battle. It does not appear he [Putnam] brought any troops on to the field, or gave a command to a field officer that day, or ever gave an order or a command to Colonel Prescott."[12]

Likewise, Samuel Abbott Green, a Groton physician and the mayor of Boston in 1882, pointed out in the proceedings of the Massachusetts Historical

Society from November 1909 that "there is no evidence that Prescott received any order from others in that memorable engagement [the battle of Bunker Hill], while he himself acted under orders from Artemas Ward."[13] Green went on to state, "Captious critics have tried to deprive the Old Revolutionary soldier of the credit of this command; but it was the universal testimony of his army comrades, that the supreme authority in that action rested with him alone." Green supported his statement by indicating that this fact is alluded to in a letter from none other than Artemas Ward to John Adams, written on October 30, 1775, four months after the battle.

Once Bunker Hill achieved legendary status, Prescott's recognition and standing began to rise beyond the narrow confines of parochial attention. This more appreciative attitude was ably captured by Henry Lee of Virginia—known affectionately as Light Horse Harry Lee, who was a military hero in his own right and father of Robert E. Lee—when he wrote:

> The military annals of the world rarely furnish an achievement which equals the firmness and courage displayed on that proud day [June 17, 1775] by the gallant band of Americans; and it certainly stands first in the brilliant events of the war. When future generations shall inquire where are the men who gained the highest prize of glory in the arduous contest which ushered in our nation's birth, upon Prescott and his companions in arms will the eye of history beam.[14]

Generations of Prescotts proved to be highly effective and respected leaders. When the first colonial settlements were still on feeble legs and failure was a constant concern, the early Prescotts proved to be very resourceful, reliable, and energetic. They were remarkably resilient, highly trusted, and faithful to their communities. They worked the land, they helped build the infrastructure for successful settlements, and they took up arms when their settlements needed defending. As a result, they quickly made their marks and were held in very high esteem by their fellow colonists. One hundred thirty-five years after their arrival in Massachusetts, one of their own was poised to play a courageous and heroic role in some of the most dramatic and consequential events that the adolescent colony would encounter up to that point in time.

Courage

Of the many attributes used to describe Colonel Prescott—his extraordinary character, integrity, and leadership—perhaps the one most often cited is his unflinching courage. Certainly, anyone who stood on that hill in Charlestown or along the defensive line that descended to the Mystic River could be considered brave, especially since they were squaring off against the more numerous, better equipped, and better trained British regulars. But it was particularly Prescott's bravery that is most recalled from that battle, as he was on the field for the entire fight, in which he literally came face-to-face with the enemy.

On June 17, 1775, Prescott displayed extraordinary physical courage, since the risk of bodily harm and even death was a distinct possibility, if not a likely probability. Where does such courage come from? What distinguishes a person who is courageous from a person who is not? Is the quality of courage inherent in a person? Is it always there, ready to spring forth when circumstances warrant, or is it a trait that needs to be learned? Does it live in the heart or the mind?

Basic biology tells us that courage emerges from a primal struggle between the brain's decision-making hub, the prefrontal cortex, and the amygdala, the focal point of fear.[15] When we find ourselves in an unexpected and dangerous situation, the amygdala sends a signal to the prefrontal cortex that interferes with our ability to reason clearly. In extreme cases, that interference "can be paralyzing," says Daniela Schiller, at the Mount Sinai School of Medicine in New York. But, she notes, the brave do not succumb to fear. In some cases, Schiller points out, the brave are strengthened by the muscle memory that comes from intense training in how to deal with fear. Certainly, Prescott had control of his amygdala, as he surely was not afflicted by paralyzing fear; quite the contrary, he seemed to become more focused by his proximity to it.

Psychologists have also studied courage closely, as it is a much valued, though not universal, trait of human behavior. Courage, a synonym of bravery, has been defined by psychologists in several ways. It is typically described as the quality or state of having or showing mental or moral strength to face danger, pain, or difficulty while overcoming fear.[16] One of the earliest psychological definitions of courage comes from H. G. Lord, who, in 1918, four years into World War I, argued that courage occurs when the more base sentiment of fear is overwhelmed by a more noble sentiment.[17] He thus elevates courage to a higher-level virtue, much like Winston Churchill who, echoing Lord's attitude, said, "Without courage all other virtues lose their meaning." Churchill also remarked, "Fear is a reaction. Courage is a decision."[18]

Present-day psychologists C. L. S. Pury and S. Saylors define courage as "taking a worthwhile risk."[19] Like Lord, they feel that courage should be ascribed to actions in pursuit of a noble goal, but they add that another part of the definition involves the likelihood that the courageous action will succeed. In their view, actions that succeed should be rated higher than those that fail. This seems to me to be a distinction without a difference. You can't tell me that the first responders who climbed the World Trade Towers on 9/11 to rescue trapped citizens and who perished when the towers collapsed were any less courageous than those who were able to lead some citizens out of the building to safety.

Pury and Saylors also note that there are various kinds of courage—not only physical courage, but forms such as moral courage (standing up for someone or for an ideal against others), civil courage (having the goal of enforcing social and ethical norms despite a range of risks to oneself), and social courage (where the individual risks damaging personal relationships or social image).[20] Each of us can recognize courage when we see it. Prescott exhibited all of these types.

Prescott's gallantry seems, at least in part, to have been influenced by the actions and attitudes of his ancestors, who, for decades, were all very active civic leaders and who were willing to take up arms to protect their communities. When circumstances warranted it, these predecessors took extraordinary actions in the face of mortal danger. If this behavior was not inherited by Prescott, he nonetheless seems to have assumed the persona of a brave soldier and rose to the occasion without hesitancy. He did not shrink at risk but almost seemed to embrace it. His comportment was so calm and bold that, as was said of him, he could not help but inspire confidence and awe.

While Prescott may have been carrying on the militaristic tradition of his ancestors, it is hard not to think that he also possessed some innate courage. He clearly knew the danger that he and his men faced on Breed's Hill. He could have placed the redoubt on safer ground farther away from Boston and been less provocative, but he did not. Neither did he shy away from his duties when the British began their terrifying cannon bombardment at the beginning of the battle. He was at his post through the thick of the fighting and never left the field. And at the apex of the fight, when the combat shifted to hand-to-hand, he was still in the redoubt fighting with his sword. He did not flinch from the danger. He overcame whatever fear he felt—and it would have been highly unusual for him not to have felt fear—and did what he could to fulfill his duty and protect his men, even while his own life was in question.

No doubt Colonel William Prescott was the man of the hour on Breed's Hill. His actions, carried out under the most severe distress, danger, and tragedy, were marked by truly extraordinary valor. As historian Paul Lockhart put it, "No one would deny Prescott's calmness under fire and his *unpretentious heroism* [italics added]."[21] However, we cannot ignore the courage Prescott displayed during the New York campaign, facing terrible odds in a highly vulnerable position. We cannot discount the courage Prescott exhibited when he heeded the call for reinforcements to fight Burgoyne's army in upstate New York. Nor can we disregard the courage he showed in Concord during Shays's Rebellion, when Prescott opposed a hostile mob, armed and ready to commit violence.

A final comment on William Prescott's personality, which might go hand-in-hand with his undisputed courage. It is hard to think of William Prescott as anything but an avid adventurer. As opportunities presented themselves, he almost jumped at the chance to leave home and take part in various exciting, albeit hazardous, exploits. He did not fall back on excuses to avoid danger. He unhesitatingly signed himself up for the assignment and strapped on his sword. This began when he enlisted for King George's War, as well as the French and Indian War. He was quick to react to the Concord Alarm and followed this action with his willingness to lead the provincial troops to Bunker Hill. He traveled great distances to participate in the defense of New York City and the effort to stop Burgoyne's advance upstate. These experiences spanned 30 years of his life, a remarkable period. I don't think Prescott regretted his military life; I think he relished it.

The End of My Search

My search to "find" William Prescott concluded with his burial in October 1795. I had learned as much as I could about this largely forgotten American hero and understood better who he was and why he did what he did during the extraordinary second half of the 18th century. There were no more leads to track down, no more events to examine where I could dig up additional relevant facts of his life. I had assembled a host of primary source materials in Pepperell's Lawrence Library and Town Hall vault, the Massachusetts Archives, the American Antiquarian Society, and the Registry of Deeds. I had surfaced Prescott's orderlies' records and his own paybook in the files of W. H. Prescott at the Massachusetts Historical Society, and extracted key information from several other historical societies. I assembled information from genealogical records and rare histories like the one of Governors Island. I drew on the views of the United States Army. I leveraged the knowledge of experts in farming and land development, military tactics, town government, and revolutionary-era American history through interviews and examinations of their work. Still, as much as I learned, I wanted to know more. Though gaps in Prescott's story remained, I had to content myself with what I amassed and with what that information told me about him. Prescott had captured my attention through his actions at Bunker Hill, but discovering what he did before that battle and, even more so, after it, enabled me to gain a greater perspective on his broader, well-lived life.

After spending many months researching William Prescott, uncovering original documents in his hand, and reading speeches and other remarks about him, I felt I got to know him pretty well. I came to hear his voice in my head, moving about the redoubt on Breed's Hill amidst the disorienting smoke and cacophonous blasts from the musket fire, shouting out orders and showing the meaning of courage. I could see him rallying his troops as they prepared the defensive position on Governors Island in New York harbor and telling the men to be alert as British warships sailed by. I could visualize him bivouacking with other privates in the misty morning at Saratoga and later standing tall at the Concord courthouse in the rain. I could envision him regaling war veterans at his Pepperell home in the last years of his life.

What has eluded me, however, is understanding precisely what he was thinking during those events. Prescott didn't document the reasons he chose to do what he did, or his feelings regarding certain issues and people, or even his reactions to particular outcomes. It is a shame he didn't have a bit of Joseph Plumb Martin in him; how rich might have been his descriptions of the critical events of his life, how he felt about them, and how they affected him.[22]

For instance, what did he think about Artemus Ward, Israel Putnam, and John Stark? He might have been frustrated by Ward, who was overly cautious at Bunker Hill and slow in his decision-making. We know he was angered by what he thought was Putnam's dereliction of duty on June 17, but did that opinion shift over the months in New York when Putnam was directing the defenses of the city? What was Prescott's view of Stark? I believe he would have found him a kinsman, someone who was as patriotic as he was and equally courageous. Can you imagine their conversation after Bunker Hill, reflecting on the incredible carnage of the battle?

What was Prescott's opinion of the dashing Dr. Joseph Warren? Was he an admirer? Or did he think Warren was recklessly foolish? How did he react to Warren's death? I think he would have seen Warren as a brave man who died too young. I think he would have appreciated Warren's leadership potential and possibly even regretted that he did not force Warren to leave the Bunker Hill battlefield when he had the chance before the fateful third assault.

Only a little is known about Prescott's activities in the New York campaign, and that is another missed opportunity. If Prescott had the inclination and foresight, he could have used his orderly, Johnson Moulton, or another scribe to record his thoughts in a running commentary of his stay in the city. Alas, it would be another hundred years before the invention of the tape recorder.

What did Prescott think about being isolated on Governors Island? Did he believe he and his troops could really do anything to stop the British from sailing up the East River and bombarding the Continental troops in Brooklyn Heights and Manhattan? Was he afraid he and his men would be annihilated by the British navy and marines if they decided to attack? His note to General Heath calling for more support is an expression of his anxiety.

What did Prescott think of George Washington, whom he was around for a year and a half? Was he awed by Washington, as so many were, or did he see the faults that plagued the commander during the early years of the war, the rashness at times and the hesitancy at others? I do not see Prescott being critical of the general. Prescott knew only too well the difficulty of war, how the lack of reliable information could wreak havoc on decision-making. So, he might have given Washington a pass on some of his more controversial decisions. Prescott would have been more admiring of Washington's sense of duty, his integrity, his adherence to a code of honor. Moreover, I think Prescott would have sneered at the detractors who plotted to have Washington removed from command and been disgusted by their duplicitousness. He might also have been somewhat reluctant to leave Washington in January 1777 when he decided to head home as Washington fled into New Jersey. I can see how he might have thought he was abandoning his leader at a critical time, and that would have eaten at him.

Perhaps one of the more interesting things Prescott could have explained would be why he came out of retirement to head to Saratoga. Maybe his patriotism and wanderlust were simply too much to ignore and, when he heard the call for men to join Gates in upstate New York, he leapt at the chance to head off on another adventure. He was not dissuaded by regrets of leaving behind his family. His urge to be a part of another high-stakes endeavor, venturing far from home to a territory he was not familiar with, would not be suppressed. What would he have thought of the climactic confrontation against Burgoyne's army? Did he wish he could have been part of the fighting?

What ran through Prescott's mind as his former comrade, Job Shattuck, threatened the judges—including his two brothers—in Concord? How did he feel about the many economically hard-pressed farmers who were drawn to Shays's Rebellion, especially those in Groton and Pepperell where he had lived? Did he care his opposition to their actions would seriously injure his reputation?

Was he shocked when Daniel Fisk, Pepperell's convention delegate, voted against the ratification of the Constitution? Was he annoyed or embarrassed that his town, the town that he had devoted his life to, voted that way?

Ultimately, was he content with the new republican form of government? Was he disappointed the blight of slavery had been accommodated instead of eliminated? Did he worry that the new government might fail?

Prescott's grandson, William Hickling Prescott, the famous historian who hadn't been born when the Colonel died, must have regretted not being able to encourage his grandfather to tell his side of so many historic events and probe his attitudes toward the war, independence, and the new government. Regretfully, there are many questions still unanswered. But detective stories often end this way, with no comprehensive revelations. Motives and opinions are often left unresolved.

When all is said and done, Prescott's life reminds us of what it takes to secure and maintain liberty and self-determination. The sacrifices, the commitment, the integrity, the bravery—he embodied all of these. That's why now, whenever I pass the Prescott statue on the hallowed ground of Breed's Hill, I reflect on the achievements born out of Prescott's actions and tip my hat to him.

Epilogue

A solitary statue stands prominently about 15 yards from the southern side of the majestic, 221-foot Bunker Hill Monument in Charlestown, Massachusetts. The memorial is not of a generic soldier, as you often see on battlefields or in certain honored settings, but of Colonel William Prescott.

The statue, sponsored by the Bunker Hill Monument Association (BHMA) and sculpted by William Wetmore Story, is bronze and roughly eight feet tall.[1] It was cast in Rome in 1880 and dedicated in Charlestown in 1881, about 38 years after the more noted obelisk that towers above it. The figure stands on a red and gray granite pedestal that is six feet high. On its base is a short inscription that simply says:

Colonel
William Prescott
June 17, 1775

The statue depicts Prescott adorned in a lightweight banyan cloak and a stylish, full-brimmed hat, jauntily tipped higher over his right ear. A cravat is tied at his neck and spills over a tight-fitting vest. He is wearing button-down boots that ride slightly above his knees. His right leg is extended about a stride ahead of his left. Since there were no known portraits of Prescott, his great-grandson, Arthur Dexter, who was living in Rome at the time the statue was being made, served as its model. At Prescott's feet are a pickaxe and shovel, symbolic of the entrenching tools that were used to build the redoubt in the defense of the hill. There is also a tri-corner hat with cockade and a folded, heavy military coat, which it is believed Prescott wore in the cooler midnight hours before the battle. In his right hand, Prescott has a sword, which extends forward and declines from his body at roughly a 45-degree angle, like he is about to wield it toward an enemy. His left hand also extends slightly from his body and behind in counterbalance, fingers splayed. He looks downward as if eyeing the British troops that rushed uphill that day, hoping to evict the Americans from their hastily constructed dirt fort. Prescott's visage is focused and stern. His is not the posture of the victor, martial and upright, looking skyward.

After all, the Americans lost the battle, something many visitors to the site do not realize. No, Prescott's posture is that of the challenged, the defender, and, most assuredly, the fighter. His stare is intimidating and draws your attention. Prescott seems to be saying to the British: *We know you are coming, we are ready for you, we will not back down.*[2] Altogether, Prescott's statue cuts an impressive figure, which is apropos, because by all accounts he was steadfast on a day of profound impact for the Americans' emerging quest for independence. He was proud, fearless, determined, calm, and unquestionably brave.

William Prescott's statue was unveiled on Breed's Hill in Charlestown on June 17, 1881, the 106th anniversary of the battle. Perhaps no greater tribute could be paid to Prescott than that made by the estimable Daniel Webster, who stated, "And by placing the statue of Colonel William Prescott in the very front of our noble monument, thus recognizing him in his true relation to the grand action which it commemorates, and of which he was nothing less than the commander...if it was proper to give the battle a name, from any distinguished agent in it, it should be called 'Prescott's Battle.'"[3]

Others voiced additional praise. In his address on the occasion, Robert Winthrop, Massachusetts lawyer and onetime Speaker of the U.S. House of Representatives, said: "Prescott with his little band is seen standing undaunted at bay; displaying still as ever, as Ebenezer Bancroft of Tynesborough, a captain in Bridge's regiment, who fought bravely and was wounded at his side, bore special witness that he [Prescott] had displayed during the hottest of the fight, a coolness and self-possession that would do honor to the greatest hero of any age."[4] Winthrop also referred to Prescott as "a man of strong mind, determined will, benevolent as he was brave, liberal even beyond his means, of courteous manners, the pride of his neighborhood, delighting to show kindness and hospitality to his old fellow-soldiers."[5] Prescott's respect and concern for war veterans—for years, he invited them to his home to reminisce—was echoed years later, when author George Hillard noted, "He [Prescott] was generous of temper, and somewhat impaired his estate by his liberal spirit and healthy hospitality."[6]

It is telling that Prescott's statue is the only one on the Bunker Hill battlefield, an obvious honor. To the citizens of Massachusetts and the associations formed to preserve the memories and achievements of the renowned battle, Prescott was their hero. John Stark, Israel Putnam, and Thomas Knowlton also played important roles as leaders of their respective troops during the fight, but they were out-of-staters and not the concern of the local citizens or societies. So, the sole tribute went to Prescott, whose likeness has adorned the battlefield for nearly a century and a half.

In eloquent language meant to inspire the crowd that had come to see the new statue, Winthrop punctuated his oration by saying this about the battle Prescott commanded:

> ...it was only when from all of the American Colonies there had come voices of congratulations and good cheer, recognizing the momentous character of the battle, the bravery with which it was fought, and the conclusive evidence it had afforded that the undisciplined yeomanry of the country were not afraid to confront the veteran armies of Old England at the point of a bayonet in defense of their rights and liberties, it was only then the true importance began to be attached to the battle of Bunker Hill, as the first battle of the American Revolution and the most eventful in its consequences.[7]

Winthrop may also have had the crowning statement of the day, however, when he left no doubt as to how Prescott should be remembered:

> He [Prescott] has returned, not with three fresh regiments only, as he proposed, but with the acclamation of every soldier and every citizen within the sound of what is being said, or within any knowledge of what is being done, here, today. He has retaken Bunker Hill; and, with it, the hearts of all who are gathered on it at this hour, or who shall be gathered upon it, generation and generation, in all the centuries of the future.[8]

Fourteen years later, on October 13, 1895, the centenary of Prescott's death, the BHMA held another noteworthy celebration in Charlestown. A number of dignitaries gave short speeches, but the main address was delivered by U.S. Congressman William Everett of Massachusetts, the son of the great orator, Edward Everett, who spoke for several hours at the dedication of the Gettysburg cemetery ahead of Abraham Lincoln's far shorter, but more memorable, address.

Signifying the special nature of the event and the connection to the Revolutionary War era, William Everett was introduced by the Honorable Frederic W. Lincoln, the great-grandson of Paul Revere. Everett noted that what happened in Boston set the stage for the oncoming Revolutionary War when he said, "The change in [Great Britain's] policy toward America which in twenty years turned one Prescott and one Washington of 1753, the Prescott of the Bay of Fundy and the Washington of the Monongahela, into the Prescott of Bunker Hill and the Washington of Dorchester Heights."[9] Everett added that Prescott "lived to the last loved and honored in his own town not merely for what he had done, but for what he was—a man who could not help charming all who knew him."[10]

Everett also alluded to remarks given at the battle's centenary on June 17, 1875 by General William Tecumseh Sherman, the great Northern warrior of the Civil War. While acknowledging the actions of Warren and Putnam, he said of Prescott, "He was the commander, and he was the only one that exercised the functions of a commander throughout the day."[11] Settling the debate about who was in charge at Bunker Hill, Everett said that "from that [Sherman's] sentence, provided by such a soldier at such a time, there can be, there ought to be, no equal."[12] Everett then quoted Sherman as having said, "If there is any glory in that day, if, as at Thermopylae, the victor for the moment was the vanquished in the result…if Bunker Hill is as unalloyed a source of exaltation as Dorchester or Trenton, as Saratoga or Yorktown, or alloyed by the loss of Warren alone, it is because we had on that day, commanding men unused to military orders, unwilling to do anything for a master, but ready to do all for a leader [Prescott]…"[13]

Beyond statuary, it is well established that art, too, can aggrandize historical figures. Tour any major art museum and you will find scores of paintings of renowned figures from across the ages. Unfortunately, in spite of his importance, Prescott has been largely bypassed in this area. There are no known portraits of Prescott—however, he does appear in two iconic paintings of the Revolutionary War, both by John Trumbull, the famous Connecticut artist of the late 18th and early 19th centuries.[14] Of relevance here, one is *The Death of General Warren at the Battle of Bunker's Hill, June 17, 1775*, first painted in 1786 and which can be found at the art gallery at Yale University.[15] A second, much smaller version of that painting was commissioned by the Warren family in the early 1800s and can be found in Boston's Museum of Fine Arts. Still a third painting was completed in 1834 and hangs in the Hartford's Wadsworth Atheneum. However, in each of these paintings, Prescott is not very conspicuous. For instance, Trumbull depicts fellow Nutmeggers Israel Putnam, Thomas Grosvenor, and especially Thomas Knowlton much more prominently than Prescott.

The other celebrated Trumbull painting in which Prescott is depicted is the massive 1821 painting *The Surrender of General Burgoyne at Saratoga*, which now graces the rotunda of the United States Capitol. In the painting are Horatio Gates, John Stark, Rufus Putnam, Philip Schuyler, John Glover, and Daniel Morgan. Supposedly, Trumbull later admitted he erred unconsciously in not showing Prescott more noticeably in the Bunker Hill painting. To make amends, Trumbull placed Prescott, musket in hand, in the principal group of American figures on the right side of *The Surrender of General Burgoyne* painting, even though Prescott had a minor role there and was not involved in the fighting.[16]

The Bunker Hill Monument and The Lodge

Originally, the BHMA, formed in 1823, purchased the Breed's Hill battle site, roughly 15 acres, with the intent of erecting a shrine to the epic fight.

Solomon Willard, a carver and builder in Massachusetts, was chosen to design and oversee construction of the obelisk, the first such monument erected in the United States. The cornerstone of the Bunker Hill Monument was laid on June 17, 1825 by the French aristocrat, military officer, and celebrated American ally with the long appellation Marie-Joseph Paul Ives Roch Gilbert du Motier, Marquis de Lafayette, who was on a 14-month tour of the United States. Lafayette, as he simply became known, was a close aide to General George Washington and had commanded American troops in several battles in the American Revolution, including the siege of Yorktown.[17] He was 68 years old when he came to Charlestown on the fiftieth anniversary of the famous battle. Alan Hoffman, who translated Auguste Levasseur's journal, published in 1829, about Lafayette's trip to the United States in 1824 and 1825, told me that Lafayette reputedly wanted to be buried with some soil from the battlefield. So, a hogshead of the material was shipped to France for that purpose in 1834. At least once more, in the early 2000s, an additional cannister of soil was delivered to France for Lafayette's grave by the Ancient and Honorable Artillery Company of Boston, the oldest chartered military organization in North America.

On June 17, 1743, more than 100,000 people attended the Bunker Hill Monument's dedication, including incumbent U.S. President John Tyler, who arrived in a carriage with Daniel Webster. Both men gave orations. For Webster, his two speeches provided bookends to the construction of the Monument. Behind Tyler in a second carriage was John Quincy Adams, the ex-President, followed by members of Tyler's cabinet. Attending the ceremony were 107 soldiers who were in the Revolutionary War, including 13 who were at the battle of Bunker Hill and were now in their 80s and 90s.[18] When the Monument was completed it was the tallest structure in the United States.

In 1902, another structure—and the last—was erected on the Bunker Hill Monument National Park site. This building is "The Lodge" that sits adjacent to the Monument on its north side and is the portal visitors use to get inside the obelisk itself. It was the King Solomon's Lodge of Freemasons, who, in 1794, erected the first monument at the Bunker Hill site, a wooden column, and who subsequently asked the BHMA to build a more permanent structure.[19]

Today The Lodge doesn't contain much, just a few artifacts as well as portraits of New Hampshire commander John Stark, British General Henry Clinton, and British naval officer John Linzee. But the center of attention is a large marble statue of Dr. Joseph Warren, a mason himself and the most prominent American to die in the battle. The statue of Dr. Warren was commissioned in the 1850s to commemorate his personal sacrifice. It was sculpted by Henry Dexter and dedicated on June 17, 1857. The statue stands behind a brass railing and is set off on its sides by an American flag and a Charlestown battle flag.

The Monument, as well as the two statues of Warren and Prescott, were not funded from public coffers but by private subscription.[20] Appropriately, two streets in Charlestown are named after Joseph Warren and William Prescott. Furthermore, in 1856, the William Prescott School was built just a few blocks from Bunker Hill Monument National Park; it is now the Warren-Prescott School, honoring both men.[21] The two patriots, forever linked because of the battle and what it meant for the course of history, now stand in their honored forms a mere 50 feet from one another on the heights they fought together to defend.

Remembering William Prescott

Even though Bunker Hill has been immortalized, William Prescott has not. His fame is mostly parochial and probably does not extend much beyond his hometown of Pepperell. School children in the town still learn about Prescott, and recently there was a small movement there to erect a Prescott statue that died out when the head of that effort moved from Pepperell.[22]

On Memorial Day, Boy and Girl Scouts perform a brief ceremony at the Wolcott Memorial, also called the Bunker Hill Bench, in the center of town across Main Street from Town Hall. This semicircular, polished granite structure came about due to the generosity of Edith Prescott Wolcott, a descendant of Colonel Prescott and the spouse of then-Governor Roger Wolcott. It was dedicated on November 1, 1899. The memorial was unveiled by William Brown Prescott, the great, great, great grandson of the Colonel.[23] Governor Wolcott delivered the dedication speech, the Reverend E. E. Hale made a historical address, and the 6th Regimental Band played "Yankee Doodle," "Stars and Stripes," and "America the Beautiful." The memorial is "To the Men of Pepperell" who fought at Bunker Hill, and is inscribed with the names of the eight Pepperell soldiers who died in the battle. Each year, after the Memorial Day ceremony, the scouts then place flowers on the graves of all the veterans buried in the adjacent Walton Cemetery, including Colonel Prescott's grave.

However, even the citizens of Pepperell admit that activities in town associated with Bunker Hill Day, June 17, have declined over the years. This might not have bothered William Prescott, who was consistently governed by personal humility. As a testament to this fact, George Hillard commented that there was never "any reason to suppose that Colonel Prescott himself ever looked upon his conduct on June 17 as anything to be especially commended, but only as the performance of a simple piece of duty, which could not have been put by without shame or disgrace."[24]

John Adams said that American independence changed the world. He was remarkably prescient, as subsequent revolutions, including the French Revolution in 1789 and others to the present day, seemed to have been inspired by the American experience. William Prescott could not have envisioned this at the time, nor do I think he would have cared. However, Prescott's leadership and bravery at Bunker Hill enabled the Americans, at a critical time, to claim victory out of a bloody defeat. His deeds on that singular day, in the context of his entire, patriotic life, deserve to be recognized for their profound influence on American history, and his memory should not be allowed to fade away.

Endnotes

Introduction

1   Bill Parrow, a National Park Service ranger, reports the park had 325,000 visitors in 2019, conducted 1,150 battle talks, and held 100 musket firings. Since the Covid-19 epidemic, the figures have been far smaller.

Prologue

1   Benson Bobrick, *Angel in the Whirlwind: The Triumph of the American Revolution* (New York: Penguin Books, 1998), 140–41.

2   Richard Frothingham, *The Battlefield of Bunker Hill: With a Relation of the Action by William Prescott and Illustrative Documents*, printed for the author (Boston, 1876), 18, Paul Lockhart, *The Whites of Their Eyes: Bunker Hill, The First American Army, and the Emergence of George Washington* (New York: HarperCollins Publishers, 2011), 194, and Rick Atkinson, *The British Are Coming: The War for America, Lexington to Princeton, 1775–1777* (New York: Henry Holt and Company, 2020), 92.

3   Robert Middlekauff, *The Glorious Cause: The American Revolution 1763–1789* (Oxford: Oxford University Press, 1982), 284.

4   Paul Lockhart, 223.

5   Samuel Swett, *History of Bunker Hill Battle* (Boston: Monroe and Francis, 1826), 22; Lockhart, 224–27.

6   Richard Wheeler, *Voices of 1776: The Story of the American Revolution in the Words of Those Who Were There* (New York: Plume, 1991), 41; also cited in Bobrick, 141.

7   Swett, *History*, 22; also cited in Atkinson, 95.

8   Lockhart, 226.

9   Short swords dated to ancient times and served as secondary weapons. While the straight one was good for thrusting, the curved one was good for slashing.

10   Richard Frothingham, *The Battlefield of Bunker Hill*, 19–20, as told by William Prescott, Jr.; also cited in Nathaniel Philbrick, *Bunker Hill: A City, A Siege, A Revolution* (New York: Penguin Books, 2013), 201.

11   Henry B. Carrington, *Battles of the American Revolution* (New York: Promontory Press, 1974), 101; also cited in Atkinson, 99–100.

12   Frothingham, *The Battlefield of Bunker Hill*, 26.

13   Richard Ketchum, *Decisive Day: The Battle of Bunker Hill* (New York: Doubleday, 1962), 127. Ketchum notes that "The rebels fell down when they saw the flash of a cannon and resumed work as soon as the ball had landed." This was gleaned from an enclosure to a letter from Richard Reeve to Sir George Howard on June 22, 1775, found in the County of Buckingham Record office, Howard-Vyse deposit.

14   Keith Brough, *General Ward's Colonial Army* (Rehoboth, MA: Timothy Walker's Regimental Press, 2015), 23.

15   Richard Frothingham, *History of the Siege of Boston and of the Battles of Lexington, Concord, and Bunker Hill* (Boston, MA, 1903), 126 and Ketchum, *Decisive Day*, 127. Also cited in Lockhart, 227n.

16   Frothingham, *The Battlefield of Bunker Hill*, 26.

17   Frothingham, *The Siege of Boston*, 126 and Ketchum, *Decisive Day*, 127. Also cited in Lockhart, 227n.

18   Ketchum, *Decisive Day*, 127.

19   William Prescott, M.D., *The Prescott Memorial or a Genealogical Memoir of the Prescott Families in America, in two Parts* (Boston: Henry W. Dutton and Son, 1870), 59.

20   In Greek mythology, Cerberus is the three-headed dog of King Hades that guards the underworld in order to keep the dead from escaping.

21   Edward Barrington De Fonblanque, *Political and Military Episodes From the Life and Correspondence of the Right Honorable John Burgoyne* (London: Macmillan Press, 1876), 140 and Atkinson, 96–97.

22   Middlekauff, 281. Middlekauff notes, "The presence of the three Britch generals indicated the ministry's dissatisfaction with General Gage's conduct."

23   Lockhart, 211–12.

24   Ira D. Gruber, Troyer S. Anderson, et al., *A Journal Kept in Canada and Upon Burgoyne's Campaign in 1776 and 1777 by Lieutenant James Hadden* (Albany, NY: J. Munsell's Sons), 44, 45–48, 56–58; also cited in John Ferling, *Almost A Miracle* (Oxford: Oxford University Press, 2007), 52.

25   Ketchum, *Decisive Day*, 121 and Lockhart, 214–16.

26   Samuel Adams Drake, *Bunker Hill: The Story Told in Letters from the Battlefield* (Boston: Nichols and Hall, 1875), 10.

27   Middlekauff, 281.

28   Lockhart, 216. Lockhart notes that "the British generals' council adjourned some time before seven o'clock in the morning." Lockhart also points out that General William Howe would be responsible for essentially the entire battle plan for the attack.

29   Joseph Ellis, *Revolutionary Summer: The Birth of American Independence* (New York: Vintage Books, 2013), 44. Ellis offers that Ira D. Gruber's *The Howe Brothers and the American Revolution* is the definitive source on the Howe brothers. Ellis also cites Troyer S. Anderson's *The Command of the Howe Brothers During the American Revolution*.

30   Lockhart, 156.

31   David Hackett Fischer, *Washington's Crossing* (New York: Oxford University Press, 2004), 67–71; and Maldwyn A. Jones in Billias, *George Washington's Opponents*, 43–48. Also found in Ferling, *Almost A Miracle*, 53.

32   Bobrick, 140.

33   The discussion of 18th-century battlefield tactics is drawn from https://tschmidtrevolutionarywarproject.weeby.com/the-tactics.html.

34   Richard Frothingham, *The Centennial Battle of Bunker Hill* (Boston: Little Brown, 1875), 29 and also cited in Atkinson, 97.

35   Letter from Peter Brown to his mother, June 28, 1775, in George F. Sheer and Hugh F. Rankin, *Rebels and Redcoats: The American Revolution Through the Eyes of Those That Fought and Lived It* (Da Capo Press, 1987), 60. Also found in Middlekauff, 284.

36   Franklin Bowditch Dexter, *The Literary Diary of Ezra Stiles*, D.D., L.L.D., Vol. 1 and 2 (New York: Charles Scribner and Sons: 1901), 595; also in Atkinson, 95.

37 Lockhart, 228, citing William Prescott's son, Judge William Prescott's account.

38 *A Particular Account of the Battle of Bunker Hill, or Breed's Hill, on the 17th of June, 1775, by a citizen of Boston*, 12–13, as cited by Lockhart, 229 and Brough, 34.

39 Letter from Colonel William Prescott to John Adams, August 25, 1775, in Massachusetts Historical Society, and cited in Henry Steele Commager and Richard B. Morris, *The Spirit of Seventy-Six: The Story of the American Revolution as Told by Participants* (New York: Bonanza Books, 1983), 125–26 and Lockhart, 201.

40 John B. Hill, *Bi-Centennial of Old Dunstable* (Nashua, NH: E. H. Spalding, 1878), 59–60, provides the description of American cannon, as cited in Lockhart, 239.

41 William Heath, *Heath's Memoirs of the American War* (New York, NY, 1904), 28; also cited in Lockhart, 241–42. Bunker's Hill was named after George Bunker and Breed's Hill was named after Ebenezer Breed, two landowners in Charlestown.

42 Brough, 34.

43 Swett, *History*, 24–25 and Allen French, *The First Year of the American Revolution* (New York, Octagon Books, 1934, reissued 1968) 23–25. Also cited in Lockhart, *The Whites of Their Eyes*, 230.

44 Swett, *History*, 24–25 and Allen French, *The First Year of the American Revolution*, 23–25. Also cited in Lockhart, 230.

45 Richard Frothingham, *The Life and Times of Joseph Warren* (Boston: Little Brown, 1866), 512–14 and Atkinson, *The British Are Coming*, 95.

46 Samuel I. Knapp, *Biographical Sketches of Eminent Lawyers, Statesmen, and Men of Letters* (Boston, 1821), 116 and also cited in Christian DiSpigna, *Founding Martyr: The Life and Death of Dr. Joseph Warren, The American Revolution's Lost Hero* (New York: Crown Publishing, 2018), 81. DiSpigna provides this description of Warren: "Even from his Harvard days performing military drills as a precursor out of the Marti-Mercurians, Warren for several years was preparing himself by study and observation to take a conspicuous rank in the military arrangements which he knew must ensue."

47 Knapp, *Biographical Sketches*, 116 and DiSpigna, *Founding Martyr*, 181.

48 Lockhart, 232. According to Lockhart, General Ward presented his dilemma to Richard Devins, who headed the Committee of Safety.

49 Swett, *History*, 25 and also found in Atkinson, 96.

50 George Ellis, *Battle of Bunker Hill* (Boston: Lee and Shepherd Publishers, 1895), 57–58.

51 Ketchum, *Decisive Day*, 138–39. Ketchum describes the timing of the troop landings from logbooks of the British warships and the accounts of various eyewitnesses.

52 Thomas S. Kidd, *God of Liberty: A Religious History of the American Revolution* (New York: Basic Books, 2010), 1–2 and Atkinson, 99.

53 Samuel A. Green, *Three Military Diaries Kept by Groton Soldiers in Different Wars* (Cambridge, MA: University Press, 1901), 90. Farnsworth may have misremembered when the British set fire to Charlestown, which other accounts placed after the first assault.

54 Samuel Adams Drake, *Bunker Hill*, 16.

55 Lockhart, 231. Lockhart makes the point that, until General Ward had better information regarding what the British were going to do, he didn't want to spare any more men to Colonel Stark than his original two hundred.

56 Brough, *General Ward's Colonial Army*, 34.

57 Ben Z. Rose, *Maverick General* (Waverly, MA: Treeline Press, 2007), 4–5. Rose also provides aspects of Colonel Stark's fighting style, noting he displayed tactics of stealth and surprise learned at an early age from his Native American neighbors.

58 John Ferling, *Almost A Miracle*, 36.

59 Atkinson, 100.

60 John R. Cuneo's *Robert Rogers of the Rangers* is the source for Ben Rose's description; see pp. 26–31.

61 "John Stark," Wikipedia, last modified September 16, 2024, https://en.wikipedia.org/wiki/John_Stark.

62 Caleb Stark, *Memoir and Official Correspondence of General John Stark, with Notices of Several Other Officers of the Revolution* (Heritage Books, 2007), 346 and Rose, 5.

63 Charles Henry Jones, *History of the Campaign for the Conquest of Canada in 1776* (Philadelphia: Porter and Coates, 1882), 2; and Rose, 51.

64 Rose, 59. Rose notes that the "rebels no doubt began to experience a sense of fear and horror, as the thunder and metallic smell of cannon fire began to envelop Charlestown."

65 Henry Dearborn, *An Account of the Battle of Bunker Hill* (Legare Street Press, 2002), 183 and also Lockhart, 257.

66 Bobrick, 141. Bobrick describes the New Hampshire troops arriving at Charlestown Heights. He notes, "Spectators thronged to every elevated point which afforded a view of the scene—to Copp's Hill, rooftops, church steeples, the masts of vessels anchored at the wharves. They so far outnumbered the combatants that the whole area appeared like unto an amphitheater in which the battle was to be staged."

67 Thomas J. Fleming, *Now We Are Enemies: The Story of Bunker Hill* (New York: St. Martin's Press, 1960), 210 and also Rose, 58–59.

68 Bobrick, 141.

69 Drake, *Bunker Hill*, 12.

70 Philbrick, *Bunker Hill*, 203. Philbrick notes that Gage thought that Howe had a far less risky plan. They would coordinate the plan with the high tide at three o'clock in the afternoon.

71 Richard V. Polhemus and John F. Polhemus, *Stark: The Life and Wars of John Stark, French and Indian War Ranger, Revolutionary War General* (Delmar, NY: Black Dome Press, 2014), 168.

72 Frothingham, *The Siege of Boston*, 186–87 and Lockhart, 256.

73 Henry Schenawolf, "The First Shots of the American Revolution That Were Not Heard Round the World," *Revolutionary War Journal*, October 29, 2018, https://www.revolutionarywarjournal/the-first-real-shots-fired-of-the-american-revolution-dec-14-1774.

74 Middlekauff, 288.

75 Drake, *Bunker Hill*, 16.

76 Drake, *Bunker Hill*, 18.

77 From Amos Farnsworth's diary, Massachusetts Historical Society, and www.historycentral.com/Revolt/battleaccounts/BunkerHill/Amosdiary.html. Farnsworth responded to the Concord Alarm in April and fought at Noodle Island.

78 Ketchum, *Decisive Day*, 138.

Chapter 1

1 Daniel Kahneman received the Nobel Prize in Economics in 2002 for work in the field of behavioral analysis, and would have shared the award with his collaborator, Amos Tversky, except he passed away before the award was granted.

2 The Boston Public Library, established in 1848 by an act of the General Court of Massachusetts, was the first large, free municipal library in the United States.

3 The MHS holds vast collections of presidential papers and letters from all presidents through George H. W. Bush. It also houses the Adams Family Papers (John 1735–1826, Abigail

1744–1818) and the Coolidge Collection of Thomas Jefferson Manuscripts, the largest assemblage of private papers, correspondence, manuscripts, and architectural drawings of America's third president. Interestingly, each year the MHS and the National Society of the Colonial Dames of America present the William Hickling Prescott Award for Excellence in Historical Writing.

Chapter 2

1   Prescott, M.D., 31. Many of the details in this chapter are drawn from the *Genealogical Memoir of the Prescott Family in America.*
2   Prescott, M.D., 32.
3   David Jaffee, *People of the Wachusett: Greater New England in History & Memory 1630–1860* (Ithaca: Cornell University Press, 1999), 44.
4   Barbados grew to 44,000 settlers by mid-century, far more than the 23,000 that inhabited New England.
5   Richard Brookhiser points out that information on the first Morrises is found in the *New York Post*, "Famous New York Families: The Morrises," May 11, 1901, see Notes, 223.
6   Prescott, M.D., 35.
7   See "John Adams & the Massachusetts Constitution," Mass.gov, www.mass.gov/guides/john-adams-the-massachusetts-constitution.
8   Prescott, M.D., 36.
9   Todd MacAlister, *New England Frontier: The Prescott Garrison—1692* (West Conshohocken, PA: InfinityPublishing.com, 2008), 19.
10 Prescott, M.D., 36.
11 The life of Anne Hutchinson is well portrayed in Eve LaPlante's book *American Jezebel* (New York, Harper Collins, 2004). Hutchinson was eventually, some might say belatedly, pardoned by Massachusetts Governor Michael Dukakis in 1987, reversing the order by Governor John Winthrop 350 years earlier. A statue of Hutchinson with her young daughter, Susanna, stands on the grounds of the Massachusetts capitol on Beacon Hill in Boston.
12 Jaffee, 53–54.
13 Jaffee, 54.
14 Prescott, M.D., 37.
15 Prescott, M.D., 37.
16 Prescott, M.D., 38.
17 Prescott, M.D., 39.
18 Prescott, M.D., 39.
19 Prescott, M.D., 38.
20 Prescott, M.D., 42. John Prescott's third child, named after him, was born in 1634, before the family came to America, but he died in the same year. The following year, John and his wife had another son, who they also named John.
21 This reference and others in this section are from Prescott, M.D. *Genealogical Memoir.*
22 Samuel A. Green, *The Boundary Lines of Old Groton* (Cambridge, MA: University Press, 1885), 2.
23 MacAlister, 1–3.
24 MacAlister, 19.
25 MacAlister, 3, and "Groton, Massachusetts," Wikipedia, last modified November 1, 2024, https://en.wikipedia.org/wiki/Groton%2C_Massachusetts. This conflict was also known as the Great Narragansett War or the First Indian War.

26 MacAlister, 3.

27 MacAlister, 3.

28 Prescott, M.D., 42–44.

29 Prescott, M.D., 42–44.

30 MacAlister, 23–24.

31 Prescott, M.D., 44. As the memoir makes clear, the colonists stood on their own and had to rely on only themselves for support and protection.

32 Prescott, M.D., 44.

33 Jaffee, 167.

34 Green, *The Boundary Lines of Old Groton*, 39.

35 Green, *The Boundary Lines of Old Groton*, 51.

36 Prescott, M.D., 110.

37 Samuel A. Green, *Groton During the Revolution* (Legare Street Press, rereleased 2022), 227. Mrs. Rockwood was born in Groton on November 11, 1785, which made her 10 years old when William Prescott died. Her father was Rev. Daniel Chaplin of Groton and her mother was Susana, the eldest daughter of Judge James Prescott, brother of William Prescott.

38 This war was the third of the four stages of the wars with France that had spilled onto the new continent. It followed King William's War (1688–97) and Queen Anne's War (1702–13), and preceded the French and Indian War (1756–63).

39 Albert Marrin, *Struggle for a Continent: The French and Indian Wars, 1690–1760* (New York: Macmillan Press, 1987), 58–62.

40 Lockhart, 189–90.

41 Lorenzo Blood, from a paper titled "Pepperell," found in the Pepperell Town Hall files.

42 Lorenzo Blood, from a paper titled "Pepperell," found in the Pepperell Town Hall files.

43 Katherine Blood Hills, "The Fletcher Picnic," in *A Pepperell Reader* (The Pepperell Historical Society, reissued 2005), 129. William's land inheritance amounted to 120 acres. By practice, James, William's older brother, as first son, received a double share of the inheritance left by his father.

44 Charles Edward Potter, *Genealogies of Some Old Families of Concord* (Janaway Publishing, 2011), 105, 110 and Susan Kurland, *A Political Progress: Process of Democratization in Concord, MA, 1750–1850* (Senior Thesis, Brandeis University, 1973), 96; also cited in Robert A. Gross, *The Minutemen and Their World* (New York: Hill and Wang, 1976), 82.

45 Daniel Scott Smith, "Parental Power and Marriage Patterns: An Analysis of Historical Trends in Hingham, Massachusetts," *Journal of Marriage and the Family*, XXXV (August 1973), 412–29, as well as cited in Gross, 78.

46 From an untitled article of unknown origin found in a file of newspaper and other clippings on William Prescott at the Lawrence Library in Pepperell, Massachusetts.

47 Michael Zuckerman, *Peaceable Kingdoms: New England Towns in the Eighteenth Century* (New York, 1970), 32–45 and Gross, *Minutemen*, 10.

48 MacAlister, 48.

49 Although all citizens of Massachusetts Bay were obligated by law to attend church, not everyone adhered to this dictum. Typically most of those attending church, often up to three-quarters, were women. Moreover, only a small percentage of the population were actual "members" of the church. Church membership was a privileged position in the community, and only members were allowed to vote on church matters and hold church office. Furthermore, becoming a member was an exceedingly arduous process. The existing elders and ministers of the church would examine the credentials of a candidate to determine if his or her religious knowledge or experience was adequate to merit membership. This is why membership conferred such status.

50 Lorenzo Blood, from a paper titled "Pepperell," found in the Pepperell Town Hall files.

51 Abram Brown, *Footprints of the Patriots Beside Old Hearth-Stones* (London: Forgotten Books, Classic Reprint, 2017), 16. A passage in this book confirms Prescott's affiliation with the church. It says: "Rev. Mr. Emerson [the deacon in Pepperell] the zealous apostle of liberty in the town, found a faithful coworker in William Prescott, one of his parishioners."

52 Lorenzo Blood, from a paper titled "Pepperell," found in the Pepperell Town Hall files.

53 Lorenzo Blood, from a paper titled "Pepperell," found in the Pepperell Town Hall files.

54 Fred Anderson, *Crucible of War: The Seven Years' War and the Fate of Empire in British North America* (New York: Vintage Books, 2000), 138–39.

55 Samuel Abbott Green, *Colonel William Prescott and Groton Soldiers in the Battle of Bunker Hill, From the Proceedings of the Massachusetts Historical Society, November 1909* (Cambridge: John Wilson and Son, University Press, 1909), 4.

56 Walter R. Borneman, *The French and Indian War: Deciding the Fate of North America* (New York: Harper Collins, 2006), 207.

57 Green, *Colonel William Prescott and Groton Soldiers*, 4–5. This was the action that was mentioned earlier that Prescott's brother-in-law, Abijah Willard, was involved in.

58 William Everett, *Oration in Honor of Colonel William Prescott*. Delivered in Boston, October 14, 1895, by the Invitation of the Bunker Hill Monument Association (Published in Boston by the Association, 1896), 44.

59 Everett, *Oration*, 44.

60 Thelma Bennett, "The Early Schools," in *A Pepperell Reader* (The Pepperell Historical Society, 2005), 87.

61 Bennett, "The Early Schools," 87.

62 Lorenzo Blood, "Colonel Prescott and the Battle of Bunker Hill," in *A Pepperell Reader* (The Pepperell Historical Society, 2005), 51.

63 Prescott, M.D., 57–58.

64 Prescott, M.D., 75.

65 Everett, 44.

66 Prescott, M.D., 76.

67 Prescott, M.D., 76.

68 Unfortunately for those who supported this move, after General Andrew Jackson defeated the British in the battle of New Orleans, effectively ending the War of 1812, popular sentiment for the country swept through New England and the separatist activities of the convention were harshly denounced.

69 Prescott, M.D., 76.

70 Prescott, M.D., 107.

Chapter 3

1 Claudia Durst Johnson, *Daily Life in Colonial New England* (Westport, CT: Greenwood Press, 2002), 60.

2 William Prescott received 120 acres of land in Groton's West Parish as an inheritance from his father, but he expanded the farm to 250 acres according to records in Pepperell's Town Hall.

3 Massachusetts was the first British colony to legalize slavery in 1641. Slavery was not outlawed in the state until 1783, though it was the first state to do so.

4 Johnson, *Daily Life in Colonial New England*, 61. This hypothetical schedule describes the typical day of a worker on a small farm in central Massachusetts in the 17th century, as reported by Stephen Innes in *Labor in a New Land* (Princeton, NJ: Princeton University Press, 2014).

5   https://legacy.sites.fas.harvard.edu/~hsb41/masstax/masstax.cgi, accessed January 15, 2025. This was used to investigate the town-by-town and taxpayer-by-taxpayer information.

6   Information is from the Massachusetts Valuation of 1771, Town of Pepperell, Middlesex County, William Prescott property.

7   Jonathan Nourse noted that one of his great ancestors, Joel Nourse, was an accomplished blacksmith who invented the Nourse Eagle Plow in 1842 that was designed to withstand the rocky New England soil. It was the bestselling plow in America for a decade, and an example of that plow now resides in the Smithsonian Museum of American History.

8   The transaction can be found in the Registry of Deeds for South Middlesex County, Grantee Book 1639–1799, Volume 6, Book 177, pages 143–45. Also, typically hay, an extremely important product of colonial farms and one of Prescott's main outputs, was stored in barns from December to April to keep it out of the rain, cold, and other inclement weather. Farmers who did not have a barn had to preserve it using haycocks in the field, conical heaps of hay often seen dotting ancient farms. It's simply inconceivable that Prescott did not have a barn.

9   Massachusetts Historical Society, William Hickling Prescott Papers, Box 25.

10 Thomas Keefe Callahan, *The Voice of the People of This Country: The Birth of Popular Politics and Support for the Shaysite Insurrection in Groton, Massachusetts*, Master's Thesis in the Field of History for the Degree of Master of Liberal Arts in Extension Studies (Harvard University, June 1991).

11 As an example of the predominance of apples in New England, Jonathan Nourse reports that, in the late 1800s, 57 different varieties of apples were grown on the Nourse Farm. Some of the apples were so delicious that their clients in England had them shipped across the ocean.

12 Joshua Vollmar, "Reflections on Juneteenth: Groton's History of Enslavement & Abolition," *The Groton Herald*, June 16, 2023, 1. Vollmar's article notes that Governor John Winthrop helped draft the code that legalized slavery in Massachusetts, making the state the first British colony to adopt the practice.

13 This document can be found in the Pepperell Town Hall, in a vault next to the office of the town clerk.

14 "Colonel William Prescott," Revolutionary War (website), www.revolutionary-war.net/colonel-william-prescott. Although Prescott's farm injury is mentioned by several sources, I have not been able to find any details about the nature of his injury.

Chapter 4

1   A word about the Lawrence Library. Pepperell's first athenaeum, housed in Town Hall and called the Pepperell Social Library, was founded in 1795, ironically the very year the education-advocate William Prescott died. This repository was replaced by the Lawrence Library in 1901. The library now states as its mission, "to promote quality services, resources, and lifelong learning opportunities through books and a variety of other formats to meet the informational, educational, cultural, and recreational needs and interests of Pepperell residents."

2   The Pepperell town records are not generally numbered, so references to them do not always indicate page numbers.

3   www.classroom.synonym.com/about-colonial-life-in-Massachusetts-12081170.html, accessed January 15, 2025.

4   Jackie Mansky, "The History of the Town Hall Debate," *Smithsonian Magazine*, October 6, 2016, available online at: https://www.smithsonianmag.com/history/history-town-hall-debate-180960705/, accessed January 15, 2025.

5   Kurland, Chapter 3, and Robert E. Brown, *Middle-Class Democracy and the Revolution in Massachusetts, 1691–1780* (New York, 1935), 80–81. Also cited in Gross, *Minutemen*, 11.

6   Mansky, "The History of the Town Hall Debate."

7   Even today, getting citizens to vote can be problematic. Australia has compulsory voting; those who don't vote pay a fine. The country typically boasts voting rates of over 90 percent. By comparison, in the United States, getting more than 50 percent to vote is difficult in most elections.

8   Mansky, "The History of the Town Hall Debate."

9   Merrill Jensen, *The Founding of a Nation: A History of the American Revolution* (New York, 1968), 3–35; R. C. Simmons, *The American Colonies: From Settlement to Independence* (New York, 1976), 150–205; and Gordon Wood, *The Radicalism of the American Revolution* (New York: Vintage Books, a division of Random House, 1993), 77–92. Also cited in John Ferling, *Whirlwind: The American Revolution and the War That Won It* (New York: Bloomsbury Press, 2015), 4–5.

10   Letter from John Adams to Nathan Webb, October 12, 1755, in Taylor et al.; John J. Waters, Jr., *The Otis Family in Provincial and Revolutionary Massachusetts* (Chapel Hill Omohundro Institute of American History, 1968), 103. Also cited in Gordon Wood, *The Radicalism of the American Revolution*, 4.

Chapter 5

1   Ferling, *Whirlwind*, 7.

2   Ferling, *Whirlwind*, 4.

3   The Sugar Act was intended to end the smuggling of sugar and molasses from the French and Dutch West Indies in the Caribbean. The Stamp Act placed taxes of various amounts on legal documents, newspapers, pamphlets, licenses, and bills of lading. It also stipulated that the revenue was to be used exclusively for the colonies' defense.

4   John Tyler, *Smugglers and Patriots: Boston Merchants and the Advent of the American Revolution* (Boston: Northeastern University Press, 1986), 91 and Ferling, *Whirlwind*, 20. Following Tyler, Ferling points out that in an essay in the *Boston Gazette*, James Otis broadened the scope of his attack by indicting Britian's mercantilist system for putting the colonists in a "dependent state."

5   Letter from John Adams to William Tudor, March 29, 1817, cited in Ferling, *Whirlwind*, 20.

6   Ferling, *Whirlwind*, 42–44.

7   Pepperell Town Records 1742–1809, Volume 1.

8   Pepperell Town Records 1742–1809, Volume 1.

9   Even though the Stamp Act was revoked relatively quickly, according to historian Bernard Bailyn, it was after this anti-tax controversy that colonial resistance turned into an organized strategy.

10   Roger J. Champagne, *The Sons of Liberty and the Aristocracy in New York Politics, 1765–1790*, unpublished Ph.D. dissertation (University of Wisconsin, 1960), 207, 249–75; Richard Walsh, *Charleston's Sons of Liberty* (Columbia, SC, 1959), 49–50; and from reports in the North Carolina Sons of Liberty in the *South Carolina Gazette* on July 5 and August 9, 1770, as cited by Pauline Maier, *From Resistance to Revolution: Colonial radicals and the development of American opposition to Britain, 1765–1776* (New York, W. W. Norton & Company, 1991), 116.

11   First, Townshend suspended the New York Assembly until it complied with the Mutiny Act, which dealt with the quartering of soldiers. Second, he created the American Board of Customs, which was designed to streamline the prosecution of violators of the prevailing trade laws. And third, he passed the Revenue Act of 1767, which placed duties on British china, glass, lead, paint, paper, and tea. The Townshend Acts rekindled the organized colonial resistance

movement embodied in the actions of the Sons of Liberty that had emerged during the Stamp Act crisis. Yet while this new resistance posture was intended to be peaceful, it morphed quickly into a more serious objection to British authority.

12 Maier, *From Resistance to Revolution*, 114–15.

13 Dickinson declared that if Parliament succeeded in taxing America, "Our boasted liberty would be [merely] a sound and nothing else." Dickinson was not a wild-eyed radical. For instance, he did not argue that Parliament had no authority over the colonies, but he clearly sided with James Otis regarding taxation.

14 The event started with a confrontation that broke out between a loyalist sympathizer and suspected informer, Ebenezer Richardson, and a crowd outside his house in Boston. In defending his house, Richardson shot pellets from his window that struck two people, including an 11-year-old boy, Christopher Seidel, who was killed.

15 Robert Allison, *The Boston Massacre* (Beverly, MA: Commonwealth Editions, 2006), 50. Allison notes British soldiers Hugh Montgomery and Matthew Kilroy had their thumbs branded on December 14 and were then released.

16 Bernard Bailyn, *The Ideological Origins of the Revolutionary Revolution* (Cambridge, MA: Harvard University Press, 2017), 109. Bailyn says the Hutchinsons, the Olivers, and their ambitious allies had managed, by accumulating a large plurality of offices, to engross the power of all branches of the Massachusetts government, enabling a "foundation on which to build a tyranny."

17 Middlekauff, 215–16.

18 Pepperell Town Records 1742–1809, Volume 1.

19 Pepperell Town Records 1742–1809, Volume 1.

20 Ruth P. Liebowitz, "The Early Settlers," *A Pepperell Reader* (The Pepperell Historical Society, 2005), 29.

21 Ferling, *Whirlwind*, 73. Ferling notes that in the late 1760s, nearly twice as much smuggled tea was being sold in England, Ireland, and America as was being sold by the East India Tea Company. In 1767, Parliament had offered to help by reducing the East India Company's tax burden, but it was the same year that the Townshend duties levied a tax on tea in the colonies, blunting the effect of Parliament's action.

22 Allison, *The Boston Massacre*, 57.

23 Prior to the law, the East India Company was required to sell its tea through London where it was taxed and duties assessed. Under the new law, the company could sell directly to the colonies without the added cost of the taxes. To make the law more palatable to the colonists, the English tea was effectively discounted. But this maneuver did not satisfy the colonists, who, once again, felt they were being abused by Parliament and having their liberties curtailed by eliminating the choice of tea products. As a result, Samuel Adams and other hardliners insisted that Bostonians not purchase East India tea.

24 Ferling, *Whirlwind*, 76–78. Ferling suggests Thomas Hutchinson's refusal to order the tea ships to return to England, "may have been his way of settling old scores with Samuel Adams and the other radicals that tormented him for years in Boston."

25 Pepperell Town Records 1742–1809, Volume 1.

26 Ferling, *Whirlwind*, 79–82. Ferling cites scores of reactions from the British government. I recommend that any interested readers read Notes 1–7 to Chapter 5 of *Whirlwind*.

27 Pepperell Town Records, 1742–1809, Volume 1, 152.

28 Robert Winthrop, *The Unveiling of the Statue of Colonel William Prescott on Bunker Hill June 17, 1881* (Cambridge: John Wiley and Son, Cambridge University Press, 1881), 21.

29 Winthrop, 21–22.

30 Winthrop, 21.

31 Blood, "Colonel Prescott and the Battle of Bunker Hill," 46.

32 Ferling, *Whirlwind*, 87. Ferling emphasizes that the Massachusetts citizenry loathed the people whom General Gage had appointed to the new governing council. He notes that crowds in the hundreds and thousands gathered to force the newly appointed councilors to resign.

33 An excellent biography of Dr. Joseph Warren is *Founding Martyr: The Life and Death of Dr. Joseph Warren, The American Revolution's Lost Hero*, by Christian DiSpigna.

34 DiSpigna, 31–50. This chapter of DiSpigna's book focuses on Warren's years at Harvard.

35 On October 26, 1774, the Provincial Congress adopted a comprehensive military program based on the militia. It created the Executive Committees of Safety and of Supplies and gave the Congress the power to order out the militia in an emergency. It also directed militia officers to reorganize their commands into more efficient units, to conduct new elections, to drill according to the latest British manual, and to organize one-quarter of the colony's force into "minute companies" or rapid deployment forces. However, not everyone was thrilled with the new, and ominous, military preparations. The most conservative colonists were shaken by the direction being taken and warned that the colonists were not capable of defeating the British regulars, which would lead to even more draconian measures.

36 Thomas Jefferson, "Draft of Instructions to the Virginia Delegation in the Continental Congress, July 1774," in the *Papers of Thomas Jefferson*, 1:121–135, and cited in Ferling, *Whirlwind*, 108.

37 These resolves laid out charges that the representatives at the convention had against the British and recommended a number of key provisions. First, they called for a boycott of British goods, the curtailment of exports, and a pledge to refuse to use British products. They proposed that the colonists pay "no obedience" to the Massachusetts Government Act or the Boston Port Bill and demanded the resignations of those who were appointed to positions under the Massachusetts Government Act. The resolves supported a colonial government in Massachusetts free of royal authority until the Intolerable Acts were repealed. Prophetically, too, they also called for the colonies to raise militias of their own people and begin war preparations.

38 Bailyn, 126. Bailyn notes that there were repeated cries that Parliament's action was "intended to take away the colonists' liberty and to enslave them." Bailyn goes on to wonder why Parliament was giving so much attention to the provinces in America. He suggests that one explanation was that the court, having largely run out of opportunities for patronage and spoils in the British Isles, sought a quarrel with the colonies as an excuse for confiscating their wealth.

39 "Suffolk Resolves," US History Primary Sources (blog), August 1, 2009, available at: https://us1primarysources.blogspot.com/2009/08/suffolk-resolves.html.

40 James P. Byrd, *Sacred Scripture, Sacred War: The Bible and the American Revolution* (New York: Oxford University Press, 2013), 39–63 and T. H. Breen, *American Insurgents, American Patriots: The Revolution of the People* (New York: Hill and Wang, 2010), 243, 249–51, as cited in Ferling, *Whirlwind*, 52–53.

41 Tensions in the colonies regarding how to view Parliamentary power and the increasingly severe British actions continued to ratchet up in late 1774 and early 1775. Much of the debate played out in both transparent, as well as anonymous, exchanges in newspapers and other documents. One notable argument occurred between Samuel Seabury, an Anglican priest, and Alexander Hamilton, then a precocious young student at King's College (later Columbia University) in New York City. Seabury declared that war would break out if Americans followed the designs of its Congress. For his part, Hamilton did not seem to fear a war; in fact, he very nearly embraced one.

42 Letter from Thomas Gage to Lord Dartmouth, September 2, 1774 and letters from Thomas Gage to Lord Barrington, September 26, October 3, and November 2, 1774, as cited in Ferling, *Almost A Miracle*, 28–29.

Chapter 6

1 Jensen, *The Founding of a Nation*, 554–55, 584 and Allen French, *The Day of Concord and Lexington: The Nineteenth of April, 1775* (Boston, 1925), 12–14, 39–40, as cited in Gross, 110.

2 Gage got intelligence from a civilian spy named John Howe that Worcester was too far away from Boston for action (it was 50 miles away), but Concord, at half that distance, was a better objective. In a note, Howe also told Gage, with amazing foresight, that "500 mounted men might ride to Concord at night and destroy the armaments and return safe, but to go with 1,000 foot…the country would be so alarmed, that the greater part of them [the troops] would be killed or taken." While Gage was impressed with Howe's report, he had no cavalry under his command and thus had to take his chances with soldiers on foot.

3 Ferling, *Whirlwind*, 100.

4 Louis Birnbaum, *Red Dawn at Lexington* (Boston: Houghton Mifflin Harcourt, 1986), 148 and Ferling, *Almost A Miracle*, 29.

5 On April 5, Gage asked the navy to prepare boats that could move troops across the Back Bay to Cambridge. He also sent a party of British officers out of Boston to examine the roads leading to Concord. These movements alerted the vigilant colonists, who passed the intelligence along to the local leaders.

6 Green, *Groton During the Revolution*, 4.

7 David Hackett Fischer, *Paul Revere's Ride* (New York: Oxford University Press, 1994), 89. Fischer notes, ironically, that the patrolling British officers, whose assignment was to stop the American night riders, had the effect of alerting the colonists themselves.

8 Arthur Tourtellot, *Lexington and Concord: The Beginning of the War of the American Revolution* (New York: W. W. Norton, and Co., 1959), 91.

9 DiSpigna, 166.

10 The British started to muster around nine o'clock on the evening of April 18. There were delays, however, and it wasn't until between midnight and one o'clock in the morning on the 19th that approximately 800 British troops rowed across the Charles River to Phipp's Farm in East Cambridge, and it wasn't until two o'clock before they began their march west. The expedition was already doomed to failure, however, as the colonists had already started to disperse the armaments in Concord to other neighboring towns.

11 Fischer, *Paul Revere's Ride*, 98–103.

12 Tourtellot, 93.

13 Reverend Jonas Clark, *Opening of the War of the Revolution, 19th of April, 1775, a Brief Narrative of the Principal Transactions of that Day*. This document was appended to a sermon given by Jonas Clark in Lexington on the first anniversary of the engagement, delivered on April 19, 1776. This source was cited in Tourtellot, *Lexington and Concord*, 99. Also Stacy Schiff, *The Revolutionary: Samuel Adams* (New York: Little, Brown, and Company, 2022), 18. Clark had moved to Lexington in 1755 when he was 24 years old, just three years out of Harvard College. The 44-year-old Clark was the pastor of the Church of Christ in Lexington and a sympathizer to the revolutionary cause.

14 Frank Warren Coburn, *The Battle of April 19, 1775* (Lexington, MA, 1912), 554–55, 584, as well as French, *The Day of Concord and Lexington*, 85–86, 88–90. Also cited in Gross, 116.

15 Tourtellot, 19. Tourtellot notes that Captain John Parker and others knew the British were on their way to Concord, but that they had to pass through Lexington first.

16 Schiff, 19. William Dawes arrived in Lexington around 1:00 p.m., even though he left Boston roughly two hours before Revere.

17 According to the Prescott Genealogical History, Dr. Samuel Prescott was later taken prisoner and sent to Halifax, Nova Scotia, where he died on a prison ship.

18 Although William Dawes, like Revere, never made it to Concord, he fought at the battle of Bunker Hill two months later and joined the army for the siege of Boston.

19 Gross, 118. Elements of this story were also supplied by Archer O'Reilly, the longtime Secretary of the Massachusetts Society of the Order of the Cincinnati. Archer is a descendant of Dr. Samuel Prescott and a proud admirer of Colonel Prescott. He is also a graduate of Harvard, as were all of his male predecessors dating back to 1645. Archer actively studies the Revolutionary War era and can occasionally be found impersonating General Henry Knox at various events in Boston.

20 DiSpigna, 168.

21 French, 95–99 and Tourtellot, 129–30, 139. Also cited in Gross, 117.

22 Tourtellot, 125–26. Tourtellot notes that Captain Parker made no attempt to get his men into nearby positions in pastures and woodlands, from which they could have watched the British approach and had the element of surprise and mobility when fighting broke out.

23 Middlekauff, 269.

24 Fisher, *Paul Revere's Ride*, 190–91 and Gross, 117.

25 DiSpigna, 168.

26 Ferling, *Almost A Miracle*, 30. Ferling notes that Lieutenant Colonel Smith had refused to call off the expedition, but he did send a messenger to General Gage asking for reinforcements.

27 By this time, about 150 men had assembled on Concord Common waiting for news from Lexington. Finally, Reuben Brown galloped into town with an eyewitness report on the shooting there. "Were they shooting bullets?" asked Major Buttrick. "I do not know," replied Brown. In his haste to get back to Concord, he had neglected to determine the outcome of the confrontation. This was more than just unfortunate, as the soldiers in Concord would now have to face the British without knowing for certain whether their fellow Americans had fought back or if blood had been shed.

28 Prescott, M.D., 57.

29 Massachusetts Archives Collection, v. 99, 440–42, no date, *c.* 1771. This document shows William Prescott as captain of the militia company in Pepperell. After the battles at Lexington and Concord, Prescott would be elevated to colonel.

30 Blood, "Colonel Prescott and the Battle of Bunker Hill," 47. Other details in this section were reported in Lorenzo Blood's account.

31 The British move against Concord was not wholly unexpected. The observed movement of British troops in the days before, as well as intelligence from assorted spies, had created a sense of anticipation among citizens. In fact, on April 17, the Committee of Safety and Supplies had voted to transfer four six-pounders (cannon) from Concord to Groton and put them under the care of Oliver Prescott. The following day, it was decided that certain ammunition, as well as a large number of tents and two medicine chests, would also be sent to Groton for their safety.

32 French, *The Day of Concord and Lexington*, 162–66 and Allen French, *General Gage's Informers* (New York: Greenwood Press, 1968), 33, as cited in Gross, *Minutemen*, 120–21.

33 Tourtellot, 163. Tourtellot notes that there were six companies of minutemen—two from Concord and one each from Bedford, Lincoln, Action, and Carlisle.

34 Ferling, *Almost A Miracle*, 31. Ferling makes the point that militiamen, farmers, and artisans arrived in Concord not to defend an American union but to defend their province of Massachusetts against what they believed to be "the malevolent intentions of a far-off imperial government."

35 Josephine Hosmer, "Memoir of Joseph Hosmer," in Concord Antiquarian Society Papers, Concord Free Library, Shattuck, 111, cited in Gross, *Minutemen*, 125, and Tourtellot, *Lexington and Concord*, 161.

36 Tourtellot, *Lexington and Concord*, 163–66. Other details in this section are drawn from Tourtellot's account.

37 Mary Beth Norton, *1774: The Long Year of Revolution* (New York: Alfred A. Knopf, 2020), 341.

38 French, *The Day of Concord and Lexington*, 220 and Tourtellot, 178, cited in Gross, 129. Gross also cited Letter from Sutherland to General Gage, April 27, 1775, in General Gage's Papers.

39 On the border between the towns of Lincoln and Lexington, the British were attacked again with troops from Captain John Parker's Lexington Company, some of whom had been on Lexington Green in that morning's confrontation. The British took more casualties until a British flanking party cleared the area. But shortly thereafter, John Parker himself—along with more men from his company, including some with bloody bandages wrapped over wounds they had sustained on the Green roughly 10 hours earlier—began firing from a steep hillside as the British passed by. Lieutenant Colonel Smith was hit in the thigh and tumbled off his horse before Major Pitcairn drove the provincials from their position. Smith survived, but more of his troops were lost. That hillside is now referred to as Parker's Revenge.

40 DiSpigna, 169.

41 Middlekauff, 272.

42 Fischer, *Paul Revere's Ride*, 262.

43 Heath, 33 and Lieutenant John Barker, King's Own Regiment, "A British Officer in Boston," in the *Atlantic Monthly*, XXXIX, 389ff, as cited in Tourtellot, 202 and Gross, 130.

44 Bobrick, 120.

45 Fischer, *Paul Revere's Ride*, 281–82.

46 Blood, "Colonel Prescott and the Battle of Bunker Hill," 47.

47 From an undated article of unknown origin found in a file of clippings on William Prescott, located in Lawrence Library in Pepperell, Massachusetts.

48 Massachusetts Archives Collection, Volume 140, 44. Minutes of the Committee of Safety May 26, 1775: "Coll William Prescott was recommended to the Congress to have his Regiment commissioned."

49 Pepperell also contributed a memorable side note to the history of Lexington and Concord when district resident Prudence Cummings Wright, wife of local resident David Wright, led a party of patriotic women in capturing Captain Leonard Whiting. Whiting was a Tory spy who was riding through town several days after the fighting on April 19, carrying intelligence for the British in his boots. Acting like a female company of minutemen, Prudence and her compatriots—dubbed Mrs. David Wright's Guard—assembled in the dark near a prominent local bridge. When Whiting eventually rode by, the women surrounded his horse and compelled him to dismount. After searching his person, the "treasonable papers" he was carrying were found and Whiting was taken prisoner.

50 Gordon Wood, *The Creation of the American Republic 1776–1787* (Chapel Hill: University of North Carolina Press, 1998), 3–4.

51 Atkinson, 86. As tensions continued to climb, the Second Continental Congress met as planned in Philadelphia on May 10. This was less than a month since the first outright fighting between the British and Americans erupted in the farming towns of Lexington and Concord.

52 DiSpigna, 172.

Chapter 7

1 Lockhart, 173. Lockhart notes that Generals Gage, Howe, Clinton, and Burgoyne saw Dorchester Heights as the more important elevation to capture. Their plan was to capture Dorchester Heights first then launch an attack on General Thomas in Roxbury. Then, and only then, would they turn their attention to Charlestown. Cambridge would be their next objective.

2 Since it was difficult to tell apart those who were loyalists and those who sided with the insurrectionists, a lot of intelligence was picked up merely by listening to conversations on the street between soldiers who were privy to British plans. The information was passed along from one person to the next until it made its way to someone connected to the Committee of Safety or even the Provincial Congress.

3 Atkinson, 92.

4 Drake, *Bunker Hill*, 9 footnote 1.

5 Atkinson, 91.

6 A brief review of Benjamin Franklin's activities in London prior to the war is described in John Ferling's book *Whirlwind*, 22, 101–4.

7 DiSpigna, 150. DiSpigna notes that the Suffolk Resolves professed loyalty to King George in an effort to pacify the more centrist and conservative Whigs.

8 Blood, "Colonel Prescott and the Battle of Bunker Hill," 47.

9 A brief profile of Israel Putnam can be found in Philbrick, *Bunker Hill*, 57 and Lockhart, 148–49.

10 Ferling, *Almost A Miracle*, 35 and Atkinson, 88–89. Ferling describes how Putnam dropped his plow when he heard the news about Lexington and Concord, mounted his horse, called for his minutemen, and rode to Concord, though he arrived the day after the battle, when the British were long gone.

11 Atkinson, 88–89.

12 In a meeting with Artemas Ward and Joseph Warren before Bunker Hill, Ward said to Putnam, "As peace and reconciliation is what we seek for, would it not be better to act only on the defensive and give no unnecessary provocation?" To this, Putnam replied, "You know, Dr. Warren, we shall have no peace worth anything, till we gain it by the sword" (see Robert Ernest Hubbard, *Major General Israel Putnam: Hero of the American Revolution*, (Jefferson, NC: McFarland and Company, 2017), 119).

13 In 1758, during the French and Indian War, Putnam was captured by Mohawk Indians and nearly burned at the stake. Fortunately, a rainstorm and a French officer intervened at the last moment.

14 Philbrick, *Bunker Hill*, 182. Putnam was not known to be a strategic military thinker, leading a Hessian officer in the Revolutionary War to say, "This old gray-beard may be a good, honest man, but nobody but the rebels would have made him a general."

15 Lockhart, 149–50. Lockhart points out that Artemus Ward was a close friend of both Samuel Adams and Joseph Warren.

16 Ferling, *Almost A Miracle*, 35. Ferling cites Charles Martyn, *The Life of Artemas Ward, the First Commander-in-Chief of the American Revolution* (New York: Kennikat Press, 1921) as a prime source for the information on Ward's earlier years.

17 Martyn, *Artemas Ward*, 89–91 and Lockhart, 20–25.

18 Lockhart, 20.

19 DiSpigna, 181. DiSpigna notes that on June 16, Joseph Warren was summoned from a meeting of the Provincial Congress and received secret dispatches from Reverend Mather, who had given them to his teenage daughter, Hannah, with secret instructions to deliver them only to

Dr. Warren. DiSpigna speculates that those dispatches may have contained intelligence alerting Warren of General Thomas Gage's intended movements.

20 George Ellis, 30 and Philbrick, *Bunker Hill*, 195.

21 William Cutler, *The Life of Israel Putnam, Major General In The Army Of The American Revolution*, Kennikat Press, 1850, reissued in 1970, 161–62.

22 William Cutler, 163.

23 George Ellis, 29–30. In Rick Atkinson's account, he says that the Committee of Safety voted that "the hill called Bunker's Hill in Charlestown be securely kept and defended," adding that Dorchester Heights would have to wait until more gunpowder could be stockpiled. As General Artemas Ward eventually sent troops to both areas, it may be concluded the additional powder indeed became available.

24 Middlekauff, 282.

25 George Ellis, 38–39. The orders given to William Prescott were written but not very detailed, leaving some decisions up to Prescott and the other commanders sent to Charlestown.

26 James Prescott, the Colonel's older brother, was very involved in the Provincial Congress and the Board of War. He knew Artemus Ward personally, and it is entirely likely that James would have talked with Ward about his brother, William.

27 Middlekauff, 282.

28 Lorenzo Blood, from an undated paper titled "Pepperell," found in the files of the Pepperell Town Hall.

29 W. H. Temple, *History of Framingham, Massachusetts, Early Known as Dansforth's Farms, 1640–1880* (Legare Street Press, 2022), 292, as cited in Atkinson, *The British Are Coming*, 93–94.

30 Atkinson, 99.

31 George Ellis, 196 and Drake, *Bunker Hill*, 9.

32 Cutler, 164. The heights of the three hills—Bunker's, Breed's, and Morton's—vary slightly from those quoted in other documents.

33 Middlekauff, 283. In addition to no uniforms, the provincials did not fly any battle flags, even though some were included in later paintings of the battle. Middlekauff notes that a soldier was supposed to carry a pack, rations for a day, and entrenching tools.

34 Details in this section are drawn from Lockhart, 195 and Brough, 33.

35 Green, *Three Military Diaries*, 89. Captain Nutting commanded the company of Pepperell minutemen.

36 Letter from Samuel Gray to Mr. Dyer, July 12, 1775, in Frothingham, *The Siege of Boston*, 393–95; also cited in Lockhart, 194. Lockhart notes that tradition has blamed Israel Putnam for the placement of the redoubt on Breed's Hill, saying, "Putnam the wolf-killer, man of action, the eternal boy, wanted battle without thinking of the consequences. Prescott, on the other hand, was cool and logical." Lockhart adds that Putnam never pulled rank on Prescott and acknowledged Prescott's authority as commander of the expedition. Historian Thomas Fleming in *Now We Are Enemies*, 13–14, reports a conversation between the three senior officers in which Gridley agreed with Putnam on placing the fort on Breed's Hill and it was Prescott who was reluctant to do so. Fleming does not document his source for this, and I haven't seen this interpretation anywhere else.

37 Philbrick, *Bunker Hill*, 197–99. Philbrick makes the point that we will never know who made the decision to build the redoubt on Breed's Hill, but he notes that Prescott was the one in charge and therefore was the one who was responsible for the location of the fort. In his endnotes, Philbrick quotes Richard Frothingham, *The Battle of Bunker Hill*, 29, who reported that William Prescott Jr. said that his father, Colonel Prescott, took responsibility.

38 Drake, *Bunker Hill*, 11 and 54.

39 Lockhart, 195. Lockhart posits that Breed's Hill altered the dynamics of the contest, noting that General Gage could have ignored it if he wished because the Americans did not have enough heavy artillery to make Breed's Hill a real threat.

40 Cutler, 165–66.

41 Cutler, 165–66.

42 Brough, 33.

43 *Selected Quotations: U.S. Military Leaders* (Office of the Chief of Military History: U.S. Army, 1964), 6; pdf available at: https://history.army.mil/Research/Reference-Topics/Military-Quotations/.

44 Bobrick, 141.

45 Ketchum, *Decisive Day*, 137.

46 Allen French, *The First Year of the American Revolution*, 222 and Ketchum, *Decisive Day*, 121, as well as Lockhart, 209.

47 Atkinson, 99.

48 Ketchum, *Decisive Day*, 119.

49 David How, *Diary of David How, A Private in Colonel Paul Dudley Sargent's Regiment of the Massachusetts Line* (Morrisania, NY, 1865), as cited in Lockhart, *The Whites of Their Eyes*, 227.

50 Ketchum, *Decisive Day*, 143.

51 Brough, 34.

52 Frothingham, *Life and Times of Joseph Warren*, 515, as cited in Christian DiSpigna, 177.

53 Cutler, 171.

54 Knapp, *Biographical Sketches*, 117.

55 Frothingham, *Life and Times of Joseph Warren*, 317, as cited in DiSpigna, 14.

56 Margaret Wheeler Willard, *Letters on the American Revolution*, 150 and Drake, *Bunker Hill*, 50, as cited in Christian DiSpigna, 182.

57 Drake, *Bunker Hill*, 18.

58 Ferling, *Almost A Miracle*, 56. Ferling cites how soldiers in other wars spoke of the terror of the last seconds before the battle: "a seeming eternity…of…supremely agonizing suspense"; "broke out in a cold sweat"; "stomach tied in knots"; "had a lump in their throat and only swallowed with great difficulty"; "knees nearly buckled," etc.

59 Richard Frothingham, *The Battlefield of Bunker Hill*, 20.

60 Drake, *Bunker Hill*, 43.

61 Lockhart, 272. Lockhart notes that officers "Stark, Wyman, and McClary walked quietly behind their men, soothing them in hushed voices, calming them, and reminding them to aim low and keep their fingers off their triggers until the British were very close."

62 Lockhart, 280; also Atkinson, 103. Atkinson notes that the "whites of their eyes" reference had been used by Austrians, Prussians, and possibly other warring armies earlier in the century.

63 Atkinson, 98.

64 Lockhart, 272. Lockhart notes that the British light infantry did not stop in the field but were intent on rushing in with their bayonets as they were trained.

65 According to historian Paul Lockhart, "The fences in the field were not the kind that could be trampled down easily, and soon the hands of the grenadiers were torn and bleeding from dismantling them." See Lockhart, 270–71.

66 Ferling, *Almost A Miracle*, 56.

67 Lockhart, 265 and Bobrick, 142.

68 David Price, *John Haslett's World: An Ardent Patriot, the Delaware Blues, and the Spirit of 1776* (New York: Knox Press, 2020), 88.

69 Williams, *Discord and Civil Wars*, 21–22, as cited in Lockhart, 266–67. Lockhart points out that "it took the kind of discipline that reduces men to unthinking, unfeeling automatons, to carry a bayonet charge through to victory."

70 Price, 89.

71 Price, 183.

72 Some sources contend that the musket was lethal up to about 175 yards.

73 Middlekauff, 289. Middlekauff notes that once the light infantry and grenadiers had broken through on the right, they would pivot to the left and attack inland.

74 Richard Frothingham, *The Battlefield of Bunker Hill*, 10.

75 Middlekauff, 288–89. Middlekauff notes that, "The old casual feeling of superiority that puffed up imperial heads when they dealt with the provincials may have clouded his [Howe's] judgment."

76 Drake, *Bunker Hill*, 18.

77 Ketchum, *Decisive Day*, 144, as cited in Rose, *Maverick General*, 60. Ketchum states that Putnam was in command on Bunker Hill (although he was not the overall commander; that distinction went to Prescott, who was at Breed's Hill), adding that Stark was not going to take orders from any Connecticut officer.

78 Joseph Ellis, *Revolutionary Summer*, 45.

79 Middlekauff, 290. Middlekauff notes that "John Stark watched the British light infantry and grenadiers come from behind the barriers of staves and kept his men silent."

80 George Ellis, 70.

81 Richard Frothingham, *The Battlefield of Bunker Hill*, 11. Frothingham cites John Burnham and E. Bancroft on this issue of the relative commencement of the firing.

82 Lockhart, 272. Lockhart notes that for a while the British troops continued to advance toward the stone wall by the beach. "The light infantry of the 4th Foot—the King's Own—stumbled over the wounded and dead to get to the wall, where they were met with more musketry."

83 Ketchum, *Decisive Day*, 158.

84 Rose, 60–61. Rose notes that once the front row of American troops fired their volley, they would kneel to reload.

85 Lockhart, 271. This was a British tactic as well, and Stark may have earned it fighting with the British. In a British assault, the first row of soldiers would typically fire from a kneeling position and then give way to subsequent rows of troops, who would do the same while the first row reloaded.

86 Middlekauff, 290. Middlekauff notes, "The grenadiers also fell in thick grotesque piles."

87 Drake, *Bunker Hill*, 19–20.

88 Sheer and Rankin, *Rebels and Redcoats*, 56, as cited in Bobrick, 142.

89 Wheeler, *Voices of 1776*, 48, as cited in Bobrick, 142.

90 Brough, 36.

91 DiSpigna, 182.

92 Carrington, 108, as cited in Rose, 61.

93 Ketchum, *Decisive Day*, 160.

94 Edward Everett, *Life of John Stark*, 61, as cited in Rose, 61–62.

95 Ketchum, *Decisive Day*, 160.

96 Lockhart, 276. Lockhart notes that observers of the battle were shocked by the suddenness of the conflagration.

97 George Washington Warren, *The History of the Bunker Hill Monument Association during the first century of the United States of America* (Boston: James R. Osgood & Company, 1877), 4.

98 Blood, "Colonel Prescott and the Battle of Bunker Hill," 49.

99 Ketchum, *Decisive Day*, 163.

100 Middlekauff, 291.

101 Brough, 35. This was the only instance I came across that placed General Putnam near the firing line.

102 Brough, 36.

103 Ketchum, *Decisive Day*, 162.

104 Middlekauff, 291.

105 Drake, *Bunker Hill*, 20–21.

106 Letters from William Howe to Adjutant General Harvey, June 22 and 24, 1775, in Commager and Morris, *The Spirit of Seventy-Six*, 132, as cited in Lockhart, 282–83.

107 Brough, 37.

108 Ketchum, *Decisive Day*, 169.

109 Brough, 36.

110 Drake, *Bunker Hill*, 21.

111 Drake, *Bunker Hill*, 21.

112 The British may have also been aware of this, as it has been reported that one or more provincials loudly shouted this fact during the interim between assaults (see George Ellis, 79).

113 Lockhart, 290–91.

114 George Ellis, 80–81.

115 Prescott knew that by the time the British were preparing for the third assault, the provincials were exceedingly low on powder. But he was in no position to organize a retreat, and besides, his orders may have forbidden him from doing so. Thus he tried to convince his remaining troops that victory was at hand if they could withstand another attempt by the British to take the fort. See Frothingham, *The Battlefield of Bunker Hill*, 20.

116 Ketchum, *Decisive Day*, 172.

117 Brough, 36–37.

118 Brough, 37.

119 Atkinson, 107. Atkinson notes that William Prescott told his men to wait to fire until the British vanguard was within 30 yards of the redoubt.

120 Frothingham, *The Battlefield of Bunker Hill*, 27.

121 Drake, *Bunker Hill*, 21 and Brough, 37.

122 William Cutler, 180. In addition, according to David Hackett Fischer, Pitcairn was mourned even by his enemies, who called him a "good man in a bad cause."

123 There is some dispute whether Pitcairn was shot atop the redoubt or on the battlefield and never made it to the redoubt.

124 Account of Adjutant Walles, Royal Marines, in Drake, *Bunker Hill*, 29–30, as cited in Lockhart, 296. Walles recalled, "When we came immediately under the work, we were checked by the severe fire of the enemy, but did not retreat an inch." It was reported that the African American militiaman who shot Major Pitcairn was Salem Prince, a veteran of the April 19 fighting as well. However, in Green, *Groton During the Revolution*, 201, it is reported that former slave Peter Salem was the one who shot Major Pitcairn. The issue is still in doubt.

125 Brough, 37–39.

126 I. Ward, Allen French, and Bernard Knollenberg, "Bunker Hill Re-viewed: A Study in the Conflict of Historical Evidence," Massachusetts Historical Society, Procs., 72 (Boston, 1963), 84–100, as cited in Middlekauff, 292.

127 Bobrick, 143.

128 Ketchum, *Decisive Day*, 177.

129 This account was published privately by Amos Farnsworth. This reference can be found at https://genealogytrails.com/mass/middlesex/revwarjournalfarnsworth.html.

130 Ketchum, *Decisive Day*, 181.

131 Brough, 38. Claudius Buchanan Farnsworth, "*Matthias Farnsworth and his Descendants in America: A Monograph*," published privately by the author, 1891. This reference can be found at https://genealogytrails.com/mass/middlesex/revwarjournalfarnsworth.html.

132 Jedidiah Morse and Elijah Parish, *A Compendious History of New England* (Printed by S. Etheridge, 1820), 281, as cited in Atkinson, 109.

133 Prescott, M.D., 59.

134 Letter from James Warren to John Adams, June 20, 1775, in Warren-Adams Letters, 62–64; Swett, *History*, 45; Dearborn, *An Account of the Battle of Bunker Hill*, 6; and *London Evening Post*, July 13–16, 1775, as cited in DiSpigna, 186–87.

135 Atkinson, 108. Atkinson cites Christian DiSpigna's biography of Joseph Warren, *Founding Martyr*.

136 DiSpigna, 189. DiSpigna notes that British officers dismissed the initial reports of Warren's death, refusing to believe he would risk his life in the fight.

137 William Gordon, *History of the Rise, Progress, and Establishment of the Independence of the United States of America: Including an Account of the Late War; and of the Thirteen Colonies, from Their Origin to that Period*, 4 Volumes, (London, 1788), Vol. 2: 49–50; DiSpigna, 189.

138 Letter from Benjamin Hichborn to John Adams, December 10, 1775, John Adams Papers, Series 3, 323–24; Letter from Lieutenant Walter S. Laurie to John Roebuck, June 23, 1775, as cited in DiSpigna, *Founding Martyr*, 188.

139 Winthrop, 13.

140 Prescott, M.D., 57.

141 Blood, "Colonel Prescott and the Battle of Bunker Hill," 50.

142 Everett, 64, as cited in Rose, 63.

143 Charles Coffin, ed., *History of the Battle of Breed's Hill*, 22, as cited in Atkinson, 109

144 Rose, 65.

145 *The Boston Gazette*, June 19, 1775.

146 Brough, 40.

147 Brough, 39.

148 H. Butterfield, *Adams Family Correspondence*, as cited in Atkinson, *The British Are Coming*, 109.

149 Atkinson, 114. Atkinson notes that Burgoyne later claimed that "the Bunker Hill bloodletting had at least affirmed the imperial principle, in doubt after the rout at Concord, that trained troops are invincible against any numbers or any position of undisciplined rabble."

Chapter 8

1   This letter from William Prescott to John Adams on August 25, 1775 is found in the Massachusetts Historical Society.

2   The letter from William Prescott to John Adams on August 25, 1775 is found in the Massachusetts Historical Society.

3   Francis Jewett Parker, *Colonel William Prescott: The Commander In The Battle Of Bunker's Hill, Honor To Whom Honor Is Due* (Boston: A. Williams and Company, 1875), 18.

4   Letter from James Warren to John Admas, June 20, 1775, in Warren-Adams Letters; letter from James Warren to Samuel Adams, June 21, 1775, as cited in Lockhart, 317–19.

5   Sheer and Rankin, *Rebels and Redcoats*, 61, as cited in Atkinson, 112.

6   Herbert Treadwell Wade and Robert A. Lively, *This Glorious Cause: The Adventures of Two Company Officers in Washington's Army* (Princeton University Press, 2016), 20, as cited in Atkinson, 112.

7   Claude H. Van Tyne, *The War of Independence: American Phase* (Houghton Mifflin Company, 1929), 53, as cited in Atkinson, 113.
8   Winthrop, 14.
9   Winthrop, 14.
10 Winthrop, 14.
11 Letter from James Knowles to his wife, June 18, 1775, as cited in Lockhart, 319.
12 Letter from John Stark to Matthew Thornton, June 19, 1775, in Nathaniel Bouton, *Provincial Papers: Documents and Records Relating to the Province of New Hampshire*, as cited in Lockhart, 319.
13 Lockhart, 306.
14 Ellis, *Revolutionary Summer*, 45. Ellis notes that before the battle, Howe was unimpressed with the prowess of the American militia and assumed "the assault would be a waltz."
15 Rick Atkinson suggests that the figure was one in eight or about 12 percent (p. 110), while Lockhart sites the percentage as one-quarter (p. 307).
16 Frothingham, *The Siege of Boston*, 195, as cited in Lockhart, 278–79.
17 Lockhart, 314. Lockhart notes that Prescott's regiment lost 43 killed or missing, 46 wounded; Bridge's 17 killed, 25 wounded; Frye's 10 killed, 38 wounded, four missing; Stark's 15 killed, 45 wounded.
18 Samuel Abbott Green, *Colonel Prescott and the Groton Soldiers*, 8.
19 Lorenzo Blood, from an undated paper entitled "Pepperell," found in the Pepperell Town Hall files.
20 Letter from Nathanael Green to Jacob Green, June 28, 1775, in *Papers of General Nathanael Green*, I, 92, as cited in Lockhart, 319.
21 *The Boston Gazette*, June 19, 1775.
22 Prescott, M.D., 58.
23 Prescott, M.D., 58.
24 Drake, *Bunker Hill*, 25.
25 Drake, *Bunker Hill*, 28.
26 Drake, *Bunker Hill*, 40.
27 Drake, *Bunker Hill*, 41.
28 Ellis, *Revolutionary Summer*, 44.
29 *Massachusetts Spy*, June 28, 1775, as cited in DiSpigna, 185.
30 William Howe to a fellow unnamed officer, June 22 and June 24, 1775, in Commager and Morris, *The Spirit of Seventy-six*, 132; and cited in Kevin Weddle, *The Complete Victory: Saratoga and the American Revolution* (Oxford: Oxford University Press, 2021), 8.
31 Winthrop, 16–17.
32 Force, American Archives, 4/2:1094; Letters from William Howe to Adjutant-General Harvey, June 22 and 24, 1775, in Commager and Morris, *The Spirit of Seventy-six*, 132, as cited in Lockhart, 311.
33 Letter from General Thomas Gage to Lord Dartmouth, June 25, 1775, as cited in Atkinson, 114.
34 Joseph Ellis, *The Cause: The American Revolution and Its Discontents* (New York: Liveright Publishing, 2021), 19. In his book *1776* (New York: Simon and Schuster, 2005), David McCullough attributes a similar quote to Brigadier General James Grant: see p. 71.
35 T. C. Hammond, ed., *The Parliamentary History of England*, 30 Vols. (London: 1806–20), Vol. 18, 149–59, as cited in Ellis, *Revolutionary Summer*, 8
36 Hammond, Vol. 18, 223, 263, 304, and 335, as cited in Ellis, *Revolutionary Summer*, 8.
37 In brief, game theory is a branch of mathematics concerned with the analysis of strategies for dealing with competitive situations where the outcome of one person's choice of action depends critically on the actions of other participants. This interdependence causes each participant to consider the

other participants' possible decisions, or strategies, in formulating his or her own strategy. For this reason, game theory has been called the science of strategy. Game theory was founded by mathematician and polymath John von Neuman and the economist Oskar Morgenstern, who published their seminal work *Theory of Games and Economic Behavior* in 1944. Since then, game theory has been applied in a variety of contexts, such as business, biology, and war.

38 In recent years, decision-making, particularly *under uncertainty*, using statistical analysis and the examination of whether individuals make rational decisions, has advanced planning, strategy, and choice architecture (how choices are presented to individuals) in many areas, including the military. In fact, Daniel Kahneman and Amos Tversky, pioneers in the burgeoning study of behavioral economics, gained many of their "behavioral" insights working with the Israeli military.

39 https://www.history.army.mil/books/AMH-V1/ch03.htm.

40 https://www.history.army.mil/books/AMH-V1/ch03.htm.

41 https://www.history.army.mil/books/AMH-V1/ch03.htm.

42 https://www.history.army.mil/books/AMH-V1/ch03.htm.

43 Drake, *Bunker Hill*, 10.

44 https://www.history.army.mil/books/AMH-V1/ch03.htm.

45 Ketchum, *Decisive Day*, 147.

46 Force, American Archives, Series 4, 240–41, as cited in DiSpigna, 197.

47 Winthrop, 16. It is worth noting, as historian Christian DiSpigna points out, that despite all that had happened over the prior 10 years, to many colonists in 1775, the idea of armed rebellion was still an "unspeakable option." In fact, most delegates at the Second Continental Congress opposed such a step, preferring to petition King George III with the aim of reaching an amicable resolution to the conflict. This evidenced itself in the Olive Branch Petition of July 5, 1775, in which the delegates declared their loyalty to the Crown while asserting their rights as British citizens. See DiSpigna, 17.

Chapter 9

1 From Massachusetts Archives, Orderly Book: Capt. Abijah Wyman's Co., Col. Wm Prescott regiment, from August 5 to December 30, 1775. Although the date range of this file is from August to December, this entry is labeled July 7.

2 Brough, 443.

3 The Massachusetts Archives, Massachusetts Archives Collection, *Revolutionary War*, Vol. 59, 551.

4 The Massachusetts Archives, Massachusetts Archives Collection, *Revolutionary War*, Vol. 77, 3. Sewall's Point began to change in 1821 when the Mill Dam was built between it and Boston Common. The idea then was to use the tides in the Charles River to power factories in the area. The plan never succeeded, and eventually the Back Bay was filled in for residential development. The dam was not destroyed, and it still exists below the roadway. Today, Kenmore Square is on the edge of the Boston University campus, but it's probably best known for being a very short walk to Fenway Park, the home of the Boston Red Sox.

5 Thomas Paine was a native Englishman who moved to America in 1774, where he began to formulate his ideas about monarchical government and the rights of individuals. He was relatively unknown, but he would soon be one of the most recognized citizens in the country. Paine's treatise, which would irrevocably change the calculus in dealing with England, sold an astounding 150,000 copies and took direct aim at hereditary monarchy in general and King George III in particular.

6   Gordon Wood, *Power and Liberty: Constitutionalism in the American Revolution* (New York: Oxford University Press, 2021), 1.

7   Wood, *Power and Liberty*, 29–30.

8   Thomas Paine, *Common Sense, The Rights of Man, and Other Essential writings of Thomas Paine* (New York: Meridian Books, 1969), 40.

9   Paine, 50.

10 Letter from George Washington to Joseph Reed, January 31, 1776, in *Papers of George Washington* Revolutionary War Series, 3:228, as cited in John Ferling, *Apostles of Revolution: Jefferson, Paine, Monroe, and the Struggle Against the Old Order in America and Europe* (New York: Bloomsbury Publishing, 2018), 49.

11 Elizabeth was also the beautiful blonde wife of Joshua Loring Jr., a prominent Boston lawyer and loyalist. The Lorings had fled their comfortable home in Roxbury and sought refuge in Boston when things turned violent. The good lawyer had a valued relationship with the British, selling provisions to the garrison before he was also appointed commissary of prisoners and then sheriff of the town by General Howe. It was obvious to everyone near him that General Howe's will to fight had diminished since Bunker Hill, and rumor had it that the presence of Elizabeth was a significant contributing factor.

12 Ellis, *Revolutionary Summer*, 30. Ellis calls the Boston siege, "Less a battle than a prolonged tactical minuet."

13 French, *The First Year of the American Revolution*, 655 and North Callahan, *Henry Knox: George Washington's General* (New York: Rinehart Publishing, 1958), 40–41, as cited in David McCullough, *1776* (New York: Simon and Schuster, 2005), 82.

14 French, *The First Year of the American Revolution*, 40–41, as cited in McCullough, *1776*, 82–83.

15 Barnet Schecter, *The Battle of New York* (New York: Walker Books, 2002), 66.

16 Schecter, 66 and https://revolutionarywar.us/year-1775/siege-of-Boston/#.

17 Lieutenant Johnson Moulton's orderly book, Governors Island, New York, 20 July 1776, as found in William Hickling Prescott Papers, Massachusetts Historical Society, Boston, Massachusetts, Box 25. As the American Revolution Institute notes, orderly books are one of the most valuable primary resources for scholars studying the operations and progression of the Revolutionary War.

18 From the summary describing William Prescott's orderly book on the ABIGAIL database at the Massachusetts Historical Society.

19 McCullough, 89. Based on the Bunker Hill experience, about 2,000 casualties were anticipated, so hand barrows were set up to transport the wounded from the battlefield. Harvard College and Prospect Hill were established as hospital wards.
    To speed the erection of the defenses on the heights, Rufus Putnam, a self-taught engineer and nephew of Israel Putnam, oversaw the construction of "chandeliers": wooden frames that could be moved up to the overlook and quickly filled with bundled sticks (fascines) and wicker baskets filled with stones and gravel (gabions).

20 Atkinson, 261. Atkinson notes that George Washington was anticipating a British lunge toward Dorchester.

21 Archibald Roberston, March 4, 1776, in *Archibald Roberston: His Diaries and Sketches in America, 1762–1780*, 74 and Franch, *The First Year of the American Revolution*, 660, as cited in McCullough, 93.

22 McCullough, 95. McCullough notes that it was Reverend William Gordon who quoted George Washington.

23 Atkinson, 260. Atkinson notes that more than 700 cannonballs were collected by rebel scavengers on March 6, 1776, the day after the bombardment.

24 McCullough, 99. McCullough notes, "When a single sloop from the West Indies did make it to the harbor, it was learned that more than seventy food transports…had been blown off course that winter and were tied up in Antigua."

25 When the British did not leave the city when Washington expected, he felt he had been duped. He ordered two units into action: one was to enter Boston by way of the Roxbury Neck and the other, which was led by John Stark, was to cross the Charles River to capture the British battery on Copp's Hill.

26 Atkinson, 266. No doubt the troops who left Boston, while perhaps feeling glad to be away from potentially heavy fighting, felt stung by their humiliating defeat at the hands of what they perceived was a far inferior fighting force of scruffy Americans. The mighty British Empire would soon be without a single deep-water port on the east coast from Canada to Florida.

27 Actually, as a precautionary measure, the first troops who entered Boston were about 1,000 soldiers that were smallpox survivors. Wary of British subterfuge, they were tasked with looking for signs of pestilence (see Atkinson, 267).

28 DiSpigna, 20. Another account says that Warren's body was identified by Dr. Jefferies, who noticed the loss of a joint on one finger, which had been broken off early in life (see Warren, *The History of the Bunker Hill Monument Association*, 13).

29 Brough, 62.

30 Massachusetts Archives, General Orders dated Headquarters March 23 and March 28, 1776, Vol. 77, 34, 36.

31 Massachusetts Archives, Vol. 58, page 134, file 22.

32 Letter from John Latham to his parents, March 17, 1776, as cited in David McCullough, *1776*, 112. McCullough notes, "Most men welcomed being on the move, even though they had no idea they were headed to New York." McCullough adds that in John Latham's letter to his parents, he asks them to "send a pair of shoes as quickly as possible, for I expect I shall march off soon, but whither we shall go I do not know nor can I tell."

33 According to Edmund Banks Smith, the original inhabitants of New York, the Dutch, called the island Noten Eylandt, later Anglicized to Nutten Island, because of all the nut trees there. In 1698, the island was set aside by the British to be "part of the Denizens of His Majestie's fort at New York for the benefit and accommodations of his Majestie's Governors for the time being." The British started calling it The Governor's Island, but eventually the "The" and the apostrophe were officially dropped in 1784. I've used Governors Island here, except when citing correspondence that spells the island with the apostrophe.

34 Brough, 63.

35 Until its Coast Guard station was closed in 1997, Governors Island was the oldest continuously operated military post in the United States, having been manned there since 1799.

36 Edmund Banks Smith, *Governor's Island: Its Military History Under Three Flags* (New York, published by the author), 1913, 43.

37 Edmund Banks Smith's history of the island notes that on June 7, 1775, the British decided to withdraw its forces from New York, feeling they were unable to continue its occupation. They relocated to Canada to replenish supplies before attempting to retake the city behind the Howe brothers' forces.

38 Edmund Banks Smith, 39–40.

39 If General Putnam had been annoyed by Prescott's harsh words after Bunker Hill, this would be a good way to get back at him.

40 The various ferries to Governors Island run every day year-round and depart from the Battery Maritime Building in lower Manhattan and other locations, with stops at Wall Street, Brooklyn Bridge Pier 6, Red Hook, and various wharfs.

41 Letter from George Washington to Charles Lee, May 9, 1776, in *Papers of George Washington*, IV, 245, as cited in McCullough, *1776*, 128.

42 Edmund Banks Smith, 41.

43 Edmund Banks Smith, 43.

44 Michael Stephenson, *Patriotic Battles: How The War Of Independence Was Fought* (New York: Harper Publishing), 231–32, as cited in Joseph Ellis, *Revolutionary Summer*, 41.

45 George Washington to Militia Colonels in Western Connecticut, August 7, 1776, in W. W. Abbott, Dorothy Twohig, and Philander Chase, eds., *The Papers of George Washington*, Revolutionary War Series, 12 Vols.; and letter from George Washington to John Trumbull, August 7, 1776, in *The Papers of George Washington*, 5: 615–16, as cited in Ellis, *Revolutionary Summer*, 102.

46 Edmund Banks Smith, 160.

47 Pauline Maier, *American Scripture: Making the Declaration of Independence* (New York: Vintage Books, 1997), 35. Maier notes, "Athens, Rome, and England's own Commonwealth of the 1650s had not survived and in general republics were said to be short-lived..."

48 At the time, in a newspaper letter signed "Republicus" and dated June 29, the letter's author wrote, "I would choose rather to be conquered as an Independent State than as an acknowledged rebel." The anonymous author added that the time had come for Americans "to call ourselves by some name," and then suggested "the United States of America."

49 The vote was a tense affair and the reader is advised to read a detailed account of the final tally.

50 Independence was not fully complete. Each state needed to make sure that its inhabitants were behind the declaration. For instance, roughly two months earlier, on May 10, the Massachusetts assembly asked the inhabitants of each town to discuss their feelings toward independence and advise their representatives to come to the next General Court and address how they stood on the proposition, asking: Would they "solemnly engage with their Lives and Fortunes to Support the Congress in the Measure?"

51 However, it was only on January 18, 1777, after American victories at Trenton and Princeton, that Congress sent authenticated and signed copies of the Declaration of Independence to the states.

52 Maier, *American Scripture*, 156.

53 Maier, *American Scripture*, 156–57.

54 Pepperell Town Records, 1742–1809, Vol. 1, 181.

55 Around this time, the Howe brothers, who had been given authority from the king to find a diplomatic solution to the crisis, decided to reach out to Washington. To their dismay, none of their entreaties were successful.

56 Edmund Banks Smith, 41.

57 Edmund Banks Smith, 42. William Alexander was a Scottish American who claimed he was heir to the title through his paternal lineage, although the House of Lords overruled Scottish law and denied him the title of Lord Stirling in 1762.

58 Edmund Banks Smith, 48.

59 On August 27, the British captured over 1,000 American troops in a decisive battle at Gowanus Creek in Brooklyn. Washington watched from Brooklyn Heights near the East River as 400 Marylanders fought valiantly to repel a British force of 2,000. As a slaughter ensued, Washington cried out, "Good God! What brave fellows I must lose this day." Fortunately, General Howe did not follow up this rout, although it appeared he could have, right then and there, bagged Washington's entire force in Brooklyn. This prompted Israel Putnam to joke, "General Howe is either our friend or no general."

60 William Gordon, *History*, 2: 102–4, as cited in Schecter, *The Battle of New York*, 159. Washington arranged for his army to be removed surreptitiously through the night with the

help of a flotilla of vessels quickly assembled under the direction of Brigadier General John Glover of Marblehead, Massachusetts.

Also in that meeting were Major Generals Israel Putnam and Joseph Spencer, Brigadier Generals Thomas Mifflin, Samuel Parsons, John Scott, James Wadsworth, and John Fellows. In fact, Washington had already decided to evacuate Brooklyn after an earlier meeting with Joseph Reed, his aide, and Mifflin.

61 William Gordon, as cited in Barnet Schecter, 165.

62 Edmund Banks Smith, *Governor's Island*, 47.

63 William Gordon, as cited in Schecter, 165.

64 Edmund Banks Smith, 47. In his history, Edmund Banks Smith reports, "In the evening of the same day [August 29] a detachment of the rebel Army went from New York to Nutten Island with a number of boats and carried off the troops, the stores, artillery, and provisions." But this seems in conflict with other information about when Governors Island was evacuated.

65 Keith Brough, 63.

66 https://www.fold3.com/image/11162128/prescott-william-page-1-us-revolutionary-war-service-records-1775-1783. This information was provided by Linda Geiger, certified genealogist. The site requires membership for access.

67 Lorenzo Blood, from an undated paper titled "Pepperell," found in the files of Pepperell Town Hall.

68 Edmund Banks Smith, 47.

69 Schecter, 153.

70 On November 25, 1783, at the war's end, the British troops withdrew from New York City. For the next century, that date was recognized as "Evacuation Day," as March 17 had been recognized as Evacuation Day in Boston.

71 Prescott, M.D., 59.

72 Schecter, 210–16 and Everett, 43–44.

73 Orderly book of Lieutenant Colonel Johnson Moulton, Massachusetts Historical Society, W. H. Prescott Papers, Box 25, Vol. 7.

74 George Washington's instructions to Charles Lee, quoted in Carrington, 245, as cited in Schecter, 245.

75 On November 20, British General Charles Cornwallis, one of Howe's most able commanders, had crossed the Hudson into New Jersey with a formidable force. It wasn't long before he picked up Washington's scent and began pursuit. Washington may have gone to New Jersey to protect the state, but now the silver fox was on the run. Cornwallis was intent on finishing off Washington's army, whose numbers were rapidly depleting as soldier enlistments expired. It was not the kind of picture Washington had envisioned for his weary troops, racing away for their lives and wondering what their ultimate fate would be.

76 Orderly book of Lieutenant Colonel Johnson Moulton, Massachusetts Historical Society, W. H. Prescott Papers, Box 25, Vol. 7.

77 https://www.fold3.com/image/11162128/prescott-william-page-1-us-revolutionary-war-service-records-1775-1783. Again, this information was provided by Linda Geiger, certified genealogist. The site requires membership for access.

78 Orderly book of Lieutenant Colonel Johnson Moulton, Massachusetts Historical Society, W. H. Prescott Papers, Box 25, Vol. 7.

79 This information is from William Prescott's paybook, which may be found at the Massachusetts Historical Society, in the W. H. Prescott papers. Prescott's paybook contains entries for Prescott's time in the army, as well as for transactions on his farm in Pepperell.

80 Pepperell Town Records 1742–1809, Vol. 1, 190.

81   The Massachusetts Archives, Massachusetts Archives Collection, Revolutionary War, Muster Rolls 1775–1783, Vol. 19, 177.

82   Richard Ketchum, *Saratoga* (New York: Henry Holt and Company, 1999), 390–448. This citation covers the entire battle of Saratoga. The number of captured British and Hessian troops can be found on page 437.

83   In Keith Brough's book *General Ward's Colonial Army*, he states that "General Glover was selected to guard and conduct [the British prisoners] to Cambridge." William Prescott does not seem to have been a party to that action.

84   https://wikipedia.org/wiki/William_Prescott, accessed December 10, 2024.

Chapter 10

1   Wood, *The Creation of the American Republic*, 356.

2   Jack Rakove, *Beginnings of National Politics: An interpretive history of the Continental Congress* (Knopf Publishing, 1979), 144–45, 155 and Wood, *The Creation of the American Republic*, 35, as cited in Michael Klarman, *The Framers' Coup: The Making of the United States Constitution* (New York: Oxford University Press, 2016), 13–14.

3   Articles of Confederation of the United States of America, Article II, DHRC, 1:86; Wood, *The Creation of the American Republic*, 354–59, as cited in Klarman, *The Framers' Coup*, 14.

4   www.massmoments.org/moment-details/massachusetts-approves-state-constitution, accessed December 10, 2024.

5   John Hancock was unanimously elected the first president of the Provincial Congress in October 1774. At the time of Bunker Hill, Dr. Joseph Warren was the president.

6   www.massmoments.org/moment-details/massachusetts-approves-state-constitution, accessed December 10, 2024.

7   Pepperell Town Records 1742–1809, Vol. 1. While many pages of these records are not numbered, this reference is labeled p. 215.

8   Thomas "Tip" O'Neill, Massachusetts politician and former Speaker of the House of U.S. Representatives, is most associated with the phrase "All politics is local," although he did not originate it.

9   Pepperell Town Records, 1742–1809, Vol. 1, 195, 199, 210–11.

10   Bobrick, 287. Bobrick notes that the village of Valley Forge "having steep hillsides and the swift Schuylkill River helped fortify the perimeter of the wooden plateau where the army built its huts."

11   Letter from George Washinton to John Bannister, April 21, 1778, in *The Papers of George Washington*, Revolutionary War Series, edited by Philander Chase, 14: 577–78, as cited in Nathaniel Philbrick, *Valiant Ambition: George Washington, Benedict Arnold, and the Fate of the American Revolution* (New York: Viking Penguin, 2016), 187–88.

12   https://en.wikipedia.org/wiki/Valley_Forge, accessed on January 15, 2025. Detailed descriptions of Washington's time at Valley Forge can be found in Bobrick, 286-312; Ferling, *Almost a Miracle*, 274–82; and Middlekauff, 411–17.

13   Despite the area being a regional breadbasket, food was scarce that winter, and clothing, which the troops desperately needed, was extremely hard to obtain. The local farmers were more willing to sell their provisions to the British in Philadelphia than to the army because they paid in pound sterling, which was more reliable than Continental currency.

14   Quoted in Benson John Lossing, *The Lives of the Signers of the Declaration of Independence* (Wallbuilder Press, 1995), 167, as cited in Bobrick, *Angel in the Whirlwind*, 287.

15 Joseph Ellis, *American Creation*, 63.

16 The economic situation in the country was also deteriorating significantly. The value of Continental currency began a long slide, such that by 1779 it was trading at just 5 percent of its face value (see Klarman, *The Framers' Coup*, 17). This was why farmers were more eager to sell their goods to the British.

17 Joseph Ellis, *American Creation*, 60–61.

18 A wonderful description of Arnold's actions is contained in Nathaniel Philbrick's *Valiant Ambition*.

19 Letters from General Cornwallis to General Clinton, May 26 and June 30, 1781; An excellent discussion of the war in the southern states is contained in *Nathaniel Philbrick, In the Hurricane's Eye: The Genius of George Washington and the Victory at Yorktown, (New York, Viking, 2018)*, and Benjamin F. Stevens, *ed., Campaign in Virginia, 1781:* An Exact Reprint of Six Rare Pamphlets on the Clinton-Cornwallis Controversy, (London, 1888); 1:488, 2:35–36, as cited in Ferling, *Whirlwind*, 298.

20 Letter from George Washington to Lafayette, August 21, 1781, in John Fitzpatrick, ed., *The Writings of Washington*, 39 Vols. (Washington D.C.: U.S. Government Printing Office, 1931–44), as cited in Ferling, *Whirlwind*, 302.

21 The French wanted the treaty to be a multilateral pact with the victorious Allies pressing the British on terms. But the Americans orchestrated their own terms, much to the French's outrage. Benjamin Franklin, who was the most trusted American delegate, later apologized to the French.

22 France objected strenuously to these last two provisions, as it wanted to prohibit American competition in the fisheries. Because Franklin suffered from a bout of kidney stones and Laurens only arrived at the end of the peace talks, Adams and Jay were the primary negotiators of the accord.

23 While French involvement in the war was extensive and is well known, Spain's role was much smaller and of less consequence. Spain had officially joined the war as an ally of the French when it signed the Treaty of Aranjuez in April 1779, but it had surreptitiously been providing financial support, as well as supplies and munitions, to the Americans since the early stages of the war in 1776. Importantly, in 1781, Spain provided funds to the Americans that helped in the crucial siege of Yorktown.

24 Prescott, M.D., 57.

25 Pepperell Town Records, 1742–1809, Vol. 1, 268.

26 James Bowdoin was the governor of Massachusetts from 1785 to 1787, between John Hancock's terms. An excellent review of Shays's Rebellion is provided in Leonard L. Richards, *Shays's Rebellion: The American Revolution's Final Battle* (Philadelphia: University of Pennsylvania Press, 2002).

27 As an example of this, in legislation that would be passed on November 10, 1786 after several months of forced court closings, the state gave the governor and his council the authority to imprison "all persons whatsoever who in their opinion were dangerous to the safety of the Commonwealth." Richards, *Shays's Rebellion*, 19. Richards notes, "The law also denied those viewed to be dangerous the right of habeas corpus until July 1, 1787."

28 This statement appears on the AAS website at www.americanantiquarian.org. Its website also declares that it houses the largest and most accessible collection of books, pamphlets, broadsides, newspapers, periodicals, children's literature, music, and graphic art material before the 20th century in what is now the United States, and a substantial collection of secondary texts, bibliographies, and digital sources and reference works.

29 Callahan, *Voice*, 19, as cited in Richards, 20.

30 The information in this section comes from Callahan, *Voice*.

31 Commonwealth v. Shattuck et al., Middlesex, April term, 1782, Supreme Judicial Court File Book, 148930; Thomas Keefe Callahan, *Voice*, 38; Van Beck Hall, *Politics Without Parties,*

1780–1791 (Pittsburgh: University of Pittsburgh Press, 1972), 187; Massachusetts Archives 190:253–60a, 318:13–16, as cited in Richards, 20.

32 Gary Shattuck, *Artful and Designing Men: The Trials of Job Shattuck and the Regulation of 1786–1787*, 235. Shattuck notes that they discussed the legality of the governor's authority to call out the militia.

33 Gary Shattuck, 235. Shattuck notes that Oliver Prescott and Samuel Phillips Savage were concerned about "a traitorous and armed body rising from within the Middlesex militia."

34 David P. Szatmary, *Shays's Rebellion: The Making of an Agrarian Insurrection* (University of Massachusetts Press, 1984), and Richards, 90, as cited in Gary Shattuck, 238.

35 *New York Packet*, September 21, 1786 and *Pennsylvania Packet*, September 23, 1786, as cited in Gary Shattuck, 243–44.

36 Lemuel Shattuck, *Memorials of the Descendants of William Shattuck: The Progenitor of the Families in America That Borne His Name* (Legare Street Press, 2022), 125 and the *Daily Advertiser*, September 21, 1786, Vol. II, Is, 490, p. 2, New York, as cited in Gary Shattuck, 246.

37 Massachusetts Archives Collection, Vol. 318.

38 Gary Shattuck, 249.

39 Thomas Keefe Callahan, *Voice*, 52, as cited in Gary Shattuck, 245.

40 Prescott, M.D., 57–58.

41 Massachusetts Archives Collection, Vol. 318, 15.

42 Massachusetts Archives, Vol. 190, 255a, as cited in Gary Shattuck, 250.

43 Gary Shattuck, 251. Shattuck notes that the judges were not ready to make this decision.

44 Gary Shattuck, 251.

45 Szatmary, 59, as cited in Gary Shattuck, 254.

46 Massachusetts Archives, Vol. 189, 41a, as cited in Gary Shattuck, 283.

47 Richards, 20–21.

48 Richards, 21. Richards notes that rumor had it the cavalry also committed other atrocities, including against women and children.

49 Massachusetts Archives, 189:36, 38, 41a, 44, 45, 402; *Worcester Magazine*, first week in December 1786, second week in December 1786, second week in January 1787; Shrewsbury Town Petition, January 15, 1787, Shays's Rebellion Collection, American Antiquarian Society; Callahan, *Voice*, 54; and Szatmary, 83, 93, as cited in Richards, 21.

50 Massachusetts Archives, Vol. 1039, File 149717, as cited in Gary Shattuck, 301.

51 Clifford K. Shipton, "Benjamin Lincoln: Old Reliable," in George Allan Billias, ed., *George Washington's Generals*, 202–3, as cited in Richards, 23.

52 Massachusetts Archives, Vol. 189, 81, as cited in Shattuck, 301.

53 Information comes from town records from Groton and Pepperell, the New England Genealogical Society, as well as from Thomas Keefe Callahan of Groton and Jeanne Palmer of Lawrence Library in Pepperell, as cited in Richards, 89–90.

54 Franklin Russell Mullaly, *The Massachusetts Insurrection of 1786–87*, Master's Thesis (Smith College, 1947), 53 and other sources, cited in Richards, 18–19.

55 Maier, *Ratification: The People Debate the Constitution 1787–1788* (New York: Simon and Schuster, 2010), 15–17.

56 Richards, 39. Richards notes it took roughly two months for Northampton, Worcester, and Concord counties to sentence 14 insurrectionists to death.

57 This document, prepared by William Prescott, along with a similar one written by Oliver Prescott in Groton, are held in a folder labeled Valuable Old Special Papers, in a vault in Pepperell's Town Hall. Both documents are dated March 23, 1787.

58 Letter from Oliver Prescott to the Massachusetts Council, June 18, 1787, Boston Public Library, Mss. Acc. 682 (12), as cited in Gary Shattuck, 342–43.
59 Governor's Council Executive Records, Vol. 30, 235–36, as cited in Gary Shattuck, 349–50.
60 The Vermont Republic, which had been formed in January 1777 as an outgrowth of the contested New Hampshire Grants region, harbored Shays from a Massachusetts petition to extradite him back to the state.

Chapter 11

1 Maier, *Ratification*, 17, as cited in Fergus Bordewich, *The First Congress: How James Madison, George Washington, and a Group of Extraordinary Men Invented the Government* (New York: Simon & Schuster, 2016), 7.
2 Two major issues drove Madison and Washington to this initiative: the articles' lack of a taxing authority and their inability to regulate trade. Being associated with a new and unproven nation, the United States' currency had shaky value, and Great Britain refused to trade with its now-departed American cousins. Spain also only had limited trade with the United States. This put severe strains on the American economy. The lack of taxing authority was also a major deficiency, since it undermined the country's ability to shore up its finances. Under the Articles of Confederation, Congress could not impose taxes on the states, only make requisitions for revenue, which was a weak and ineffective alternative.
3 However, they kept this notion under wraps while they solicited support for a constitutional convention. Not surprisingly, Virginia was the first state to support a convention, and by March 1787, 10 of the 13 states had signed on to the meeting and selected delegates who would assemble in Philadelphia. Eventually, 12 states would send delegates, with only the persistently recalcitrant Rhode Island refusing to participate. The state's main concern was that the convention intended to eliminate its right to print its own currency.
4 For instance, Jonathan Dayton was 36, Alexander Hamilton was 30, James Madison 36. There were two notable exceptions. George Washington, who was unanimously elected president of the convention, was an elder statesman at 55, and Benjamin Franklin was two generations removed from most delegates at age 81.
     In what was a precursor of things to come, 35 of the 55 delegates were lawyers and 13 were involved in commercial trade. Ominously, for the course of the discussions, 12 delegates, or over 20 percent, either owned or managed plantations worked by slaves.
5 This rule left many delegates exasperated, as on numerous occasions progress was halted as one or more delegates decided that certain provisions needed to be revisited.
6 Madison, who was a principal architect of the Virginia Plan, said a federal government operates on the states, while a national government operates on individuals. The convention, he suggested, should debate the rights of states but not the rights of man, which he considered inviolate.
7 Throughout the convention, many suggestions were proffered and many issues were debated, sometimes multiple times. Citizens today would marvel at some of the items that were proposed. These can be found in books by Catherine Drinker Bowen, David O. Stewart, and the Colliers (see Bibliography).
8 Finally, on July 26, the Committee of Detail was appointed and given until August 6—just 11 days—to aggregate and streamline all the suggestions, propositions, and amendments into a workable structure that would be acceptable to the delegates. The five members of this committee included Randolph of Virginia, Wilson of Pennsylvania, Gorham of Massachusetts,

Ellsworth of Connecticut, and was led by Rutledge of South Carolina, all of whom played significant roles during the convention.

9   While debates on the Constitution continued through August, momentum was building to finish the work as soon as possible. One of the last items to be decided was how the Constitution would be amended. Rutledge's committee authorized that amendments could be considered if two-thirds of the states called for a convention. However, a different mechanism was substituted, requiring three-quarters of the states to ratify amendments. This last-minute change has been the way all 27 amendments of the Constitution have been adopted.

10   Gouverneur Morris's preamble is one of the most famous passages of any American document from the revolutionary era. Morris's ancestors came to New York from England via Barbados and did very well. They bought 500 acres of land from a Dutch farmer named Jonas Bronck, whose large property holdings would later be known as the Bronx.

11   Catherine Drinker Bowen, *Miracle at Philadelphia* (Boston: Back Bay Books, 1986), 254–55. She notes that Benjamin Franklin doubted that a second convention, which some delegates wanted, could do any better.

12   Within days of the convention's close, objections began to be raised. Some delegates, such as Randolph, began arguing for a second convention. Others, like Elbridge Gerry, lobbied for a Bill of Rights. Then, on September 28, a little over a week after the convention vote, Congress recommended that each of the states call their own convention to vote on ratification of the new government. In October, as opposition from anti-federalists increased, a series of 85 essays in defense of the Constitution began to be published in the New York papers. Penned by James Madison, John Jay, and, primarily, Alexander Hamilton, but published under the name Publius, this collection of writings became known as the *Federalist Papers* and went a long way toward bolstering public opinion behind the new government. Still, it was not a foregone conclusion that the Constitution would be adopted.

13   James Madison had been so worried about whether Massachusetts would ratify that he asked George Washington to write to someone he knew in the state and let his pro-Constitution feelings be known. Washington contacted his old friend and fellow soldier, Benjamin Lincoln, and said there was "no Alternative between Adoption of the Constitution and Anarchy."

14   Maier, *Ratification*, 139.

15   Criticism of the proposed Constitution appeared in Boston's *American Herald, Independent Chronicle, Massachusetts Gazette*, and *The Boston Gazette*.

16   The discussion of the process of selecting delegates is discussed in Maier, *Ratification*, 142–45.

17   Oath of Allegiance, Massachusetts Archives, 190:170; Green, *Groton During the Revolution*, 185; Green Epitaph for the Old Burying Ground in Groton, as cited in Richards, 144–45. Also, see Massachusetts Ratification Project: The Great Debate of '88, found at the Massachusetts Archives, which lists the votes of each delegate by county and town.

18   Pepperell Town Records 1742–1809, Vol. 1, 310.

19   Maier, *Ratification*, 125–53. The reader is advised to read this section of Maier's *Ratification* to learn about the debates that occurred in Connecticut and Massachusetts before the ratifying conventions.

20   Maier, *Ratification*, 155.

21   The report was labeled Agency series #955, MA Advisory Commission to Commemorate Bicentennial of the U.S. Constitution, Presented to MA Archives, August 1989.

22   It is not clear why James Fowle Jr. from Woburn abstained from voting, but for some reason he apparently couldn't decide which way to go.

23   Account of the Massachusetts Convention to Ratify the Proposed Federal Constitution, Monday January 7–February 9, 1788, transcribed by Keith Kaplan, Hancock Scholar at Belchertown High School, Robert J. Hansbury, Jr. Hancock Fellow, Completed December 20, 1987.

24 Each state determined who would be eligible to vote on ratification, which is why the number of delegates at the state conventions varied so widely, as in the case of Rhode Island's first tally.

25 In a land where written constitutions were everywhere that governments were being formed, the ratification of the federal Constitution was an exceptional achievement. This has led one observer to note, "The written constitution has been one of the United States' most important assets."

26 www.mountvernon.org/library/digitalhistory/digital-encyclopedia/article/presidential-election-of-1789, accessed November 22, 2024.

27 Letter from James Madison to Thomas Jefferson, June 30, 1789, Documentary History of the First Federal Congress, 16:890, as cited in Bordewich, 5. To begin with, there was little agreement as to what President Washington's new job entailed. Washington essentially had to invent the presidency, which he did haltingly at first. While cognizant of the importance of his every move, Washington was intent on infusing the presidency with enough power to pry it away from the domination of Congress. He also began to define the parameters of the office that would endure for generations to come.

Chapter 12

1 This deed can be found in Pepperell Town Hall in a vault next to the town clerk's office. The deed is in a folder labelled Valuable Old Special Old Papers. The deed is dated February 10, 1792.

2 This report is contained in a file at the Lawrence Library in Pepperell, Massachusetts. The report was transcribed by Franek J. Kiluk.

3 Blood, "Colonel Prescott and the Battle of Bunker Hill," 51.

4 Information on Prescott's home and farm was provided on December 2, 2022 by Frank Schembari, the assistant assessor of the town of Pepperell.

5 This description of Colonel Prescott's home appears in a file in Pepperell Town Hall in a report titled Homestead of Colonel William Prescott.

6 Ferling, *Almost A Miracle*, 27. Congress also stipulated that "one-third of the men of their respective towns, between sixteen and sixty years of age, be ready to act at a minute's warning." The Congress also recommended that these *minutemen* "should be immediately equipped with an effective firearm, bayonet, pouch, knapsack, thirty rounds of cartridges and balls, and that they be disciplined [trained] three times a week, and oftener, as opportunity may offer." In truth, the minutemen were a specialized, handpicked force, typically about one-quarter of the militia, that were required to be highly mobile and be able to assemble quickly.

7 George Hillard, *Little Journeys to the homes of American Authors, Prescott* (New York: Putnam and Sons, 1896), 111.

8 Ferling, *Almost A Miracle*, 49. Ferling notes that William Prescott had fought in two previous wars in armies raised by Massachusetts, serving as a rifleman in King George's War and as a junior-grade officer in the French and Indian War.

9 See Nancy Koehn and Eugene B. Kogan, "History teaches 3 critical leadership lessons for our current crises," Fast Company (website), June 2, 2020, available at: https://www.fastcompany.com/90511885/history-teaches-3-essential-leadership-lessons-for-our-current-crisis.

10 In Barnet Schecter's book *The Battle For New York: The City at the Heart of the American Revolution*, he refers to General Israel Putnam as "a hero of both the Seven Years War and the Battle of Bunker Hill (see p. 88). Likewise, in his book *The Glorious Cause: The American Revolution 1763–1789*, Robert Middlekauff, after praising Colonel Prescott, says, "Putnam proved as brave, riding between Bunker and Breed's [Hills] and twice to Cambridge to demand reinforcements and supplies from Ward" (see p. 286).

11 Parker, *Colonel William Prescott*, 9.

12 Frothingham, *The Battle of Bunker Hill*, 24.

13 Green, *Colonel William Prescott*, 5–6. Green was also the librarian of the Massachusetts Historical Society from 1868 to his death in 1919, and he also served as its vice president from 1904 to 1918.

14 Winthrop, 18.

15 Jeff Wise, "The Fascinating Psychology of Bravery: What Makes Someone Brave?," The Healthy (website), updated August 20, 2019, www.thehealthy.com/mental-health/what-makes-people-brave. In the *Laches*, a Socratic dialogue written by Plato in 380 BC, he presents a dialogue between Socrates and two Athenian generals, Laches and Nicias, that addresses courage. Laches feels that courage comes from within the person, that it is either present naturally or it is not. On the other hand, Nicias thinks that courage has to be learned. While they all agree that courage is a lofty virtue, Socrates refers to courage as endurance of the soul, but he demonstrates to Laches that even courage can be foolish and produce greater risks for the collective society, as the courageous person can act more rashly and cause (military) defeat. The participants in this dialogue also discuss courage's relationship to fear. Socrates's view is that courage is less valuable when arrived at without fear. In other words, for those whose courage comes naturally, courage is less meaningful. That is, not all bravery is the same.

16 Cynthia L. S. Pury and S. Saylors, "Courage, courageous acts, and positive psychology," in D. S. Dunn (ed.), *Positive Psychology: Established and Emerging Issues* (New York: Routledge, 2018), 153–68.

17 Pury and Saylors, 154.

18 https://somethingofvalue.com/winston-churchill-quotes, accessed December 10, 2024.

19 Pury and Saylors, 154.

20 Pury and Saylors, 159.

21 Lockhart, 320.

22 Joseph Plumb Martin's *A Narrative Of A Revolutionary Soldier* (New York, New American Library, 2001) is a classic memoir written by a private in the Continental Army, and it provides a firsthand account of the trials and tribulations endured by a soldier in the Revolutionary War.

Epilogue

1 The idea for a statue of Colonel Prescott came about in the mid-1800s. This effort was also backed by the BHMA, which had supported the construction of the Bunker Hill Monument. It raised the requisite funds to start the project and secured William Wetmore Story as the architect. Story was from Salem, Massachusetts, and he attended Harvard University and Harvard Law School. His father, Joseph Story, was an acclaimed jurist who served on the U.S. Supreme Court from 1812 to his death in 1845. His son, William, was extraordinarily accomplished as well, spurning a promising law career and instead becoming a successful poet, art critic, and editor, as well as an internationally recognized sculptor. When his father died, a committee was formed to honor him with a statue to be placed in the memorial chapel at Mount Auburn Cemetery in Cambridge, Massachusetts. In an unexpected move, the committee offered William the commission, even though he had no formal training. William accepted, provided he could first study art in Italy, where he went in 1847. Poignantly, Story's statue of his father now resides in Langdell Hall at the Harvard Law School.

Story also sculpted statues of the great Massachusetts orator Edward Everett, legendary Chief Justice of the Supreme Court John Marshall, and author of the "Star-Spangled Banner," Francis Scott Key.

2   At least one observer has said that the statue's pose indicates Prescott holding back his troops from firing until he gives his command, but, in my view, that is subject to interpretation.

3   Winthrop, 19.

4   Winthrop, 12.

5   Winthrop, 24. A note in a Pepperell town file echoes this observation, noting Prescott was a generous man, who, it was said, "never refused anything asked by a soldier who fought under his command."

6   Hillard, 110.

7   Winthrop, 17.

8   Winthrop, 31

9   Everett, 33–34.

10 Everett, 43.

11 Everett, 40.

12 Everett, 40.

13 Everett, 42.

14 See Irma B. Jaffe, *John Trumbull: Patriot Artist of the American Revolution* (Boston: Little, Brown, and Co., 1975).

15 The three Trumbull paintings of the death of Joseph Warren at Bunker Hill show essentially the same scene. However, the paintings differ in size and in other observable ways, such as the color of the American battle flag and some of the figures depicted.

16 Jaffe, 247. Colonel William Prescott is listed in the painting's legend.

17 George Washington had an extremely close relationship with General Lafayette, treating him like a son.

18 Elisha D. Eldridge, *Personal Recollections of the Completion and Dedication of Bunker Hill Monument* (Boston: Boot and Shoe Recorder Press, 1907), 11.

19 https://en.Wikipedia.org/wiki/Bunker_Hill_Monument, accessed November 22, 2024.

20 Proceedings of the Bunker Hill Association, June 17, 1893, 21.

21 At least one other school has been dedicated to William Prescott. The William Prescott Elementary School of Scranton, Pennsylvania, was built in the 1890s and replaced by a new building in 1966. Teams at the school are known as the Patriots.

22 Based on several conversations and correspondences in 2020 with Frank Kiluk of Pepperell.

23 Based on information contained in an undated document on file in Pepperell Town Hall.

24 Hillard, 111.

Bibliography

A Pepperell Reader. Published by the Pepperell Historical Society and the Daughters of the American Revolution. Pepperell, MA, reissued in 2005.

Alden, John R. *General Gage in America*. Baton Rouge, LA: LSU Press, 1948.

Allison, Robert. *The Boston Massacre*. Beverly, MA: Commonwealth Editions, 2006.

Anderson, Fred. *Crucible of War: The Seven Years' War and the Fate of Empire in British North America*. New York: Vintage Books, 2000.

Anderson, Troyer S. *The Command of the Howe Brothers During the Revolution*. New York: Hassell Street Press, 1936, reissued 2021.

Atkinson, Rick. *The British Are Coming: The War For America, Lexington to Princeton, 1775–1777*. New York: Henry Holt and Company, 2020.

Bailyn, Bernard. *The Ideological Origins of the Revolutionary Revolution*. Cambridge, MA: Harvard University Press, 2017.

Bennett, Thelma. "The Early Schools." *A Pepperell Reader*. The Pepperell Historical Society, 2005.

Billias, George Allan. *George Washington's Generals and Opponents: Their Exploits and Leadership*. Boston: Da Capo Press, 1994.

Birnbaum, Louis. *Red Dawn At Lexington*. Boston: Houghton Mifflin, 1986.

Blood, Lorenzo. "Colonel Prescott and the Battle of Bunker Hill." *A Pepperell Reader*. The Pepperell Historical Society, 2005.

Bobrick, Benson. *Angel in the Whirlwind: The Triumph of the American Revolution*. New York: Penguin Books, 1998.

Bordewich, Fergus M. *The First Congress: How James Madison, George Washington, and a Group of Extraordinary Men Invented the Government*. New York: Simon & Schuster, 2016.

Borneman, Walter R. *The French and Indian War: Deciding the Fate of North America* (New York: Harper Collins, 2006.

Boston Gazette. June 19, 1775.

Bowen, Catherine Drinker. *Miracle at Philadelphia*. Boston: Back Bay Books, 1986.

Breen, T. H. *American Insurgents, American Patriots: The Revolution of the People*. New York: Hill and Wang, 2010.

Brookhiser, Richard. *Gentleman Revolutionary: Gouverneur Morris—The Rake Who Wrote the Constitution*. New York: Free Press, 2003.

Brough, Keith. *General Ward's Colonial Army*. Rehoboth, MA: Timothy Walker's Regimental Press, 2015.

Brown, Abram. *Footprints of The Patriots Beside Old Hearth-Stones*. London: Forgotten Books, Classic Reprint, 2017.

Brown, Robert E. *Middle-Class Democracy and the Revolution in Massachusetts, 1691–1780*. New York: Harper, 1935, reissued in 1969.

Butterfield, L. H. *Adams Family Correspondence, Volumes 3 and 4: April 1778–September 1782*. Cambridge, MA: Belknap Press, 1973.

Byrd, James. *Sacred Scripture, Sacred War: The Bible and the American Revolution*. New York: Oxford University Press, 2013.

Callahan, North. *Henry Knox: George Washington's General*. New York: Rinehart Publishing, 1958.

Callahan, Thomas Keefe. *The Voice of the People of This Country: The Birth of Popular Politics and Support for the Shaysite Insurrection in Groton, Massachusetts*. Master's Thesis in the Field of History for the Degree of Master of Liberal Arts in Extension Studies. Harvard University, June 1991.

Carrington, Henry B. *Battles of the American Revolution*. New York: Promontory Press, 1974.

Champagne, Roger J. *The Sons of Liberty and the Aristocracy in New York Politics, 1765–1790*. Unpublished Ph.D. dissertation. University of Wisconsin, 1960.

Coburn, Frank Warren. *The Battle of April 19, 1775*. Lexington, MA: independently published, 1912.

Coffin, Charles, ed. *History of the Battle of Breed's Hill*. Santa Fe, NM: Legare Street Press, 2022.

Collier, Christopher and James Collier. *Decision in Philadelphia: The Constitutional Convention of 1787*. New York: Random House, 1986.

Commager, Henry Steele and Richard B. Morris. *Spirit of Seventy-Six: The Story of the American Revolution as Told by Participants*. New York: Bonanza Books, 1983.

Cuneo, John R. *Robert Rogers of the Rangers*. New York: Oxford University Press, 1970.

Cutler, William. *The Life of Israel Putnam, Major General in the Army of The American Revolution*. Port Washington, New York: Kennikat Press, 1850 (reissued in 1970).

Daniel, Seth. "Enemies Become Family: Years After Bunker Hill, the Prescott and Linzee Families Were United and Reconciled." *Charlestown Patriot Bridge*, June 17, 2020.

Dearborn, Henry. *An Account of the Battle of Bunker Hill*. Boston: Legare Street Press, 2002.

DeFonblanque, Edward Barrington. *Political and Military Episodes From the Life and Correspondence of the Right Honorable John Burgoyne*. London: Macmillan, 1876.

Dexter, Franklin Bowditch. *The Literary Diary of Ezra Stiles*, D.D., L.L.D., Vols. 1 and 2. New York: Charles Scribner and Sons, 1901.

DiSpigna, Christian. *Founding Martyr: The Life and Death of Dr. Joseph Warren, The American Revolution's Lost Hero*. New York: Crown Publishing, 2018.

Donahue, Brian. *The Great Meadow: Farmers and the Land in Colonial Concord*. New Haven: Yale University Press, 2004.

Drake, Samuel Adams. *Bunker Hill: The Story Told in Letters from the Battlefield*. Boston: Nichols and Hall, 1875.

Drake, Samuel Adams. *History of Middlesex County, Massachusetts, Containing Carefully Prepared Histories of Every City and Town in the County, by Well-Known Writers; and a General History of the County, from the Earliest to the Present Time*. 2 Volumes. Boston: Estes and Lauriat, 1880.

Eldridge, Elisha D. *Personal Recollections of the Completion and Dedication of Bunker Hill Monument*. Boston: Boot and Shoe Recorder Press, 1907.

Ellis, George. *Battle of Bunker Hill*. Boston: Lee and Shepherd Publishers, 1895.

Ellis, Joseph. *American Creation: Triumphs and Tragedies at the Founding of the Republic*. New York: Alfred A. Knopf, 2007.

Ellis, Joseph. *Revolutionary Summer: The Birth of American Independence*. New York: Vintage Books, 2013.

Ellis, Joseph. *The Cause: The American Revolution and Its Discontents*. New York: Liveright Publishing, 2021.

Everett, Edward. "Life of John Stark." *The Library of American Biography*. Boston: Hilliard, Gray and Company, 1834.

Everett, William. *Oration in Honor of Colonel William Prescott, Delivered in Boston, 14 October 1895, by the Invitation of the Bunker Hill Monument Association*. Boston: Bunker Hill Monument Association, 1896.

Farnsworth, Amos. *Diary of Amos Farnsworth*. Massachusetts Historical Society.

Ferling, John. *Almost A Miracle*. Oxford: Oxford University Press, 2007.

Ferling, John. *Apostles of Revolution: Jefferson, Paine, Monroe, and the Struggle Against the Old Order in America and Europe*. New York: Bloomsbury, 2018.

Ferling, John. *Whirlwind: The American Revolution and the War That Won It*. New York: Bloomsbury, 2015.

Ferling, John. *Winning Independence: The Decisive Years of the Revolutionary War 1778–1781*. New York: Bloomsbury, 2021.

Fischer, David Hackett. *Paul Revere's Ride*. New York: Oxford University Press, 1994.

Fischer, David Hackett. *Washington's Crossing*. New York: Oxford University Press, 2004.

Fitzpatrick, John C., ed. "7 August 1782, General Orders." *The Writings of George Washington*. Washington, D.C.: Government Printing Office.

Fitzpatrick, John C., ed. "27 April 1783, General Orders." *The Writings of George Washington*. Washington D.C.: Government Printing Office.

Fitzpatrick, John C., ed. "8 June 1783, General Orders." *The Writings of George Washington*. Washington D.C.: Government Printing Office.

Fleming, Thomas J. *Now We Are Enemies: The Story of Bunker Hill*. New York: St. Martin's Press, 1960.

Force, Peter. *American Archives, Containing a Documentary History of the English Colonies in North America, From the King's Message to Parliament of March 7, 1774 to the Declaration of Independence by the United States*, Series 4: 240–41.

French, Allen. *General Gage's Informers*. Westport, CT: Greenwood Press, 1968.

French, Allen. *The Day of Concord and Lexington: The Nineteenth of April, 1775*. Boston: Eastern National Park & Monument Association, 1925, reprinted 1984.

French, Allen. *The First Year of the American Revolution*. New York: Octagon Books, 1934, reissued 1968.

Frothingham, Richard. *History of the Siege of Boston and of the Battles of Lexington, Concord, and Bunker Hill*. Boston: Little, Brown, 1903.

Frothingham, Richard. *The Battlefield of Bunker Hill: With a Relation of the Action by William Prescott and Illustrative Documents*. Boston, 1876. Printed for the author.

Frothingham, Richard. *The Centennial Battle of Bunker Hill*. Boston: Little, Brown, 1875.

Frothingham, Richard. *The Life and Times of Joseph Warren*. Boston: Little, Brown, 1866.

Goodwin, Doris Kearns. *Leadership in Turbulent Times*. New York: Simon & Schuster, 2018.

Gordon, William. *History of the Rise, Progress, and Establishment of the Independence of the United States of America: Including an Account of the Late War; and of the Thirteen Colonies, from Their Origin to that Period*, 4 Volumes. London, 1788.

Green, Samuel Abbott. *Colonel William Prescott and Groton Soldiers in the Battle of Bunker Hill, From the Proceedings of the Massachusetts Historical Society, November 1909*. Cambridge: John Wilson and Son, University Press, 1909.

Green, Samuel Abbott. *Groton During the Revolution*. Boston: Legare Street Press, re-released 2022.

Green, Samuel Abbott. *Groton Gore and the Provincial Line*. Cambridge, MA: University Press, 1885.

Green, Samuel Abbott. *The Boundary Lines of Old Groton*. Cambridge, MA: University Press, 1885.

Green, Samuel Abbott. *Three Military Diaries Kept by Groton Soldiers in Different Wars*. Cambridge, MA: University Press, 1901.

Gross, Robert A. *The Minutemen and Their World*. New York: Hill and Wang, 1976.

Gruber, Ira. *The Howe Brothers and the American Revolution*. New York: Atheneum Press, 1972.

Hadden, James and Horatio Rogers. *A Journal Kept in Canada and Upon Burgoyne's Campaign in 1776 and 1777 by Lieutenant James Hadden*. Albany, NY: J. Munsell's Sons.

Hall, Van Beck. *Politics Without Parties, 1780–1791*. Pittsburgh: University of Pittsburgh Press, 1972.

Hammond, T. C., ed. *The Parliamentary History of England*, 30 Vols. London, 1806–20, Vol. 18: 149–59.

Hill, John B. *Bi-Centennial of Old Dunstable*. Nashua, NH: Forgotten Books, reissued 2018.

Hillard, George. *Little Journeys to the Homes of American Authors, Prescott*. New York: Putnam and Sons, 1896.

Hills, Katherine Blood. "The Fletcher Picnic." *A Pepperell Reader*. The Pepperell Historical Society, 2005.

Hosmer, Josephine. "Memoir of Joseph Hosmer." *Concord Antiquarian Society Papers*. Concord Free Library.

How, David and Henry Barton Dawson. *Diary of David How, A Private in Colonel Paul Dudley Sargent's Regiment of the Massachusetts Line*. New York, 1865, reprinted by Nabu Press, 2010.

Hubbard, Robert Ernest. *Major General Israel Putnam: Hero of the American Revolution*. Jefferson, NC: McFarland and Company, 2017.

Hudleston, F. J. *Gentleman Johnny Burgoyne: Misadventures of an English General in the Revolution*. Garden City Publishing, 1927.

Innes, Stephen. *Labor in a New Land*. Princeton: Princeton University Press, 2014.

Jaffe, Irma, B. *John Trumbull: Patriot Artist of the American Revolution*. Boston: Little, Brown, 1975.

Jaffee, David. *People of the Wachusett: Greater New England in History & Memory 1630–1860*. Ithaca: Cornell University Press, 1999.

Jefferson, Thomas. "Draft of Instructions to the Virginia Delegates in the Continental Congress, July 1774." *The Papers of Thomas Jefferson*, 1:121–35.

Jensen, Merrill. *The Founding of a Nation: A History of the American Revolution*. New York, 1968.

Johnson, Claudia Durst. *Daily Life in Colonial New England*. Westport, CT: Greenwood Press, 2002.

Johnston, Henry Phelps. *The Campaign of 1776 around New York and Brooklyn including a new and circumstantial account of the battle of Long Island and the loss of New York, with a review of events to the close of the year*. Brooklyn: Long Island Historical Society, 1878, reissued 2011.

Jones, Charles Henry. *History of the Campaign for the Conquest of Canada in 1776*. Philadelphia: Porter and Coates, 1882.

Kahneman, Daniel. *Thinking Fast and Slow*. New York: Farrar, Straus, and Giroux, 2011.

Ketchum, Richard, M. *Decisive Day: The Battle Of Bunker Hill*. New York: Doubleday, 1962.

Ketchum, Richard, M. *Divided Loyalties*. New York: Henry Holt and Company, 2002.

Ketchum, Richard, M. *Saratoga*. New York: Henry Holt and Company, 1999.

Kidd, Thomas S. *God of Liberty: A Religious History of the American Revolution*. New York: Basic Books, 2010.

Klarman, Michael, J. *The Framers' Coup: The Making of the United States Constitution*. New York: Oxford University Press, 2016.

Knapp, Samuel I. *Biographical Sketches of Eminent Lawyers, Statesmen, and Men of Letters*. Boston, 1821, reprinted by Kessinger Publishing, 2010.

Koehn, Nancy and Eugene B. Kogan. "History teaches 3 critical leadership lessons for our current crisis." Harvard Business School website at Harvard.edu.

Kurland, Susan. *A Political Progress: Process of Democratization in Concord, MA, 1750–1850*. Senior Thesis. Brandeis University, 1973.

LaPlante, Eve. *American Jezebel*. New York: Harper Collins, 2004.

Letter from Benjamin Hichborn to John Adams, December 10, 1775. In John Adams Papers, Series 3, 323–24. Adams Family Papers, Massachusetts Historical Society.

Letter from Colonel William Prescott to John Adams, August 25, 1775. Held at the Massachusetts Historical Society, Boston.

Letter from George Washington to Lafayette, August 21, 1781. John Fitzpatrick, ed. *The Writings of Washington*, 39 Vols. Washington D.C.: US Government Printing Office, 1931–44, as cited in John Ferling, *Whirlwind*.

Letter from George Washington to Joseph Reed, January 31, 1776. *Papers of George Washington* Revolutionary War Series, 3:228.

Letter from John Adams to Nathan Webb, October 12, 1755. Papers of John Adams, Massachusetts Historical Society I:5.

Letter from John Adams to William Tudor, March 29, 1817. Massachusetts Historical Society.

Letter from James Knowles to Wife, June 18, 1775. James Knowles Papers, Ms. S 730a, Massachusetts Historical Society.

Letter from James Warren to John Adams, June 20, 1775. Warren-Adams Letters, Massachusetts Historical Society.

Letter from James Warren to Samuel Adams, June 21, 1775. Massachusetts Historical Society, 14 (1875–76): 81.

Letter from John Stark to Matthew Thornton, June 19, 1775, in Nathaniel Bouton, ed. *Provincial Papers: Documents and Records Relating to the Province of New Hampshire, from 1764–1776*, 7 Vols. Concord, NH (1867–73), 7:523.

Letter from Lieutenant Walter S. Laurie to John Roebuck, June 23, 1775.

Letter from Nathanael Green to Jacob Green, June 28, 1775. The Papers of Nathanael Green, 1:92.

Letter from Peter Brown to his Mother, June 25, 1775. Massachusetts Historical Society.

Letter from Thomas Gage to Lord Dartmouth, June 25, 1775. UK NA CO 5/92, f. 187.

Letter from William Sutherland to General Thomas Gage, April 27, 1775. Thomas Gage's Papers.

Letters from General Cornwallis to General Clinton, May 26 and June 30, 1781. As cited in John Ferling, *Whirlwind*.

Letter from William Prescott to John Adams, August 25, 1775. Massachusetts Historical Society.

Letters from William Howe to Adjutant General Harvey, June 22 and June 24, 1775. Commager and Morris, *Spirit of Seventy-Six*, 132.

Liebowitz, Ruth. "The Early Settlers." *A Pepperell Reader*. The Pepperell Historical Society, 2005.

Lieutenant John Barker, King's Own Regiment. "A British Officer in Boston." *The Atlantic Monthly* (XXXIX): 389ff.

Livingston, William Farrand. *Israel Putnam: Pioneer, Ranger, and Major General, 1718–1790*. New York: Putnam's Sons, 1901.

Lockhart, Paul. *The Whites of Their Eyes: Bunker Hill, The First American Army, and the Emergence of George Washington*. New York: HarperCollins Publishers, 2011.

London Evening Post. July 13–16, 1775.

Lossing, Benson John. *The Lives of the Signers of the Declaration of Independence*. Wallbuilder Press, 1995.

MacAlister, Todd. *New England Frontier: The Prescott Garrison—1692*. West Conshohocken, PA: InfinityPublishing.com, 2008.

Maier, Pauline. *American Scripture: Making the Declaration of Independence*. New York: Vintage Books, 1997.

Maier, Pauline. *From Resistance to Revolution: Colonial radicals and the development of American opposition to Britain, 1765–1776*. New York, W. W. Norton & Company, 1991.

Maier, Pauline. *Ratification: The People Debate the Constitution 1787–1788*. New York: Simon and Schuster, 2010.

Marrin, Albert. *Struggle for a Continent: The French and Indian Wars, 1690–1760*. New York: Macmillan, 1987.

Martin, Joseph Plumb. *A Narrative of a Revolutionary Soldier*. New York: New American Library, a division of Penguin Group, 2001.

Martyn, Charles. *The Life of Artemas Ward, The First Commander-in-Chief of the American Revolution.* New York: Kennikat Press, 1921.

Massachusetts Archives. General Orders, dated Headquarters, March 23 and March 28, 1776. Vol. 77.

Massachusetts Archives. Oath of Allegiance, 190:170.

Massachusetts Archives. Massachusetts Archives Collection. *Revolutionary War*, Vol. 59, 551.

Massachusetts Archives. Massachusetts Archives Collection, Vol. 189.

Massachusetts Archives. Massachusetts Archives Collection, Vol. 190.

Massachusetts Archives. Massachusetts Archives Collection, Vol. 318.

Massachusetts Archives. *Orderly Book: Capt. Abijah Wyman's Co., Col Wm Prescott regiment, from August 5 to December 30, 1775.*

Massachusetts Archives. Vol. 58, Page 134, File 22.

Massachusetts Spy. June 28, 1775.

McCullough, David. *1776.* New York: Simon and Schuster, 2005.

McLoughlin, William G. *New England Dissent 1630–1833: The Baptists and the Separation of Church and State.* Cambridge, MA: Harvard University Press, 1971.

Middlekauff, Robert. *The Glorious Cause: The American Revolution 1763–1789.* Oxford: Oxford University Press, 1982.

Mobs, Dean. "The ethological deconstruction of fear(s)." *Current Opinion in Behavioral Sciences,* Vol. 24, (December 2018): 32–37.

Moore, Howard Parker. *A Life of General John Stark of New Hampshire.* Boston: Spaulding-Moss, 1949.

Morse, Jedidiah and Elijah Parish. *A Compendious History of New England.* Printed by S. Etheridge, 1820.

Moulton, Johnson. *Orderly Book, Governor's Island, New York, 20th July 1776.* William Hickling Prescott Papers. Boston: Massachusetts Historical Society, Box 25.

Mullaly, Franklin Russell. *The Massachusetts Insurrection of 1786–87.* Master's Thesis. Smith College, 1947.

Nili, Uri, Hagar Goldberg, Abraham Weizman, and Yadin Dudai. "Fear Thou Not: Activity of Frontal and Temporal Circuits in Moments of Real-Life Courage." *Neuron*, Volume 66, Issue 6 (June 2010): 949–62.

Norton, Mary Beth. *1774: The Long Year of Revolution.* New York: Alfred A. Knopf, 2020.

"Opening of the War of the Revolution, 19th of April, 1775, A Brief Narrative of the Principal Transactions of that Day." Appended to a Sermon Preached by Reverend Jonas Clarke in Lexington, April 19, 1776. Lexington Historical Society.

Paine, Thomas, *Common Sense, The Rights of Man, and Other Essential writings of Thomas Paine* (New York, Meridian Books), 1969

Parker, Francis J. *Colonel William Prescott: The Commander In The Battle Of Bunker's Hill, Honor To Whom Honor Is Due.* Boston: A. Williams and Company, 1875.

Pepperell Special Old Papers, Pepperell Town Hall, Pepperell, MA.

Pepperell Town Records, 1742–1809, Vol. 1, Lawrence Library, Pepperell, MA.

Philbrick, Nathaniel. *Bunker Hill: A City, A Siege, A Revolution.* New York: Penguin, 2013.

Philbrick, Nathaniel. *In the Hurricane's Eye: The Genius of George Washington and the Victory at Yorktown.* New York: Viking, 2018.

Philbrick, Nathaniel. *Valiant Ambition: George Washington, Benedict Arnold, and the Fate of the American Revolution.* New York: Viking Penguin, 2016.

Plato. *Laches.* Benjamin Jowett, trans. Originally published in 1892, reprinted in Las Vegas, 2021.

Polhemus, Richard V. and John F. Polhemus. *Stark: The Life and Wars of John Stark, French and Indian War Ranger, Revolutionary War General.* Delmar, NY; Black Dome Press, 2014.

Potter, Charles Edward. *Genealogies of Some Old Families of Concord.* Santa Clara, CA: Janaway Publishing, 2011.

Prescott, William. Paybook. William Hickling Prescott Papers, Massachusetts Historical Society, Box 25.

Prescott, William, M.D. *The Prescott Memorial or a Genealogical Memoir of the Prescott Families in America,* in two parts. Boston: Henry W. Dutton and Son, 1870.

Price, David. *John Haslett's World: An Ardent Patriot, the Delaware Blues, and the Spirit of 1776.* New York: Knox Press, 2020.

Pury, Cynthia L. S. and S. Saylors. "Courage, courageous acts, and positive psychology." D. S. Dunn (ed.), *Positive Psychology: Established and Emerging Issues.* New York: Routledge, 2017, 153–68.

Quintal, George. *Patriots of Color at Bunker Hill and the Siege of Boston, 17 June 1775.* Self-published, 2024.

Rakove, Jack N. *Beginnings of National Politics: An interpretive history of the Continental Congress.* Knopf Publishing, 1979.

Registry of Deeds for South Middlesex County, Grantee Book, 1639–1799, Volume 6, Book 177, Pages 143–45.

Richards, Leonard L. *Shays's Rebellion: The American Revolution's Final Battle.* Philadelphia: University of Pennsylvania Press, 2002.

Robertson, Archibald. *His Histories and Sketches in America, 1762–1780.* New York: New York Public Library, new edition 1971.

Rose, Ben Z. *Maverick General.* Waverly, Massachusetts: Treeline Press, 2007.

Scheckter, Barnet. *The Battle of New York.* New York: Walker Books, 2002.

Schiff, Stacy. *The Revolutionary: Samuel Adams.* New York: Little, Brown, 2022.

Shattuck, Gary. *Artful and Designing Men: The Trials of Job Shattuck and the Regulation of 1786–1787.* Mustang, Oklahoma: Tate Publishing and Enterprises, 2013.

Shays's Rebellion Collection. American Antiquarian Society, Worcester, Massachusetts, 2022–23.

Sheer, George F. and Hugh F. Rankin. *Rebels and Redcoats: The American Revolution Through the Eyes of Those That Fought and Lived It.* Boston: Da Capo Press, 1987.

Smith, Daniel Scott. "Parental Power and Marriage Patterns: An Analysis of Historical Trends in Hingham, Massachusetts." *Journal of Marriage and the Family,* XXXV (August 1973): 419–28.

Smith, Edmund Banks. *Governor's Island: Its Military History Under Three Flags.* New York: published by the author, 1913.

Staiti, Paul. *Of Arms and Artists: The American Revolution Through Painters' Eyes.* New York: Bloomsbury, 2016.

Stark, Caleb. *Memoir and Official Correspondence of General John Stark, with Notices of Several Other Officers of the Revolution.* Heritage Books, 2007.

Stephenson, Michael. *Patriot Battles: How the War of Independence Was Fought.* New York: HarperCollins, 2008.

Stevens, Benjamin Franklin, ed. *The Campaign in Virgina, 1781: An Exact Reprint of Six Rare Pamphlets on the Clinton-Cornwallis Correspondence.* London, 1888.

Stewart, David O. *The Summer of 1787: The Men Who Invented the Constitution.* New York: Simon & Schuster, 2007.

Swett, Samuel. *History of Bunker Hill Battle.* Boston: Monroe and Francis, 1826.

Szatmary, David P. *Shays's Rebellion: The Making of an Agrarian Insurrection* (University of Massachusetts Press, 1984.

Taylor, Robert J. *Massachusetts, Colony to Commonwealth.* New York: W. W. Norton & Company, 1961.

Temple, J. H. *History of Framingham, Massachusetts, Early Known as Dansforth's Farms, 1640–1880*. Boston: Legare Street Press, 2022.

Tourtellot, Arthur, B. *Lexington and Concord: The Beginning of the War of the American Revolution*. New York: W. W. Norton, and Co., 1959.

Tyler, John W. *Smugglers and Patriots: Boston Merchants and the Advent of the American Revolution*. Northeastern University Press, 1986.

Van Tyne, Claude H. *The War of Independence: American Phase*. Boston: Houghton Mifflin, 1929.

Vollmar, Joshua. "Reflections on Juneteenth: Groton's History of Enslavement & Abolition." *The Groton Herald*, June 16, 2023.

Wade, Herbert Treadwell and Robert A. Lively. *This Glorious Cause: The Adventures of Two Company Officers in Washington's Army*. Princeton: Princeton University Press, 2016.

Walsh, Richard. *Charleston's Sons of Liberty*. Columbia, SC: University of South Carolina Press, 1959.

Ward, I., Allen French, and Bernard Knollenberg. "Bunker Hill Re-viewed: A Study in the Conflict of Historical Evidence." Massachusetts Historical Society (1963), Procs. 72.

Warren, George Washington. *The History of the Bunker Hill Monument Association during the first century of the United States of America*. Boston: James R. Osgood & Company, 1877.

Watson, John L. *Paul Revere's Signal: The True Story of the Signal Lanterns in Christ Church*. Boston: Legare Street Press, 2021.

Weddle, Kevin. *The Complete Victory: Saratoga and the American Revolution*. Oxford: Oxford University Press, 2021.

Wheeler, Richard. *Voices of 1776: The Story of the American Revolution in the Words of Those Who Were There*. New York: Plume, 1991.

Wheildon, William W. *History of Paul Revere's Signal Lanterns, April 18, 1775 in the Steeple of the North Church*. Boston: Legare Street Press, 2022.

Willard, Margaret Wheeler, ed. *Letters on the American Revolution, 1774–1776*. Boston, MA: Houghton Mifflin Company, 1925.

Willcox, William, ed. *American Rebellion: Sir Henry Clinton's Narrative of His Campaign, 1775–1782, with an Appendix of Original Documents*. New Haven: Yale University Press, 1954.

Willcox, William. *Portrait of a General: Sir Henry Clinton in the War of Independence*. New York: Alfred Knopf, 1964.

William Hickling Prescott Papers. Massachusetts Historical Society, Box 25.

Williams, Lieutenant. *Discord and Civil Wars; being a portion of the journal kept by Lieutenant Williams of His Majesty's Twenty-third Regiment*. Buffalo: Easy Hill Press, 2018.

Wilson, Rufus Rockwell. *Heath's Memoirs of the American War*. New York: Wentworth Press, reissued 2019.

Winthrop, Robert. *The Unveiling of the Statue of Colonel William Prescott on Bunker Hill June 17, 1881*. Cambridge: John Wiley and Son, Cambridge University Press, 1881.

Wood, Gordon, S. *Power and Liberty: Constitutionalism in the American Revolution*. New York: Oxford University Press, 2021.

Wood, Gordon, S. *The Creation of the American Republic 1776–1787*. Chapel Hill: University of North Carolina Press, 1998.

Wood, Gordon. *The Radicalism of the American Revolution*. New York: Vintage Books, a division of Random House, 1993.

Yale University Open Courses. "Economics: Game Theory." Online course taught by Ben Polak, Fall 2007.

Zuckerman, Michael. *Peaceable Kingdoms: New England Towns in the Eighteenth Century*. New York, 1970.

Online Sources

https://classroom.synonym.com/about-colonial-life-in-massachusetts-12081170.html, accessed January 15, 2025.

https://en.wikipedia.org/wiki/Barbados, accessed Novembre 22, 2024.

https://en.wikipedia.org/wiki/Battle_of_Long_Island, accessed December 10, 2024.

https://en.wikipedia.org/wiki/Battles_of_Saratoga, accessed December 10, 2024.

https://en.wikipedia.org/wiki/Bunker_Hill_Monument, accessed November 22, 2024.

https://en.wikipedia.org/wiki/Henry_Clinton_(British_Army_officer,_born_1730)https://en.wikipedia.org/wiki/Henry_Clinton(British_Army_officer,_born_1730, accessed November 23, 2021.

https://en.wikipedia.org/wiki/Henry_Knox, accessed December 10, 2024.

https://en.wikipedia.org/wiki/John_Burgoyne, accessed November 23, 2021.

https://en.wikipedia.org/wiki/John_Stark, accessed February 13, 2020.

https://en.wikipedia.org/wiki/Joseph_Warren, accessed December 10, 2024.

https://en.wikipedia.org/wiki/Richard_Gridley Reference note #2, Huntoon, Daniel T. V., History of the Town of Canton, Norfolk County, Massachusetts, Friends of the Little Red House, 1975, accessed December 2, 2021.

https://en.wikipedia.org/wiki/Richard_Gridley, Reference note #3, United States Army Corps of Engineers, *Colonel Richard Gridley, First Chief Engineer: The Forgotten Soldier of the Battle of Bunker Hill*, 1775, accessed December 2, 2024.

https://en.wikipedia.org/wiki/Thomas_Gage, accessed November 22, 2024.

https://en.wikipedia.org/wiki/Thomas_Knowlton, accessed November 22, 2024.

https://en.wikipedia.org/wiki/Valley_Forge, accessed on January 15, 2025.

https://en.wikipedia.org/wiki/William_Howe,_5th_Viscount_Howehttps://en.wikipedia.org/wiki/William_Howe,5th_Viscount_Howe, accessed November 23, 2021.

https://en.wikipedia.org/wiki/William_Prescott, accessed December 10, 2024.

https://genealogytrails.com/mass/middlesex/revwarjournalfarmsworth.html, accessed December 11, 2024.

https://history.army.mil/Research/Reference-Topics/Military-Quotations, accessed January 24, 2025.

https://history.army.mil/books/AMH/AMH-V1/ch03.htm, accessed January 16, 2025.

https://legacy.sites.fas.harvard.edu/~hsb41/masstax/masstax.cg accessed January 15, 2025.

https://www.azquotes.com/author/2886-winston-churchill/tag/courage, accessed January 21, 2025.

https://US1primarysources.blogspot.com/2009/08/suffolk-resolves.html, accessed November 22, 2024.

https://en.wikipedia.www.massmomemorg/wiki/Andrew_McClary, accessed December 10, 2024.

https://en.wikipedia.org/wiki/Artemas_Ward, accessed November 23, 2021.

https://en.wikipedia.org/wiki/Israel_Putnam, accessed November 23, 2021.

https://en.wikipedia.org/wiki/Shays%27_rebellion, accessed December 10, 2024.

https://en.wikipedia.org/wiki/Siege_of_Boston, accessed December 10, 2024.

www.historycentral.com/Revolt/battleaccounts/BunkerHill/Amosdiary.html, accessed November 22, 2024.

www.massgov/guides/John-Adams-the-Massachusetts-Constitution, accessed January 21, 2025.

www.mountvernon.org/library/digitalhistory/digital-encyclopedia/article/presidential-election-of-1789, accessed November 22, 2024.

www.revolutionary-war.net/colonel-william-prescott, accessed December 11, 2024.

www.revolutionarywarjournal.com/british-army-command-structure-in-the-american-revolution, accessed November 22, 2024.

www.smithsonianmag.com/history/history-town-hall-debate, published October 6, 2016, accessed December 11, 2024.

www.thehealthy.com/mental-health/what-makes-people-brave, accessed November 22, 2024.

Index